The Politics and Poetics of Journalistic Narrative investigates the textuality of all discourse, arguing that the ideologically charged distinction between "journalism" and "fiction" is socially constructed rather than natural. Phyllis Frus separates literariness from aesthetic definitions, regarding it as a way of reading a text through its style to discover how it "makes" reality. Frus also takes up the problem of how we determine both the truth of historical events such as the Holocaust and the fictional or factual status of narratives about them.

Frus first examines narratives by Stephen Crane and Ernest Hemingway, showing that conventional understanding of the categories of fiction and nonfiction frequently determines the differences we perceive in texts, differences we imagine are determined by common sense. When journalists writing about historical events adopt the Hemingway-esque, understated narrative style that is commonly associated with both "objectivity" and "literature" (John Hersey is one example), the reader sees the damage done by the wholesale construction of literature as a "pure," nonfunctional art: it leads to an audience unable to face the historical and social conditions in which it must function. She interprets New Journalistic narratives by Truman Capote, Norman Mailer, Tom Wolfe, and Janet Malcolm, suggesting by her critical practice ways to counter the reification of modern consciousness to which both objective journalism and aestheticized fiction contribute.

The Politics and Poetics of Journalistic Narrative

The Politics and Poetics of Journalistic Narrative

The Timely and the Timeless

PHYLLIS FRUS
Vanderbilt University

CAMBRIDGE
UNIVERSITY PRESS

Published by the Press Syndicate of the University of Cambridge
The Pitt Building, Trumpington Street, Cambridge CB2 1RP
40 West 20th Street, New York, NY 10011-4211, USA
10 Stamford Road, Oakleigh, Melbourne 3166, Australia

First published 1994

Printed in the United States of America

Library of Congress Cataloging-in-Publication Data
Frus, Phyllis.
The politics and poetics of journalistic narrative : the timely
and the timeless / Phyllis Frus.
p.   cm.
Includes bibliographical references and index.
ISBN 0-521-44324-5
1. American prose literature – 20th century – History and criticism.
2. Politics and literature – United States – History – 20th century.
3. Reportage literature, American – History and criticism.
4. Journalism – United States – History – 20th century.   5. Nonfiction
novel – History and criticism.   6. Narration (Rhetoric).   I. Title.
PS366.R44F78   1994
818.'50809 – dc20
                                                                    94-6273
                                                                    CIP

A catalog record for this book is available from the British Library.

ISBN 0-521-44324-5 hardback

To my parents, Roy Frus and Nelle Bennett Frus,
and my son, Craig McCord:
"it was more than enough"

Contents

Preface: True Stories

We are obliged to receive the majority of our experience at second hand through parents, friends, mates, lovers, enemies, and the journalists who report it to us.
　　　　　　　　　　　　– Norman Mailer, *Some Honorable Men*

This is a book about both journalism and fiction, specifically about the relationship between the two narrative modes over the course of the twentieth century. By "journalism" I mean writing that appears in periodicals; I also include book-length nonfiction which tells of recent events but which may not have appeared first in a magazine. (*In Cold Blood* did, but *The Executioner's Song* did not.) Some of my examples are conventionally called "nonfiction novels" or true-life novels; others, especially those published since the 1980s, are not. Their immediacy, the research the writer has done, and her relationship with her subject make works like Janet Malcolm's three nonfiction books journalistic to me. Unlike Thomas Connery, who excludes essays and commentary from journalism, I use the term in its broadest sense to mean "writing about newsworthy subjects." Because writers make whatever they are interested in "news" to others, they in effect make their subjects journalistic by writing about them.

　Most of what I say theoretically about journalism applies to nonfiction in general, but that is a large category, and I wanted to choose a more limited category, for practical reasons. My historical approach suggested journalism because that is the kind of nonfiction Stephen Crane and many other American writers practiced and that is how many of them still start out. I began this study many years ago by taking journalistic narrative as a place to consider what we mean by literature. Why do we set off some prose in a special category, rather than considering writing critically in all its diverse modes, in what Raymond Williams calls its "multiplicity" (*Marxism* 146)? Rather than trying to locate an essential quality that defines literature (which in prose is synonymous with "fiction"), I came to use Williams's conception of literature as a socially constructed category of works that developed its current meaning by the end of the nineteenth century: a privileged realm of works embodying timeless truth and transcendent values (*Marxism* chap. 3). This does not solve the problem of how to regard and evaluate what have been regarded as "crossover" texts in this hierarchy of prose modes (nonfiction treated like fiction, well-written history and biography), but it does guide me toward a historical and contextual framework for considering these examples.

Although my main focus is on texts by canonical American writers who have published journalism as well as fiction (narratives usually regarded as blurring the boundaries between literature and reportage), I do not use the term "literary journalism," because I cannot accept the valuation that results from separating some examples of journalistic narrative from general coverage of current events and issues. Designating narratives as "literary" places them within an objectivist and essentialist framework that inevitably affects our readings of these works: it implies some aesthetic judgment and tends to remove the text from historical or political analysis. We usually overlook the fact that "literature," as currently defined, is produced in a "gate-keeping" process involving publishers, critics, teachers, and professional journals. Historicizing the concept of making literature produces an alternative definition: "Literature comprises works with a history of critical readings that emphasize their universal characteristics or aesthetic aspects." The result of this aestheticizing process is to render literary narrative something we regard as "neither true nor false."

Once the tension between nonfiction and fictional tendencies signaled by a given narrative has been resolved in favor of literature, the text becomes nonpropositional, and thus unlikely to be a factor in the politics of ordinary life, the domain of social experience and public expression where change is possible. The particular, local claims of a literary work are subsumed under its universal qualities, whereas a narrative on the border keeps its readers (if it continues to attract them) because they are interested at least partly in its truth claims, that is, in its referentiality. This is a readership to be desired, for the notion that literature is too pure to be useful in gaining particular ends inevitably constructs an audience unable to face the historical and social conditions in which it must function. This is why I struggle to represent the complexity of truth claims inherent in narratives on the border and to resist either celebrating these texts' stylistic attributes for their own sake (which is to begin the process that will lead them to the literary category) or emphasizing their factuality and accuracy (thus beginning the process that leads to nonliterary status). My goal is to counter the tendency of literary critics and historians on one hand and media critics and journalist-reviewers on the other to reduce problematic narratives to either factual or fictional status and to lament the muddying of distinctions that have not always been clear anyway.

This puts my study squarely in the midst of the current debate in the humanities over whether the "canon" (defined narrowly as "literature itself") should be conceived more broadly or whether the formalist notion of literature will prove difficult to dislodge or modify because of its ability to exclude deviant forms and incorporate or co-opt alternatives. Because I regard the hierarchical categories of literature and non-literary forms, fiction and "other" prose modes, as pernicious to the development of the complex public discourse necessary in a well-functioning democratic society, I oppose the aesthetic judgments these high-low distinctions rest on and would do away with the canon altogether. But I also understand the resistance to such leveling tactics on the part of conservatives, who view them as threatening the ground of meaning, of absolute standards, and of coherent structures that provide stability and the basis for moral judgments in society.

Because there is no winning this battle in the current climate – as indicated by the recent governmental, judiciary, and media backlash against liberal scholars (in the National Endowment for the Humanities as well as the National Endowment for the Arts), against women who do not accept their "natural" place or biological roles (see Faludi), and against First Amendment protection of artistic expression – I would turn the discussion to a different issue, one obscured by the argument over the weakening of standards and the assault on the canon by what are labeled "radical" or "diluting" forces. To insist on the importance of maintaining universal, "natural," and aesthetic standards for art in the face of calls for diversity, pluralism, and an openness to popular forms avoids the historical and political issues raised by these energetic and democratizing alternatives. In whose interest is it to preserve an elitist canon, moral absolutes, high aesthetic standards? And – a corollary question – why are the groups in ascendancy content to conduct the debate on the grounds of taste, aesthetic value, and the moral force of art?

One answer is that the canon of great American literature and the values necessary to preserve it mesh very well with the dominant myths of our American past, which seem to illuminate our progress to the status of a powerful and influential nation. If we lose those myths and the values they imply, or even if they are seriously questioned, we may lose that place (or we may be forced to admit that it is being steadily eroded). James Carey suggests that the "national media give public and identifiable form to symbols and values of national identity and also

block out of public communication areas of potential conflict" ("Communications" 25). Perhaps the strongest argument against the perpetua-
tion of these naturalized categories of myth and art is the argument from
history, but although those in support of the status quo may pay lip
service to history (usually a nostalgic or mythic version), they seem to
be invested in promulgating myth, rather than in real historical analysis.

What are we missing out on when we do not preserve the nonliterary,
the popular, the nonfictional text? Preserving texts is, after all, what the
canon process is about: publishers keeping books in print and reprinting
journalism, booksellers distributing them, critics and scholars creating a
body of criticism about them, teachers and administrators choosing
them to teach. The brief answer is that we lose the ability to discuss the
complex political and historical issues they raise. Under the guise of
requiring works to satisfy criteria of permanent and universal interest,
we may lose texts (and even particular subgenres) of importance, but
certainly a number of writers and works will disappear because they
are considered radical, irrelevant, "feminine," subcultural, or lowbrow.
(Lauter ["Race"], O'Brien, and Ohmann ["Shaping"] describe the influence that categories named by these adjectives have on canon formation.) One reason to be grateful for the canonical status of a work like
Norman Mailer's *Armies of the Night,* for example, is that anyone reading
the second half of that novel cannot readily dismiss the antiwar activists
of the sixties as improvising radicals, or hippies and freaks, as easily
happens when students pick up their knowledge of that decade from
television and films and learn popular myths from conservative parents.
Being canonical means that this text is likely to be read – perhaps even
assigned for a course in history, literature, sociology, or political science – and thus carefully analyzed.

Similarly, if we emphasize only the literary style or techniques of
journalistic and other nonfictional narratives, we risk overlooking their
context, message, and argumentative strategies and what they can teach
us about complex argument and political discourse. As Donald Lazere
points out in an important essay, "Literacy and Mass Media," both
conservative and leftist groups have an interest in raising the level of
public discourse by working to change the superficial banalities of mass-
journalistic forms and the passivity and "universal regression of reasoning capacities" to which they apparently lead (288). He argues that
teaching literature and literary criticism can help to improve Americans'
abilities to contribute to public discourse and participate in democratic
institutions, but he is not talking about approaching literature as an
autonomous realm filled with works that are "good" for us. Rather, he
is asserting the connection between the study of literature and other
areas where advanced cognitive development is important.

Journalist-critic Sven Birkerts seems to have reached a similar conclusion about the interrelationship of critical thinking and literary criticism, based on his experience of teaching introductory expository writing to Harvard freshmen. He describes struggling to find ways to improve the quality of reading and the level of discussion and expression of his students. (Lazere reports that, according to their teachers, upper-middle-class, suburban white students are not immune to the deficiencies in cognitive development and to "media-induced illiteracy" that researchers have found in students from lower social classes, from oral cultures, or mired in the "culture of poverty" ["Literacy" 299–300].) A good method for teaching advanced literacy, Birkerts discovered, is to encourage close reading of essays and of their geographical, historical, social, and political contexts. If his approach begins in New Critical interpretive strategies, it does not remain there, but moves on, like Mark Miller's analyses of television, publicity, films, shopping malls, and the arrival of 1984, to backgrounds such as the women's movement, neocolonialism, and theories of propaganda.[1]

My point here is that the ahistoricism of our mass media (especially television news but also print journalism in its daily, objective form) is not corrected by the ahistoricism of predominantly New Critical interpretive strategies taught to masses of students in secondary and postsecondary schools and applied to "superior" examples of well-researched and prestigiously presented magazine articles and trade books. Therefore I reject the approach implicit in all critical strategies emphasizing "literary journalism" or "literary nonfiction." By and large, journalists and their productions are assimilated to the literary canon on the basis of essentialist criteria, as the titles of two collections edited by Norman Sims indicate: *The Literary Journalists* and *Literary Journalism in the Twentieth Century*. These "canonical" examples of journalism or nonfiction are sometimes used to illustrate techniques of postmodernism, such as fabulism and metafiction (Hellmann, Zavarzadeh) and new strategies for reviving the near-moribund novel in the late twentieth century (Birkerts 149; Wolfe, "Stalking"). Although I too treat journalistic narratives that have been much discussed by other critics (what an early reader of this manuscript called "the same old new journalistic works") – *In Cold Blood, The Executioner's Song,* and *The Electric Kool-Aid Acid Test* – I do it not to increase their canonical status but to show their politics, and I read even the self-conscious strategies I find there as more than stylistic attributes. Most previous readings of these novels have emphasized their rhetoric, and many have read them against the turmoil of the sixties and seventies, but they also generally regard the interesting border crossings as occurring as a discrete phenomenon within a finite period (Wolfe, Introduction; Hollowell; Hellmann).

My strategies for self-conscious and historical readings of these journalistic narratives emphasize the importance of activating readers to become co-creators, rather than passive consumers of either pleasure or information. Because journalist-novelists exploit the tension between the referentiality and the form of their productions, this is one source of readers' pleasure. Readers can also emphasize these two levels, as when they read the content of any narrative through its form. We do this when we discover how a text, through its style, "makes" reality. Thus when we read texts in relation to the conditions that have given rise to them, we engage in the process of producing literature. Reading narratives historically is therefore one way of countering the aesthetic criteria of the canonization process. I demonstrate this in Chapter 1, where, unlike nearly every other critic of Stephen Crane's "The Open Boat," I read this story as autobiographical, revealing Crane's obsession with the idea of immortality but trying to suppress it within the context of yellow journalism and the idea of the freelance writer as a "man of business" rather than simply a "man of letters."

This is a rather theoretical approach to the problem of border-crossing genres. I have taken this path out of a desire to shift the discussion away from the issue of whether these texts are factual or fictional, nonfictional or literary. I want fiction to take on some of the intellectual and political power of nonfiction – its propositionality, or ability to make statements that influence the way we frame and interpret our experience, and that locate it in particular social processes and contexts. At the same time, I advocate reading journalism so that it crosses over to share fiction's emphasis on its own materiality – not so that it will achieve the label of "literature," with its status and prestige, but so that it will attract the serious readings we give to fiction. In Murray Krieger's words, "Literature, losing its definition and reduced to an egalitarian status with all texts, is returned to the greater privilege of providing the model for a mode of interpretation to which all texts are now made eligible" (21).

Because all narratives have the same status as texts, and because the language structures of formal realism take priority over the reality they produce, "true-life" narratives ought to be judged as fictional ones are: according to their coherence and correspondence to a world we recognize, that is, as they correspond not to the events themselves but to other narratives. We naturally do compare the events that we derive from different narratives, but once events have happened we can recover them only through narratives about them (considering memory, too, as a kind of narrative), and so they are secondary to the plots in which they are embedded. In other words, narratives, whether recited to ourselves in our mind's ear, told aloud, or read, are not representations of reality but in some sense prior to the happenings that supposedly gave rise to them. In an age of electronic as well as mechanical reproduction, instant replay, news simulations, docudrama, multiple transmission sites (cable), and burgeoning video and computer technologies, it is the rare reader or viewer who has not been confused about the reality of some representation or felt the secondariness of even "original" experience. If mass-media forms are not creating a new "reality," they may be restructuring the way we experience it by affecting the way we perceive the world.

There is a dark underside to this insight, which may be responsible for the virulence of the antitheory sentiment among journalists and some sectors of the academy, which in turn is part of what Lazere says is a "long-running assault by conservative politicians, journalists, and scholars on the American academic left, particularly in literary and cultural studies" ("Literary Revisionism" 49). This is the fear, usually repressed, and detectable mainly in the unreasonable temper of the response, that what leftist theorists and cultural revisionists have been saying about the relation between texts and reality may be correct – for example, their skepticism about our ability to "know" anything for certain and even to pursue knowledge and disseminate the results of our search free from the political view within which we undertook it. It is probably always difficult to learn that there are very few uncontested facts in the world, and almost impossible to admit how one benefits from the common belief that supporting things as they are is not a political position, whereas criticizing the existing form of government, economic relations, or class system, or suggesting alternatives to particular social forms such as heterosexual marriage or the nuclear family, is clearly regarded as partisan and biased, and somehow un-American (Lazere, "Literary Revisionism" [54]).

A new collection of pieces by Joan Didion, *After Henry,* well illustrates the practical implications of the messages that have been filtering through the thick screen of conservative resistance to recent theory. In the book's opening section, as she focuses her incisive personal, New Journalistic style in what only appears to be scattershot recording of isolated scenes of the Reagan presidency and the 1988 presidential campaigns, it becomes clear that the press coverage of this significant national office and the process of electing someone to fill it has moved to a level far beyond mere "pseudoevent" or manipulation of the voting public. She shows this to be in large part the result of the press corps's complicity in transmitting "the images their sources wish transmitted," even to the point of being willing "in exchange for certain colorful details around which a 'reconstruction' can be built . . . to present these images not as a story the campaign wants told but as fact" (58). This "reconstruction" is, of course, the news story that will fill the reporter's employer's need for neutral but interesting coverage in order to sell enough papers or magazines to justify the rates charged to advertisers. (We may have moved away from partisan political coverage, but surely not from economically "interested" reporting.)

One of her most effective strategies is cumulative: she shows the transformation, through three reporters' accounts, of a Democratic presidential candidate "casually" throwing a baseball on an airport tarmac into an iconic representation of "He's just a regular guy." Any reader of Didion's account of this transformation can hardly fail to see that the abuses of "objective" journalism are far greater than any benefit in the form of information the public might get. Here is Didion's concluding analysis of this construction of a "real moment":

> What we had in the tarmac arrival with ball tossing, then, was an understanding: a repeated moment witnessed by many people, all of whom believed it to be a setup and yet most of whom believed that only an outsider, only someone too "naive" to know the rules of the game, would so describe it. (64–5)

Such collusion also renders this supposedly objective coverage far more fictive than the sophisticated political reporters convey through their modest self-referentiality. (David S. Broder began the tarmac story for the *Washington Post* with this sentence: "Dukakis called out to Jack Weeks, the handsome, curly-haired Welshman who good-naturedly shepherds us wayward pressmen through the daily vagaries of the campaign schedule" [64].) Coverage from such a deceptively self-aware viewpoint does not even manage to contradict the illusion of objectivity, which is defined as the coverage from "nobody's point of view" (as Edward Epstein quotes a producer of television news, giving Epstein his title *News from Nowhere*). Instead of taking responsibility for their agreement to "overlook the observable in the interests of obtaining a dramatic story line" (Didion 65), the reporters mask their collusion by their disingenuous references to the process of covering the story. They do not go so far as admitting that they contributed to the story, however.

This ability to co-opt criticism by incorporating the techniques of one's critics but using them to bolster the illusion one is creating may be an indication that objective journalism, rather than giving up its goals in the face of repeated assaults on its legitimacy, is adapting to the critique and in fact gathering strength. Didion's indirect reference to herself as the "naive" outsider, in the passage quoted earlier, and other allusions to her detached observation – in contrast to the other reporters, who apparently accepted the premise that "the winning of and the maintaining of public office warranted the invention of a public narrative based at no point on observable reality" (82) – contributes to a different kind of self-consciousness. Unlike the aesthetic strategy of the self-deprecating, compromised establishment journalist, she reveals her political bias, as well as the construction of her attitudes and the criticism they lead to.

It may be that only the devastating irony of a Didion or extensive analysis like Miller's of the "preemptive" self-derision of television, which protects its power by mocking its critics' derision, can reveal the complicity between consumer advertising, journalism and other mass media, and the capitalist status quo. Didion's collection (comprising pieces that appeared in the *New York Review of Books,* the *New Yorker,* and the now-defunct *New West*) is at the least a reminder that critical, political New Journalism is going strong, despite the paucity of references to it, and her results are evidence that it is needed more than ever.

The story I tell in the chapters that follow traces the separation of journalism and fiction as narrative categories (via such oppositions as "nonfiction" versus "literature," "factual" versus "literary," "real" versus "invented"), and the various ways writers and texts on the border have muddied these neat distinctions and questioned their basis. But in turn I also treat the way critics have interpreted and categorized those border-questioners – most characteristically, in terms of formalist or aesthetic norms. At each stage of the history of the relationship, things could have gone differently. There was nothing inevitable about either the separation of the two modes or the publishing, editing, teaching, and criticism that fostered and reinforced the separation, accepted the legitimacy of journalistic objectivity, and favored the production and reading of fiction in formalist terms. But because the relationship developed as it did, literature is today primarily an aesthetic category, its structuring devices are rendered invisible, and we exclude from the canon most political or historical novels and interpretations that emphasize politics or history. (As evidence, consider that the "historical novel" is now regarded primarily as a mass-market genre, and that contemporary historical novels by Didion, E. L. Doctorow, and Toni Morrison are rarely considered in that light; Birkerts's essays provide a recent, casual example of that tendency.) At the same time, criticism of nonfiction is dominated by the questions "Is it true?" "Did this really happen?"

The story starts in an earlier time, a period in which what writers produce when they write for periodicals was not viewed as very different from their fictional output. "Journalism," Carey says, "was traditionally conceived as a literary genre rather than as a species of technical writing" ("Communications" 32). The move of journalism from a sub-genre of literature to a mode dominated by objective reporting meant a loss of independence for the reporter; he (in the majority of cases, it was a "he") could no longer be a clear advocate and social critic. From writing what readers must have been aware was observed from a subjective viewpoint, journalists moved to a position of complicity with the status quo. Objective journalism rarely acknowledges its role in actively shaping our environment; instead it asserts conventions of invisibility and the naturalness of fact.

I begin with a journalist from the old school, Stephen Crane, who cared so little about whether something he wrote was a sketch, or tale, or front-page reporting that his editors have had a hard time sorting it out. By comparing interpretations of two 1897 Crane narratives – "The Open Boat" and the piece of journalism he wrote about the same incident – I show the effect of the paradigmatic assumptions about fiction and journalism on our reading practice. Characteristics we find in the short story, such as third-person point of view and hierarchy of narration, are associated with fiction, and so all the things we "know" about fiction come into play in that reading. Thus I demonstrate how we tend to universalize the fictional.

The usual view is that realism in fiction, from Twain to Hemingway, developed out of the major realists' experience as journalists, so that the techniques of American realism are those of the newsroom and the reporter. Because I define literature differently, I can see in Hemingway's 1920s narratives the construction of the illusion of objectivity – which then is elevated to the status of transcendent, universal truth, above the contingency of history, through strategies of omission, understatement, and indirection. This minimalist form of realistic fiction, which conceals its methods along with the temporality, particularity, politics, and history inherent in a nonfictional discourse like journalism – indeed excises "discourse" itself in favor of "pure" or ostensibly objective narration – thus works by ideology, defined by Roland Barthes in *Mythologies* as "what goes without saying" (11).

Although we use the term "objective" to describe the form of modernist realism perfected by Hemingway, this kind of realism did not grow out of journalism, for the journalism practiced by the likes of Crane, Dreiser, Cather, and Hemingway was subjective and personal, filled with signs of the presence of the observer or reporter and with references to its own production. Fictional objectivity is better seen as both a reaction to the commodification of artistic production and an expression of it. That is, the alienation of labor inevitable in the Taylorized workplace results in the obliteration of signs of work from the product; the corollary in artistic production is the autonomous art object, which conceals "the fact that it is itself a human construction," in Adorno's analysis (quoted in Jameson, *Marxism and Form* 408).

Next I tell the story of the rise of journalistic objectivity in the Anglo-

American tradition, likewise under the pressure of a society rapidly being transformed, first by monopoly and then by consumer or commodity capitalism. I contrast the doctrine of objectivity with literary and sociological notions of reflexivity, in order to undermine the notion that facts speak for themselves and to show how the "real" is produced through "news." Two readings demonstrate the difference between "reflexive" and "objective" (or pragmatic) reading of journalism and fiction. These include Hemingway's "Japanese Earthquake," a self-conscious interview with earthquake survivors, which shows the journalist "alienating the apparatus of production" and thus revealing the conventions of survivor interviews; and *Hiroshima,* by John Hersey, which suppresses them in a transparent form that Hersey is at pains to distinguish from fiction ("The Legend on the License").

In Chapters 4 through 6, although I continue to integrate my critical readings of journalistic narrative with history and theory, I apply my theoretical and historical theses to the journalistic narratives that have been popular in the United States since 1965. Although 1960s New Journalism and nonfiction novels have been called "literary" genres, because of their self-conscious style and techniques supposedly borrowed from fiction, I see them as an identifiable category of nonfiction, because of the way they have been treated – by the mainstream media, academics, and critics, in a labeling and stereotyping process designed to set them apart from the dominant practice. They comprise narratives that have been noticed precisely because they call attention to what has been suppressed in the separation of journalism and fiction.

The usual explanation of these practices is that they blend the factual and the literary; to Mas'ud Zavarzadeh, for example, the nonfiction novel has "the shapeliness of fiction and the authority of reality" (56). Conceiving of the new nonfiction as a hybrid form that is ultimately literary (and designating it "literary journalism" or "the literature of fact") not only splits form from content but asserts the prior claims of the world on narrative, rather than the other way around, for the devices borrowed from fiction are supposedly applied to stories of actual people and events. By regarding New Journalism as a hybrid mode, these critics sidestep the important epistemological question of the relation between discourse and reality, and the ideological implications of transparent realism. As I suggest in Chapter 4, a nonfiction novel like Tom Wolfe's *The Electric Kool-Aid Acid Test* gives instructions on how to read not only itself but the practice that it helps define. Following that process, one can read even history reflexively.

I also take up the problem of accounting for the appeal of nonfictional narratives in general and stories of sensational events in particular. The most common explanation for the popularity of New Journalism and the nonfiction novel in recent decades is that, as Philip Roth said in 1960, reality is outdoing the novelist's imagination; these genres suppos- edly answer the need for credibility that the traditional realistic novel can no longer take for granted, given the absurdity of modern life. I examine this view, expressed by novelists from Roth to Wolfe, sug- gesting that at least part of the new nonfiction's power derives from its acknowledgment of the role that language and the conventions of mime- sis play in structuring "reality" by structuring our consciousness of it. Using two nonfiction novels of crime, I show that these are different from fictional ones at the level of the story we derive from them ("what happens"), not at the level of plot, or "how the reader learns of what happens," for this is the level of narrative itself, which cannot be divided neatly into factual or fictional categories.

The story we derive from Capote's *In Cold Blood* is radically different from that of Mailer's *Executioner's Song,* for Capote suppresses his rela- tionship to the killers. Besides, his third-person, impersonal narration presents cause–effect explanations and tidies up the sociological case study in the manner of a realistic novel with closure. Mailer's massive novel accounts for its own production (the second half presents the story of the media's involvement, including that of Larry Schiller, who got Mailer to write the novel), leaves many unanswered questions, and avoids psychological explanation. The ubiquitous true-crime novel (the default nonfiction novel, to some critics) seems more closely connected to antecedents such as novels of sensation, gothic novels, and detection fiction, popular since the earliest novels published in the United States, than to documentary nonfiction or journalism. The new element that has been added to the triad of criminal or villain, victim, and sleuth (law enforcement officer or private eye) is the journalist, who recounts the whole story and then either reminds us of his particular observer's point of view (Mailer) or suppresses his role in uncovering "the facts" (Capote).

In Chapter 6 I use psychoanalytic theory to focus on the reader as fourth party to the narrative transaction. I treat Janet Malcolm's reports and essays on psychoanalysis, including *In the Freud Archives,* and a highly fact-based journalistic narrative, Wolfe's *The Right Stuff,* as well as Freud's own texts. In the case study of the "Wolf Man," Freud refuses to locate reality in events; rather, he defines a category of structural or "psychical" reality or experience: "something which has all the consis- tency of the real without being verifiable in external experience" (see Laplanche 33). Here, too, is the clearest expression of Freud's concept of *Nachträglichkeit,* or belatedness: when we alter events afterwards, have experiences before we could have had them, and derive causes from effects. In the case of our present-day "Wolfe Man," Tom, *The Right*

Stuff is a problematic and ambiguous narrative about the relationship between journalism and history, read in terms of belatedness. In his description of the Cold War rivalry between the United States and the Soviet Union to win the "space race," the "Right Stuff" turns out to be a euphemism for the death instinct, the longing to return to an earlier state of innocence and unity, with no gap between the "real" and our perception of it. But Wolfe's attention-getting, opaque style reveals his desire to leave signs that he was here, of his originality, of his anxiety at having something new to say about the overly media-exposed astronauts. Meanwhile, the first seven astronauts desperately create themselves as the first space pioneers, despite their knowledge that test pilots like Chuck Yeager were their heroic forerunners and their awareness that the space flights do not live up to the elaborate training simulations that formed the original of their belated "actual" experience. In short, we see events appropriated by texts that become "prior" or original, and the dominant interpretation (which we call "narrative history") in the process of being constructed.

My goal throughout the study is to show ways of reading contemporary narratives so as to illuminate the construction of the myths that dominate our public and private lives. A secondary aim is to help readers realize that they can learn to interpret critically and even against the implications of the formative cultural experiences that constitute their environment and determine their beliefs. As my epigraph suggests, many of these experiences come in the mediating forms of journalism, conceived in the largest sense, not simply as news that stays new, relevant, or influential.

Acknowledgments

The result of having written a book that demonstrates the effects on interpretation of reading nonfiction content through form is that I find myself paralyzed at the thought of acknowledging the many people who have contributed to this project by composing a narrative essay, which relies on sequence and therefore privilege. Many of those I want to thank are my readers, who have proved themselves adept at the practice of what I call reflexive reading and will not be fooled by a deceptively objective style into overlooking the politics of precedence or the hierarchy of effusiveness any such essay inevitably entails. And so the form I have chosen is a list, subject to interpretation primarily for its politics of inclusion or omission.

I gratefully acknowledge all those who contributed to this project, in no order save alphabetical, with four exceptions. The exceptions are my dedicatees, my family, whom I thank for their love and support (in the tangible forms of fresh garden vegetables, frequent shipments of baked goods, and regular cooking and caretaking); my wonderful friend Stanley Corkin, collaborator for a decade, whose ideas I can hardly distinguish from my own when I read anything I wrote during that period; my dissertation adviser Perry Meisel, who started me off down this road with powerful advice and challenging questions; and my patient and encouraging mentor at Vanderbilt University, Michael Kreyling, who has read this study in many different forms and has always said the right thing.

The "A" list: Chris Anderson, the anonymous readers for Cambridge University Press, Margaret Bass, the late William Buckler, Ellen Caldwell, Susan Chang, Joyce Chaplin, Mary Jane Doherty, Shelley Fisher Fishkin, Barbara Foley, Larry Frus, Teresa Goddu, Julie Greenblatt, Josephine Hendin, William Howarth, Mark Jarman, Paula Johnson, Christine Kreyling, Nancy Kranich, Larry Lerner, fine copy editor Christie Lerch, Joan Lichtman, Ilse Dusoir Lind, Vara Neverow-Turk,

James Olney, Elisabeth Perry, Jack Prostko, Gary Richards, Dennis Rygiel, Ronald Schleifer, Jane Schwartz, Richard Schweid, Marilyn Frus Schweitzer, Eric Sundquist, Jim Toplon, Valerie Traub, Roger Trefousse, Rashelle Trefousse, Nancy Walker, James Young, Dorothy Young, and students in my courses at New York University, Hunter College of the City University of New York, the Juilliard School, and Vanderbilt University.

The author acknowledges the kind permission of Southern Illinois University Press to reprint, in altered form, an essay that appeared in *Literary Nonfiction,* ed. Chris Anderson, which forms part of Chapter 1; and *Genre,* which first published an essay adapted here in Chapter 5. The Vanderbilt University Research Council awarded two summer grants for work on this manuscript. Permission to reprint four lines of "I'll Never Forget the Day I Read a Book," by Jack Barnett and Jimmy Durante, was graciously granted by the Jack Barnett Estate and Jimmy Durante Music Publishing.

Introduction:
What Isn't Literature?

"I'll Never Forget the Day I Read a Book"

It wasn't a history,
I know because it had no plot.
It wasn't a mystery,
Because nobody there got shot.
      – Jack Barnett and Jimmy Durante

There may be no gods, but there is a pattern: names by themselves
may have no magic, but the *act* of naming, the physical utterance,
obeys the pattern.
                                – Pynchon, *Gravity's Rainbow*

Despite the recent efforts of some academic literary theorists and philosophers to break down the barriers between literature and "Other" categories of discourse – that is, between fiction and nonfiction – and the insistence of a few writers that what they are doing makes these distinctions meaningless, most critics and readers continue to respect the terms, especially in regard to news on the one hand and novels on the other.[1] No matter what criteria theorists specify to define the "literary," it appears that journalism in general does not meet them. Because journalism is dependent on the occasions that bring it into being, supposedly only those seeking evidence from the past, such as historians, will find its reports useful when our interest in these occasions wanes. It is thus easily dismissed because of its ephemerality. Related to this is Aristotle's distinction between history, which is tied to actuality and thus to the "particular," and poetry's representative, and therefore "universal," subject matter and appeal; journalism, by definition, has merely "local" interest. It is also difficult to argue that journalism shares with literature ba commitment to "pleasure rather than truth," in Coleridge's phrase, and thus to make a case for its being considered literary in a straightforwardly aesthetic framework. If we use the category of "fiction" to describe literary prose, what journalists write obviously cannot be con-

1

sidered literary, because they have pledged to report events, not to embellish them. Even when the concept of fictionality is stretched to mean "transcendent of its context" or having a value apart from contingent facts (Rader, "Literary Form" 38), journalistic writing hardly qualifies, for it is tied to everyday life and is thus hampered by its pragmatic function, which is to provide information. In contrast to fiction's imaginative freedom and creativity, journalism is discursive and mundane. It is objective where fiction is subjective, and more like science than literature in its transparent, rather than self-conscious, form. And as a popular form with mass appeal, it is considered inferior to an elitist "Literature," defined defensively and comparatively, "against all other modes" (Williams, *Marxism* 51).

There are some exceptions to this exclusion of journalism from literature, for there are various journalistic works from the eighteenth and nineteenth centuries which are now considered to have literary value. In every case, however, the text has either been designated a member of some literary genre, such as the essay or satire, or has been labeled "literary nonfiction." Thus the journalistic text has crossed over into literature by meeting at least one of its criteria. For example, a text is said to have passed the test of time when we read it for its formal beauty or the universal truth it expresses, after our interest in its content has waned (Frye 307); thus Johnson's *Rambler* essays, Swift's "Modest Proposal," Hazlitt's description of a boxing match, and Twain's travel correspondence are eighteenth- and nineteenth-century examples of literary journalism. Because of the "endurance" criterion, not much journalism from even the first half of the twentieth century has become "literary," judging from anthologies and criticism. (It is probably safe to say that journalism by Crane, Hemingway, Cather, and others has been collected and reprinted not for its intrinsic merit but because we are interested in the relation between these writers' journalism and their realistic novels, or simply because these writers are important novelists.)

In the case of contemporary journalistic narratives, the situation is similar to the one in which we wait to see which of the many novels published each year become candidates for inclusion in the canon of literature. As Richard Ohmann has shown, conferral of this "precanonical" status on a novel depends on its selling in large numbers, being kept in print, receiving scholarly attention in literary journals, and being taught to students in high schools and colleges (in part by being included or excerpted in anthologies). Most of the novels published each year, which are regarded as "literary" by virtue of being fictional, are soon relegated to the category of mass or popular literature. This selection has little to do with a work of fiction's intrinsic value (which would enable us to predict its status as a classic), because, as Ohmann points out, what we mean by "excellence" or the best in literature is "a constantly changing, socially chosen value" ("Shaping" 73), dependent on economic and intellectual "markets."

The process by which literary status is conferred is even more necessary (and lengthier) in the case of nonfiction, and the determining socioeconomic forces are even more likely to be repressed or ignored in favor of the endurance criterion. This is because market forces are associated with the timeliness of the content (readers want to know only about what is "new" or relevant), and literariness with aesthetic criteria. Critics assume that the determining aesthetic factors are essentially present in the work, and that time will reveal them after the inevitable loosening of its ties to particular social and cultural phenomena. James Wolcott's comments on *The Electric Kool-Aid Acid Test* may be typical in this regard. In his view, the alternatives regarding Tom Wolfe's best-selling, highly acclaimed novel, fourteen years after its publication in 1968, were that it would either become "a true landmark of brain-fried Sixties sensibility" or would finally be regarded as an unreadable "word-monster" (23).

Although readers may have naturalized these categories of fiction and nonfiction, literary and "other" kinds of writing, and seem to sort them out instinctively, despite the rationalizations of the categories provided by literary critics and academics, there are signs that these commonplace distinctions are not self-evident, and that readers and viewers at the end of the twentieth century find them problematic. We have not only an array of tabloid newspapers, with their headlines of imagined Elvis sightings and improbable births, but tabloid television, which blurs the line between entertainment (fiction) and news programming (nonfiction or fact), puts journalists into prominence as newsmakers, and reduces the distance between viewers and journalist-entertainers and their subjects by utilizing live audiences as participants and interlocutors. Thus presentation on television takes precedence over content, which is gradually emptied out. At the beginning of the 1990s, network news programs featured simulations and "re-creations" of news events: "CBS Evening News" had been accused of showing staged reenactments of war scenes in Afghanistan, and pictures of oil-soaked cormorants supposedly injured by the Iraqi sabotage of pipelines on the Saudi coast during the Gulf War were revealed to be reruns of footage shot after a 1983 spill during the Iran-Iraq War (Ireland). We are inundated with "docudramas," televised dramatizations of recent events, a form that, according to the *New York Times,* "usurps" the authenticity of the "real" journalistic medium of the "documentary" and betrays the ideal of objectivity by refusing to give all sides ("Chicanery"). Since the late 1960s, while media critics, reviewers, and journalists were debating the validity of so-called hybrid forms like the New Journalism and the nonfiction novel, many techniques from these forms were being discreetly assimilated by mainstream journalism.

Such phenomena, and the reaction to them in both popular and academic criticism, suggest that the line separating news from novels ought to be reconsidered, especially in view of recent literary theory that makes the fiction–nonfiction distinction the locus of many issues, among them the nature of realism or the relation between language and reality, the contrast between subjective experience and objective knowledge, and the problem of the status of the subject as well as of the text. These concerns are already implicit in any discussion of nonfictional texts, for these narratives, by highlighting the illusion of reality while effacing themselves as discourse, seem to be "the thing itself" – that is, to capture the world or give certain knowledge of the object – while all the time only "signifying" reality. As Roland Barthes says, historical narratives assert "*this happened,* but the meaning conveyed is only that someone is making that assertion" ("Historical Discourse" 154). Fictional narrative also asserts "what happened," but nonfictional narratives are overdetermined, that is, doubly "real": their materials are verifiable by other means, so that we take their subjects to be actual, and they are narrated with the rhetorical strategies we group under the label of "realism." Which domain, then, has priority: the text, or events in the world? Is there an unbridgeable gap between our subjective experience and our objective observation of events in the world? Does language enable our sense of a unified life, because of our habitual experience of coherent texts that have a beginning, middle, and end and are narrated in a rising and falling pattern?

"Nonfictional" or "true-life" narratives are a likely place to consider these questions and to develop a reflexive reading practice that, in theorizing the satisfactions or problematics of narrative, moves beyond formalism to historicize what are usually figured as the "universal," "transcendent" properties of narrative and the pleasure and knowledge we take from them. Because nonfiction (especially journalism) does not come prewrapped in an aesthetic package, with universal relevance implied, as does any novel, its ties to its particular context are not easily loosened, and generalizations about universal human nature are not readily abstracted from the particulars. A new conception of literariness would view these ties as valuable, instead of something to transcend; the reader would regard the text's referents as inseparable from its formal means and would make this dynamic relationship central to a reading. To arrive at this kind of reading of journalism is difficult, under the dominant conceptions of literature today, for only certain nonfictional narratives – some New Journalism and nonfiction novels, for example –

are regarded as belonging to literature, and their designation by special terms such as "literary journalism" and "the literature of fact" shows that they are exceptions. Honoring only selected forms of journalism as literature emphasizes the line that separates the two modes, confirming the late-nineteenth-century notion of literature that arose specifically to exclude journalism and other factual narrative, defining literature as a collection of timeless works of universal value and appeal. In other words, only works that transcend their context need apply for the category.

If we look at some of the ambiguities in the positions of those who would set journalism off from literature, we may see why the separation is vulnerable to reading as well as writing practices that blur it; then a theory that would collapse all discourse back into one category – such as the one I am proposing – may seem more appropriate. My goal is to break down the hard line between literature, specifically novels and short stories, which we regard as created fictions, and nonliterary texts – journalism, biography, history, essays – which we think of as records of actuality. I propose to substitute for the concept of "literariness" the practice of what could be termed "literary reading" but which, for clarity, I shall term "reading for the process," or "reflexive reading." In brief, I will argue that as readers we produce what we call "literature" when we read to discover how a text, through its style, "makes" reality, that is, when we read its content through its form. By this means we enter what Henry James calls the "world in which we know nothing except by style" (148), so that the most obviously "literary" prose is narrative that acknowledges its basis in imagination.

This practice avoids the pitfalls of defining the literary object and listing its intrinsic properties (or those inherent in the literary reading situation), so long as the reader or critic can avoid reifying the process by attributing what we produce or enact in this reading to properties of the text. Although reflexive readings are by definition self-conscious, this is not to privilege self-conscious texts or formally interesting ones (in a reflexive reading all forms are interesting, even those that efface themselves as form), but to emphasize the reading whereby we uncover the processes of production of any text. To do this, we must render its language palpable rather than transparent and then apprehend the message via that opaque form. This level of attention to the text combines a naïve or referential reading (when the illusion created is regarded as real) and an autoreferential one (which notes how the language itself works to create the illusion) into what Karlheinz Stierle calls a "pseudoreferential" reading – one in which we consider almost simultaneously both the illusion and how the text produces that illusion and signals this process to us (89–90).

It may be argued that this approach is not new, that good readers and critics have always read as though form and content were inseparable. I contend that although there always have been readings of this kind, this practice has not been paradigmatic under the New Criticism, the dominant twentieth-century school of theory and criticism, which, because it developed around poetry, promotes the aestheticization of narrative and isolates particular canonical works apart from their social and political contexts. Of course this emphasis on form was itself an attempt to counter both the illusory or naïve readings that realistic novels commonly receive at the hands of untrained readers and the criticism, dominant at the beginning of English studies, that emphasized the biographical and historical roots of literary works. Similarly, structuralism and linguistic-based criticism are varieties of formalist criticism (see Tompkins 225–6), and deconstruction has been discredited, at least in part, because of its tendency toward an essentializing formalism.

Therefore I want to advocate what I call a process of "reading reflexively" as the basis for conceiving of literariness, and ultimately as a way to erode the status of "literature" as a category, for I believe the approach to defining literature taken by formalist theorists has perpetuated an exclusionary, apolitical, largely ahistorical objective category. This in turn has led to an essentialist reading practice that assimilates even innovative, critical, radical texts to a normalizing view of groups and events and of "human nature."[2] In other words, the dominant conception of literature constructs a mythology around texts (Barthes, *Mythologies* 134–7). As Barthes points out, when literature becomes a timeless or essentialized category it also becomes an ideological concept, because the connections of particular texts to the conditions of their production are lost. "A conjuring trick has taken place; [myth] has turned reality inside out, it has emptied it of history and has filled it with nature" (142).

This is not the place for an all-encompassing survey of theories of literature.[3] Books have been written about the problem of defining the literary object (Hernadi) or proposing and explaining a single theory of literariness (Hämburger, Banfield, Pratt), and "What is literature?" has been called the primary question of "bourgeois criticism," if not of literary theory (Bennett 170). Historically, it is evident that the concept of "literature," in its present sense, arose by the end of the nineteenth century, largely in order to set off the novel as an aesthetic form, along with poetry. Evidence that "literature" became equivalent to the older category "poetry" is that the two terms have become interchangeable in discussions about the poetic principle, literary techniques, poeticality or literariness. The category of literature is now applied retroactively to include narrative from Homer on, making it even more difficult to define, because it includes so many different modes of writing. But the fact that it did come to apply retroactively to a particular class of texts gives it a historical meaning that needs to be considered.

This after-the-fact construction of a class designated as "literature" and the difficulty of determining which contemporary works will be part of the literary canon suggests that instead of constructing a definition to set literature off from what then becomes an undifferentiated mass of "Other" discourses, it will be useful to describe the effects of such discriminations on our judgment – our reading and criticism – of what have been considered "nonliterary" narratives. Rather than examine the definitions to see if journalism can sometimes cross over to literature, perhaps we can reconceptualize writing so that it is not dependent on naturalized notions of "literary" and "Other" (and on the separation of subject and object). These theories of literariness have hampered our reading of fictional narratives, as well as making nonfictional discourse decidedly secondary. The question seems no longer to be "What is literature?" but "What is *not* literature?" or perhaps "What has been the effect of the categories of 'literary' and 'nonliterary' texts on our reading of nonfictional discourses, as well as of novels and short stories?"

Of all the rationales for excluding journalism from literature, the most obvious one, literature's fictionality, rests on what is called the different ontological status of the referents of fiction and journalism. The commonplace observation is that the journalist deals with actual characters and with events that have occurred; the novelist is free to invent both, as well as to refer to historical ones. As John Hersey succinctly puts it, the legend on the journalist's license says, "None of this was made up" ("Legend" 2).

No matter how "natural" this distinction seems, however, it is not an innocent one. In the first place, those referents are nowhere near the text, much less there on the page, and so unless the reader has firsthand knowledge of the subjects she has no way of knowing what is actual, unless it is verified by other narratives.[4] This has led some critics to develop the notion of a text's "frame" and the "contract" the frame puts into effect between writer and reader (Hellmann chap. 1; Foley, *Telling*), so that the reader knows whether the subjects are invented or historical and reads the text appropriately as fiction or as journalism. Evidence of a work's status may be supplied by a subtitle or label on the contents page or jacket copy, in a preface or afterword by the author or editor, by its library classification, or, in the case of a first-person narrative, by the narrator's "identity or non-identity with the author under whose name the narration has been published" (Cohn 13).

But to read a narrative as fictional, under most definitions, is to accept the nonexistence of the referents outside the text that brought them into being; what, therefore, of the apparent truthfulness of the recognizably factual statements that the narrative also makes: for example, its use of proper names? The problem of fiction's mixture of invented and historical referents has led to the claim that fictional narratives are not propositional, because judgments of truth or falsity are suspended. In this definition, the world that novels or short stories refer to is acknowledged as a creation, even though these works may be set in a recognizable place and, occasionally, have characters who can be identified with real-world people (sometimes with names changed). Conceding the text's ability to create alternative worlds has the effect of making its referential level secondary to its inner coherence, for these hypothetical creations are not usually meant to be read allegorically, that is, as referring primarily to the external world (although they may be, as are romans à clef). Thus many theorists declare that "literary works do not pretend to describe or assert"; instead, they turn inward toward their own form (Frye 74).[5]

This move from fictionality (defined as "giving the illusion of reality") to aesthetic form is also implied by other definitions of literature. According to speech-act theory, for example, fictional discourse does not refer to actual people and events; it imitates "natural" discourse (B. Smith 30), and the interest is presumably in the qualities of the imitation. Ohmann says, "Since the quasi-speech-acts of literature are not carrying on the world's business – describing, urging, contracting, etc. – the reader may well attend to them in a non-pragmatic way, and thus allow them to realize their emotive potential" ("Speech Acts" 17).

This peculiar means of asserting the nonreferentiality of fiction, when applied to those supposedly "nonfictional" narratives that have been accepted as literary because of our interest in their style, involves us in an obvious contradiction. Texts such as James Agee's *Let Us Now Praise Famous Men* must be considered fictional in some sense, even if it means giving up the possibility of vouching for the factualness of its statements, because literary prose is considered to be fiction. Paradoxically, works that start out as "nonfiction," purporting to tell the truth about the world, no longer can be said to make truth claims once they have been classified as literature, and so literature, Hatlen argues, can be defined as "what we are no longer interested in."[6] It is clear that narrative does give up its nonfictional status when it is enshrined in the canon of literature, even if this happens within a few decades of publication (as in the case of Agee's putative exercise in sociological journalism), because nonfiction is thought of as the realm of discourse where true and false are important distinctions, and literature is thought of as the realm where, even when a work represents the world, its truth or falsity is irrelevant. Not so incidentally, this makes the term "literary nonfiction" logically contradictory, for under these notions of literature a narrative can be either nonfictional or literary, but not both. (The term thus joins "true stories" and "nonfiction fiction" in my list of most meaningful oxymora.)

Aesthetic criteria dominate another form of discrimination between literature and nonliterary categories as well. As anyone who has taken a literature course knows, although literary prose is generally conceded to be fictional (for the reasons just given), not all fiction is considered literary. Much popular or generic fiction, such as detective, gothic, and romance novels, as well as didactic, sentimental, or otherwise "flawed" examples, are not deemed worthy of the category, which is evidence that the terms "fiction" and "literature" have narrowed to include only *aesthetically interesting* mimetic prose. Not only does this define the term by one of its properties – art is what is artistically rendered – as Todorov points out ("Notion" 8), but the only way the category can be maintained is by careful discrimination according to standards like formal beauty and the expression of universal truth (Williams, *Marxism* 51).

From even this brief summary of the principal definitions of literature, two dominant conceptions emerge. The primary tendencies are to emphasize either a work's imitation of reality or its self-display, that is, its rhetorically organized features. Other definitions easily fit into one or the other of these frameworks. For example, Mary Louise Pratt mentions four criteria usually used to define the category: literature is fictitious, autonomous or self-focused, pleasure-oriented, and world creating (99). The first and last are varieties of fictionality, and the middle two are aspects of the rhetorical.

These two kinds of definitions – and the problems in applying them, indeed the instability of the category – result from the relatively recent historical development of literature as a specialized realm of texts embodying universal values and "higher" truths. Raymond Williams has given the best account of literary fiction's historical roots: its relation to economic and cultural conditions and its status as a "specializing social and historical category . . . a particular form of the social development of language" (*Marxism* 53). Williams shows literature beginning in the eighteenth century and settling in by the end of the nineteenth, in a subtle process inseparable from the growth of mass journalism, the elevation of positivist science, and the technologizing of much of life as well as labor (*Marxism* 46–54). He accounts for the development of this specialized category by pointing out that, as the way a writer's productions reached their audience shifted from patronage to subscription publishing to modern commercial distribution (and, in the 1980s, to the consolidation of most publishers into a few giant corporations), by analogy with other forms of production the work of the writer became a business; the novel readily became a "commodity" and literature "a trade" (*Culture and Society*, 52–3). Not only did artists, poets, and writers react to being thought of merely as producers of a "commodity" by describing themselves as "specially endowed" but, together with critics, they emphasized "the embodiment in art of certain human values, capacities, energies, which the development of society towards an industrial civilization was felt to be threatening or even destroying" (53–4; and see Hough xvii).

Thus, to set some forms of narrative prose above the commercial, the nonpropositional quality of literature was promoted; and so, in most definitions of "fiction" (whether it is regarded as mimetic or rhetorically governed), fiction is said not to make assertions. Fiction is world-creating discourse brought about by narrators of imitation, or "quasi," speech acts (Pratt 87; Ohmann 14); or fiction consists of "feigned reality statements" (Hämburger 313). To philosophers of language, fiction is narrative in which "noun phrases with virtual reference have no actual reference," and so it is not false but instead constitutive of "fictional reality which can only be taken as fictionally true" (Banfield 258).

Also, because the term "fiction" retains its earlier meaning of "false," "lying or feigning," fiction pretends merely to be imitating what it actually invents. But at least since the Renaissance hardly anyone has wanted to view fiction as defined by its false relation to the world, and so an important asserted characteristic of fiction becomes its ability to tell a "higher truth" – to transcend questions of truth or falsehood by expressing essential, universally held values and insights about the human condition (see Nelson). The habit of using the term "fictional" to cover both of these meanings is probably motivated by logical fictionality, such as the obvious fictivity of invented referents, impossible subjective knowledge indicated by represented consciousness, or the presumed nonidentity of narrator and author. Because to common logic these textual features appear to be fictional, they have been identified by some theorists as sure signs of fiction.

In a larger sense, however, fictionality can be subsumed into the aesthetic, that is, can itself be regarded as a rhetorical category. In this view, language is constitutive or fictive in its social use, and so the various examples of fictivity are the result of particular rhetorical effects. In the case of referents, the represented world created in realistic narrative is the product of tropes of imitation, that is, of a particular group of rhetorical figures and specific narrative structures (for example, self-effacing narrator, verisimilar characters, hierarchy of narration, sequences of plot events leading to closure). Similarly, free indirect speech is always imagined, whether by a fictional narrator or a historical one;

and both of these narrative personae are fictional, that is, projections of characters, even when they have a real-world counterpart, because we derive our knowledge of them from texts. Consequently, fictional narrative cannot be distinguished from nonfictional narrative on the basis of the fictivity of any of its elements, for even fictivity must be represented in language. Rhetorically, no state or condition is more imaginary than any other: all characters and personae are created; the world is constituted after the fact by texts; and in a manner of speaking "all speech acts are imitation speech acts" (Culler 215).

As we know, however, this distinction between fiction and nonfiction is made all the time and on just this basis (fiction is more imaginary or imaginative), which shows that the formalist distinction has been naturalized to the point that it will take a more developed theory and a demonstration of its validity to convince readers that all narratives have the same status: that they are textually indistinguishable and that their fictionality or literariness depends on the way they are read and in what context. Whether separated into two distinct notions or collapsed into an inevitably formalist one, the dominant conception of literary fiction sets it apart from ordinary discourse as somehow unreal, and the effect of the aestheticized category is to distance the literary work from the particular situation in which it was written and is being read. The precariousness of the category is revealed, however, by the continuous critical effort to justify and perpetuate it, to rationalize the existence of a category posited as natural. The multiplicity of definitions and explanations has succeeded at least in determining the form of the argument, for it is almost impossible to move literary and narrative theory off this point of intersecting interests: its concern with defining the literary object and in ranking texts according to their beauty or truth value (Williams, *Marxism* 146).

What if we did not take the existence of literature for granted, as most definers of literature do before working backward to construct a definition that accounts for its characteristics? In Chapter 1, rather than seek a broadened definition of the literary object, one that would include at least some forms of journalism, I examine the effect on our interpretations of defining literature as a separate realm (and justifying it in myriad ways) by comparing two texts that fall into different categories as a result of the separation.

1

Writing After the Fact: Crane, Journalism, and Fiction

A man said to the universe:
"Sir, I exist!"
"However," replied the universe,
"The fact has not created in me
A sense of obligation."
– Stephen Crane, *War Is Kind*

It is by now a common strategy of critics to set two works from the domains of fiction and nonfiction side by side in order to test the distinction between the two realms or to account for differences in terms of a particular theory. Two well-known exercises of this type are John Searle's comparison of a novel with a story from the *New York Times* (325–6) and Barbara Herrnstein Smith's juxtaposition of a biographical passage from a history and the similarly biographical introduction of the title character in Tolstoy's *Death of Ivan Ilyich* (29–30). Both critics decide that it is not possible to distinguish between the nonfictional example and the literary one on the basis of particular properties in the texts themselves. Instead, they conclude, evidence of a work's category must be gathered from other aspects of the discourses, such as expressions of authorial intention and their influence on the reader's decision about how to approach the work (for example, responding to the "frame"). The fictional work, in each case, is ultimately distinguished by its suspension of truth claims. While the factual text asserts propositions meant to be taken as meaningful, the fictional one only imitates "natural" discourse or only pretends to refer.

David Lodge has performed a similar comparison, in this case using two nonfictional examples, to see why we categorize as literature some works that do not foreground their fictionality or express "an intentionality to write literature," while we regard others as merely good journalism (or biography, etc.). Like most formalist or structuralist definers of literature, he bases his conception on the belief that we read a work as literature when we read it " 'as if ' the criteria of truthfulness did not apply" (*Modes* 9, 8). Thus he determines that a New Zealand journalist's account of a hanging is not literary because it "depends on our trust that it is historically verifiable," whereas George Orwell's essay "A Hanging" is an effective piece of fiction because it does not require a factual or real-life basis (12). Lodge's attempt to show more systematic foregrounding of artistic elements in Orwell's piece and his emphasis on its coherent internal structure at the expense of references to historical time and place make this split of aesthetic and referential aspects seem inevitable in literary works with historical signifieds.

Dividing narrative along these lines is especially problematic for journalism because of journalism's historical referents. Readers have a difficult time separating these particulars from reality because they are likely to read of the same characters and events in other contemporary accounts; thus the "reality" of these narratives is overdetermined, and despite the fact that these "real signifieds" are "available" only in textual form, they are connected more strongly with the referential than with their aesthetic or textual dimension. Lodge's method thus virtually precludes classifying journalism as literature.

Then, too, Lodge's conclusion follows from the examples he has chosen; all the effects he notes can be explained more satisfactorily by the fact that he believes Orwell to be a better writer than the New Zealand journalist he compares him with. Lodge's determining criteria turn out to be normative: nonfictional works are literary when they respond "with credit" to a fictional reading (7), for Lodge implies that nonfiction writing is "good" when it has the effect of making the question of whether something happened irrelevant. There are other variables besides these that determine the different effects the two pieces have on us, such as different authors, but probably the most important factor is the different contexts in which Lodge reads them. Lodge admits that the reprinting of Orwell's story in different settings caused him to reconsider his opinion of the story's dependence on factuality, and he makes an attempt to find out whether Orwell actually witnessed a hanging (but decides ultimately that it does not matter whether he did or not). What Lodge does not admit is that because he "knows" "A Hanging" to be literature already (on the evidence of its reprinting in various contexts and its being the object of a variety of commentary), he is predisposed to find proof of it according to his theory.[1]

It may be that the categories of fiction and nonfiction, literature and other, actually determine the differences we think we notice by common sense. What would be the effect of separating these naturalized categories from our reading of two prose narratives that are commonly distinguished as routine journalism on the one hand and a masterpiece of short story literature on the other? To accomplish this exercise we will have to suspend our belief in the myth of literature, that is, remind ourselves that literature is a socially constructed category rather than a natural one. Although we cannot read as though our minds were blank slates, with no knowledge of conventional assumptions about the distinctions between literary and nonliterary texts, we can read with a different intention: to see what our interpretations might be if we did not accept or assume the different status of the two categories. This turnabout may be more useful when the two works in different genres are by the same writer. I have chosen Stephen Crane's famous story "The Open Boat" and his journalistic account of the same incident, "Stephen Crane's Own Story," which appeared on the front page of the *New York Press* on 7 January 1897 (datelined January 6). ("The Open Boat" appeared in *Scribner's* in June 1897 but had been submitted by February 25.) By treating two narratives not only by a single writer but about the same incident, written and published only months apart, we reduce the number of variables that Lodge had to deal with considerably. Then we do not have to consider the results of evaluating two writers' styles differently, and we are not isolating short passages out of longer texts to prove a point.[2]

Both narratives are accounts of the events surrounding the sinking of the ship *Commodore,* which was "filibustering" by illegally carrying weapons and munitions from Florida to Cuba, aiding Cuban rebels in an insurrection against Spanish rule. Crane was aboard, disguised as a crew member, in order to cover the story for his newspaper. (Journalists were banned from such expeditions because the United States was officially neutral.) In "Stephen Crane's Own Story," Crane narrates events (in the first person) from the time he went aboard the *Commodore* in Jacksonville, Florida, on New Year's Eve, 1896, to the ship's sinking (possibly as a result of sabotage) the next day, an event which he and three comrades watched from their precarious position in a 10-foot dinghy. "The Open Boat" derives from the thirty hours Crane spent in the tiny boat with the oiler, cook, and captain of the *Commodore* as they fought the Atlantic swells and steered for the Florida coast. When no one on shore spotted them to send a rescue craft out, they swam for the beach; three of them made it safely, but the oiler was drowned.

In comparing these two narratives, I find no objective properties of text, such as rhetoricity or fictionality, that enable us to distinguish fiction from nonfiction (although I am not predisposed to find them, any more than Lodge, Searle, or Smith is, for like them I am looking for something other than properties to account for the difference). Both narratives use figurative language, predominantly simile (especially in the *Press* article), metaphor (more frequent in the short story), personification, and irony. Neither invents characters or events. Both narratives follow the historical sequence of events surrounding the *Commodore* disaster that can be verified in other contemporary newspaper reports, the ship's log and other shipping records, and accounts by witnesses (Stallman, *Biography,* chaps. 14–15; apps. 5–7). Both proceed chronologically, with some digressions and foreshadowing. However, the news story telescopes the outcome, merely mentioning in the final two paragraphs the thirty hours "in an open boat," the bravery of the *Commodore*'s captain and the oiler, Billy Higgins, and Higgins's death. Thus the later narrative, "'The Open Boat," for all practical purposes picks up where the detailed journalism leaves off, with the four men in the boat in heavy seas. Neither story invents facts or characters, although both narratives inevitably proceed by invention – in the rhetorical sense of producing the subject matter according to previous literary models while appearing to copy from nature or reality ("Invention").

The news story dispenses with many of the "who, what, when, where, and why" conventions of journalism; few particulars are given after the ship gets under way (partly because this is the "following" story, supplementing the *New York Press* reports of January 4, and announced in a "sidebar" on Crane and his work that appeared that day on page 2).[3] For example, we do not know how many men were on the ship and how many were lost, and there are other mysteries. Proper names are more in evidence in the journalistic account: six participants are named, including the *Commodore*'s Captain Murphy. But the oiler, Billy Higgins, is named in both versions, and in both some figures are named only by their roles: "the cook," "the Cuban leader," "the chief engineer," and "the correspondent." Although both narratives use techniques that we associate with fiction, it does not seem likely that we would say about either that its truth claims do not matter, for the by-lined correspondent of "Stephen Crane's Own Story" wants to tell us, as the headline says, "how the *Commodore* was wrecked and how he escaped," and in *Scribner's* the following subtitle appeared below the title "The Open Boat": "A tale intended to be after the fact: being the experience of four men from the sunk steamer *Commodore*." This subtitle was repeated when the story was reprinted in a collection, which Crane dedicated by name to his three companions in the ordeal (Levenson lxvi n.).

In short, literature cannot be separated from other kinds of texts by making literariness an inherent property of the writing. (Texts do have qualities, but literariness is not one of them.) Some narratives nevertheless seem to receive literary readings as a matter of course. If literary interpretations are demanded by some texts and encouraged by others, but possible in all discourse, what conventions of reading account for our predisposition to regard these two narratives in different ways and to evaluate one as superior to the other? Although "Stephen Crane's Own Story" probably had more readers than the *Scribner's* story in 1897, "The Open Boat" has doubtless had many more readers since then, for it is widely anthologized and regularly called a masterpiece of naturalistic fiction (Cady 151; Walcutt 67); the piece of journalism, on the other hand, is reprinted primarily to show how Crane "transformed" a true experience into art – an exercise that already seems less predictable than it at first appeared. Are these normative differences the result of our culture's valuation of literature, or are there also differences owing to the speed with which the first "dispatch" (an apt label) was written or to the differences in form of publication?

Matthew Arnold is reputed to have described journalism as "literature in a hurry," and so perhaps readers find the short story superior merely because it was written "after the fact," when Crane had had time to reflect and consider, to digest the experience. But all historical narrative is deferred in relation to its subject, and if the time lapse between these two narratives is indeed a factor in the short story's literariness, then there ought to be features in the text of "The Open Boat" that affect our perception of it as different, as "literary."

There are changes in "The Open Boat" which we associate with our reading of fiction: besides the illusion of the real, there is the convention of closure and a complex system of narration (Belsey 70). These are sometimes regarded as literary qualities because of the kinds of readings they stimulate. And as we shall see, "The Open Boat" fits the conventions and codes of "naturalism," the intensified form of realism that lent itself to the aestheticization of fiction in the first decades of the twentieth century. We can see this from the way "The Open Boat" has become an exemplary text of New Criticism – for instance, in Caroline Gordon and Allen Tate's *House of Fiction*. Because Gordon admired the dramatically new way of seeing that Crane introduced into American literature, she focused primarily on the technical innovations that facilitated it, such as variations in narrative perspective and point-of-view technique. While she was interested in technique, in order to teach student readers about form in fiction – that is, form in and of itself – we seek textual features that enable the thematizing of naturalism and the universalization of a very specific "true story." Our first clue comes in the significant change from first person (in the news story) to third, which offers the narrator and reader an external perspective on the men in the boat. This shift also makes it possible for the implied author of the short story to vary the distance between the narrator and the characters and events he speaks about, and to mediate among the various discourses within the text, including the free indirect discourse of the protagonist, the "correspondent." We can account for these effects by using descriptive linguistic categories developed by Emile Benveniste.

Benveniste, discussing French texts, makes a distinction between history (*histoire*) and discourse (*discours*), based on the use of two types of past tense for narrative in French (the simple past and the perfect) and on the corollary absence of the first and second persons in the simple past. Roland Barthes also has noted the effect of a distinctive past tense (with the accompanying use of third person) for written French texts (*Writing* 29–40). Although the distinction is not linguistically the same in English, the terms have also been used by contemporary theorists of narrative to distinguish between two types of narration: the story which seems to narrate itself without the intervention of a speaker, and the discourse of the narrator which implies a reader or listener and refers to the act of speaking (the "enunciation") as such. In Benveniste's explanation, with the system of historical narration (which uses primarily the simple past and the third person) "we can imagine the whole past of the world as being a continuous narration." The author remains "faithful to his historical purpose" and proscribes "everything that is alien to the narration (discourse, reflections, comparisons). As a matter of fact, there is then no longer even a narrator. The events are set forth chronologically, as they occurred. No one speaks here; the events seem to narrate themselves" (208).

In contrast, "discourse" assumes a speaker and a hearer and the speaker's "intention of influencing the other in some way." Obviously all kinds of oral discourse are intentional in this sense, and so are the genres that derive from oral discourse, such as diaries, letters, autobiographical novels, "all the genres in which someone addresses himself to someone, proclaims himself as the speaker, and organizes what he says in the category of person" (208–9). The primary signals of discourse are either the first person or the perfect tense, but all tenses are possible, except the simple past, or aorist. When the simple past is used, the narration has shifted to *histoire*. Many such shifts are of course likely in any text, for purely historical narration cannot be maintained for very long; it is the dominance of one of these forms in a given genre or text that concerns us.

Despite the fact that English has no corollary literary tense, we can use the basic dichotomy of the two levels of narration (what Todorov in *The Poetics of Prose* calls the "two distinct levels of the speech-act") to explain our perception of two kinds of communication in realistic narratives: the transparent representation of "reality" (*histoire*) and the reference to the communication itself (discourse), which implies a speaker (a subject) and a listener. Todorov (*Poetics* 25) assures us that "each language possesses a certain number of elements which serve to inform us exclusively about the subject and the other elements of the speech-act and which effect the conversion of language into discourse; the others serve exclusively to 'present the phenomena which have occurred' [Benveniste's definition of *histoire*]."

It is this self-referential aspect of discourse that prevents the reader from regarding such prose as transparently "real," as Lionel Gossman emphasizes. "The tenses of [discourse] all maintain a relation to the present and direct attention to the subject, to the act of speaking (*l'énonciation*), and to the present relation between narrator or speaker and reader or listener, rather than exclusively to the events being narrated (*l'énoncé*)" (21). This description of discourse enables us to see why "Stephen Crane's Own Story" can be told chronologically, following journalistic conventions, and yet achieve all the variety that shifting tenses makes possible. As Benveniste insists, the perfect is "the tense that will be chosen by whoever wishes to make the reported event ring vividly in our ears and to link it to the present" (210). This makes possible hindsight and foreshadowing, as when the three whistle blasts of the departing *Commodore* are remembered by the narrator as being impressively sad wails, and when the cook has premonitions of the ship's destruction.

Another effect of the first-person discourse, predominantly in the perfect, is that we know the source of the double view (of the past, from the platform of the present). It is always the journalist-narrator who speaks, even when he uses the simple past to relate events chronologically. The premonitions, interpretations of events, and judgments are always attributable to this voice, and it is also the source of the coherence of the narrative. Most importantly, the constant reminder of the speaker and his production of the story he tells so eloquently precludes our taking the events narrated to be the actuality. We are always aware that it is an interpretation, a version told from hindsight, although this realization does not detract from the narrative's vividness. The narrator does not assert "what actually happened," as twentieth-century "objective" journalism claims to do, but only claims to give Crane's "own story," his subjective account, in the tradition of late-nineteenth-century personal reportage.

When critics emphasize such features as the "tonal objectivity" of this report, in which Crane supposedly adopts a "reportorial stance" in order to suppress his emotions (particularly horror [Katz xvii]), they seem to be ignoring its similarities to the short story he was to write in the next few weeks and the absence of the very journalistic conventions that would support their point. Indeed, they seem to locate in the newspaper account what their expectations of reportage lead them to find, as when

Eric Solomon calls its prose "unadorned, measured," and labels it a "documentary article" that "sticks to the facts . . . without distortion or heightening" (151, 152).

That this is not an accurate description of "Stephen Crane's Own Story" is obvious from reading the opening paragraph.

> It was the afternoon of New Year's. The *Commodore* lay at her dock in Jacksonville and negro stevedores processioned steadily toward her with box after box of ammunition and bundle after bundle of rifles. Her hatch, like the mouth of a monster, engulfed them. It might have been the feeding time of some legendary creature of the sea. It was in broad daylight and the crowd of gleeful Cubans on the pier did not forbear to sing the strange patriotic ballads of their island. (*Reports* 85)

Apparently Crane assumes the reader will know the facts from the previous news stories, so that he can merely refer to incidents without explaining their significance. (We never find out, for example, why water was coming into the engine room, only that the men were forced to form bucket brigades to bail out it and the fireroom, nor do we have any idea how long any of this lasted before the decision to abandon ship was made and everyone was evacuated.)

The narrative's reliance on inference and its vagueness of reference have another effect, however. We realize that Crane is signifying the absence of meaning, of a determinate commonsense explanation, by his style: the lack of transitions, of time and place markers, and of explanations of various events. He conveys instead the confusion of being on the verge of an imminent disaster which no one will explain or even acknowledge. (Amid talk of lowering the lifeboats, for example, an "unknown" man suggests to the mate that they send up a flare, and he replies, "What the hell do we want to send up a rocket for? The ship is all right" [90].) Crane has only fragmented knowledge of the crisis, and that is how it comes to us, piecemeal, instead of completed, filled out, explained and interpreted. This is not because the journalist is writing in a rush, unable to take the time to fill in details of what he knows; it is a conscious stylistic choice, for his account of going down the river toward the Atlantic is leisurely enough, and he gives quite full descriptions of natural phenomena and of the scene in the engine room. "As darkness came upon the waters, the *Commodore* was a broad, flaming path of blue and silver phosphorescence, and as her stout bow lunged at the great black waves she threw flashing, roaring cascades to either side" (87–8).

The steady fading away of any outline of what is happening, in the newspaper report, beginning with the ship's arrival in the open sea after she has twice ignominiously run aground in the river below Jacksonville, disappoints our expectations of a newspaper story's factuality. The journalist is unable to sleep, and he has premonitory conversations with the cook ("the old ship is going to get it in the neck, I think") and with an "old seaman" named Tom Smith, who announces that this is his last trip, "if I ever get back safe this time" (88–9). Most of the action during the emergency is mysterious, and the final section, telling of the doomed men whom the captain tries to coax off the *Commodore* and onto make-shift rafts before the ship goes down, is all the more horrifying for its restraint: "One man had his arms folded and was leaning against the deckhouse. His feet were crossed so that the toe of his left foot pointed downward. There they stood gazing at us, and neither from the deck nor from the rafts was a voice raised. Still was there this silence" (93). The men in the dinghy try vainly to tow the first raft ("a tugboat would have [had] no light task in moving these rafts"), when they suddenly realize they are going backward, because the black man on the raft is pulling the line hand over hand in a frenzied attempt to get aboard the tiny boat. "He had turned into a demon. He was wild, wild as a tiger. He was crouched on this raft and ready to spring. Every muscle of him seemed to be turned into an elastic spring. His eyes were almost white." No longer speaking only for himself, the narrator repeats what all four men in the 10-foot boat know, "that the touch of a hand on our gunwale doomed us. . . . The cook let go of the line." Still no one cries out. The *Commodore* sinks, and the rafts are "suddenly swallowed by this frightful maw of the ocean" (93–4).

Crane adds two paragraphs summarizing the fate of the four men in the dinghy and alludes to a possible "sequel": "The history of life in an open boat for thirty hours would no doubt be instructive for the young, but none is to be told here now" (94). "Stephen Crane's Own Story" does seem headed toward the point where the whole will be intelligible and order will be reinstated (some of the men will reach shore safely). This return to security is hinted at in the antepenultimate paragraph: "The lighthouse of Mosquito Inlet stuck up above the horizon like the point of a pin. We turned our dingy [*sic*] toward the shore" (341). The text never reaches that "point," instead breaking off to summarize briefly what happened afterward.

Conceding that there is a lesson to be learned from the experience the survivors were soon to undergo is not the same as drawing a moral from the story already told, however. Hayden White connects our desire for closure to the longing to understand morally, "to have real events display the coherence, integrity, fullness, and closure of an image of life that is and can only be imaginary" ("Value" 23). Apparently, realism of representation requires not only objectivity of perception but the production of desire, which drives the narrative toward resolution and the "establishment of that moral authority without which the notion of a specifically social reality would be unthinkable" (23).[4] Because of our experience of reading nonfiction novels and autobiographical novels, we know that this definition can describe texts with historical referents, and from our comparison of Crane's newspaper story and "The Open Boat" we know that both use accurate historical details, even proper names. Therefore a journalistic narrative might fit this definition of short story or "nonfiction fiction" (the human interest story, for example, moves toward closure and the establishment of "moral authority"); and yet "Stephen Crane's Own Story" does not.[5]

Desire appears in other explanations of the power of realism, for example the concept of "represented action" developed by R. S. Crane and Sheldon Sacks. According to Ralph Rader's refinement of this concept of an action of the "realism-plot-judgment" sort, "the author pits our induced sense of what will happen to a character against our induced sense of what we want to happen to him, our hopes against our fears, in order to give the greatest pleasure appropriate to their resolution" ("Defoe" 34).[6] "Stephen Crane's Own Story" is naturalistically related, including dialogue, description, and concrete details, but the gaps in the narrative, and the lack of explicit cause-effect relations (owing to the absence of historical narration – especially apparent once the ship leaves the security of shore) make it difficult for readers accustomed to the conventions of realism to experience it as a short story or represented action. This should make us look even more closely at the effects of the shift to third-person narration (with its apparently transparent representation of reality) on our perception of "The Open Boat" as fictional or literary. Because we know that many individual features can occur in both fiction and nonfiction (e.g., third-person transparent narration, first-person discourse, closure, depth characterization, rhetorical patterning), these individual characteristics cannot be determining of a text's status. There must be a history of interpretation and critical judgment that teaches us to recognize and then to categorize prose according to a hierarchy that has also been devised over time. It is difficult to locate this process in a particular moment or in specific texts, that is, to recover the history of the myth of literature in our culture.

My argument is not that the concept of literature was established at the end of the nineteenth century in the United States, only that our idea of what is literary changed, as it always does with variations in historical conditions, for literature is a contingent rather than a universal concept (McHale, "Unspeakable" 43). Our conception is altered by changes in the conditions of production and consumption – including attitudes toward writers, their representation of relations between men and women and the world, and the reception of the products of their labor or creativity. In the last decades of the nineteenth century, literature was associated with the emergence of new modes of realism and naturalism and their strategies of representation. Certainly, late-nineteenth-century realism represents one brick in the wall separating nonliterary genres from literary ones, despite the fact that the realistic novel purported to be democratic and inclusive and might have been expected to encompass other nonfictional, realistic narrative appearing in periodicals. Apparently there were other, at least partially defensive, factors that led novelists to elevate their fiction to a realm separate from the commercial system that determined its economic value and put them on the same level as producers of other commodities. (I take up some of these factors later in the present chapter, and in Chapter 2, with respect to Ernest Hemingway's career.)

We must not miss the ideological implications of the system of historical or impersonal narration, which led to the universalization of realism/naturalism in the twentieth century. Barthes suggests that when events are set down in sequence in the preterite they take on the appearance of being related causally and of being ordered, even if they happen by chance: "This is why it is the ideal instrument for every construction of a world; it is the unreal time of cosmogonies, myths, History and Novels. It presupposes a world which is constructed, elaborated, self-sufficient, reduced to significant lines, and not one which has been sent sprawling before us, for us to take or leave" (*Writing* 30). This is ideological work because we do not see the act of construction, only the appearance of the world as fact.

The significance of the change to third-person narration in "The Open Boat," then, is that it makes possible hierarchy of narration. In the first place we are introduced to a voice which becomes authoritative by hiding itself as discourse ("events seem to narrate themselves"). It is an impersonal voice, not attributable to the correspondent or any of the other characters, or even to the narrator of the discourse in other passages. The famous first sentence of "The Open Boat" is an example of this historical narration: "None of them knew the color of the sky."

In the next paragraph the present-tense verb announces a shift to discourse, and we are aware of a narrator who is capable of reflection, comparison, and opinion: "Many a man ought to have a bath-tub larger than the boat which here rode upon the sea. These waves were most wrongfully and barbarously abrupt and tall, and each froth-top was a problem in small-boat navigation." This narrator is the source of the discourse spread throughout the text that expresses the gap between the way things ought to be and the way they are (certainly the boat is acting like a bathtub in holding water and "bathing" the men, but it "ought" not to).

The third-person narration also makes it necessary to speak of the correspondent from the outside, as one of four men in a small boat on the open sea, for the narrator here is not telling his "own story"; it also makes possible varying viewpoints and distance from the characters – along with the technique of a central intelligence, or focalizer.[7] The narrator (of the discourse as a whole, the subject of the enunciation) has regular access to the correspondent's mind, and via this reflective consciousness he at times surmises what the others are feeling. For example, he offers occasional speculations about the group mind, at the beginning of part III (for example, that their "brotherhood," though unspoken, can be felt) and in part IV:

> As for the reflections of the men, there was a great deal of rage in them. Perchance they might be formulated thus: "If I am going to be drowned . . . , why, in the name of the seven mad gods who rule the sea, was I allowed to come thus far and contemplate sand and trees? Was I brought here merely to have my nose dragged away as I was about to nibble the sacred cheese of life?" (*Tales of Adventure* 77)

When this sentiment recurs (near the end of part IV and the beginning of part VI), it is not assigned to anyone but merely placed inside quotation marks. Is the narrator attributing the question to the correspondent or to all the men?

We associate the ambiguity inherent in free indirect discourse (the question of where the narrator's voice leaves off and the voice or thought of the character begins) with fiction, and some theorists of narrative (e.g., Cohn) make represented consciousness the distinguishing feature of fiction told in the third person. It is not the presence of focalization that makes "The Open Boat" a short story (for I will argue throughout that fiction has no defining properties), but focalization is doubtless one of the causes of the fictional effect of "The Open Boat," since we associate that feature with classic realist novels.[8] The narrator of this discourse, however, scarcely departs from what would be "knowable" and reportable in a factual discourse. Crane has not adopted the multiple points of view common in omniscient narration, and his insight into even the correspondent's mind is rather limited.[9] Not coincidentally, this fits naturalism's tendency to confine narration to "accurate external representation" (R. Williams, *Keywords* 183), with its emphasis on seeing and reporting exactly how things looked. This story's focalization provides information about the correspondent's attitude toward his predicament and his realization that this was "the best experience of his life" (73); offers some ironic generalizations about previous actions, such as the fact that some men row for amusement; and reproduces a poem he memorized in his childhood, which now provides an ironic gloss on his possible imminent death. That is, free indirect discourse, like the discourse of the narrator, in this story serves mostly the effect of irony.

Another kind of ambiguity results from the fact that we cannot always be sure whether to attribute a particular discourse to the correspondent or to the narrator. Distinctions among the discourses are important, for, as Barthes and others have pointed out, the historical narrative becomes authoritative, the privileged "source of coherence" of the whole, by effacing itself as a discourse (Belsey 71–2). In Barthes's words, as "the cornerstone of Narration," the preterite (or in English the third-person "impersonal" narrator) "aims at maintaining a hierarchy in the realm of facts" (*Writing* 30). In general, the use of impersonal narration implies that all accidents of chance or fate have meaning simply because they are told, explained in a story. In this particular text, significance is imposed on a sequence of random, meaningless occurrences by the very act of relating them in a coherent pattern, the emptiness of which is not apparent unless the last sentence is read ironically: "When it came night, the white waves paced to and fro in the moonlight, and the wind brought the sound of the great sea's voice to the men on shore, and they felt that they could then be interpreters" (92). The absence of reference to the narrative situation in the historical narration, coupled with the illusion of realistic representation and the tendency to reconcile the contradictory elements in a rounded-off ending, fixes the world the way it is depicted here, and the reader tends to accept it as presented (Belsey 70–6).

These characteristics doubtless produce the interpretations of "The Open Boat" as a work of literary realism: those that see the oiler's death as "redeem[ing] the significance of life" or the story as unified by Crane's "understanding of the indifference of Nature that comes to men through the comradeship of suffering, through the meaningless confusion of death" (Katz xviii; Going 82). As this reading insists, although nature is "flatly indifferent" (as well as splendid and "serene amid the struggles of the individual"), those who have suffered but held together can still be "interpreters." That is, from a privileged position the men presumably will mediate between the emptiness of a blank universe and their fellows who desire to understand how life and death are related, or to know how we are related to nature. The only comforting way to do this, however, would be to be deceptive about what "the great sea's voice" said to them, because, when the correspondent was awake alone the night before, the voice of the wind over the waves "was sadder than the end" (83). Perhaps the narrator believes that it is comforting to know the worst: here, in view of the oiler's death, "the futility of life itself" (Autrey 101). Most readers do seem to find this lesson reassuring, perhaps simply because it comes in the last line, and thus meets White's definition of closure as the *"moral"* represented "under the aspect of the *aesthetic"* ("Value" 23). This seems to hold even when the illusion of ordinary existence (here, restored by the comforts of "blankets, clothes, and flasks, and women with coffee-pots" that are the land's welcome to the three survivors) keeps men from facing what Monteiro calls "that piece of bone-chilling knowledge": the fact that "an immense sea assails man at every instant" (335).

Nevertheless we have one explanation of why we perceive "The Open Boat" as fiction: it works as realism, while "Stephen Crane's Own Story" does not. Realism is not what gives a factual or complete record, but what produces an illusion of a world we recognize as real. And so the short story, although it reveals "just how it happened, and how [the men] felt," transcends mere factuality to give what Edwin Cady calls "the truth of experience," while the journalistic piece seems limited and tentative, if not as "flat" as Cady says it is (151).[10] It does not affirm or reestablish order, and the first-person narration reminds us that the viewpoint of personal journalism (whether eyewitness or participant) is partial, rather than "what actually happened" (as historical narration would assert). It is just a step from responding to the pattern of realism and accepting the factuality of the world it asserts to regarding this created world as somehow universally valid and the verisimilar events encoded in plots as transcendent expressions of human experience. To show why we take this step, I will examine interpretations of "The Open Boat" which emphasize Crane's naturalism, for one explanation of how he transformed a biographical experience into art is that he made it seem exemplary by coding it in terms of naturalist narrative.

To a naturalist like Crane, says Lee Mitchell, the universe appears random, amoral, irredeemable. Naturalism posits the inability of characters to learn from their environment, or even to act as autonomous characters, for nature – in the form of heredity or social laws as fixed as those of biology or physics – determines not only their actions but their desires. Therefore, they are "enslaved no less by conventions than by circumstances" ("Naturalism" 536). Supposedly that is why characters in a naturalist text cannot learn that the only meaning they can find in a deterministic universe is what they bring to it. Naturalist readings of "The Open Boat" thus emphasize the gap between the men, who assert the significance of their survival in the face of what they must have learned (i.e., that it was a matter of chance), and an indifferent, impersonal nature (which they apparently will continue to personalize). Mitchell's observation that throughout the story Crane alternates the narrator's perspective with the characters' inside view helps to explain the irony of the last line of "The Open Boat" and why it seems to sum up the world view of naturalism.[11] He says this technique reveals "the gap between actual consequences and the futile intentions behind them, between impersonal events and the guilt or pride they feel. Nothing more than circumstances enmesh characters in fictional worlds they are unable to alter" (*Determined* 98).[12]

The assumptions of such a world view might be characterized as follows: nature replaces God in a restored universe of absolutes; naturalism increases our certainty that, as realism implied, the world exists apart from and prior to our experience of it and texts only copy or imitate this ordered universe; as readers we are confirmed in popular naturalism's fatalistic attitude (this is the way the world is, this is the way people are) by the objectivity of the narrator (I am only recording what I observe) (Scholes, *Textual* 37). These features are strikingly similar to the formalist "virtues" by which, according to Paul Lauter we recognize literature: "economy, irony, well-articulated structure, and the like." Although we frequently take the congruence of modernist and New Critical desiderata for granted (as Lauter does in reciting this "modernist catechism"), the roots of these two movements in naturalism are usually overlooked. For example, the definition of literature as "a form of discourse that 'has no designs on the world,' that represents things rather than trying to change them," seems modernist, but it is a viewpoint that continues naturalism's distanced narration and objectivity. Lauter also notes our tendency to universalize such standards as "complexity and detachment," the latter of which certainly derives from naturalism (*Canons* 104).

Perhaps the broadest tendency of naturalism on its way to modernism is to replace history by myth, that is, untie the narrative from its moorings in a particular time and place in the process of abstracting a universal, noncontingent "truth" or thesis. Such an autonomous "work" then no longer depends for its understanding or power on facts of only local interest that will soon "date" and require footnoting. "The Open Boat" has been systematically naturalized or mythicized in this way, as a result of a series of formalist tenets and procedures. These include the practice of viewing the text as complete in itself, and so unlikely to be improved by knowledge of the social or political context of the story; the New Critical warning against the biographical fallacy, so that Crane's life or career at this time is disregarded; and the necessity most critics feel to distinguish the short story from the piece of reporting, because of their interest in defining the literary object and accounting for its distinctiveness. It must also be said that Crane contributes to this universalization (and to the story's elevation as art) by leaving out many historical and political details, such as an explanation of how the men came to be on a ship that sank and who was in the other boats that are mentioned (he omits the filibustering expedition and its connection to the Cuban insurrection). It may be that, as Alfred Kazin insists, Crane "cared not a jot which way the world went," so that revolutions had no meaning save as "something foreigners attempted that Hearst would pay good money to report" (*Native Grounds* 68). Or this may be drawing the wrong conclusion from narratives like "The Open Boat"; aesthetic aspirations, not lack of interest in politics, may have dictated what Crane left out.

Whether Crane was interested in world events primarily as occasions for freelance work or chose to play up the artful shape of incidents, situations, and historical actors rather than to analyze them makes little difference. Realist and naturalist narratives, though originating in anti-literary impulses, are easily described in aesthetic terms because these narratives downplay historical and political contexts (even when the characters' environment is emphasized, it is universalized as determining) and stress the appearance of things more than their causes. They empty reality of its history and substitute "nature" or universal human nature (Barthes, *Mythologies* 142–3). Once a formalist conception of literature dominates interpretation, economic and political and cultural processes are turned into "givens," which highlights the essentializing features of realism and naturalism. For example, in reading "The Open Boat" the particular social and political forces that have led four men to their precarious position as struggling survivors in an inadequate "lifeboat" are reduced to a hostile or indifferent nature, with the men as its pawns; this renders futile their efforts to save themselves, for their survival will be determined by forces beyond their control. It is inevitable, then, that the repetition of sentences, of actions, of refrains of desire or warning in "The Open Boat" will be regarded as turning characters into machines for rowing and as removing the semblance of will from their actions by making the notion of "progressive behavior" an illusion (see Mitchell, *Determined* 22).

A number of critical statements from this period show the gradual elevation of "nature" over a particularized culture, that is, form over history. One was made by Crane himself in an 1894 letter rehearsing his invention of a "little creed" of realism all his own and his subsequent discovery that he had allies in Hamlin Garland and William Dean Howells; together their "beautiful war" pitted realism against the inflations of romance. His side claimed that "art is man's substitute for nature and we are the most successful in art when we approach the nearest to nature and truth" (*Correspondence* 63). Was the battle against romance "beautiful" because its aim was the establishment of realism as the dominant aesthetic mode? This, at any rate, was the project pursued by

Howells as editor and critic, as well as novelist, throughout the 1880s and 1890s. When Howells asserts in *Criticism and Fiction,* his 1891 manifesto of realism, that "in the whole range of fiction" he knows of "no true picture of life – that is, of human nature – which is not also a masterpiece of literature," he is claiming for the realistic approach to genre the highest status – indeed, insisting that a sure way to make literature is to picture human nature (49). In his first column as editor of *Harper's Monthly,* in January 1886, Howells proclaimed the virtues of this creed, calling the "good" novel the one disposed to "regulate our life without the literary glasses so long thought desirable" and to represent "character as it abounds outside of all fiction" (*Editor's Study*).

Although Crane echoed many of Howells's precepts, claiming that ever since his youthful apprenticeship his goal had been to reflect life "accurately" and "give to readers a slice out of life" (*Correspondence* 230), in practice he hit on a technique with a different emphasis. While Howells pretended to inclusiveness and an egalitarian attention to all forms of social life, Crane differed from those ideals, most notably in his narratives' concision and simplicity, and in his ability to leave things out – in short, in his work's suitability to canonization by New Criticism. Although neither writer believed in preaching or making a moral lesson explicit, it is in Crane's few pronouncements to his correspondents, including editors, on what he was up to that we catch glimpses of that impulse toward omission, simplicity of expression, and objectivity that becomes the hallmark of post–World War I fiction and that so well suits the formalist/modernist aesthetic that, as perfected by Anderson, Cather, and Hemingway, it has been enshrined as *the* type of literary prose. From the beginning, Crane tells the editor of *Demorest's Family Magazine,* he has tried "to observe closely, and to set down what I have seen in the simplest and most concise way. I have been very careful not to let any theories or pet ideas of my own be seen in my writing." And he (mis)quotes Emerson: "There should be a long logic beneath the story, but it should be kept carefully out of sight" (*Correspondence* 230; and see 322–3). Crane also anticipates Hemingway in claiming that it is his desire "to write plainly and unmistakably, so that all men (and some women) might read and understand. That to my mind is good writing" (99).

Howells's role as critic was explicitly to create realistic literature as a transcendent form, yet he did it in a businesslike way. When he delineates a set of techniques by which readers can recognize realistic fiction and writers can deliberately produce it, it is difficult to avoid the inference that he is issuing blueprints which perhaps even an uninspired writer could follow. Realism seems to require only the workmanlike skills of observation, the ability to record "manners and customs," and an ear for ordinary speech, including the dialect of characters who were now likely to be drawn from any class (C. Wilson 12). In an "Editor's Study" column (Dec. 1887), Howells empowers the "common, average" man as critic, able to hold writers to a "strict accounting, and verify their work by the standard of the arts which we all have in our power, the simple, the natural, and the honest." In fact, Howells defines realism against the "effectism" of neo-romanticism and historical romance by characterizing it as without technique, as working "through the direct, frank, and conscientious study of character" (his comment on the view of the Spanish realist Armando Palacio Valdés) (*Howells as Critic* 167). In addition, such leveling forces as the growth of mass-circulation magazines and the professionalization of letters at the end of the nineteenth century threatened the older conception of the writer as creative artist, for the newer model of the writer as realist/naturalist made it difficult to avoid the conclusion that writers were laborers, with their productions contracted for by agents, editors, and publishers, and their worth determined by the market.[13]

In defense, novelists and critics (who were sometimes, like Howells or Henry James, one and the same person) moved to reserve a space for the nonutilitarian, the noncommercial, the "more than real" literary production, that is, for works that transcended their ties to the immediate occasion, their association with the market, and their appeal to an uncritical mass public. From our vantage point, it is clear that in seeking to elevate realism, Howells had his work cut out for him: when the dominant aesthetic is to depict "what is," how can this goal be made to seem attainable by only a few writers? Howells's response was to mystify realism's techniques, largely by promoting morality and elevating the physical fact to the level of philosophical truth, thereby making it timeless. He argues for Keats's "Beauty is Truth" over "A thing of beauty is a joy forever," asserting that the highest ideal is to be true to life, not to art. "No author is an authority except in those moments when he held his ear close to Nature's lips and caught her very accent," he concludes ("Editor's Study," Dec. 1887).

Another technique of asserting realism's moral value was to emphasize its transparency. Because it was supposedly an antiliterary form, Howells could say little about specific techniques. He advised that the writer must not simply map life but "picture" it (*Criticism* 15). Thus another strategy was to associate its goals with other machines for "invisibly" capturing truth, such as the spectroscope, the camera, and, especially, the apparatus for projecting "moving pictures." Stanley Corkin quotes the awed response of George Parsons Lathrop (Hawthorne's son-in-law) to the "kinetograph," an early version of the motion picture camera, in 1891: "Edison's machine . . . reproduces the movement and appearance of life with such truth of action that if colors could only be given at the same time, the illusion that one was looking at something really alive would be absolute"; and he explicitly connects the goal of inventors like Edison to Howells's project of producing "a means of dispensing 'information' – that is, ideologically neutral fact" (*Realism*, chap. 3).

The result of the realists' successful repression of the process of producing realism was to set off a category of works from ordinary prose and justify its elevation by elaborating on some aspect of a text's verbal art or "style" or by citing its elevation of the mysteries of human experience. As Robert Shulman characterizes the criticism that has resulted from this habit of mind,

> Intelligent and influential critics of "The Open Boat" have placed an unwarranted normative stress on objectivity and absolutes. . . . The emphasis has distracted attention from the complexity of Crane's achievement in "The Open Boat," distorted his basic concerns, and often undermined our confidence in his characters and in our own ability to read and understand without a special interpretive key to unlock the mysteries of a story allegedly so hedged in ironic and epistemological qualifications as to be inaccessible to the uninitiated. (449)

This critical framework has also resulted in a narrow range of interpretation. "The Open Boat" has been called an example of symbolism, imagism, impressionism, and existentialism as well as of realism and naturalism; its underlying concerns have been identified variously as epistemological uncertainty or the absurdity of the human condition. And yet there is no great variety in these readings, no matter what philosophy or approach critics posit to explain Crane's success in transforming the story of his experience. Even when the critic looks outside the story to relate its "lesson" to American social history – for example, Shulman gives one answer to Tocqueville's characterization of Americans as isolated by democratic social structures by maintaining that Crane's tale shows a highly developed sense of the "value of human community" – he cannot avoid the fact that the four men who learn the value of community are themselves isolated from their fellows and "alienated from the land" (441). Shulman apparently does not see the irony in this failure to tie the men to their society in any significant way. He calls the brotherhood the men share "a central human value in the face of the impersonal elements" (459), thus essentializing it rather than analyzing it as a community derived from particular social institutions such as marine law and custom. Why do only the oiler and correspondent row, for example? Why are the captain's orders obeyed without question, even though the men have to "flounder out here all night"("Open Boat" 373)?

Clearly we need a different approach to interpretation, one based on a conception of literariness that considers a text in relation to its context. Like Fredric Jameson's "dialectical criticism," my method does not take a system of literary characteristics to a text, in the hope of finding those features there, and interpret according to the categories instead of considering the text's "inner coherence" and historical context. Jameson defines dialectical criticism as the practice of adapting one's mode of analysis to the characteristics of the text under discussion, for "to the degree that each work is the end result of a kind of inner logic or development in its own content, it evolves its own categories and dictates the specific terms of its own interpretation" (*Marxism* 333). My term for this approach is "reflexive reading": a dynamic method of putting form in the place of content and reading with attention to the text's process of production, which is viewed as inseparable from the text and available to some extent to readers of any period. By "process of production" I mean the historical conditions that give rise to the text, including the social and political context of the writing and the writer. As Robert Scholes says, "The interpretation of any single literary text, if pushed seriously, will lead us not to some uniquely precious exegetical act but to cultural history itself" (*Textual* 35). Under this contextual framework, then, literature is the result of reflexive reading, and we can enlarge the category to contain all the texts we choose to read in this manner. This is much less exclusive than the current one based on canonicity: the body of works read for their style, and therefore considered "timeless."

To develop this reading practice I draw on Roman Jakobson's conception of the literary as (in Barthes's summary) "that type of message that takes as its object not its content but its own form."[14] A reflexive reader pays attention to the way the message is expressed, that is, analyzes its tropes as they support or contradict or distract her from the referential function. The function of the text that is thereby emphasized is its autoreferentiality (see Stierle 89–90), the act of putting the form of the message in the place of the subject. Under this theory there is no particular rhetorical strategy that is inherently literary. Narratives that emphasize a particular rhetorical pattern, even the self-effacing tropes of transparent realism, can be regarded as defamiliarizing, or "laying bare" the conventional ways of representing reality. In Howells and Crane's time, the novel was dominated by conventions of romance and sentimental narrative, and so by contrast realist conventions include reticent narrators, the foregrounding of character over plot, and the use of free indirect discourse to dramatize characters' subjectivity.

A theory of reflexive reading can account for the fact that what we regard as literature changes over time and can also help to explain why some works seem self-evidently literary. Some texts dictate the terms of their own apprehension, and so we easily take our reading cues from the texts themselves. The most obvious example is self-conscious narrative, or metafiction.[15] At the opposite pole is high realism, which so effaces itself as narrative that fictional definitions of literariness may have arisen in order to justify its inclusion as a special category of writing. In sum, we produce literary texts by reading them in a particular way, by acknowledging their self-conscious or estranging function and highlighting the nonidentity of sign and object – the gap between word as word and word as thing, where history and society enter and influence language.[16] This restores the dialectic and transforms what we mean by style; style is no longer what it became to the New Critics, "an essential and constitutive component of the literary work," but foregrounded language, viewed relationally (Jameson, *Marxism* 333).

It is not just syntax and semantics, sound and sense, that we attend to alternatively, but such aspects as the decisions made by the writer to dramatize the author function or how much attention to call to that construction (the emotive in relation to the poetic function), or the effect of the context on the reader's understanding, that is, the conative in relation to the referential function. (An example is considering whether proper names and particular incidents in historical fiction are invented or actual, the source of much pleasure in a novel like E. L. Doctorow's *Book of Daniel,* which is based on the 1950s Rosenberg case.)[17] Furthermore, the elements in storytelling – the organization of narrative, delay or retardation of disclosure, forward or backward movement and digression, relation of tenses, the pace and rhythm of the reading – are the results of decisions and have implications for the message we perceive, and equivalent aspects are brought to the text by the reader in different historical and social contexts.[18]

As a relational process rather than a reified quality of texts, reflexivity reinserts a text, genre, or mode into the conditions which gave rise to it. A demonstration very much to the point here would be to read naturalism reflexively, specifically in relation to realism, placing both against the context of late-nineteenth-century culture. By noticing that naturalism makes realism's self-effacing narration overt, emphasizes the "thingness" of the world, even its surface, and exaggerates the meaningfulness of objects, we can see that naturalism, read reflexively, lays bare what realism only implicitly asserts: the truth of appearances, the inevitability of the world posited as prior to narratives about it, and the reduction of human characters to "a system of value based on appearance and acquisition" (see Corkin, chap. 2). Because formalism describes the characteristics of texts and categorizes them empirically, naturalism in

this framework emphasizes features such as metaphors drawn from
nature to describe characters lacking personal freedom and a detached
narrator who enters characters' consciousness only to show their lack of
autonomy because of the influence of environment and heredity on
their desires.

A reflexive reading makes apparent what naturalism does: it shows
effects without their causes and "naturalizes" historical processes; that
is, it makes them seem inevitable – including the process by which
things as they are have become universalized as "the real." This process
involves focusing on naturalist narratives' totalizing world view, concrete representations, and the distance between narrator and characters.
Reflexive reading also shows what the formalist conception has done:
emptied naturalism of its history, of the forces that led to this conception
of literature as above or outside history in a transcendent realm. Naturalism's historical context includes, besides the mechanization of the workplace and the alienation of labor, a growing mass culture dominated by
advertising, with its intentions of creating the consumers that an advanced industrial society needs for its increase in manufactured goods.
In the usual conception of naturalism, the effect of these material causes
may be noticed, but they are likely to be attributed to transcendent
natural forces such as an immutable universe that embeds characters in
their actions, allowing them no autonomy. Thus in various ways naturalism in its dominant conception reifies the results of specific economic
and political and cultural forces.

Then, too, we ought to see the relation of naturalism to Progressive
politics, which dominated this turn-of-the-century period. When we
recognize that Progressivism's goals tended toward reform and accommodation, the maintenance of order, and the stability of a business and
financial system based on monopoly capital, rather than the radical
restructuring of relations between classes and the redistribution of capital, we realize that it must be in society's interest to have cultural forms
that assert the inevitability of the way things are, to naturalize the
hierarchies of men over women, clocks over sun time, bosses over
workers (see Wiebe).[19] We can well understand how naturalism, as
ordinarily defined and read, in various ways reifies the results of those
economic and political and cultural processes. It accepts them as
"given," as they appear, rather than showing them in process. For
example, it does not show the history of the metonymies that dominate
labels applied to characters but accepts the rationalization of men and
women who are defined in relation to their function, that is, to the work
they do (as "workers," or even "hands"). Nor does it question the
fatalism and hopelessness with which characters bear their condition
instead of agitating for reform. That is why Rebecca Harding Davis's

Life in the Iron Mills can be read as a naturalist novella as well as an early realist one (and why we cannot periodize naturalism too neatly as a turn-of-the-century mode).

If we view turn-of-the-century naturalism as an intensification of realism, which "lays bare" realism's devices and brings out its hidden assertions, then we are more likely to read a text like "The Open Boat" to discover its contexts, to notice its relation to the cultural undercurrents of the age, and to detect the competing ideologies under-lying the correspondent's self-conception – for example, his ideas of what kind of work a correspondent does and of how he came to be there in the little dinghy. The differences between "Stephen Crane's Own Story" as a journalistic report and "The Open Boat" as an "after the fact" version, couched in conventions we associate with a naturalistic short story in the aesthetic tradition, are bound up with certain historical processes apparent in the 1890s: the desire of writers to distinguish creative acts and "inspired" writing from popular, commercial narratives; the wish that their audiences would learn to discriminate "higher," or moral, realism from the merely "photographic" (the term often used for low and vulgar, or Zolaesque naturalism); and the attempt to remove the determination of literary value from the marketplace, where it seemed likely to be decided within a commercial society.

The first step in a reflexive reading of a text where the referential function is dominant – for example, a realistic narrative like "The Open Boat" – is to render the linguistic sign palpable. Here the effect of emphasizing the poetic function is not to "obliterate" the reference but to make it "ambiguous." This does not mean that the text no longer refers,[20] but that it becomes more "peculiar, intricate" (Jakobson, "Closing" 371). Promoting the "palpability of signs" deepens the gap between signs and referents (356). Focusing on language as a verbal structure rather than allowing it to become transparent works against the illusion that signs and objects are connected naturally and that words refer to objects that are somewhere "out there" in an external reality. Realizing this, we see why the realist/naturalist implication that the world exists first and texts capture it in more or less transparent narra-tive is untenable.

It is but one step from this insight to the realization that once a narrative is told or written, it can be apprehended only through the text, or what the Russian Formalists called "plot" (*sjuzet*), as distinguished from "story" (*fabula*).[21] By insisting that plot, as the arrangement of events rather than the action itself, is part of composition ("how we learn of what happens") instead of thematic ("what happens," which is story or content), they showed that *how* we learn determines *what* we learn (Eichenbaum 116). There is no way to hold, therefore, that stories exist outside their embodiment in textual form (whether told, written, mimed, or danced). There is no prior "original" story that exists anywhere, because we cannot apprehend it except through texts.[22] Everything we talk about in a narrative is a result of plot, of the inseparability of what happens from how we learn about it; therefore story (or "story-stuff," the translation of *fabula* given by Matejka and Pomorska) becomes hypothetical and secondary.[23]

As readers we order events as they "must have happened," thus producing a coherent, chronological story, but it is always after the fact, and apparently we learn how to do it by practicing: that is, by listening to, watching, and reading narratives. The process is equally creative whether the text is a journalistic narrative (or biographical, a memoir, or history), when the story we infer is historical, with actual characters and circumstances as referents; or imaginary, with invented ones; or a mixture. In every case we construct an orderly sequence of events, which take place in a world similar to the one we think we know, where acts have consequences, characters grow up, they succeed or fail in work and in love, and so on. Thus our experience of reading stories about characters and events that we know (from other sources) actually existed or have happened is the same as that of reading about invented ones (including narrators), and this is why I emphasize the similarity of fictional and nonfictional narratives as texts. The primary determining difference between them is at the level of the story we construct from their "plots."

Not only are "Stephen Crane's Own Story" and "The Open Boat" both historical, but their "stories" form a seamless whole. When a story we derive is historical, it is continuous with everything that happens in what we call "history" or "the past" (from which nonfictional narratives select referents, positing cause-effect relations and other relations among them). Because the story-stuff of "The Open Boat" is historical, we can extend the story that we infer from it by connecting it to other circumstances from its period, particularly those surrounding its protagonist and author. We derive them, in turn, from other historical narratives of the same period – letters, diaries, eyewitness testimony, legal records, and secondary sources such as memoirs, biographies, histories – thus gradually filling out "what must have happened" and constructing a more complete and satisfactory "story." In this historical story, the correspondent and Crane (in his role of reporter under contract to the Bacheller syndicate) are the same. Although the correspondent, as a character in the text, is only one version of Stephen Crane, the historical person whom we know about from other texts as novelist and journalist, he does have a history, as do the other men, as does the "open boat." (*Its* history is that it was a dinghy, but for reasons of metaphor – the "vulnerable" boat? – and euphony, it became what the title says it is.)

Apparently because they have been taught not to confuse the author with the fictional character, formalist critics cannot ordinarily bring themselves to connect the events in "Stephen Crane's Own Story" to the thoughts and emotions of the men in "The Open Boat"; they are particularly reluctant to identify the journalist Stephen Crane who wrote the report with the correspondent who is the focalizer of the story. That would be to commit the biographical fallacy. Cady says, for example, that "to identify Crane himself with 'the correspondent' in the fiction is naïve," and he calls the biographical events "at best the occasions for the tale" (151).[24] Most critics refer to the correspondent as a character who "exists" only in the text, and they cast around for ways to explain the oiler's death (rarely calling it "Billy Higgins's death," as if they would rather Crane had not named one of the characters, reminding us of his historical status). They write as though the author had decided that man would be the one to die, and therefore decided to foreshadow his death on the first page, with the image of the oiler's "thin little oar" that seemed "ready to snap."[25] And they argue over what "causes" his death, as well as over its significance, rather than attributing it to the facts of the story Crane had to work with; the donnée of the narrative is, after all, historical. They regard Higgins's death as resulting from mere chance; as caused by a capricious or even hostile Nature; as ironic, because Higgins is the "wily surfer" and a stronger swimmer than the others; as punishment, because he struck out on his own rather than coming to the overturned boat with the others; or as an appropriate sacrifice to "the seven man gods who rule the sea."[26]

The difference in a reflexive reading, however, is that the reader acknowledges that the story derived from "The Open Boat" is continuous with that of "Stephen Crane's Own Story." Considering the journalistic survivor's account makes a difference in interpretation, because the reader of both knows what is left out or only obliquely referred to in "The Open Boat"; this makes one particular interpretation of the oiler's death more likely and explains why the men might feel they can "then be interpreters." Unless the reader considers the events told of in "Stephen Crane's Own Story," she cannot understand the reference in the sixth paragraph of "The Open Boat" to the "scene in the grays of dawn of seven turned faces" that has impressed itself on the captain's face. This is the only reference in "The Open Boat" to the seven men aboard the *Commodore* or on one of the two makeshift rafts when it sank, whom the four have abandoned. Readers who treat the two narratives as continuous and on the same historical level can explain why the men feel they can be interpreters: they may understand the oiler's death to be the appropriate sacrifice of their best in order to propitiate a vengeful Nature or God, and thus begin to alleviate their guilt at having survived. Thus what the men will "interpret" to others is the appropriateness of the ending, the meaning that is provided by the oiler's death. Without the context, the last sentence is merely mysterious.

Critics generally have read both narratives when they begin to write about "The Open Boat" (they are printed side by side in many anthologies), and so they comprehend the reference, but because of formalist dogma and the commonly held view that the news story is inferior because it is "factual," and therefore not relevant, they do not call attention to the effect the memory of this scene apparently has on the men in the vulnerable dinghy. They repress the knowledge that the survivors have something to feel guilty about and therefore may feel that the oiler's death is an appropriate sacrifice that will help to expiate their sin; thus critics suppress the recognition that the "subtle brotherhood" of the four survivors is particular to them, not a general one embracing all men. In effect they do read the correspondent as a representation of the writer of both narratives; they just do not admit that they are doing so, and therefore they do not support their interpretation with the evidence necessary to be convincing – namely, that the men feel some guilt for having abandoned the men on the ship and in the rafts.

Christopher Benfey, Crane's most recent biographer, does read the two narratives together, and because to him "Stephen Crane's Own Story" is as "literary" as "The Open Boat," he is alert to the implications of Crane's including this "harrowing and morally ambiguous" scene of the abandonment of the men in the *Press* report but omitting it in the short story (189). He calls the oiler's death "a substitute sacrifice to the monstrous sea" (199), which allows Crane to be reunited with his new love in Jacksonville, Cora Taylor (later Cora Crane). Benfey regards Crane's writings as the source of information about his "real life," rather than the other way round, because "[i]n Crane's world, written narratives tend to precede experience, rather than the reverse" (6). He claims that Crane went so far as to try "to live what he'd already written," "to make his life an analogue of his work" (5).[27] Detecting this pattern is the result of reflexively reading Crane's life, that is, putting form in content's place (substituting Crane's writings for the material experience of his life) and, because there are so few primary materials for a biography, giving Crane's published output as much weight as biographers or historians usually give to documentary evidence.[28]

This is an interesting take on Crane's life, for biographical interpretation does influence Crane criticism, whereas perhaps it ought to be the

other way round. Because it has been for the most part faulty information, based on romantic legends originating during his lifetime and
perpetuated by Thomas Beer's inaccurate, partially fabricated biography
in 1923, it has contributed to our misconceptions about Crane's goals in
"The Open Boat" and about the difference between his methods of
observing and representing experience when he was acting as a journalist
and when he was writing masterpieces of fiction.[29] For example, after
Crane's death in 1900 Willa Cather was eager to remember Crane as the
artist torn by the tensions of his age, which she expressed as the conflict
he felt between wanting to write literature that would endure and having
to write journalism to live. Therefore, she remembered the newspaper
report as "lifeless as the 'copy' of a police reporter" ("When I Knew"
16; see also Crane, *Correspondence* 90–1).

Even more significant is the mystification of the artist which renders
Crane only a serviceable journalist – because he was more interested in
the telling detail than in the large picture – but a masterful fiction writer,
when he could get the time away from hack work undertaken to meet
the bills run up by Cora. This influential view probably has led to the
dozens of articles about "The Open Boat" that assume, because it seems
so different from "Stephen Crane's Own Story," that it must transcend its time and place, and therefore cannot be "about" the work
of reporting. It must be a story of a supreme test, not about the mis-
adventures of a journalist under contract to a major syndicate with
a hefty advance in gold, who lost the moneybelt but saved his own
life.

By considering Stephen Crane in history, as the Bacheller-syndicated
reporter described in the *New York Press* "advance" story on January 4
as having turned to writing stories because "his nature revolted at the
slavish devotion to facts" required of a journalist (*Stories and Tales* 247)
and thus as the correspondent of "The Open Boat," I can account for
many of the plot details and the polyphonic voices of the story. That is,
I can show how the narrative's reflexivity becomes an alternative to its
literariness, which is based on aesthetics or some notion of transcendent
truth. Therefore I can posit an equally plausible reason for its interest to
us – its "superiority" to other sketches, tales, and vignettes – without
depriving it of reference to a particular time and place. I am not proposing the empiricist treatment of the narratives of "The Open Boat" and
"Stephen Crane's Own Story" that Cyrus Day attempts in "Stephen
Crane and the Ten-foot Dinghy." By taking each incident, action, and
implied fact out into the world to test it against the historical record,
Day reverses the priority of plot over story and takes Crane to task for
misrepresenting the actuality of what Day believes was not a very trying
adventure. For example, Day suggests that the oiler's "thin little oar" is

not only logically unlikely but carries the connotations of "a W. C. Fields movie short," and he objects to the famous opening sentence, for he is sure that at least the captain and the oiler would have been anxiously scouting the dawn sky and remembering old sailors' maxims such as "Red in the morning, sailors take warning" (211, 210).[30]

What I am suggesting is that Crane is trying to reconfigure for his own use an inherited conception of the writer as genius, dependent on inspiration, although his avowed aim is now realism, an "antiliterary" form, which requires only the ability to record information and then distill it into a revealing scene or conversation or quotation – the talents displayed by the journalist, in other words. If we follow Crane's lead, that is, if we read "The Open Boat" as an autonomous work of art, we consent to his aestheticization of his experience, and therefore to the mystification of realism and the validation of the story's lesson in universal terms. Read reflexively, on the other hand, the narrative offers insight into an interesting moment in Crane's career when we can detect the labor and production practices in which his writing was grounded (he was under contract, with his output subject to editors' requirements, and with an agent to place it appropriately). This is in contrast to the way the story is usually read: as though the text itself were serenely transcendent of such mundane matters, absent signs of production, and as Crane said was his means, with the "long logic beneath the story . . . kept carefully out of sight" (*Correspondence* 230).

The two roles in dialectical relationship not only illuminate the particular social system that led to the correspondent's presence in the dinghy (the "age of the reporter" and the rise of yellow journalism), but show how the narrative enacts a model of textual production. Specifically, it reveals the transformation of the "real" into the "literary." Such a reading also shows the dominant realist/naturalist reading to be asserting the immanence of language, accepting the way things are, and putting such texts above ordinary political reality, where their suppositions are not subject to criticism and controversy. Rather than dramatizing the abrupt, chance confrontation of universalized "man" with brutal, elemental nature, this narrative presents an encounter mediated by social custom, legal contracts, international relations, the professionalization of reporting, the Christianity of the correspondent's parents, his habit of reading popular narratives of shipwreck, the influence of Kipling – in short, by cultural as well as literary practices.

The first question we can answer by situating Crane in history is the one uppermost in the correspondent's mind as the narrator introduces him in paragraph 5, after describing the actions of the cook and the oiler: "The correspondent, pulling at the other oar, watched the waves and wondered why he was there" (68). Although this instance of represented consciousness raises a good question, the reader does not get an answer, even the hint of one, only the remark that "shipwrecks are *apropos* of nothing." According to the discourse of the narrator, the men have not trained for this one and therefore have not slept nor eaten well in preparation (74). From the subtitle ("being the experience of four men from the . . . *Commodore*"), the reader knows that the correspondent was on a ship that sank and from "Stephen Crane's Own Story" that it was filibustering. From another *New York Press* story on January 4, contemporary readers learned that Crane had been scheduled to report about the "war" in Cuba, and that although he had been shipwrecked they could soon expect "a treat from his versatile pen" (Crane, *Stories and Tales* 247). It is necessary to turn to the historical story, or diegesis, for much of this information, however. Most critics, taking their cue from the narrator's offhand comments about the way ships go down "willy-nilly" or at inappropriate times, treat the loss of the *Commodore,* and Crane's happening to be on it, as pure chance. Since this could happen to anybody, the correspondent appropriately represents all of us, for he tells a universal story of "man *in extremis*."[31] Although the text encourages us to share the perception of the men, that they have had bad luck, we can read against those particular cues and note signs that these were not simply chance events.

For starters, the correspondent's presence there was not accidental but had real social and economic "causes." As the narrator points out, being in a ten-foot boat in high seas is beyond "the average experience, which is never at sea in a dinghy" (69). Rather than being a fluke, the ship's sinking likely had a particular cause (perhaps sabotage by the Spanish or the captain's negligence, for we know from the historical story that the ship twice ran aground on its way out to sea, without anyone inspecting for damage). Besides, no one innocently goes aboard a known filibustering ship; presumably all the men knew the risks. It seems particularly pertinent, therefore, to pick up on the correspondent's tantalizing reflection, "How did I get myself into this mess?" (my guess as to his interior speech as he was wondering "why he was there"). It is impossible to understand why Crane *was* there in the small boat without some knowledge of the "new journalism," or "yellow journalism," of the 1880s and 1890s, introduced to New York by Joseph Pulitzer, who bought the *World* in 1883, and joined in 1895 by William Randolph Hearst, new owner of the *New York Journal.* These publishers openly courted popular approval by mixing news and entertainment, breezy headlines and illustrations, crusades and stunts, exposés and promotions (such as raising money to build a base to support the Statue of Liberty). When the two engaged in a circulation war that included

Hearst's hiring away much of Pulitzer's staff, the sensationalist battle was joined.[32]

Most readers probably associate yellow journalism with the public outcry that put pressure on the U.S. government to intervene in the Cuban insurrection against Spain, which led to the Spanish-American War. Hearst and Pulitzer did fan these flames, for various reasons, including increased sales as well as expansionist sentiment, but the new journalism did more than warmonger.[33] Charles Brown reports that "by 1898 almost one-half the daily newspapers in twenty-six major cities were of the blatantly yellow variety," or "at least a primrose hue" (19), which meant that readers all over the country were treated to sensationalist stories of scandal and disasters; large-type, sloganeering headlines; reform efforts of investigative editors; self-advertisements boasting of circulation increases and subscriber contributions to campaigns; and by-lined stories by celebrity writers (by-lines were not the norm in most papers until the 1930s – see Schudson, *Discovering* 68, 145). Other important innovations, all of which form the context of Crane's career in journalism, were the growth of newspaper publishing as a business, the increasing professionalism of journalism, the self-conscious appeal to what was primarily an urban phenomenon of mass readership, and the supplanting of big-name editors and publishers by writers and correspondents, to the point that journalism histories call these decades the "age of the reporter" (Brown 20; Schudson, *Discovering* 68–70).

The reporters became well known from their by-lines, but not only for their writing: in many cases they became actors in the dramas they reported. Two histories detailing the role of the press in the Spanish-American War give central place to journalists, as is obvious from their titles: *The Correspondents' War* and *The Yellow Kids;* Crane is prominent in both. Beginning in 1895, many of the correspondents in Cuba were also participants, serving as scouts (and sometimes spies) to determine the extent of the insurrection, acting as liaisons to rebel leaders before the United States went to war, carrying messages on "dispatch boats" hired by their publishers, even digging trenches and firing on enemy soldiers (Brown vii). One of the reasons Crane was there off the coast of Florida was that he was a well-known, even notorious, figure at the time of the *Commodore* disaster, and such "star" reporters were paid well to get to the scene of revolution (or disaster or worker exploitation), to investigate matters and to report what they saw. One paragraph in the *Press* advance story on January 4 begins, "Stephen Crane has been talked about more in New York than any writer of recent years" (Crane, *Stories and Tales* 247). The reference is to Crane's activities as reporter as well as novelist.

The Red Badge of Courage had made Crane suddenly famous early in 1896. (It seemed so "truthful" an account of the Civil War that a veteran claimed to have fought alongside the author, although Crane was not born until 1871.) But it was the hazing resulting from an incident during his coverage of New York City's Tenderloin District for Hearst's *Journal,* later in 1896, which made him notorious beyond his usefulness even to a yellow paper. Crane had become embroiled in a sensationalized case involving his court appearance on behalf of a prostitute, Dora Clark, and he was being harassed by the police (who resented his testimony and his investigative reporting).[34] Crane seems to have jumped at the Cuban assignment offered by Bacheller as an opportunity to get away from an impossible situation. He never returned to work in New York, making only occasional stopovers, during which he was harassed by the police, according to Edwin Cady (70, 72). He lived in England until his death in 1900. (His expatriation was probably inevitable once he decided to live with Cora Taylor, whom he could not marry because she was unable to obtain a divorce.) Although the *New York Press* and other papers running the Bacheller-syndicated reports of the ill-fated voyage of the *Commodore* dramatized him as a hero (the *Press* "advance" assured its readers that "he is not of the sort who are frightened by an experience in a lifeboat"), Cady reports that papers in other parts of the country made fun of his survival. One called him a "Jonah," and another suggested that Crane had gone filibustering in search of material, just as a few months before he had caroused in the Tenderloin. Now, it seemed, Crane would be able to say which was "the most dangerous way to get material for a realistic romance" (57). As Cady points out, Crane got no fiction out of the Dora Clark episode or out of any of his complicated affairs of the heart (58). It was necessary to seek out experience of one kind or another in order to be a freelance writer, however, no matter what form one's output took. Crane was not running away from sensationalism altogether, just from a situation where he was the butt of gossip.

Crane's view of the correspondent's function seems to have been close to his conception of the artist, and both were romantic. In the 1894 letter to Lily Brandon Munroe in which Crane describes developing "all alone a little creed of art" and then finding out it was "identical with the one of Howells and Garland," he refers to having "renounced the clever school in literature," his "Rudyard-Kipling style" (*Correspondence* 173). Noting this reference, and the likelihood that Crane had read Kipling's *The Light That Failed* at an impressionable age (it was serialized in *Lippincott's Magazine* in 1891, when Crane was nineteen), James Colvert concludes that Crane adopted the artistic principles of Kipling's artist hero, Dick Heldar, out of whole cloth and never really "renounced" them. These tenets assert the importance of absolute honesty, deem no subject unworthy of treatment by the artist, and hold that art is born out of need or privation ("Origins" 178–9). To a certain extent, the experiences one has are literary even before they are transformed by writing about them. Kiplingesque artists make of their bodies prisms through which to view the world. It follows, then, that one cannot write until he has seen everything, has come close to life in all its forms.

This attitude fits well with Crane's realist credo of faithfulness to nature and writing so that people can understand; indeed, it suggests one of the ways in which the realists elevated realistic treatment of the everyday world to art. This romantic emphasis on experience also contributes to "why he was there." Crane was acting very much in the spirit of the journalist, as what Christopher Wilson calls a "social and political pathfinder," in the 1860s and 1870s: "The reporter became America's first public agent of exposure, the high priest of 'experience,' the expert on 'real life' – all key words emerging at the heart of American popular discourse" (17). Newspapers fed the appetite for sentimental or sensationalized news stories by playing up the separation of audience from actors in the news. This correlates with polarities thrown into relief by the population shift to the cities, which others have noted: the contrast between spectacle and observer, such as a celebrity viewed by an anonymous individual in a crowd of onlookers; and the separation of production from consumption, the prosperous from the poor, which resulted in new configurations of living and commercial space and the abutting of rich and poor neighborhoods. As Crane wrote in a poem in *War Is Kind,* the newspaper

> Spreads its curious opinion
> To a million merciful and sneering men,
> While families cuddle the joys of the fireside
> When spurred by tales of dire lone agony.
> (*Poems and Literary Remains* 52)

Crane's way of dealing with these divisions in his reporting was to try to overcome the subject–object split implied by the journalism of spectacle and sensation by drawing the reader into the space occupied by his persona or narrator. He acknowledges his role in the production of perspective, referring to the process of observation (frequently in painterly or impressionist terms) and pays inordinate attention to the look of things.[35] While I do not go so far as Benfey, who says that Crane first imagined various experiences in fiction and then sought to live them, I believe that the emphasis on reporting which was prominent in this cultural moment – featuring the emotional response of people in dire circumstances, acting adventurously by seeking out unusual experience, and reproducing one's sensations for the vicarious identification of others – deeply influenced his writing. Colvert says, "What he sought was the final revelation of the mystery of existence in violent event and ultimate crisis" (Introduction, xx). Crane time and again put himself in the way of having adventures and observed himself experiencing them. More importantly, both the experience and his reporting of it transpired according to his original expectations. Other critics have characterized Crane as seeing the world in literary terms, although these would have to be qualified as deriving from what we would call "popular" literature: family magazines, adventure stories, sea stories, sentimental fiction, boys' books, religious and reform tracts (such as those written by his father, a Methodist minister, and his mother, a temperance activist), and compilations such as tales of shipwreck and *Battles and Leaders of the Civil War* (which first ran in *Century* magazine). He also contributed to many of these genres, and Eric Solomon has grounded a theory of Crane's practice of realism in his imitation and parody of these popular forms.[36]

"The Open Boat" provides an excellent example of the persistence of both realistic and Romantic attitudes toward writing. The correspondent, like Crane, seems to regard his profession as involving both work and art, although these do not separate into clear categories of journalist's work and fiction writer's art, as they will a few decades later, in Hemingway. They seem rather to correspond to two world views, two attitudes: what will save him – the work of rowing for survival – and what will enable him to survive even death – the wish of poets for immortality. Will he be open to the inspiration that will ensure his immortality, and thus "preserve" him for posterity? The correspondent carries out his job, rowing for survival, and yet hopes for inspiration that will "save" him.[37] In order to see this, the reader must note the significant portion of the narrative given over to physical details. These include reference to hours of rowing ("the oiler rowed, and then the correspondent rowed, and then the oiler rowed"), the procedure by which the oiler and the correspondent change places (72), and the exhaustion that results, which is compared at length to the "amusement" of rowing (74). Rather than tie this weary mechanical motion and the textual repetition that communicates it to a naturalist aesthetic, I view the tension between this aspect and its opposite – hope of spiritual grace or inspiration – as the repressed subject of "The Open Boat." The two styles, voices, or tonal levels guide us to the tension between work and "gifts," between the planning, scheming, the making of contracts and the uncertain payoff of writing, viewed as commercial production on the one hand and on the other as a miraculous gift which no one can earn, a moment of inspiration which results in the creation of art.

> Then the correspondent performed his one little marvel of the voyage. A large wave caught him and flung him with ease and supreme speed completely over the boat and far beyond it. It struck him even then as an event in gymnastics, and a true miracle of the sea. (91)

Throughout "The Open Boat" the reader can trace this ambivalence about work in the narrator's discourse, in the reported thoughts of the correspondent, and in the dominant trope of irony: the organization the men's survival depends on, namely the hierarchy of leader and followers; authority and those who are obedient to it; the men's arduous labor (which ought to be rewarded appropriately but may not be); what "ought" to happen versus what is happening ("Many a man ought to have a bath-tub larger than the [open] boat"); why the correspondent ought to be saved but may not be, considering fate is such "an old ninny-woman" (77).

Most biographers and critics deplore the effect of the literary marketplace, as well as the Cranes' profligate spending habits, on his talent, which they feel he abused in order to turn out hack work that would sell.[38] Indeed, "the syndrome of advances from agents and publishers and futile efforts to keep up with them became the monotonously dominating theme of his correspondence in the final year and a half of his life and resulted in an embarrassing amount of uninspired journalism," say Wertheim and Sorrentino (11–12). A letter to his brother William from London in October 1897 is representative; Crane says that he has earned close to two thousand dollars in a few months but has been paid only about one hundred twenty (*Correspondence* 301). Crane seems to have believed, however, that deprivation fostered creation. As he wrote of *The Red Badge of Courage* in 1896, "It was an effort born of pain, and I believe that this was beneficial to it as a piece of literature. It seems a pity that this should be so – that art should be a child of suffering; and yet such seems to be the case" (*Correspondence* 230–1, 323). Although Crane concedes this is not always true, he thinks that some writers would produce better work "if the conditions of their lives were harder," and he gives Bret Harte as an example (323).

Nevertheless, this guiding principle, if it was that, had serious consequences. Although Crane was apparently a sickly child and had frequent colds and coughs as an adult, we can surmise from accounts of his activities camping, tramping the streets of New York, horseback riding on a scouting expedition in Cuba, and surviving many illnesses, including dysentery and malaria, that he also had an amazingly strong constitution that might have enabled him to survive if he had suffered less abuse of his body. Although he had made a several-month trip to the West and Mexico in 1895 as a feature writer under contract to the Bacheller syndicate, his attempt to get to Cuba at the end of 1896, and the shipwreck that resulted, was the first in a series of ordeals by mishap and bad weather that he underwent during the next two years. Beginning with his trip to Jacksonville to get hired on a filibustering ship, Crane became a peripatetic freelance, moving to England with Cora in 1897; traveling with her to the Greco-Turkish War as a *Journal* and McClure-syndicated correspondent; according to Cady (67), trying to join the U.S. Navy to serve in the Spanish-American War in 1898 and, when he was rejected, covering it in Cuba and Puerto Rico for the *World* and, when fired, for the *Journal;* slipping into Havana, where he went underground for a few months, perhaps with malaria; resurfacing in New York and in the first days of 1899 returning to Cora in England, where they settled in an ancient English manor house for the last sixteen months of his life, broken only by short trips to Ireland (to gather atmosphere for a novel) and Switzerland (to place a niece in school there).

This first long ordeal apparently also had real consequences: A friend who saw Crane in New Jersey a week after the *Commodore* disaster recalled that "he looked like a man from a grave. He jerked and thrashed in his sleep, and sometimes he cried out in anguish" (*Correspondence* 263). Crane's family said he was never in good health after that (Cady 61), and yet he continued to behave recklessly, subjecting himself to bad weather and bad food, even to enemy fire in Cuba (R. H. Davis *Notes* 125). He died of tuberculosis in 1900 at the age of twenty-eight, although there is some evidence that his case was curable or at least manageable (Liebling 20). Anyone doubting the seriousness of the effects has only to learn of Cora's heart-wrenching description of Stephen's delirious ravings during his last illness, when she reported being driven to distraction by hearing him "try to change his place in the Open Boat" (Gilkes 257).

Christopher Wilson points out that Crane was not the only popular naturalist writer who died young, and at least partially from poor conditions while on assignment or seeing for himself wars and other newsworthy events. He mentions Jack London and Frank Norris and, later, John Reed (194). The pressures of the marketplace on these writers ought not be underestimated. As Wertheim and Sorrentino point out, Crane showed more tenacity in sticking to writing than Melville, who took a patronage job in the New York Customs House (11). Of course no one offered Crane a political appointment or any kind of stable work such as editing. Unlike his champion Howells, who built his career on "house" positions such as editorships and regular columns, Crane was a freelance from adolescence to his death, and, as he told an editor, that is "hopeless work. Of all human lots for a person of sensibility that of an obscure free lance in literature or journalism is, I think, the most discouraging" (*Correspondence* 232). Conceding that Crane's "improvidence" may have been a factor in his "agony," Cady nevertheless insists, "Whether pride or art or character caused it, Crane's suffering was real; and it produced important effects. It ruined his teeth, wracked his body, and doubtless presented him the tuberculosis which eventually killed him" (42).

In short, the transformation of a traumatic experience into a beautiful, multileveled narrative for which Crane received three hundred dollars from *Scribner's* marks the beginning of a transformative process that eventually led to Crane's becoming "a machine producing saleable manuscripts to pay off the bills" (Cady 73). Read with this historical context in mind, the automatic machine for rowing that the correspondent becomes in "The Open Boat" takes on new resonance. (I am reminded of Louisa May Alcott, who taught herself to write with either hand, so that when one cramped up from producing her self-prescribed output per day she could switch to the other in order to maximize production and keep to the schedule necessary to support her family.)

> In the meantime the oiler and the correspondent rowed. And also they rowed.
> They sat together in the same sea, and each rowed an oar. Then the oiler took both oars; then the correspondent took both oars; then the oiler; then the correspondent. They rowed and they rowed. (72)

This passage with its repetitive motion as well as repeated phrases may, after all, support a naturalist interpretation of what happens to characters in a determined universe. But unlike this ahistoricist assumption that the world is "just like that," that a determinist universe embeds characters in their action, a reflexive reading recovers the repressed historical causes of the correspondent's finding himself sharing the lot of workers in general: in effect becoming a repetitive motion machine.

Possibly the single most significant result of substituting reflexivity for literariness is that we define fiction or literature as texts that have been read as literature – that is, that have a history of being read by projecting form into content. This moves the division among discourses off the fact-fiction question (according to whether a text's referents are historical or invented) and locates the differences in the processes of production and reproduction, the acts of writing and reading. Once we acknowledge that some narratives suggest particular reading strategies, that is, point to the means by which they are best apprehended, then we see that we can read even realistic novels or objective journalism (which tends to hide its status as discourse) with attention to its materiality.

It is possible to read transparent realism as opaque because in effect all

primary definitions of literature can be explained as objectified extrapo-
lations from the reflexive reading process or after-the-fact rationalizations of what we have learned to do by reading narratives as literature.
Because reflexivity describes a process rather than a quality, we can take
these properties or characteristics that have been called signs of fictionality or literariness and restore dynamic qualities to them – show that
they are not essential qualities but potentially dual or dialogic ones.
When we show the reflexive or "process" basis of literariness, we can
see why theorists trying to define literature slip from the logical to the
generic sense of fiction, or merge formal and content-based distinctions.
What they are doing is recapitulating the reification evident in formalist
definitions, which turn processes or methodologies into objective properties.

For example, take the case of fictionality. Because the term "fiction,"
with its latent or repressed sense of the feigned, has connotations of
deceptiveness, some theorists prefer the term "mimesis," which implies
simply an imitation of the world as it appears to us; thus we say that
mimetic texts "reflect" the real, or create an illusion of it. "Mimesis"
has both a cognitive sense (it is a way of knowing) and an aesthetic one
(it is a way of configuring language to create illusions). There is a
methodological dimension (the question of how one knows or how
language represents) to either sense of the term, for the reader's attention
may be displaced from the world to the work by signs or gestures of its
having been made, or to the fact of knowing by the way the illusion of
factuality is expressed. That is, we may be drawn to notice the methodology of representation rather than to the objects represented (Lyons
and Nichols 3). A formalist definition represses the methodological
aspect of mimesis by emphasizing the object as represented, apart from
the observer, treating it as self-evidently there, instead of attending to
its process of coming into being or implicating the observer in that
process. In a reading that does not suppress or reify the process, mimesis
thus may be self-referential or performative as well as representational,
that is, reflexively involved rather than allowing the separation of viewing subject from represented object. This dialectical reading process
turns attention alternately toward the form the presentation takes (e.g.,
description or narration, as Lukacs describes them) and toward its content, which itself lies on a continuum from the concrete historical reality
of a historical novel to the "self-sufficient" world of science fiction or
The Hobbitt, with generalized realistic fiction somewhere in the middle
(Jameson, *Marxism* 296). It should be obvious that reflexive reading of
mimetic texts is never formulaic, because both form and content further
divide along various continuums, such as that from historical to supernatural referents, or from dramatized to "invisible" narrator. For exam-

ple, an authorial choice that affects the reader's degree of identification or "subject position" is whether to offer a nondramatized narrator as either "observing outsider" or "imaginative participant" (Jameson, *Marxism* 203). Lukacs's examples of these divergent tendencies in French literature are Zola and Balzac; in U.S. realism, the difference can be represented by Hemingway and Crane. Aesthetic or rhetorical conceptions of literature are already implicitly reflexive, because they are based on the self-sufficiency or autonomy of the literary work: it is only a small step from emphasizing a work's rhetoricity or autonomous pattern "for its own sake" to acknowledging its self-referentiality. Other ways to express the rhetorical emphasis are to note the way the text calls attention to its own form, that is, to attend to its opacity or autonomous existence.[39]

A feature frequently said to mark a narrative as literary is free indirect discourse (FID), the "sign of the thought of another." To my mind this is the rhetorical strategy that best represents our inability to know things apart from the way we know them, that is, acknowledges our capacity for reflexive "knowing." Free indirect discourse is the technique which makes point-of-view narration possible, and it is supposedly characteristic of fictionality, because its premise is that we can know the thought of a third person (or even one's own thoughts in the past), whereas this is logically impossible.[40] Not only does free indirect discourse show the inseparability of form and content by being both an overtly rhetorical device and one based on fictivity (it must always be imagined), but it is inherently dual-voiced (a narrator gives the speech and thought of one or more characters) and inevitably ambiguous. It is sometimes impossible to tell where the narration leaves off and the focalization, the speech or thought of the character, begins: free indirect discourse combines the narrator's and the character's points of view.[41] Because of this ambiguity and the difficulty of deciding who is the focalizer, the technique subtly undermines the certainty, and hence the authority, of what in other respects is transparent narrative. When the reader is aware of the ambiguity, as when she reads reflexively, the text becomes more palpable. In short, free indirect discourse illustrates the dialogism of all narratives, the way words inhabit multiple discourses and bring echoes of those other texts to the one in which they are found (see Volosinov).

Because of this "mutual interpenetration of reported utterance and reporting context" ("McHale, "Free Indirect Discourse" 263), the process of free indirect discourse models a reflexive reading. What started me off on the attempt to discover the reasons for the fictional effect in "The Open Boat" was the sense of ambiguity created by the use of third-person point of view. Because I knew that the story was autobiographical, it followed that "the correspondent" meant "Crane," and so

I expected the free indirect discourse to be limited to his consciousness. But the reader must be conscious of this decision as an active dimension of the text, of the process by which we are enabled to identify with this one character out of the four, and thus to enter into the narrative by identifying with the subjectivity of the correspondent. In short, the technique enables the observer (both narrator and reader) to enter into the objectified world, and enables the reader to realize that the narrator is also present in the character's represented thought and speech, rendering it always ambiguous rather than certain.

This is similar to what the reader does in any reflexive reading. We go into and out of the subjectivity of the character, feeling that we participate in the world rather than viewing it helplessly, unable to identify with any aspect of it (as is the case when we are closed out of the modernist objective text).[42] At the level of story or meaning we derive from the plot presented in this way (in third person with limited point of view), we then consider the tension between the "overt" message – the necessity of the solidarity of men in the face of an impersonal universe – and the refusal to render it impersonally or objectively. With the correspondent and narrator, we interact with the world of nature – waves, cold, and wind – rather than confronting it in a detached or contemplative way. The free indirect discourse allows the reader a place and reminds her that the narrative itself interprets events by giving two perspectives on them.

And yet the alternative is represented to us. Because we know only one character's reveries and memories, along with him we are isolated from his comrades in the boat. If we read unself-consciously, we remain locked within this limited perspective, instead of recognizing that our ability to interact, to participate, constitutes an act, and we are no longer passive. This may be the motive behind Crane's choice of third-person narration for "The Open Boat": it enables him to show the correspondent from inside as well as outside, and thus to split himself into narrator and character. The result is an inherent ambiguity that makes it necessary to read form in relation to content, and it is this practice that we identify as a literary reading. Literature, under this conception, is not essentialist, because it is put into effect by reading, and is not defined by its qualities, although they do encourage the reading that produces the literary "effect."

Free indirect discourse also reminds us of the "belatedness" of all narrative (in relation to an implied original), and yet, paradoxically, it depends on the priority of the text over the story (the characters and events) we derive from it. Our intuition is that we can derive free indirect discourse from indirect discourse, and indirect discourse from direct discourse, but this is an illusion fostered by "novelistic illusionism"; we cannot recover the "original" direct utterance, because it is not derived from anything but is all we have (McHale, "Free" 256; Volosinov 128–9), just as stories (or the diegesis) are always derived from plot at the material level of the text. And yet this illusion, in both cases, is so strong that theorists as well as readers perennially refer to the original version or source, the "given" story that narratives transform. Finally, the presence of free indirect discourse reinforces our sense that language is dialogic, for it is a transformation of an implied utterance – that is, indicative of language's grounding in communication, its social function.

It should be clear by now that the reflexive process does not by itself produce literature. Nor can we conceive of a literary space "between" idealized texts or naturalized ones, that is, between ideology and objectivity. Although the poles of subjectivism or objectivism are "errors" which either reduce language to the individual utterance or privilege the abstract system as a whole, literary quality is not somewhere between these. Rather, the reflexive process takes place in "meaningful activity" among social beings in language considered as forming those users as well as being constituted by them (Williams, *Marxism* 36; Volosinov 94). In short, there is no special realm of literature apart from language production as a whole. In Volosinov's words, "Linguistic creativity does not coincide with artistic creativity nor with any other type of specialized ideological creativity" (98).

The revisionist definition proposed here permits us to move outside the usual categories of literature and "other" in teaching and criticism. It requires us to acknowledge that literature is a historically produced category, and that what we view as "literary" varies according to the definition of "literature" in force at a particular time. By testing our usual definition of the literary in "The Open Boat" and other realistic stories, assessed within their historical context, we may discover that what seems to be a self-evident, qualitative conception is culturally produced, as are refinements and variations of this category. One such shift in emphasis toward aesthetic criteria in a specific time and place, again involving the separation of journalism and fiction, is the subject of Chapter 2.

2

"News That Stays": Hemingway, Journalism, and Objectivity in Fiction

> Objectivity and again objectivity, and expression: no hindside-before-ness, no straddled adjectives (as "addled mosses dank"), no Tennysoni-anness of speech; nothing – nothing that you couldn't, in some circumstance, in the stress of some emotion, actually say.
>
> – Ezra Pound, letter to Harriet Monroe (Jan. 1915)

> Literature is news that STAYS news.
>
> – Pound, *ABC of Reading* (1932)

The characteristics that lead us to regard Crane's two accounts of surviving a disaster at sea as journalism on the one hand and a short story on the other are not inherent in the texts. Although we may believe that journalism and fiction are qualitatively different, we are taking our cues from the contexts in which we find them and from particular narrative conventions that we reify as properties of fictional texts, such as third-person point of view and the existence of two levels of narration in the short story. On the basis of extrinsic factors, we identify the texts either as obviously literary (capable of conveying universal truths) or as journalistic (belonging to the medium that reports everyday facts).

These generalized distinctions, in turn, produce a particular version of literary history, such as the widely held view that the founders of realism, from Twain to Hemingway, were journalists first.[1] In this view, writers practice their powers of observation and impersonal narration at the city desk and then apply them to invented characters and to subjects with a broader appeal. Journalism is then best seen as a training ground where writers serve an apprenticeship before becoming novelists. (Tom Wolfe shows that this idea lingered in the big-city newsrooms he entered as a feature writer in the early 1960s [Introduction 5–9].)

This theory has the advantage of showing the continuity of realism over forty years, from the North American version of classic realism

53

(Twain, Howells, James), through naturalism (Crane, Norris, Dreiser, Wharton), to the objective or minimalist variety of modernism (Cather, Anderson, Hemingway). All these varieties share some form of the defining characteristics of realism, such as emphasis on the visual, separation of the observer from the observed, a consistent point of view, and avoidance of authorial intrusion. It is a plausible historical account if one accepts the secondary status of journalism or regards reporters as objective recorders of facts.

On the other hand, if we regard literature as a historical category produced by particular practices of criticism, teaching, and reading, this secondary status of journalism is not natural or inevitable. We tend to accept it unthinkingly; for us it has been "naturalized." It depends, we have already noted, on the elevation of literature to a transcendent category (based on the expressive or objective definition of art) in the nineteenth century, and the concomitant linking of nonfiction forms like journalism with the mundane world of factuality, thereby defining them as of only temporal interest. Instead of acknowledging the etymological roots the novel shares with journalism ("What's new?"), this genre, when viewed as a naturally superior category, is held to transcend them, linking the novelty" of its form to its access to a higher truth, above the mere facts and everyday – and plural – truths of journalism. Thus the division of discourses in the early twentieth century moved from the separation of poetry from prose to the separation of literature from nonliterary modes, fiction from nonfiction.

This usual history of the relationship ignores evidence that does not fit, smoothing over contradictions. For example, consider the curious results we obtained by comparing the two Crane narratives. Although our usual dichotomy has subjective fiction on one side and objective factual narrative on the other, we found that Crane's first-person journalistic narrative is more subjective, and less factual, than the objective narration produced by the impersonal narrator of "The Open Boat." Here the theory that journalism was the incubator of realism is contradicted, because news stories at the end of the nineteenth century were not yet commonly narrated in anonymous third-person objective style. Crane was known as a "literary" journalist, but this meant, not that he was crossing boundaries which had not yet been defined but that he was asked to produce his impressions of an event, to sketch the scene, including signs of his own subjectivity. The names that Crane and his editors gave to his pieces – "story, sketch, study, episode, tale" (Gullason 471) – show the tentativeness of the category of fiction, the lack of distinct criteria for news stories, and the absence of clearly defined news categories such as is represented by the later compartmentalization of news into "pages" or "beats."

"Star" reporters and big-name correspondents before the twentieth century apparently did not care what their work was called, as long as it was featured prominently. Neither did the newspapers and magazines in which their stories were published use the terms "fictional" and "nonfictional," as by setting off a category of fiction on the contents page. For example, nowhere in the June issue of *Scribner's* is "The Open Boat" labeled "a short story by Stephen Crane."[2] When the story was published the next year in collections of Crane's work put out by Heinemann in London (*The Open Boat and Other Stories*) and by Doubleday & McClure in New York (*The Open Boat and Other Tales of Adventure*), its category was still ambiguous.

Distinguishing between categories of fiction and nonfiction was not of obvious concern to Crane. He apparently regarded his sketches and tales as continuous with his reports as "local-color" journalist and as correspondent for various news syndicates, and, as with his novels, he wrote them to please himself and also for the money they earned.[3] Because the late-twentieth-century critic considers journalism an inferior form, Crane's efforts in this mode are usually denigrated in favor of his fiction. The editors of *The War Dispatches of Stephen Crane* insist, however, that he was "not the failure as a journalist that almost every critic has labeled him," and they call him "a star reporter." To them this high quality made his work seem all of a piece, and in compiling the collection they found it difficult to decide whether to label a given narrative a newspaper sketch or a short story (Stallman and Hagemann 109, 108). Cady states that although his conveying of "atmospheres" and psychological effect "rather than 'facts' dismayed editors and annoyed fellow reporters" (Introduction xxiii), peers who regarded journalism as a branch of letters appreciated his coverage. Richard Harding Davis, for example, called one of Crane's pieces from Cuba, "Marines Signalling under Fire at Guantanamo," one of the finest examples of reporting to emerge from the Spanish-American war ("Our War" 941).

Such tentative boundaries were evidently firmed up in a very short time, for in 1922 we find Hemingway complaining about the limitations of reporting and deciding to give up journalism before it ruins him for serious writing (*Letters* 62–3, 101). Sometime before 1932, when he had published only two novels and two collections of fiction, he wrote to a bibliographer who had inquired about his journalism, "If you have made your living as a newspaperman, learning your trade, writing against deadlines, writing to make stuff timely rather than permanent, no one has any right to dig this stuff up and use it against the stuff you have written to write the best you can" (*By-Line* xi).

Among Hemingway's many observations about the handicaps journalism imposes on the creative writer is one remark which mentions how easy it is to describe a newsworthy event, because "the timeliness makes people see it in their own imaginations" (*By-Line* 215). This implies that all a reporter has to do is be on the scene to record the facts and sequence, which will then have power by themselves. This apparently was his view, for in a fragment found among his papers (quoted in Donaldson 104), he assumes that reporters are born, not made, but that their natural viewing apparatus eventually wears out:

> [W]hen exposed to a murder, hanging, riot, great fire, eternal triangle or heavyweight box fight [the reporter] automatically registers an impression that will be conveyed through his typewriter to the people who buy the paper. Great feature men are constructed like color photographing plates – humorous writers are cameras with a crooked, comically distorting lens. When a reporter ceases to register when exposed, he goes on the copy desk. There he edits the work of other men who haven't yet been exposed so many times as to cease to register.

This deprecation of reporting by American journalists who become novelists is now part of popular mythology. Writers seem to feel that if they do not get out of journalism, it will sap their energy, destroy their memory, or ruin them for anything else by its "tricks" (Fenton 161).[4]

There are several consequences of our ready belief that writers serve time working for newspapers and magazines before they are released into fiction. First of all, it perpetuates journalism as a secondary mode, because journalism is the form of production that is left behind by the novelist who needs to do his "real work." As an inferior discourse, it is not worthy of being treated seriously for the particular relationship it posits among the narrator, its subjects, and its readers. Accepting the usual version of the history also leaves unquestioned the objective aesthetic that journalism supposedly gave rise to yet can no longer participate in. This aesthetic sets a high value on a style characterized by concision, concreteness, deflation of rhetoric and abstractions, understatement, contrast and juxtaposition, the absence of complex syntax, apparent moral detachment, and a lack of overtly expressed emotion. This style seems to be transparent or objective, but asserting its universality and timelessness as inevitable enables it to work by ideology. Thus it is similar to the ideology of objective journalism in that both modes depend on the repression of some materials; both transparent realism and objective journalism reify their temporal observations by separating the viewing subject from what is observed, and both share the world view of positivist science. If we continue to narrate literary history by assuming that these distinctions are natural, we cannot see the process of making literature – the process by which the criteria of modernism become normative, first to critics and then to readers.

Hemingway's work is an exemplary site to consider the results for American literary history of narrating the influence of journalism on fiction from the rise of realism to literary modernism. He practiced both journalism and fiction in the early 1920s, and the apprentice role journalism played in his developing career is considered to be typical of the realists' experience. He also described the differences and justified his investing fiction with prestige on aesthetic grounds. Hemingway's style became what Philip Young calls "unquestionably the most famous and influential prose style of our time" (172–3); its influence extended not only to other writers but to his readers. Edmund Wilson says that *The Sun Also Rises* so expressed the mood of "heroic dissipation" of the mid-1920s that "in the bars of New York and Paris the young people were getting to talk like Hemingway" (*Wound* 179). Although his objective fiction of the 1920s is not the only prose that fits the definition of literature that was soon to be refined by the New Criticism, it can stand for it, because the qualities named in praising it are those that are assumed to be "naturally" literary: its demonstration of the rigors of craft or discipline; its emphasis on form or method rather than moral or meaning; and its exploitation of the distilled image, resonant scene, or sensory object (in his case through economy and indirection, including understatement and irony).

Although there is some evidence to support a causal relationship between the writing of journalism and realistic fiction, most of it shows journalists' experience being broadened and their attitudes toward the world affected by covering both the deviancy that makes certain local events newsworthy and the wars and other international events that lure them abroad.[5] The influence is thus experiential and biographical rather than stylistic – and yet technique is the area where its influence is most cited. Along with an emphasis on accurate observation, the primary similarity between journalism and fiction noted by critics is the brevity and economy of means developed for recording those observations. Journalists from Twain and Howells through Hemingway are supposed to have learned these techniques in the newsrooms of U.S. cities.[6]

Even from a quick reading, it is obvious that the journalism of Crane, Dreiser, London, and Cather is not more spare or concise than their fiction. If the writing is similar in both modes, we cannot assume one was the proving ground for the other. Crane, we saw in Chapter 1, did not elevate his fiction as more serious; indeed, he did not comment on his craft in any significant way, as Willa Cather points out (*On Writing* 73–4). Cather is another journalist who belies the observation that the column, reviewer's essay, or editor's desk was a place to hone one's incisive language tools. For her, journalism was a place to let all the stops out, in what she called "my high-stepping rhetoric." As she said in 1927, in a private letter to the editor of the *Nebraska State Journal*, for which she had written from 1893 to 1896, the journalistic freedom allowed her there "was good for me, because it enabled me to riot in fine writing until I got to hate it, and began slowly to recover" (Bohlke 181).

It seems more likely that journalists and fiction writers at the end of the nineteenth century and in the first few decades of the twentieth were influenced by the same cultural forces, such as the domination of knowledge and intellectual inquiry by empirical science. U.S. journalism and the realistic novel may be similar in this period because both were responding to the positivism of the world view prevalent at that time, namely its concern with "objective observation, analysis, and classification of human life" (Carter 102). Stanley Corkin ("Hemingway") observes that not only novels and journalism but the emerging film medium at the turn of the century have similar formal characteristics (invisible narration, privileging of the visual) and similar behaviorist attitudes toward their subjects and audiences (human beings presented as mere objects among many others). The similarities among these forms dominated by realistic representation and a belief in objectivity may have been related to the ideology of developing industrial capitalism, whose positivistic assertion of the world as it appeared to be, disseminated in the journalism, literature, and cinema of the period, prepared readers and viewers to be subjects who would, in Althusser's words, "work by themselves" ("Ideology" 181).

If this thesis is correct, brevity, impersonality, omission of temporal and historical referents, and indirection or understatement are not inevitable qualities of literary prose; we choose to make them defining characteristics in a process that is historically recoverable. And yet these characteristics are conventionally used to distinguish Hemingway's fiction from the journalism in which his style was supposedly incubated. If we simply accept these features as virtues resulting from his work as a journalist, we miss the chance to consider the influence of Pound, Eliot, and Stein on that aesthetic; we risk overlooking the implications of Hemingway's own self-canonizing pronouncements and may fail to question their sincerity or disingenuousness; and we ignore the fact that the successful separation of realistic fictional prose from nonfictional or functional kinds coincided with the modernist construction of formalist criticism, that is, the establishment of the aesthetic basis for recognizing and analyzing literature. Last of all, we probably will not consider whether these characteristics really are virtues, whether they make fiction superior to prose anchored in the social, political, and economic issues of the time in which it is written. That is, we will not question the formalist definition of literary prose as text in which questions of truth or falsity do not matter, because fiction exists in an autonomous realm, "for its own sake."

The first realization one has after turning to Hemingway's early work with an eye to examining the usual assumptions is that, for all the effect Hemingway's apprenticeship as a cub reporter for the *Kansas City Star* and as reporter and correspondent for the *Toronto Star* is supposed to have had on his first published fiction (especially *In Our Time,* published in 1925 but largely completed in 1924), the journalism he wrote from 1920 to 1923 is quite personal and expansive. Nevertheless, critics continue to describe this journalism as concise and compact, and to suggest that Hemingway's characteristic "brevity, clarity, austerity, and directness" is derived from the "instincts and skills [he] developed as a newspaper man" (Benson, "Ernest Hemingway" 306). This description more aptly suits his very early work for the *Kansas City Star,* where he wrote according to the "formula" for straight news stories and covered the police and hospital beats. Evidence that the Toronto newspaper experience was very different from this became readily available with the publication of *By-Line: Ernest Hemingway* (1967), which includes pieces from throughout his journalistic career. Indeed, several reviewers of *By-Line* note instead its loquacious commentary, humor, and other personal qualities (Bradbury; Oldsey, "Always").

In some accounts, it was the *Kansas City Star*'s famous style sheet that did the trick for Hemingway's prose (Donaldson 89; Fishkin 137–9) by stressing "brevity and compression" and urging: "Use short first paragraphs. Use vigorous English. Be positive, not negative" (quoted in Fishkin 137). Hemingway told George Plimpton in 1958, "On the *Star* you were forced to learn to write a simple declarative sentence. This is useful to anyone" ("Art" 70). If we cannot say that these were the rules that formed Hemingway's style nor agree with Charles Fenton's conclusion that "if one worked even briefly in this world where short sentences and vigorous English were truly important things, then he would, fundamentally, write that way forever, just as he would always write with the emphasis on freshness and originality" (32), at least we can say that here are the roots of the *belief* that such a style is best. Here is the basis of the commonplace assumption that the goals of a good writer are "authenticity, precision, immediacy" (32).[7]

In general, however, Hemingway's journalism from the twenties is characterized by irony, parody, broad satire, and by a narrative persona that communicates variously authority, irreverence, expertise, and wit. As Donaldson notes, "These newspaper pieces, written from 1920 to 1923, were remarkably personal for a profession which lays claim to objectivity" (89). One reason for the difference is that for the *Star* he was writing feature stories rather than straight news, and so we must not do what many Hemingway critics do, that is, lump all his journalistic work together and draw conclusions from what we know about the way objective journalism works now. As Fenton points out, the dispatches Hemingway sent to Toronto from Europe in 1921 had an "intimate, impressionistic quality" that he would have been unable to cultivate as correspondent for a major city paper in the United States. Fortunately for him, the *Star* wanted "lively, entertaining dispatches, intimate and subjective" (119).

If we note the loquacious and self-conscious style of the pieces that are usually seen as foreshadowing the terse declarative style of Hemingway's fiction, we are likely to conclude that the objective narration of the stories and novels of the twenties was a result of a deliberate aesthetic, and that Hemingway did indeed take his fiction more seriously, regard it as "art." And yet, despite the novelist's denigration of his own journalism, as the editor of *By-Line* points out, "Not only did Hemingway use the very same material for both news accounts and short stories: he took pieces he first filed with magazines and newspapers and published them with virtually no change in his own books as short stories" (xi). We may be able to reconcile this attitude with his actions by studying those pieces that became short stories and noting the changes he made or failed to make.

My first example is the often-discussed *In Our Time* vignette depicting the evacuation of eastern Thrace during the Greco-Turkish War after the Greeks' humiliating defeat by Turkey. In this case the changes from journalism to vignette generally move toward compression, elimination of reportorial shaping of the reader's response, and understatement. The first three paragraphs of the dispatch Hemingway cabled to the *Daily Star* on 20 October 1922, datelined Adrianople (with the addition of an image supplied by a second, longer report mailed three days later and published November 3), became the single paragraph of chapter 2 of *In Our Time*, which begins "Minarets stuck up in the rain."[8]

Fenton has analyzed Hemingway's alterations in the many drafts of this sketch, beginning with the first cable and including the version published in the *Little Review* in April 1923 (where it was the third of six pieces) on the way to its revision for *in our time* (the 1924 collection of chapters which includes none of the short stories of the 1925 version) and, finally, its appearance in 1925 in *In Our Time*, the collection of alternating chapters and titled stories which has been in print ever since. The major changes Fenton describes are Hemingway's elimination of authorial "direction" and of most modifers, including many of the almost thirty adjectives in the cabled first draft. As Fenton details them, these include compound modifiers ("never-ending," "muddy-flanked");

pejorative adjectives like "ghastly"; and adjectival sequences like "exhausted, staggering," and "ripe, brown" (231).

Hemingway also reframed the sketch to emphasize the "water-logged immobility" of the procession, that is, its logjam quality, its lack of movement or progress (233–4). Much of the sketch's metaphoric power comes, Fenton believes, from the narrowing of the focus to two figures, the woman in labor and her crying daughter. (He points out that "the husband [described in the dispatch] did not survive the rewriting" [235]. Then Hemingway condenses the long list in the third paragraph of the cable into a single sentence: "Women and kids were in the cars crouched with mattresses, mirrors, sewing machines, bundles [, sacks of things]."[9]

Somewhat contradicting the "sluggish" progress of the refugees is the chapter's emphasis on present participles. (Fenton calls them "gerunds," but the effect is the same, for participles also express "movement and flow" [233].) Although Fenton does not point this out, the cable is in the present tense while the vignette sets the evacuation in a vague past, thus counteracting the timeliness of the report. He also does not discuss the three sentence fragments in the revised sketch, which avoid the question of tense completely: "No end and no beginning. Just carts loaded with everything they owned."[10] The last fragment is so isolated from its context that the reader does not know who is "Scared sick looking at it." Furthermore, most of the chapter's participles are past indefinite ("were hauling," "was running") or part of past-tense clauses ("old men and women . . . walked along keeping the cattle moving"). Altogether, then, the effect of the revision is to eliminate the present-tense immediacy of the dispatch and its ties to a particular time and place.

Although Fenton says that Hemingway removes the "excessive clutter" of the dispatch in order to "eliminate the unspecific" (235), and that this is characteristic of his career-long "concern with precision," this specificity (if it is that) does not lead to greater understanding on the part of the reader.[11] The interchapter as a whole is much less historically detailed than the cabled account. Fenton does not mention that in the vignette the reason for the evacuation is never given. Whereas the cable situates the horrific scene in eastern Thrace, where "the Christian population . . . is jamming the roads toward Macedonia," the literary version leaves the complicated political context vague: a large civilian population, defined by religion and nationality, was forced to leave their homes because the European allies had intervened in the Greco-Turkish War, awarding eastern Thrace to the Turks and giving the Greeks only fifteen days to evacuate (Baker, *Life Story* 97–9; *Dateline* 226–32). As Hemingway wrote in a dispatch from Constantinople published October 16, "the cross made way for the crescent" (*Dateline* 226). (In his five-page analysis of the transformation of the first three paragraphs of the cable, Fenton says that Hemingway did not use the last two paragraphs because they were too "general" [230]; actually, they are more specific than the vignette, for they describe relief efforts in Thrace and give the magnitude and context of the evacuation.)[12]

In moving from journalism to fiction, or in adapting newspaper reports for publication in book form, Hemingway cuts the particulars that would link his narrative to a specific time and place and produces deliberately decontextualized images that work the way photographs do: as "pieces of" the world rather than "statements about" it (Sontag, *On Photography* 26). The well-known emphasis on realism and authenticity of his fictional composition practice results from a deliberate process of editing out particular historical and temporal references and omitting signs of the observer – the journalist whose regular by-line would lend credibility to the report, no matter how far away its subject and how difficult for readers to picture for themselves "how it was." Journalism provided many of the subjects for the chapters of *In Our Time* and Hemingway's stories of the 1920s and 1930s – and perhaps their pervasively ironic attitudes, which were as common among journalistic colleagues as among other modernist writers. Their brevity, concision, and compression, however, which enable narrative to work as timeless myth or to sound like the truth of folklore or other oral traditions, come, Benson finds, from prose Imagism ("Ernest Hemingway" 286–7; 306).

More evidence that Imagism was an important influence on Hemingway's prose comes from examining articles that went from periodicals into short story collections without being changed (except the title, in one case). Evidently he could reprint these narratives as fiction while consistently regarding journalism in general as inferior, because these few pieces were, in his view, already fictional, in that they are not dependent on the timeliness of their subjects. Besides, they proceed in terms that must have defined an artful story to him: a focus on representative situations and characters, plot events corresponding to observable relationships among the facts of the world, and indirect suggestion of a universal human nature. One of these pieces is a report from the Spanish Civil War, "The Old Man at the Bridge." All Hemingway had to do with his notes to produce a story instead of a dispatch was what he did to the cable from Asia Minor gradually, in a series of drafts, to make it suitable for *In Our Time*: select and focus the materials in order to unify the narrative and make it self-contained, and remove instructions indicating how the reader ought to feel.

Other examples, such as "The Chauffeurs of Madrid" and "Italy –

1927," show that Hemingway was practicing similar techniques in both journalism and fiction, using irony, understatement, and dialogue to advance the narrative. These pieces doubtless took many revisions to perfect. For example, the reader notes him experimenting with subtle repetition and varying the rhythm and length of sentences to suit the subject.[13] As a correspondent or feature reporter, he did not have much time in which to revise, and, to avoid possible misreading or lack of clarity, he fell back on the conventions of first-person reporting, the persona of the "confidential insider" (P. Smith 363), the "one trick and another" he knew would communicate the emotion (*Death* 2). The stories he decided to reprint without change must already have seemed like fiction to him, therefore, not because they were invented but because they already lacked those characteristics we can note him removing from dispatches he did revise into fiction, such as the *In Our Time* vignettes based on journalistic pieces (discussed by Reynolds, "Two Hemingway Sources").

Another dispatch from Spain in 1938, "The Flight of Refugees," would have been a likely candidate for short story treatment, except that Hemingway had already "done" a universalized refugee piece as chapter 2 of his first collection of fiction. The families evacuating ahead of the advancing Republican army during the Spanish Civil War reminded him of those at Thrace in 1922, as his field notes for this dispatch show (reprinted in Watson, "Variorum" 98–9). It would have been a fairly easy matter to revise this scene and allow it, as Watson says, "to break out of the constraints of the article and become a story on its own" ("Old Man" 158).[14]

Another factor contributing to the belief that Hemingway's journalism was the incubator for his fiction is the repetition by critics and literary historians of the effect of the cable on Hemingway's distinctive form of declarative prose. James Carey, for example, says, "In a well-known story, 'cablese' influenced Hemingway's style, helping him to pare his prose to the bone, dispossessed of every adornment." He quotes Hemingway's later remark to Lincoln Steffens about having "to quit being a correspondent" because "I was getting too fascinated by the lingo of the cable" (Carey, *Communication* 211).[15]

Neither the "lingo" nor the fascination is evident in the pieces reprinted in *By-Line* and *Dateline: Toronto* (subtitled "The Complete *Toronto Star* Dispatches, 1920–1924"). Robert O. Stephens asserts that as European correspondent for the *Daily Star,* Hemingway "had complete freedom of movement and choice of material and was expected to cultivate a lively, intimate, and subjective approach in his articles. These conditions differed sharply from those imposed on most correspondents for American news agencies, who were expected to submit routine, objective, factual reports" (10). For a short time Hemingway did send cables of the latter sort to the International News Service (INS) from Asia Minor. In a 1934 *Esquire* article (*By-Line* 179) he complained about the limitations imposed by the cost – "three dollars a word" – which forced the writer to pare his words to the minimum. But that terse cablese (Hemingway's example is KEMAL INSWARDS UNBURNED SMYRNA GUILTY GREEKS) does not make itself felt in the 174 Toronto *Star* pieces reprinted in *Dateline: Toronto* (including the dispatch about the Thracian refugees that became chapter 2 of *In Our Time*), which he and Steffens were discussing in 1922 (Fenton 186–7).

Fenton says that in 1930 Hemingway "repressed the surviving cabelese" in chapter 2 by inserting the phrase "There was" before the fragment that read "No end and no beginning" in the versions published in 1924 and 1925 (236). But this sentence fragment is *not in* the dispatch, the first three paragraphs of which Fenton reproduces (230–1) and which is much longer, more discursive than those in chapter 2 – in short, not written in so-called cablese at all (although it may have been transmitted as such). So much for critics' determination to find effects that are simply not there.[16] The fragment, like the other two sentences mentioned earlier, is more likely the result of Hemingway's attempt to give the vignette the quality of "oral literature." In such stories, Jackson Benson says, "the tragedy of a modern event is given a timeless, mythic quality as the flat, impersonal, simplified prose, punctuated and structured by repetition, recounts the inevitable doom that overtakes nearly anonymous people in nearly anonymous settings" ("Ernest Hemingway" 286–7).

Fenton elsewhere distinguishes between "the conventional, telegraphic cabelese" Hemingway sent to the INS and "the curt but nevertheless formed cabelese" allowed by the *Daily Star* (187).[17] Hemingway was indeed interested in this formed "lingo," but primarily as a method for keeping cable costs (billed by the word) to a minimum. It is true that cablese "challenged" the writer to "transmit his ideas using a minimum number of words" (Flora 5), but the key word here is "transmit." The journalist did not have to write in a more condensed style, merely translate it into the dialect called "cablese" that resulted from the attempt to use the fewest words. (Fenton points out that Hemingway was usually paid by the word, so that he was not likely to write very "economically" for the sake of his own finances [260].) The rest of the passage from Steffens's *Autobiography* that Carey quotes has Steffens impressed by the evocative power of Hemingway's refugee cable, with the younger journalist, perhaps embarrassed by the compliment, responding, "No, just read the cablese, only the cablese. Isn't it a great language?" (834). It is likely that learning this dialect or "lingo" was a challenge to Hemingway, who was, as Fenton insists on the evidence of his newspaper work, "always intensely interested in how to do a thing. He was absorbed by method" (150). A writer who tells his readers everything they need to know to be able to fish, instructs them in bullfighting appreciation, and even describes what bootleggers do is obviously interested in process analysis. This interest in doing things correctly, Fenton concludes, was an important part of Hemingway's personal style and "fundamental to his interest in war, politics, and sport" (151).[18] An interest in the process of cablese, rather than a concern about its effect on his prose style, seems to be behind Hemingway's comments to Steffens about the allure of cablese.[19]

Watson has printed the two extant drafts, both in cablese, of a dispatch from Spain in 1938, when Hemingway was under contract to North American News Alliance (NANA), as part of a "variorum edition" to illustrate the process of composing and sending a dispatch and to show the changes made by people involved at each step: in the censor's office; at NANA, where it was translated back into standard English; and in editorial offices, where decisions about correct versions and about how much of the story to print were made. As a reader I was fascinated by the ingenuity evident in the condensed dispatches Watson reprints; it is easy to imagine Hemingway's professional interest in mastering this process of contracting subjects and verbs, attaching adjectives to their nouns, and omitting prepositions, articles, and other parts of speech.[20]

Dispatch 19 (3 Apr. 1938) begins:

> twas lovely false spring day when we started for the front smorning stop last night incoming barcelona tad been grey and foggy and dirty and sad but today twas bright and warm and the pink of almond blossoms coloured the grey hills and brightened the dusty green rows of olive trees stop. ("Variorum" 95)

No "pre-cablese" draft survives. The best of several retranslated versions from the NANA offices, Watson suggests, is the "Diplomatic Text":

> It was a lovely false spring day when we started for the front this morning. Last night coming into Barcelona it had been grey and foggy and dirty and sad, but today it was bright and warm and the pink of almond blossoms colored the grey hills and brightened the dusty green rows of olive trees. (96)

If Hemingway's fascination with cablese had more to do with the means of communication than with the final form, over which he had little control, his decision to quit being a foreign correspondent might have been the result of this very loss of control. He might have felt that it was no use composing a dispatch very carefully when by the time his cable arrived in New York "dozens of changes had been introduced into his text by unknown hands," and NANA editors contributed many more in reconstituting it for release to the newspapers they served. Hemingway's first Civil War dispatch grew from 182 to 275 words, for example (Watson, "Variorum" 94–5). Carey points out that the telegraph effectively separated the observer on the scene from the writer in the editorial office. By implication this makes the reporter more important for his powers of observation than for his writing skills (*Communication* 211). What ambitious writer will long put up with this job description?

A question that has not been asked is why, if transmission by cable and radio wireless was such an influence on the compressed prose style Hemingway perfected in the early 1920s, it did not affect writers in the last half of the nineteenth century. The telegraph was in use by newspapers by 1848, the year the first wire service, the Associated Press, was organized, and yet correspondents like Crane continued to send long, detailed, well-formed reports over the wire. "Stephen Crane's Own Story," to name just one familiar example, was telegraphed to Crane's agency, Bacheller (and perhaps to the *New York Press*) and then sent out over the wire to other papers.[21]

Technology, Michael Schudson points out, is rarely the cause of ensuing developments, although it may make them possible (*Discovering the News* 31–4). Other conditions, particularly motivation, must also be present. He notes that in Britain only the penny papers made full use of the telegraph because of their different concept of "news," which included accuracy, completeness, and timeliness; these were not necessarily emphasized by the older six-penny press (4, 34–5).[22] For the telegraph to affect the standard length of a story or the precision of style, for example, brevity and conciseness would have had to be at least implicit goals of journalism; and yet, although messages themselves were as compressed as possible, the format and length of news stories did not change dramatically until the twentieth century. (See Carey, *Communication*, chap. 8.)

For similar reasons, the experience of covering the police station, the courts, immigrant and working-class life, and other features of city life, although important to writers as material for realistic fiction and for broadening their experience, could not in themselves have created the new rhetorical strategies that would counter the style used in the genteel and sentimental fiction that prevailed at the turn of the century (see Crane, "Howells Fears"). After all, reporters had begun to get this kind of experience in the 1820s and 1830s (M. Stephens 238), yet their reports were variously subjective, leisurely, sentimental, and sensationalized all through the century. Neither did many of these reporters become novelists, and no critics speak about the contribution of the journalistic observation of the antebellum period in the United States to the rise of realism.

Most journalists who did write novels, even in the period of the rise of realism, were unable to avoid the conventions of the potboiler, including sensationalism, sentimentality, and the creation of caricatures instead of realistic characters. This is Howard Good's assessment of the "newspaper fiction" written by journalist-novelists from 1890 to 1930. In other words, the fiction about the world they knew is relentlessly unrealistic. Critics and literary historians who emphasize the role of journalism in producing fiction may be missing the larger picture simply by concentrating on the canonical writers and overlooking the pedestrian fiction produced by most journalists. If the first realists were going to represent people from all strata of life, with consistent point-of-view-narration, without authorial intrusion, and with other strategies of realism, they were going to do it with or without newspaper experience.

It seems likely that the telegraph did affect the structure of "hard" news stories; the "inverted pyramid" form, for example, probably resulted from reporters "rushing to transmit their most newsworthy information over often unreliable telegraph lines," with supporting facts following, just as they do in the news story that results (M. Stephens 253). And it doubtless contributed to the construction of objectivity in journalism by making one observer interchangeable with any other and ensuring a standardized prose not attributable to a particular writer. Fiction writers seldom write in an inverted pyramid style, however, and it is difficult to see how the telegraph influenced literary realism in general. The growing emphasis on facts and information that the telegraph facilitated instead led to the disruption of narrative (sentence sequence determined by the importance of the information rather than by chronology or logical continuity, for example) and to an "unreal" divorce of facts from context.[23]

It is against the odds the the medium of the telegraph could have brought about as distinctive a prose style as Hemingway's was in the early 1920s. It is more likely that interchangeable observers following standardized "top-down" news conventions would eventually produce a uniform colorless prose, which is what happened as journalism began to operate under twentieth-century notions of objectivity. The connection between news writing and fiction seems to stem as much from the convention of using the term "objective" to describe both Hemingway's minimalist version of realism and journalism's striving for impartial reproduction of visible facts as from any influence. If both journalism and fiction are seen as responding to the growing faith in positivist science, however, it is no surprise to find them associated. The effects of objectivity in fiction and objective journalism are similar; both work by hiding the means of representation, utilize a detached or anonymous narrator, generally adopt a consistent but limited point of view, and depend on or imply the separation of an objectified world from the observer.

There undoubtedly were many aspects of reporting that Hemingway and others disliked, and there are many ways that writing to meet journalistic conventions differed (and still does) from much of that published as fiction. Writing to deadline allows little time for revision, and Hemingway, with his interest in craft, may well have chafed at this. Journalism was undergoing professionalization in the last quarter of the nineteenth century, along with many other occupations in a complex market economy (C. Wilson 14–15), and writers aspiring to art rather than to a profession, or desiring a more bohemian lifestyle than that offered by steady work on assignment, must have disdained what was, after all, a regular job (Fenton 101).[24] No matter how often one got out into the streets, to the police station and courthouse, to the opera and theater (as Cather did in Nebraska), or out in the fields of war, writing to someone else's specifications and having one's work revised and edited without final approval must have made journalistic output – that is, words and stories – seem a kind of product or commodity like any other in a developing consumer society. The fact of a mass readership must have made the pretense of writing for a like-minded reader difficult. Furthermore, the structure of news organizations is as hierarchical as that of many workplaces (an editor or publisher is certainly a boss), and the acceptance of a freelancer's work and the placement or "play" of one's stories depends on an editorial gatekeeper.[25]

Perhaps the primary impetus for Hemingway and other formalists to posit an opposition between journalism and fiction, however, is that it creates recognizable boundaries between literature and nonliterary writing, art and life. Art is that by its relation to other forms; it is defined by difference. As Peter Stallybrass and Allon White show by tracing what Bakhtin calls "carnival" over several centuries of European social and cultural life, the hierarchy of genres, as well as of people in socioeconomic classes, is maintained by distinguishing those above on the ladder from the "low/Other." What is demystified as "low" for reasons of prestige and status, in politics and social relations generally, is actually "constitutive of the shared imaginary repertoires of the dominant culture" (6).[26]

Journalism seems to have served this purpose for Hemingway, for we see him disparaging journalism and deciding to give it up before it ruined him for serious writing, when he quit the *Toronto Star* to go back to Paris in January 1924 (*Letters* 62–3, 101). Because the characteristic feature of so-called objective fiction – clean, concrete, transparent prose – might also occur in journalism (and who would know this better than a writer who was practicing both modes?), we see Hemingway going to great lengths to distance what he does in his "real work" from his journalism. He does this even when the latter consists of well-written feature articles and dispatches from European countries that capture the mood of a particular setting, characterize a class or group of people in a few paragraphs or scenes, and share many features with his 1920s fiction.[27] With the advantage of hindsight, we can see such anxiety as this as the result of Hemingway's insecurity about the differences, for in the first decades of the century the two modes had been rather similar, and both were now becoming more so – more impersonal and less subjective. By moving toward verisimilitude, emphasizing visual observation (what could be seen by anyone exchanging places with the observer), presenting experiences easily related to by large numbers of readers, and developing methods such as consistent point of view and absence of authorial intrusion, realistic narrative shed the appearance of art: the frame, the distancing mechanisms of authorial voice, and other signs of the act of writing.

If fiction was to be "literature," it had to appear to possess superior qualities, such as the ability to express universal and timeless truths. Because the literariness of a realistic form of fiction is not obvious, its elevation was accomplished by producing a critical discourse that emphasized the artfulness of antiliterary techniques and insisted on the virtues of style – even an objective, behaviorist one. Novelists and critics thereby distinguished fiction from journalism, which was set off as a time-bound and particularized discourse, a type of "low/Other." Fiction thus became "news that stays," while journalism was identified by what were considered limiting characteristics: immediacy and sensationalism, and the use of particular, recognizable names and events.[28]

The style of fiction often described as objective arose in the minimalist experiments of Cather, Anderson, Stein, Hemingway, and other modernists. In interviews, essays, and letters, these writers defined their goals and discussed their methods, in effect instructing readers in the correct manner for reading their work. This instruction took the form of emphasizing the writer's imagination, for in the face of a growing market economy, utilitarian culture, and the factory system – all forces which seemed to threaten art conceived of as realistic, for how can art be reconciled with such a society? – the writer who could create an alternative world through force of imagination would inevitably be held in esteem. The modernist realists therefore emphasized the transformative power of craft, contrasting their imagination to reporting skills and overcoming their verisimilar form by playing up or even mystifying their particular method of conveying "the real thing."

When Hemingway described this method in his memoir of the early 1920s in Paris, he said he was starting to "break down all my writing and get rid of all facility and try[ing] to make instead of describe"; writing thus became "wonderful to do" but very difficult (*Moveable* 154). Although he was commenting many years after this formative period, and therefore from a vantage point dominated by the aesthetic he was influential in forming, this shift to a more distilled and transparent version of realism is also apparent in the prose of his contemporaries just after World War I.[29] Here is Cather in 1921, telling an interviewer, "What I always want to do is to make the 'writing' count for less and less and the people for more" (Bohlke 24).

This brings up an apparent paradox: although both writers claimed to be interested in the "real," their concern was inevitably with the method or art of conveying it. Strategies of omission (of overt connections, of explanations, of obvious art) and authorial detachment contribute to the deliberate construction of an antiliterary aesthetic. Tension then results from considering whether to call attention to the form or let it work by its seeming artlessness. The modernists' belief is that this tension, reproduced in the reading, contributes to readers' pleasure, for we also make this choice. The technique of juxtaposition as Cather described it illustrates the possibilities. Cather claimed that she refused to use "colorful rhetoric" to detract from the effect of two colorful objects set side by side but left an out for the reader trained in the formalist aesthetic (and this kind of criticism was part of the training):

> I want the reader to see the orange and the vase – beyond that *I* am out of it. Mere cleverness must go. I'd like the writing to be so lost in the object, that it doesn't exist for the reader – except for the reader who knows how difficult it is to lose writing in the object. (Bohlke 20)

The tendency to give the illusion of the real instead of being obviously literary is said to be related to a widespread distrust of language after World War I – or at least of idealistic and abstract language. Joseph Warren Beach called this group of writers "the war generation, who have learned to dislike big words because they were so much abused both during the War and in the age that prepared the War" (110). Critics cite as evidence the passage from chapter 27 of *A Farewell to Arms* in which Frederic Henry insists,

I was always embarrassed by the words sacred, glorious, and sacrifice and the expression in vain. We had heard them, sometimes standing in the rain almost out of earshot, so that only the shouted words came through, and had read them, on proclamations that were slapped up by billposters over other proclamations, now for a long time. . . . There were many words that you could not stand to hear and finally only the names of places had dignity. . . . Abstract words such as glory, honor, courage, or hallow were obscene beside the concrete names of villages, the numbers of roads, the names of rivers, the numbers of regiments and the dates. (184–5)

This is a very interesting passage, not only because a study of the manuscript by Michael Reynolds shows that it was "one of the most heavily revised passages" of the novel (*Hemingway's* 61). Reynolds found an unnumbered manuscript page with a typed quotation from that rare thing, an interview Henry James gave to the *New York Times* in March of 1915 to appeal for funds and volunteers to the American Ambulance Corps. (Leon Edel says it is clear that James rewrote the interview, not only from the orotund style but from his secretary's amusement at the picture of him "interviewing himself" over several days [527].) The passage Hemingway copied concerns the devaluation of language in the face of horrendous casualty figures in the first year of the war:

One finds it in the midst of all this as hard to apply one's words as to endure one's thoughts. The war has used up words; they have weakened, they have deteriorated like motor car tires; . . . and we are now confronted with a depreciation of all our terms, or, otherwise speaking, with a loss of expression through an increase of limpness, that may well make us wonder what ghosts will be left to walk.

Reynolds speculates, in *Hemingway's First War,* that Hemingway considered using this passage as an epigraph for his war novel but had learned from starting with two in *The Sun Also Rises* that they misled readers into reading the novel as autobiographical, a chronicle of the "Lost Generation," rather than responding to the passage (from Ecclesiastes) "about the earth abiding forever" (61–2). This is plausible, although I also believe that Hemingway would not have been eager to cede influence to a predecessor like James, and his own description of the loss of useful language is much pithier than James's circumlocution. (Hemingway quoted only part of James's paragraph, which is given by Peter Buitenhuis in *The Great War of Words* [21].)

This sense of the difficulty of writing in the face of a preposterous reality was everywhere during World War I. Edith Wharton, for example, wrote in two letters, before the end of the war, that "the face of the world is changing so rapidly that the poor novelist is left breathless and mute, unless like Mr. Wells, he can treat things 'topically,' which I never could." And this: "Before the war you could write fiction without indicating the period, the present being assumed. The war has put an end to that for a long time, and everything will soon have to be timed with reference to it. In other words, the historical novel with all its vices will be the only possible form for fiction" (quoted in R. W. B. Lewis 423–4). This emphasis on the "topical," as well as the resort to verifiable facts and documentary records, seems a logical response to the abuses not only of the body (James refers to as many as five thousand casualties in twenty minutes on the western front) but of truth, as a result of the massive propaganda effort conducted in the United States by the Office of War Information (headed by George Creel) and in Britain by C. F. G. Masterman and a stable of Britain's most famous authors (Buitenhuis, chaps. 4–6). It is surprising, then, to see Hemingway and other modernist minimalists in effect de-emphasizing history.

For that is what is lost in the substitution of names and numbers for concepts in this passage: not merely what the narrator wishes to lose – the abstraction and idealism we recognize in the first group of words – but meaning and history, for the concrete words come without context.[30] Why are these village names significant? What did particular regiments do in relation to these roads and rivers, and on what dates? It may be that those abstract words ought to be rejected, having become fraudulent from incorrect or deceptive use, and because their facile use to enlist support for governments' cynical purposes doubtless caused young men to die in the war. But simply listing the names of regiments separately from the battles they took part in, the villages they won or lost, and the roads they advanced or retreated down fails to correct the abuse, because names, like facts, are not meaningful in themselves. Both here and in his fiction throughout the twenties, Hemingway seems to acquiesce in the belief that political writing is futile. Nor does he make an effort to expose the propaganda myth that had so much effect on young Americans that they enlisted in the service of other countries before their own had made up its mind to enter.[31]

Passages such as this from *A Farewell to Arms* about the worth of concrete names (and paragraphs repeating its lesson in Hemingway criticism) enable us to see how the objective text gives the illusion of being both real and true. The idea that concrete words are more realistic is not inevitable, however, but part of a set of values that must be established. Accepting the concrete language as less "obscene" or more faithful to facts distracts us from its equally artificial or "literary" nature. For one thing, the lists in the passage are not parallel, since the second one gives no examples (as the first does of abstract words); it simply asserts the fact of names, the fact of their existence. Robert Weimann reads the passage as narrating the breakdown of representation in two ways: the shouted words are almost unheard through the rain (and the printed ones are pasted up in layers, which apparently do not last very long before being pasted over in turn); and words are meaningless when their referent has become detached from the signifier so that it is no longer "socially relevant" (211). Thus the "twofold burden on representation, iconic and discursive," has broken down, with only placenames remaining meaningful. We should note that there is very little significance in what remains. Because there is no ideological pressure to split the proper name from its referent, since it carries no more than a designating function, to confer dignity on these numerical terms or placenames is not to grant them very much in the way of shoring up the "representational function" (211).

Millicent Bell asserts that Hemingway frequently includes realistic detail for no obvious purpose, simply "to affirm the presence of the actual, whether or not truly remembered, reported, historical." She says this is a kind of "pretend" realism, for one can mimic "testimonial incorporation of the real" or make up the "real" to become "realistic" (198, 108). The passage we are analyzing may not be the best example of such accidental detail, but her point is worth quoting in full because she emphasizes Hemingway's tendency to insert information just because he had it at hand. This is the ultimate antiliterary strategy, for we assume that everything in a literary narrative is significant, and so we struggle to see the significance of what has no meaning save in inclusivity. Bell says, "In *A Farewell to Arms,* as elsewhere in his writing, Hemingway made the discovery of this secret of realist effect, and his art, which nevertheless presses toward poetic unity by a powerful if covert formalist intent, yet seems continually open to irrelevance also" (109). The effect is only increased, she notes, by his refusal to add explanation, to interpret, or to frame the objective details in any meaningful way.

That appears to have been a deliberate strategy, moreover. Hemingway, Cather, Pound, Stein, Eliot, and other founders of modernism were working out an aesthetic which favored certain modes and styles that we know as Imagism, Objectivism, and objective realism in opposition to their conception of the sentimentality or sensationalism or deceit of political discourse, propaganda, advertising and public relations, genteel fiction, and journalism. Therefore they deplored not only the idealism and "suitable" subjects of earlier realists like Howells but the full description and "ideas" of great realists like Balzac and Tolstoy. In a 1934 *Esquire* piece, Hemingway recommended skipping the "Big Political Thought passages" in *War and Peace* as "no longer true or important, if they ever were more than topical," meanwhile pointing out "how true and lasting and important the people and the action are" (*By-Line* 184). His comments are regarded as valid literary criticism by many critics, who accept the definition of literature as what transcends the particular or local, what becomes timeless and therefore of universal appeal. This is rather paradoxical, considering the cultural and political function the novel has assumed. When Howells, who admired Tolstoy above all other novelists, for a time, set into motion the mystification of realism by emphasizing its ability to convey supremely moral truths, he doubtless did not anticipate the use to which his doctrines would be put or the effect they would have before five decades had passed.

Cather was rejecting both the "interior decorator" in Balzac and the "romance of business" so common in novels after him when she wrote, in "The Novel Démeublé" (1922), "The higher processes of art are all processes of simplification. The novelist must learn to write, and then he must unlearn it" (*On Writing* 40).[32] As in Hemingway's early work, Cather's predominant method in *My Antonia* (1917) and *One of Ours* (1922) was indirection, her goal to evoke a scene "by suggestion rather than by enumeration" (40). In another passage in "The Novel Démeublé," she says:

> Whatever is felt upon the page without being specifically named there – that, one might say, is created. It is the inexplicable presence of the thing not named, of the overtone divined by the ear but not heard by it, the verbal mood, the emotional aura of the fact or the thing or the deed, that gives high quality to the novel or the drama, as well as to poetry itself. (41–2)

The similarity between Cather's desire to eliminate the elaborate "furniture" of the novel and Hemingway's theory of omission is striking. He frequently described this strategy as resembling an iceberg, once saying, "There are seven eighths of it under water for every part that shows" ("Art" 84). His version of "less is more" is, "You could omit anything if you knew what you omitted and the omitted part would strengthen the story and make people feel something more than they understood" (*Moveable* 75; and see *Death* 192.) By using these strategies in their fiction, both writers made a virtue of inarticulateness; apparently they were reluctant to express feelings, concluding that "public ideas are false and truth resides solely in unverbalized private experience" (Ziff 153). We can see the equation being formed between genuine feeling and the absence of signs of it. Apparently, truth is inexpressible. Alfred Kazin might well have added Cather to "that group of friends – Hemingway, Fitzgerald, Dos Passos, Cummings, Wilson – for whom the right words in the right order were the immediate act that cut away the falseness and inconsequence of the world" (*Bright* 11).[33]

Because this aesthetic is expressed through omission, understatement, and similar strategies of minimalism, it requires extensive critical elaboration. After all, we might mistake this writing for clever and faithful recording of the facts of the world (and, as we noted in Chapter 1, realism is the mode in which it is difficult to read content through form). Although the goal is said to be concrete language and concise expression of meaning, when a narrative style leaves out explanation and refuses to connect or interpret events, ambiguity and vagueness are a likely result – unless professional interpreters explain the significance of what is left out (see Wagner 51). This is especially necessary given the closely allied aesthetic of indirection or "discipline" (Peterson 56), which extends to distrusting extrinsic emotion. Cather and Eliot (and others, including William Carlos Williams) shared with Hemingway the belief that emotions lay in objects, and that they could be evoked in the reader by conveying the proper "sequence of motion and fact" or "chain of events" or recorded experience that would trigger the equivalent emotion in the reader. This behaviorist method is appropriately named the use of the "objective correlative" by Eliot. To Cather it involves the construction of a scene: "When we have a vivid experience in social intercourse, pleasant or unpleasant, it records itself in our memory in the form of a scene; and when it flashes back to us, all sorts of apparently unimportant details are flashed back with it" (On Writing 79–80).[34] Although it appears that the writer has little to do with the affective power of scenes that record themselves unconsciously and work by unbidden association, Cather says that her ability to have experiences that make an impression indicates her emotional and imaginative power. (Cather expresses this idea by litotes, or understatement, arguing that the "absence" of such scenes is a sign of "lack of imagination" (80).)

Hemingway explains this phenomenon on the second page of Death in the Afternoon, where he is analyzing the writing of the chapters and stories of In Our Time in the early 1920s.

> I was trying to write then and I found the greatest difficulty . . . was to put down what really happened in action; what the actual things were which produced the emotion that you experienced. . . . [T]he real thing, the sequence of motion and fact which made the emotion and which would be as valid in a year or in ten years or, with luck and if you stated it purely enough, always, was beyond me and I was working very hard to try to get it. (2)

Interestingly, Hemingway defines this artistic method in contrast to techniques of journalism. The first part of the second sentence reads, "In writing for a newspaper you told what happened and, with one trick and another, you communicated the emotion aided by the element of timeliness which gives a certain emotion to any account of something that has happened that day." The issue of temporality or ties to a particular time and place is here closely related to the difference between making and describing, between fiction's intrinsic emotion and journalism's "tricks." In 1935, Hemingway elaborated:

> When you describe something that has happened that day the timeliness makes people see it in their own imaginations. A month later that element of time is gone and your account would be flat and they would not see it in their minds nor remember it. But if you make it up instead of describing it you can make it round and whole and solid and give it life. (*By-Line* 215–16)

Thus, to Hemingway, reporting is subject to the pressure of both the occasion and the audience one writes for; it does not have the "purity" of fiction for its own sake.[35]

Possibly the most dramatic difference between a reader-oriented journalism and the objective aesthetic of modernist prose lies in the way each mode is said to produce its effects. In the view of the constructors of modernist aesthetics, the reporter does not bother to work at making readers see what happened, because they will fill in the emotion called for by the fact that the story is displayed as news. In contrast, the writer of fiction has to capture "what really happens" to produce emotion and then must state it "purely." Writers, however, do not simply express their emotions; rather they are *in* the text. Here is Cather in 1922: "The writer does not 'efface' himself . . . ; he loses himself in the amplitude of his impressions, and in the exciting business of finding all his memories, long-forgotten scenes and faces, running off his pen, as if they were in the ink, and not in his brain at all" (Bohlke 17–18). This is similar not only to Eliot's statement that "the progress of an artist is a continual self-sacrifice, a continual extinction of personality" ("Tradition" 53) but to Hemingway's belief that emotions exist in things, in "sequence[s] of motion and fact" (and of course, William Carlos Williams's "No ideas but in things").

We see these writers constructing the aesthetic conception of minimalist prose by elevating invention, imagination, and simplification over profuse description and leisurely recording of events; intrinsic form over journalism's sensational effect on the reader; omission, juxtaposition, and other forms of indirection over journalism's direct explanatory narrative; and the solidity and permanence of "made-up" scenes over the temporal and historical contexts of journalism, which are viewed as providing extrinsic or "easy" emotion. Furthermore, by recalling changes Hemingway and Cather made when moving from journalism to fiction, we can add to their repertoire of differences the techniques of repetition and compression in the interest of genuine immediacy, and the impersonality that hides the signs of writing.[36] We can thereby reconcile the problematic conjunction of modernism's interest in form (in the "how" of representing, not just the "what") with the concomitant goal of avoiding "literary" constructions – which are here associated with sentimentality, propaganda, and thus the betrayal or disguising of reality, as opposed to the "truth" of objectivity. Because this antiliterary style appears neutral or invisible, the minimalist aesthetic takes the form of an emphasis on the act of writing (Kazin, *Bright* 16), on the transcendental appeal of exactly observed actions, and on the behaviorist assertion that emotions and meaning reside in things.

"Objective" is an apt term for this method, even though it is part of a self-conscious theory of form, because the subjectivity of the perceiver or observer is denied in the objectivity of the technique. According to Larzar Ziff, in Hemingway's style "the preference for passivity and indirectness in verbal constructions heightens the objective illusion that it is all there outside us happening and flowing in and affecting us cumulatively rather than being controlled and ordered by our will (let alone a divine plan) or being received through categories imposed by the mind" (152). The implications of this objective illusion are serious. They include the separation of observer from observed, the naturalization of the world as it appears to be (rather than an awareness of the role of social, cultural, and economic practices in producing reality), and the objectification of human beings, who are reduced to their function or the roles they play.

It is difficult to see how fiction written and read in terms of this behaviorist aesthetic is different from the journalism produced by the reporter who simply registers impressions and conveys them directly to the reader, as Hemingway describes the process in the fragment quoted earlier in this chapter: "[W]hen exposed to a murder, hanging, riot, great fire, eternal triangle or heavyweight box fight [the reporter] *automatically registers* an impression that will be conveyed through his typewriter to the people who buy the paper" (emphasis added). In either case, the writer is merely the plate on which the stimulus registers, the conduit for the emotion which is *in* the world, in the events observed carefully and merely "conveyed" to the reader, whether they are published in a periodical or a novel. Neither are the events recorded in newspapers – "a murder, hanging, riot, great fire, eternal triangle," or boxing – more sensational than the subjects of *In Our Time;* except for the riot and the fire, they are all there in this fictional collection, with bullfighting substituting for the boxing match (and the roaring crowd in the bullfight vignettes, chaps. 9–14, threatening riot in response to the poor performance of the ritual). The snippets of newspaper headlines that form the cover of the 1924 volume *in our time* and were intended to surround each page clearly reinforce this relationship between news and stories.

The fact that Hemingway describes both writing processes as mechanical (in *Death in the Afternoon* the fiction writer merely records "the sequence of motion and fact which made the emotion") supports the theory that, at some level, he knew that both reporters and fiction writers observe, experience, and construct prose via the same process. But he cast his lot with the "enduring universals" of the prestigious form and set about distinguishing his literary craft from his journalistic labors in the same way that literary historians and critics began to firm up the boundaries between literature and other discourses: in order to elevate literature to a secure realm where disinterested truth is possible, in contrast to everyday, instrumental discourses, where it is subject to contingent facts, various interests, competing points of view. To do this writers must suppress the similarities, withdraw to an area clearly removed from borders where actual texts cross and recross borders, and deny the appeal of the sensational or deviant or else transform it into aesthetic experience. Fiction must be somehow beyond the messiness of history and politics; outside the economic market, where it is implicated in exchange (its value determined by demand, like any commodity); and above considerations of "use value," being distinguished by its aesthetic effect, in contrast to journalism's primary purpose of communicating information.[37]

This situation is similar to that which Roland Barthes finds at the end of the nineteenth century, when the Symbolist poets turned away from trying to influence particular readers, toward poetry for its own sake. Barthes (summarized here by Eagleton) explains why either "the purity of silence" or the "degree zero of writing" seemed to the Symbolists preferable to writing with a social purpose:

> If objects and events in the real world are experienced as lifeless and alienated, if history seems to have lost direction and lapsed into chaos, it is always possible to put all of this "in brackets," "suspend the referent" and take words as your object instead. Writing turns in on itself in a profound act of narcissism, but always troubled and overshadowed by the social guilt of its own uselessness. (*Literary Theory* 140)

Hemingway may not have felt guilty – after all, he did not abandon journalism completely – [38] but he may have experienced the ambivalence that goes along with identifying oneself with an elevated discourse that depends for its status on the realm it is setting off as low, or Other. Removing his writing to the realm of the aesthetic, where it is valuable for its own sake, may have enabled him to feel he was not just another producer of a useful commodity in a world where anyone with expertise is potentially a writer (see Benjamin, "Work" 234).

It does seem ironic, however, that at the moment when art seemed to offer a strong position from which to offer a critique of what threatened it most – a society based on commodity production and consumption that regards men and women as labor-producing machines rather than considering them in their intellectual and emotional being – to those who would elevate it, literature instead became ineffectual, because to use it for merely local or particular conflicts would be to destroy its universal appeal (see Tompkins, "Reader" 217; Hough xvii). Literature thus exalted – as a mode too pure to be useful in gaining particular social or moral ends – inevitably implies an audience characterized by passive functioning, unable to acknowledge its real conditions of existence and to analyze its actual history.

Just as fiction writers like Cather and Hemingway moved toward an objective or minimalist aesthetic as a kind of retrenchment, a way to preserve some transcendent values apart from economic, social, and political forces that seemed to threaten art by converting all men and women into assembly-line workers, and even ideas and texts into commodities, so critics, Bové explains, sought a means of reinserting order and value into a world they believed to be governed by "naturalistic science, by positivism, and by causal history" (*Destructive Poetics* 97). The solution developed by the New Criticism involved overcoming the dissociation of sensibility caused by modern science, with its logical, linear propositions and abstractions, and freeing human beings from the determinism of historical cause and effect by locating transcendent truths in the "universals of human nature" expressed by the work of art (98–9).

As I mention the role of the New Criticism in solidifying this formalist conception of literature by perpetuating it in classrooms across the country beginning in the 1930s, I am aware that their critical views can be seen as the reason for the demotion of journalism and other nonfictional genres. Deborah Rosenfelt summarized this view: "Because the New Criticism valued works that could be analyzed as autonomous, self-contained structures without reference to the artist or to the historical era, certain genres (like poetry and fiction) became more highly regarded than others (like autobiography or essay)" (21). To accept that explanation, however, is also to acknowledge the unsuitability of so-called expository or nonfictional genres to formalist interpretation or close reading, meanwhile overlooking a distinction that has been made before any reading is done. That is, the New Critics defined fiction by its difference from discursive genres; the basis on which they distinguished was literature's transcendence, its absence of extrinsic temporal, social, cultural, and political contexts – fiction's ability to float free of its ties to history. The secondary status of nonfiction was therefore not a byproduct of this conception of literature, but a condition of it.

To see that this is so, we need only consider the circumstances surrounding the composition, reprinting, and critical evaluation of "Old Man at the Bridge." It is one of the few stories Hemingway published without change (save dropping the initial article from the title) both in a magazine and in a collection of his own fiction, *The Fifth Column and the First Forty-Nine Stories* – the last to appear in his lifetime.[39] In it Hemingway tells of an encounter with an elderly man, made a refugee by the Fascist advance in the Ebro Delta during Spain's civil war. The man is worried about the animals he has left behind after being warned to flee the enemy, because if it was unsafe for him, it must be so for them as well. His plight is emphasized by his statements that he has no family and no politics and knows no one on the road to Barcelona, the direction of the retreat. Hemingway narrates the encounter in the first person, but anonymously; the narrative advances through dialogue, with little comment or interpretation. Thus the story has all the virtues of objectivity that critics have admired in Hemingway since the twenties: understatement, irony, unity, simplicity, epiphany, and universality. In Edmund Wilson's view, it is "a story which might have been written about almost any war" (*Wound* 192).

Hemingway sent the short (800-word) narrative by cable from Barcelona to *Ken,* a new anti-Fascist magazine, edited by Arnold Gingrich, for which he had promised to write articles bi-monthly, along with his regular dispatches to the North American Newspaper Alliance (NANA). It appeared in *Ken* on 19 May 1938, a month after it was sent. Although the story has an apparently uncomplicated composition history, due to the fact that it was cabled on the same day Hemingway encountered its subject near Barcelona, Paul Smith calls the question of its genre a complex one (362–3). It can be so only because Hemingway "found" the story as he narrated it, true in all its essentials (even to the poignancy of the day being Easter Sunday); he did not change any details from his notes except the man's age and the number of animals he had to leave behind in San Carlo.

To Smith, its basis in fact raises the issue of genre: the "nearly immediate transcription of experience into fiction, the story's transmission by cable, and some of its similarities with the diction and the tone of the confidential insider" (363). Once again, the logical term "fictive" seems to be a criterion of the generic sense of fiction: the story is too factual to be clearly fictional, unless the critic emphasizes its lack of newsworthiness, the author's intention to write fiction, or its formal features. Although White calls the story a "news dispatch," in his introduction to

By-Line, probably because of its transmission by cable, later in 1938 Hemingway differentiated between the two modes by saying, "[I]t was for a magazine so I could write a story about the old man and not a news dispatch" (quoted in Watson, "Old Man" 157).[40]

This is an interesting distinction, because, as William Watson shows after examining the field notes and copy of the cable passed by the censors, Hemingway wrote the story in only a few hours and seems to have decided to send it to *Ken* instead of NANA during the writing. He speculates that Hemingway saw the opportunity to meet his obligation to Gingrich and "realized, moreover, that a news story about an old man, a refugee, would have differed little in the eyes of the NANA editors from the report on refugees he had already filed at the beginning of the month [3 Apr. 1938]." Watson claims that Hemingway had realized, "much to his annoyance," that NANA would reject pieces they regarded as "repetitious or un-newsworthy" (155). In other words, he might have sent the same narrative to NANA if he thought they would have used it.

Because Watson has followed Hemingway in accepting the difference between fiction and journalism, he emphasizes the narrative's formal characteristics, including its use of dialogue, its narrow focus – the exclusion of background details such as the presence of other refugees (and doubtless other journalists) – and the indirect and understated style that produce an intense emotional response (159–61). Watson also believes that the narrative is a short story by intention, that Hemingway used his notes differently, knowing that what he wrote was going to *Ken* instead of to NANA, placing emphasis on the formal and archetypal characteristics present in the encounter that needed only to be selected and brought out.

If we start with the conception that fiction or literature is what has been regarded as such, the question is easily settled. "Old Man at the Bridge" is a fictional story because Hemingway reprinted it in a collection of short stories – not because he has changed some facts, or because he focuses on a single figure among the flood of refugees and avoids the "dispassionate observer" persona common in the dispatches (Watson 159–60).[41] The fact of its reprinting then earned the story the attention of critics, who have made it, if not "major," at least one frequently mentioned; it is sometimes grouped along with Hemingway's other Spanish Civil War stories or related to *For Whom the Bell Tolls* or *The Old Man and the Sea* (Waldhorn 169; Flora 90–2).[42] By reprinting it among his short fiction, Hemingway confirmed the worth of its characteristics: the "brevity, clarity, austerity, and directness" that critics find in his work as a "newspaper man" (Benson, "Ernest Hemingway" 306) but which is not valued there.

Because journalism is relegated to secondary status when fiction is aestheticized, critics can only see it as an influence; Pound could only "liberate" these "instincts and skills" Hemingway had developed as a journalist (Benson, "Ernest Hemingway" 306). Then, too, emphasizing the power of these techniques only when they are separated from the discourse in which they supposedly originated enables readers to overlook the abstraction and the mystification that result from the techniques of compression, simplicity, and omission. Rather than being seen as limiting or narrowing, they are said to produce universal observations and to work the magic of aesthetic and emotional truth. In this sense it is clear that Hemingway called what he wrote a "story" and not "journalism" because this was "the moment when literature was most firmly rejecting the contingent and historical, striving for the permanent, the mythic, the concrete universal of art" (Scholes, *Textual* 71).

We need to recognize that, as Robert Scholes shows, this aesthetic decision is a political act, and we must question the universalizing of emotional restraint or reticence; it is not a natural human characteristic. We have seen that Hemingway's style works in part by loading neutral, descriptive words (such as "clean," "clear," "cool") with value (Peterson 25–6ff.). Although these substitutions and associations may have developed out of a reaction to the excesses of sentimental or inflated rhetoric (as in genteel or propagandistic prose), this tendency may well be personal or psychological, developed because the writer distrusts emotion and fears the ties of responsibility or compassion to which emotion can lead. Therefore, we ought also to question the elevation of fiction as the more serious form of creative work (because it communicates higher truth) when it works by removing history, particulars, and politics and by denying the "Other" (journalism) as an important "constituent" of its own identity (see Stallybrass and White 5).

We may well ask, moreover, why a style that hides its method and perspective, its attitudes and judgments, in the assertion of the natural and "unartful" is deemed to be transcendent and permanent, and why understatement might convey truth better than direct or "over" statement. In other words, how does the simple (or what Hemingway calls the "purely stated") become the true? Is it because we have been trained under the New Critical paradigm – as Hershel Parker suggests, taught "to value showing over telling, subtlety over heavy-handedness" (21)? One of the things we have learned is that although understatement and irony signal objectivity, in themselves they are no more objective than any other rhetorical techniques, and they may be less honest. In general, when Hemingway uses this strategy to assert the transcendent humanity of Old Spain and her citizens (e.g., the Old Man becomes a synecdoche of essentialist Spain), it is a political act, but one that does not acknowledge its position, its bias.

In one sense the distinction between journalism and fiction does not matter, for the response of those who read "The Old Man at the Bridge" in *Ken* was probably not very different from that of readers who encounter it among the collected fiction. Its journalistic genre is the human interest story, which presents news in its personal rather than official or institutional aspect (see Hughes 212–13). To locate and play up the archetypal elements of such a story is, as Helen Hughes says, "to leave off writing news and to begin writing literature" (176), since such stories encourage the assumption that everyone has essentially the same nature (178), which is also implied by New Critical notions of fiction. By sticking to observable but "transportable" facts, evoking a permanent present, and remaining nonspecific about other sides, other views, both kinds of stories supposedly transcend the more discursive forms of journalism, and of history or political essays. Thus the story's reprinting as literature only heightens the ideological assumptions of this journalistic genre, which works by favoring particular observations as truths and overlooking or suppressing other possible ones.

The old man's assertion, "I am without politics," which he links to his advanced age (seventy-six) and his having reached the end of his rope after walking 12 kilometers in one day, is an example of the way an objective text can assert a debatable proposition as obvious by common consensus, or as self-evidently true. By asserting the pathos of this man's situation, the text implies that to have politics means to espouse a cause or engage in partisan activities, whereas we might prefer to define "political" to encompass a range of activities or beliefs, including the expression of support for one form of government over another or even the belief in a particular way of life. To see the bias implied by making this claim on behalf of the elderly refugee the ironic center of the story, one has only to ask whether those who actively engage in political activity in support of their beliefs deserve a bad fate any more than this man, who has not expressed a preference for either a Republican or a Fascist Spain. In what sense are there victims who are not innocent? Clearly, however, the viewpoint of this story is that a figure without politics is worthy for his own sake, much as a work of art is; of either we can say, it just *is*.

That he is a victim of war seems to be all that can be said about the old man at the bridge, for the form of the narrative prevents the reader from entering into the man's history, returning us instead to the universal "human condition" in which "man" is born, works (here, tends animals), and dies. As Roland Barthes says about a similar display of an essential human "nature," *The Family of Man* exhibition and book of photographs from the mid-1950s, "this is the reign of gnomic truths, the meeting of all the ages of humanity at the most neutral point of their nature, the point where the obviousness of the truism has no longer any value except in the realm of a purely 'poetic' language" (*Mythologies* 101). In this case the figure most celebrated by the New Critics, irony, is the means by which the author, through his surrogate, the wise narrator, stirs our emotions. Benson claims that irony makes the difference between "flat and journalistic reports" and "significant literature" (*Hemingway* 150). Our feeling of helplessness as we watch this old man, "without politics," unable to move out from under the Fascist planes offers us the "easy" emotion of fatalism as we perceive that the unstated outcome will be not only the animals' death but the old man's. Perhaps it will even include his apotheosis, for there are hints of possible martyrdom in the narrator's last-minute yoking of the date, Easter Sunday, with the fact that "the Fascists were advancing toward the Ebro." Of course, the objective technique of declarative clauses joined by the coordinate "and" makes no such overt causal connection; that is the beauty of its neutrality. It is not responsible for the connections the reader makes. (The old man is a subtle shepherd figure, and when the narrator calls his pigeons "doves," he seems to associate him with a particularly "good" shepherd.)

Writers and New Critics elevated objective narrative by emphasizing the detachment of the observer or narrator, the fact of objects in the world as meaningful in themselves, and the essential identity of word and thing, rather than the gap between them. This was the gap that they believed the subjective narrator of genteel, sentimental, governmental, or journalistic prose attempted to fill in with such methods as explanation, a style filled with adjectives and adverbs, and a political (i.e., biased) viewpoint. Then the means of these New Critics – an emphasis on interpretation of the text itself, apart from "the distractions of biography, social message, even paraphrase" (Said 138), instead focusing on aspects of form, particularly irony, analogy, and unity – led unavoidably to the neglect of history, of how things came to be the way they are.

To counter the objective rhetorical strategy of Hemingway's piece, we can read it against the assumptions of its universality by showing the construction of the old man's archetypal qualities and how the distance between narrator (a "forward observer" of some kind) and his subject is created; we can even refuse the subject position offered to the reader in which we identify with the observer. We ought to ask what is lost from this story by being narrated with the techniques of omission. One such omission is the narrator's history, which is deliberately kept vague, despite our knowing his purpose near the bridge this day. For example, we do not know his occupation. Lid assumes he is a soldier "whose job it is to locate the advancing Fascists" (402). This is a reasonable interpretation of the narrator's explanation, in paragraph 2, that "it was my business to cross the bridge, explore the bridgehead beyond and find out to what point the enemy had advanced" (57). Perhaps Hemingway viewed this slippage of the narrator's role as "forward observer" from that of reporter to military scout as a desirable consequence of reprinting the piece as a short story. His role in the front ranks of the American divisions liberating Paris in 1944 was similarly ambiguous. Was he a correspondent or a military strategist? (Baker, *Life* 408–18, 428–9).

Reinserting the story into its magazine context at least gives the piece a specific audience and the narrator a specific profession: he is a journalist sending regular reports (every two weeks) about the Spanish Civil War from the Republican side for an anti-Fascist journal. Kobler points out that Hemingway's political bias was much clearer in this forum than in the thirty-four NANA dispatches, in which, although he covered battles only from the Loyalist side, his presentation was more balanced, partly because as an accredited correspondent he was subject to censorship (89–90). Critics still argue over the degree of bias evident in these dispatches, and we cannot know how the first readers of "The Old Man" in *Ken* may have interpreted them. If they had read Hemingway's other reports, they doubtless read into this story the context provided by his openly anti-Fascist articles.

I am not criticizing the representation of the old man's situation as tragic or pathetic, only pointing out how Hemingway's style and strategy work to win our assent to a particular world view, one that is represented as inevitable. The narrative works this way whether it is regarded as journalistic or fictional, but it does so because of the power of what I am calling Hemingway's "objectivity," his assertion of a particular attitude and attribution of value to certain observations, attitudes, and beliefs to which we might want to give a different value. Then this power was reinforced by the New Criticism, which shared the assumptions and values of objective or universal prose and communicated them by its interpretive strategies and by its elevation of prose of a particular kind to literary status.

Although it is not important to me whether "Old Man at the Bridge" is considered a human interest story for a magazine or a short story – our formalist privileging of objectivity in fiction has the same effect as universalizing the "humanist" human interest story, in that essentialism underlies both – it was obviously of deep importance to Hemingway. Because I am interested in the effect of his getting his way with most critics and readers for the rest of the century, I will pursue the process by which this distinction becomes dominant. Watson quotes a letter Hemingway wrote, but apparently did not send, to Edmund Wilson, who had dared in a 1938 review to criticize his NANA dispatches while admiring the recent stories (including "Old Man at the Bridge") in *The First Forty-Nine*.[43] In the draft of the letter, Hemingway insists on the distinction between his dispatches and the piece he says he wrote as a story: "I am not ashamed of the dispatches. . . . All are true. But I do not go in for reprinting journalism" (quoted in Watson, "Old Man" 157). When Watson uses this outburst to argue for Hemingway's right to preserve "the sacred boundaries" between journalism and fiction, he supports the superiority of the "transcendent work of art" and in effect upholds a harmful distinction, because once a text has been set off as fiction or literature, its assumptions tend to go unexamined; readings tend to regard it as "without politics." Although Watson acknowledges that other writers who practice both nonfiction and fiction do not make such a distinction and are equally capable of speaking truth in both categories, he supports the right of Hemingway to absolve himself of responsibility for writing partial truths *in the guise of avoiding the charge of being partial*. I do not want to let him off the hook so quickly, for I think Hemingway retreats into art in order to deny the implications of his aesthetic politics.

   This is not to say that Hemingway was without politics in his coverage of Spain's civil war, for he viewed the war, and wrote, consistently from the Loyalist side, and his strongly anti-Fascist position was the basis for his contract with *Ken,* an openly partisan new publication that had as its mission winning support for the Republican cause in the United States. This partisanship was assumed by Gingrich, who responded enthusiastically to the "Old Man at the Bridge" dispatch by calling it one of those successful "short punches" that would help the Loyalist cause more than "volumes" of "ordinary reporting" (Watson, "Old Man" 157). Hemingway knew that most of *Ken's* readers would share his politics; they did not need to be spelled out. But when it was reprinted as fiction, the story lost its politics, except the universalizing politics of humanism. Hemingway ran from the intricacies of the political situation in Spain. It was part of his strategy of affecting the reader, but indicative of his particular type of involvement and his largely unintellectual position. In this story he was posturing a position that was almost unsupportable unless he refined it, which he chose not to do.

   Scholes says that "Hemingway found in bullfighting an absolute divorce between the political and the ethical," and it is appropriate that it was his support for the side that he believed would preserve the Old Spain of such barbaric spectacles which led him to write "Old Man at the Bridge." (Scholes calls the bullfight "the last true survivor of ancient

Roman bread and circuses" [*Textual* 72].) The essentialism that is evident in this story allowed him to support the Loyalist side unequivocally, without troubling himself to sort out for his audience the duplicity, betrayals, and compromise necessary to maintain a coalition that stretched from anarchism to leftist liberalism, and thus to tell less than he knew. Unlike George Orwell and John Dos Passos, other writers sympathetic to the Loyalists, who wrote about the complex political situation on that side (*Homage to Catalonia* and *Journeys between Wars*), Hemingway suppressed evidence of Loyalist infighting and Communist betrayals and executions that amounted at times to "civil war within a civil war" (Garrick 87), either in the belief that it would harm the Republican cause or in order not to use up the material in an inferior form.

Philip Knightley claims that "for all his compassion for the Spaniards, for all his commitment to the Republican cause," Hemingway "used the war to gain a new lease on his life as a writer." He follows Baker in charging that Hemingway saved his best material for fiction, revealing his awareness of the "carnival of treachery and rottenness on both sides" only in October 1938, before his last visit to the war, and to his editor, not his readers (Knightley 214; *Letters* 474). His overly optimistic and simplistic view persisted in his script for the documentary film *The Spanish Earth,* a work of deliberate anti-Fascist propaganda that was intended to win support for an unpopular cause in the United States and to raise dollars for ambulances (Garrick 87–8).

In short, Hemingway's support for the Loyalists was the result of a mixture of aesthetic, moral, and sentimental attitudes (see Garrick 78–81). Besides the idealization of Old Spain, the personal attachment he had for the country and its people which he projected onto the Republican cause, and the work (as war correspondent and fiction writer) he believed would come out of his presence in the country during the war, he exhibits a resentment of fascism and its outright experimenting with weapons designed to dishearten a civilian population, and so at least conveys something of an antiwar stance. Garrick notes, "[B]y early 1937 it was almost mandatory for a U.S. or British writer to support the Spanish Republic" (79). Hemingway may well have been affected by the spirit of leftist idealism, although this sympathy too was probably rooted in antifascism. At any rate, he did not publicly criticize the Communists, who made up a large part of the coalition waging the war (Knightley 213).

Nevertheless, by drawing this elderly man as the type of eternal Spanish peasant, failing to particularize the narrator beyond some vague "mentor figure," and deciding not to specify the reasons it ought to matter to the old man that the Fascists were advancing by dropping bombs from German planes on civilians, Hemingway aestheticizes the fatalism of this old man's resigned attitude, expressed in the remark, "I was only taking care of animals." That is, he gives us the emotion of determinism, rather than analyzing it or laying responsibility for it somewhere. Of course, he need not do either of these things in a specific text, but when we find over the course of his work of the twenties and thirties these techniques of aestheticizing determinism or making the reader feel the emotions of a political position rather than its substance, as Scholes suggests, then we ought to point out the pervasiveness of the pattern. Scholes says that when a "text is clearly based upon a pervasive aestheticizing of its world, our antagonistic position must challenge the position of literary art itself" (*Textual* 71). Can we see Hemingway attempting to aestheticize the "Old Man at the Bridge" by removing the story's specifically political context?

The narrator's statement in the last paragraph, the resigned "There was nothing to do about him," is an example of the fatalism expressed by the technique of detachment. Why not "I could do nothing for him"? Or a sentence that would concede the possibility of the narrator taking responsibility, or admit the political decision not to do anything, or at least claim the inability to do anything for him, such as, "I realized that I could do nothing to help him"? Here is where Hemingway's decision to depart from his more usual subjective style of journalism has its telling effect. By refusing to provide the circumstances of the encounter (on these trips out from Barcelona Hemingway was rarely alone) or relate it to other (political and strategic) facts and events, perhaps even to similar encounters, the journalist uses the strategies of omission that produce objective realism and is unable to account for his inability to do anything for the old man.

The failure to give sufficient information (as would be common in discursive genres like journalism) forces the reader to fill in from her own experience, and therefore begin to identify with a character. But which character? With the man, or with the narrator as he turns him into an objective correlative or archetype? The man's "otherness" and both the narrator's and our distance from him are preserved by reminding us that he speaks differently. Both characters' speech is stylized, rendered as literal translation of Spanish word order: "What politics have you?", the narrator asks, for example. The effect is one of archaic formality; if it is not exotic, it is at least "different." That the narrator's speech is also represented that way serves to remind us that he is using the old man's language. This too contributes to the effect of a temporary encounter, which allows the narrator to fill the role of what Earl Rovit calls the "tutor figure," the more knowledgeable, wiser, or more experienced observer, in contrast to the old man as innocent, naïve, or ignorant victim (48).

The narrator breaks the limited point of view of the present only once, when he assumes knowledge of the old man's future. The effect is ironic, because the narrator and now the reader know something that the old man does not. What he knows is that the weather is preventing the Fascist planes from flying; that and "the fact that cats know how to look after themselves was all the good luck that old man would ever have" (58). In Scholes's view, literary naturalism "almost always proffers an unearned pessimism, in that the writer is much better off than the characters whose entrapment he is lovingly presenting" (*Textual* 54). Because we identify with the narrator who is presenting the old man (that is, we fill the "subject" position implied by the first-person detached narrator), we too are better off than the old man. Through limiting the reader's position, objective realism thus forces us to identify with a value judgment we might reject if offered other choices.

In prose, we have learned to read understatement and irony as more realistic, as truer to our experience of "objective" reality. We have had to learn this, however, for these devices do not inevitably produce this effect. We have naturalized a faulty cause-and-effect analysis, because taking the opposite tack to a faulty set of circumstances does not necessarily produce the correction. For example, believing that the national press was complicit in the propaganda aims of one's government in wartime understandably makes one suspicious of its objectivity in peacetime. When propaganda and exhortations in support of the war take the form of abstractions, euphemism, and exaggeration of victories, it is also natural to turn against these techniques, and against inflated rhetoric in general. But the strategies one turns to in order to correct the abuse – using concrete language, omitting sentiment, cultivating a tone of detachment, and otherwise developing a prose of understatement and indirection – do not necessarily mean that one is being more honest or true. They may produce the illusion of this effect, but not necessarily honesty or truth. The desire to critique the discourse of propaganda and patriotism by proposing an alternative style does, however, seem a more plausible explanation of the minimalist style of Hemingway and others in the twenties than the influence of writing for a newspaper or magazine or of cablese.

3

News That Fits: The Construction of Journalistic Objectivity

> [Y]ou could only guess about reporters, they never wrote about themselves, they were just these bodiless words of witness composing for you the sights you would see and the opinions you would have without giving themselves away, like magicians whose tricks were words.
> – E. L. Doctorow, *Billy Bathgate*

Fiction in the early twentieth century (when U.S. journalist-novelists were beginning to distinguish their work in fiction and journalism as qualitatively different) was characterized by a style of purity and simplicity, achieving these effects through omission and indirection. Because of these attributes and their effect, this style has been called behaviorist and objective; although we associate these characteristics with objective journalism, they are not features of Hemingway's journalism, in the early twenties or later.

When Hemingway used journalistic material in works published as fiction, he omitted signs of its writing and much of its context and explanation. As in revising the refugee chapter from Asia Minor, he removed extraneous characters and narrowed the temporal focus to a single period. Instead of reporting the consequences of events or explaining them, he presented scenes dramatically, often concentrating on a few details that then had to bear the weight of meaning, much as an objective correlative does. In one example after another, we see him transforming news stories into fictional vignettes by simplifying, omitting details, and making formal patterns out of chaotic or random events. That is, he imposes order through formalist rituals of omission and irony, constructing an objectivity that is a way of looking at the world, as well as a style.

It is interesting to note, however, that when critics look for forerunners of the New Journalists and nonfiction novelists of the 1960s, Hemingway is among those named, because, by reworking material for novels that had appeared first in nonfiction, he seemed to blur the categories of fiction and journalism (Wolfe, Introduction 45; Josephs 315). This view is a romanticization from hindsight, however, for the distinctions were not firmly in place in the twenties. Hemingway was not blurring genres or calling attention to the problematic status of fiction and nonfiction; rather, he was contributing to their separation and, what's more, ensuring that journalism and fiction would split along hierarchical lines rather than simply diverge.

This hierarchical split has led ultimately to the conditions prevalent at the end of the twentieth century, under which fiction is the "default" literary category and journalism that aspires to lasting significance borrows its objective techniques (as though they are separable from narrative) from fiction and seeks to transcend its own ties to the quotidian, thereby crossing over into the domain of universality. So-called documentary novelists search out the archetypal characteristics of their subjects and render them in transparent prose, like Hemingway, suppressing signs of "interest," and therefore reflection and analysis, and making it unlikely that the reader will consider alternatives to the view that is presented as objectively true. Rather than acknowledging the construction of their representations, they suppress their narratives' self-accounting dimension, which would reveal their relationship to the social and cultural forces out of which they were written and enable the reader to become self-aware in turn (Barthes, "Science" 414).

Essentially, I shall argue, journalism shares the goal of objectivity which corresponds to the aesthetic ones elevated by the modernists. Because the goal of this dominant mode of journalism is to give a faithful picture of events and characters as they appear to the representative eye, rather than to acknowledge the existence of competing representations, journalists do not believe they are persuading readers and viewers to accept only one of many possible orientations toward the world; they regard themselves as neutral, rather than partisan (see Ortega y Gasset 13–16). By positing the world as objectively there and insisting on their ability to capture it accurately, practitioners of objective journalism contribute to the reification of modern consciousness.

One of the results of a half-century of this paradigm of journalism is that we have become accustomed to news as information – as top-down communication, rather than as the exchange of ideas in an ongoing conversation about whose opinions will prevail. As James Carey observes, certain "vital habits" are missing from the public's discourse in the late twentieth century, such as "the ability to follow an argument, grasp the point of view of another, expand the boundaries of understanding, debate the alternative purposes that might be pursued" (*Com-*

munication 82). The mass media's "objective" practice of news reporting has contributed to this decline in public discussion and argument and to the dominant view of news as information.

A human interest story or a *New Yorker* factual account such as John Hersey's *Hiroshima* employs many of the same conventions as Hemingway's *In Our Time:* self-effacing narrator, a tendency toward narration rather than discourse, and the reluctance to interpret, instead allowing facts to "speak for themselves." As a result, our response is reduced to a narrow emotional range, and we do not experience the subjectivity of another, for the text (with its repetition of universal truths and reified, ahistorical facts) confirms the naturalized view we already hold, the world we recognize as "actual." Because texts are organized into literary and "other" discourses, it is difficult to view writing in its full range or "multiplicity" (Williams, *Marxism* 146ff.); and journalism, though it comprises a variety of modes, is seen as deviating when it visibly escapes the boundaries of its two dominant tendencies, namely, to reproduce its impersonal observations in transparent prose, and to transcend its ties to the local in archetypal human interest stories or universalized documentary narrative. Both modes result in the loss of news media's specific political powers, not the least of which is the ability to reflect on their own status as "a form of social knowledge, a way of defining and making sense of the world" (Dahlgren 101). Once the shift was made in the twenties and thirties and readers became accustomed to the limited responses possible, this depoliticization of objective discourses – whether news or narrative – was apparently inevitable.

The examples that frame this chapter are once again two survivors' accounts: a documentary narrative that aspires to the authority and immediacy of fiction (*Hiroshima*), and a reflexive news feature, Hemingway's "Japanese Earthquake." In some senses Hemingway's decision to reprint a journalistic narrative like "Old Man at the Bridge," which celebrates the enduring human spirit through archetypal figures, and to leave a piece like "Japanese Earthquake" to languish in the morgue of the *Toronto Star* assures the production of a work like *Hiroshima* (and the *New Yorker* "fact piece" in general), for the latter's assumptions are the same as those of Hemingway's human interest feature turned short story.

Hiroshima, probably the best-known journalistic work of the post-World War II period, is an excellent example of the effect of taking aestheticized objective narration as a model, and it is not an isolated narrative. It is one of a number of similarly understated, impersonal "fact" pieces that have appeared in the *New Yorker* with relative frequency over the decades (forming a more distinctive style than *New*

Yorker fiction, which includes a wide range of story types). In these exhaustively observed factual pieces, the writers tell one everything about a person or project except "what, if anything, the parade of facts signifies" (Nocera 50). This "hands-off" narrative pose seems to be the result of deliberate editorial policy at the magazine. Although Kingsley Widmer suggests that the editing of Harold Ross and William Shawn was responsible for the "weirdly understated and depersonalized" effect of *Hiroshima,* similar effects persisted in the *New Yorker* – for example, in profiles and in long multiissue pieces by John McPhee – on into the 1980s. Presumably the absence of "personal evaluation," "intellectual reflection," "moral argument," and "poetic mediation" that Widmer found in documentary narrative in the 1940s remained the ideal of *New Yorker* nonfiction editors.[1] At any rate, by 1946 they formed a recognizable style, which Dwight Macdonald called "denatured naturalism," in which he found a "moral deficiency," a "clinical" detachment that can only objectify its subjects and provoke the reader's (as well as the writer's) condescension ("Hersey's"). (That was not the only nonfiction style permitted in the *New Yorker,* however, for Macdonald's distinctive essays appeared there regularly enough for the magazine to memorialize him on his death in 1982.)

Hersey's account of the experience of six survivors of the Hiroshima atomic attack illustrates the split between factual content and fictional form that is implicit in the separation of fiction from nonfictional genres. Critics of *Hiroshima* generally divide along the lines of form and content, depending on whether they read transparently or "aesthetically." In general, those who praise it do so for its content, believing that the news Hersey brings about the devastation wrought by the first atomic bomb dropped on a civilian population ought to be known by readers everywhere.[2] By and large these critics admire *Hiroshima's* "impartial recording," its "clear and objective reporting," and describe it as "a factual account in straightforward reportorial style" (Reviews). The mode of narration is thus not noticed or is viewed as appropriately unobtrusive.

The drawbacks of this style, Hersey's critics said, included his narrator's flat tone, his avoidance of drawing the moral or even putting the question, and the lack of shaping that would highlight one incident over another. Detractors also noted that Hersey's understatement – the deliberate avoidance of hyperbolic reporting – nevertheless results in exaggerated effects: excessive detachment, unnaturally impersonal narration, and the monotonous recording of details, none of which is "telling" or significant (see Macdonald, "Hersey's"; Widmer 143). Critics also regarded the form of narration as inappropriate to its subject. This is not a simple matter of finding the technique inadequate to the horrors the survivors describe, although that is one response: the *TLS* reviewer said that Hersey has "left the facts to speak for themselves, and they have not spoken loudly enough." Some readers feel that the ordinariness calls more attention to the misery suffered by the Japanese than would heightened language, which might not penetrate Americans' complacency (Poore 7). Readers who do not accept the separation of what is said from how it is expressed, however, will quickly realize the role the understated narration plays in *creating* those stoic Japanese who suffer without unnecessary fuss, like the minimalist who states only what is "necessary, absolutely minimally" (Karl 586). Unlike those who read transparently, they do not accept the authority of the text without seeing that the minimalist representation of suffering by these "representative" Japanese is a convention of the text, which produces the people's stoicism as a conventional response.

The representativeness of the six subjects that the journalist on assignment for both the *New Yorker* and *Life* located and interviewed a year after the atomic bomb was dropped is similarly called into question by readers who read other than transparently. As Hersey admits, he looked for survivors to fit a preconceived pattern, a meaningful cross-section of "types" of victims whose lives crossed paths and who "shared" the disaster ("Art" 227). This is a drawback of the documentary novel in general: its impersonal method of factual notation reduces characters to "random and representative topical figures" suitable to manipulation by the author (Widmer 142). Because the journalist does not regard them as actual human individuals but as "material" subject to his disinterested editorial choices, he is in effect superior to them. Even the "economy and polish and consistency of the documentary-novel" is dehumanizing, for what is in effect a form of communication by technology results in the "drastic editing down, and out, of much of human response" (Widmer 142). The characters become functions of the narrative, and because they are in effect locked into the text, depersonalized and dehistoricized, they do not represent a "problem" for historical interpretation or political action. They simply represent human beings' staying power, their capacity to endure and their desire to rebuild out of the ashes.[3]

In short, Hersey is hampered by the same positivist attitude that permeates the fiction of objectivity: a belief in "seeing is believing," or that truth is available to the observer's eye; the assurance that authorial impersonality prevents an unsuitable identification with one's subject; the conviction that a detached viewpoint offers readers and viewers an unbiased vantage point and is therefore potentially universal. When this world view is dominant, what passes for literature is narrative that emphasizes "the universality, the timelessness, the transcendence of culture." As Richard Ohmann says, literature thus defined "can hardly be expected to supply critical insight into the exercise of power and the forces that move history, precisely through the agency of class, race, gender, and other socially constructed categories" ("Kinder" 219).[4] The main effect of positivist objectivity is a passive reader, because impersonal or consensually validated objectivity tends "to isolate what happens from the realm in which it could affect the experience of the reader" (Benjamin, quoted in Trachtenberg "Experiments" 148). It is thus an "obstruction" in our efforts to develop self-conscious historical subjectivity (see Fekete 194). Hersey's detached, "neutral" style exploits its subjects much as objective fiction does, and because Hersey refuses to analyze or consider his relation to his subjects, we end up with a depoliticized journalism that reproduces "the way things are." Despite Hersey's obvious desire to avoid sensationalizing his subject, *Hiroshima* fits John Berger's definition of sensationalism as "the reducing of the experience of the other into a pure framed spectacle from which the viewer, as a safe and separate spectator, obtains a thrill or a shock" ("Another" 63).[5] This is similar to the effect naturalists get by separating narrator from subjects, as we saw in Chapter 1.

Hiroshima is regarded as an enduring work of art not because the techniques are borrowed from fiction but because the effect they achieve is normative; it is the one that defines literature. The aesthetic becomes that by "firmly rejecting the contingent and historical, striving for the permanent, the mythic, the concrete universal of art" (Scholes, *Textual* 71). The features of the narrative identified as aesthetic, as well as those regarded as authentic, result in the separation of subject and object and the consequent objectification of historical subjects. Apparently, to be distinguished aesthetically a narrative need not be admired as beautiful or artful; its recuperative humanist values, which both separate its content from its form and set those subjects off from the observer and reader who can only contemplate them, qualify it as literature.

Ironically, it is a survivor story that Hemingway wrote near the end of his fulltime journalism career which shows how journalism might have developed a different practice of objectivity, one that does not separate journalists from their materials – in short, a reflexive one. This unusual news feature apparently began in the strategies that were developing into his particular style of objective fiction, such as impersonality, spare use of names and factual details, and narrative reticence, but in laying bare the process that led to the story Hemingway produces a narrative that is also a metanarrative. It is not surprising that Hemingway adapted strategies he was experimenting with in his fiction, for he seems to have taken his journalistic writing seriously, even back in Toronto in 1923 while awaiting the birth of his and Hadley's first child. From all biographical accounts, it was the grind of working six days a week and the limitations of the *Toronto Star*'s editors and readers – "a provincial paper run in a big-town way" – that wore him down in his last four months as a journalist, and the longing for his European haunts and the company of artistic comrades that led to his derogation of the reporter's life (Fenton 250–1; Griffin 55–61).

The seriousness with which he took the interview that led to "Japanese Earthquake" is evident in an anecdote told by a *Star* colleague, Mary Lowry. In 1923, she remembers, he told her not to speak about a story they had just covered together, at least not before writing about it. "You mustn't talk about it," he said, "you'll spoil it" (quoted in Fenton 253). This is strikingly similar to a remark Jake Barnes makes to Brett in *The Sun Also Rises* when she feels compelled to discuss her recent affair with the bullfighter Romero. It is part of the code characters understand to be true, and it has been applied to Hemingway's method altogether: "You'll lose it if you talk about it," Jake says (245).[6] What Hemingway did not lose in shoptalk on the way back from the interview became "Japanese Earthquake," which ran in the *Toronto Daily Star* on 15 September 1923. This piece invokes some conventions of objectivity as they worked in the early twenties to enable the journalist to offer a distanced view of quite personal and sensational material. In order to counteract the usual assumptions that reporters who interview survivors are inconsiderate or even coldblooded, Hemingway "alienates the apparatus"; that is, he shows the process of obtaining the interview, narrating the "story of the story" in third person, and allowing access to the journalist's consciousness at brief but crucial moments. As a result the reader is offered the opportunity to identify with (that is, exchange her subjectivity with) not only the survivors but the journalists who must carry out the assignment at the risk of becoming callous or cynical. Unlike much of Hemingway's experimental fiction of this period, the narrative style of "Japanese Earthquake" allows first the narrator and then the reader to close the gap between subject and object in a form of dialectical objectivity that departs from the norm for newspaper journalism after 1920.

Because "Japanese Earthquake" has not been reprinted as a short story, our reading of it has been less shaped by the critical lenses through which we view literary works. It has had no claim on our attention, because of its unavailability before 1967 (when it was reprinted in *By-Line: Ernest Hemingway*) and the nearly complete absence of discussion of it in the critical or biographical literature.[7] Nevertheless we cannot read it without preconceptions; as late-twentieth-century readers and viewers of news, we have suffered hundreds of these stories vicariously, for survivor accounts and other disaster stories make up a significant portion of daily news coverage.[8] It is an account of two reporters – a woman and a man, apparently Mary Lowry and Hemingway – assigned to talk to two Japanese women in Toronto, a mother and her daughter, who were in Yokohama during the recent earthquake and who were able to escape on an ocean liner then in the harbor. The liner (the Canadian Pacific's *Empress of Australia,* unnamed in the narrative) had been about to set sail, but it was soon turned into a rescue ship. The women are reluctant to be interviewed, but the reporters have "lovely pictures" (of what we are never told) that arouse the curiosity of the mother. She agrees to talk on the condition that their names will not be used. The body of the narrative comprises the older woman's monologue, punctured by a few questions; she is responding to the male reporter's request to "tell us as you remember it just what happened" (84).

The account has many of the characteristics of the fiction Hemingway was writing at the time: understatement, indirection, dependence on dialogue, characters' reluctance to speak, and omission of specifics. For example, "There are no names in this story" is the opening line of the third-person narration, and the characters are "a reporter, a girl reporter, a quite beautiful daughter in a Japanese kimono, and a mother." The mother gives the sequence of events, "what really happened," when the powerful earthquake struck, leveling buildings, buckling the concrete dock the woman and her husband were standing on (they were seeing their son and daughter off on the *Empress*), and rupturing gas mains, then starting fires that killed many and hampered rescue work. She narrates scenes of chaos and of rescuers' inability to save individuals trapped in the rubble "in a dull, tired voice" (87) without adding extrinsic or unearned emotion, which we usually regard as sentiment or excess. She presents events dramatically, as scenes, rather than describing them. The dialogue even sounds like Hemingway's style of rendering it in fiction during this period. It is built out of short declarative sentences and subtle repetition:

> "They got the boy out but his back was hurt. They worked hours getting him out. But they couldn't get the French butler out. . . ."
> "They had to leave him in there alive with the fire coming on?" asked the girl reporter.
> "Yes, they had to leave the French butler in there," said the mother. "He was married to the housemaid so they had to tell her they had gotten him out."

This neutral tone and the woman's technique of implying rather than describing sensational details are appropriate to the aftermath of a natural disaster as well. Once the woman has begun to relive the story by telling it, the reporter realizes she "didn't need any prompting or questions now. . . . Now the reporter saw why she didn't want to be interviewed and why no one had any right to interview her and stir it all up afresh" (87). Her storytelling affects the responses of the reporters who, if they were inured to survivors' stories because of familiarity with them, now forget their roles as cool journalists and are moved to near inarticulateness. Near the end of the interview, the woman casts around for further details to tell the reporters, who are no longer prodding her with questions or even responding.

> Her mind was going back to Yokohama harbor. "Some of the people that had stood up all night in the water were very tired," she offered.
> "Oh, the people that had stood up all night in the water," said the reporter softly.

Hemingway blurs subject and object distinctions; as the reporter he cannot break down the barrier between himself and survivors, but he can at least refuse to turn the information gathered, the quotations, the "color," into the standard report of such interviews. These are frequently both sensational and sentimental, because the survivors come to stand for all people who have witnessed a horrific event and come back to tell about it, and the reader is a "safe and separate spectator" experiencing a "thrill or a shock" from the distanced "spectacle." In the conventions of such a report, journalists reshape material into paragraphs of predigested emotion. They preserve the barriers between reader and survivors by mediating the encounter, that is, describing how the survivors looked and acted, highlighting the sensational details, giving the effect of something different and incredible (disasters are a departure from the norm, thus characteristically deviant), and in effect telling readers how to feel. Frequently they do not call attention to themselves as mediators.

To make this story stand out, Hemingway chooses to understate the presentation, allowing the woman to speak continuously instead of reorganizing her narrative into chronological order; and creating a journalist figure (or two) with whom the reader can exchange places, giving the direct perspective of an eyewitness to the scene of the storytelling. "Japanese Earthquake" is thus less mediated than the conventional survivor story, and the reporter is apparently less in control of the interview situation, but he may be willing to give the illusion of handing over the pace of the narrative to the relentless recounting of the mother because he is in full control of the writing. We know the end is coming not only because the ship is pulling out to sea but because the dialogue recommences as both reporters ask questions which require shorter answers, ones which no longer come in the order in which things happened.

The last two sentences are an exchange between the reporters over who will write the story that the reader has just read:

> "Who's going to write the story. You or me?" asked the girl reporter.
>
> "I don't know," said the reporter.

Hemingway plays with the frame by making his piece the story of getting a story: the characters of the reporters are established and dominate the first section, but the interview itself is dominated by the oral report of the woman who tells her story without any prompting after she gets underway. Then, the reader may wonder, what is the subject? The journalistic traditions that require them to visit and interview survivors? Or the account they get from the subject?

Thus, without stating them, Hemingway demonstrates the construction of conventions of objectivity as they apply to interviews and manages a defense of the image of reporters as cold-blooded. Implied by his use of these conventions is the notion that journalists who interview people at such a time are not carrion birds but, as Dreiser says (160–1), entitled to secure their stories as a kind of service to readers. The conventions to a certain extent give the illusion that the publication is respectful, not inappropriately invading their subjects' privacy; and the audience, by identifying with the survivors, can transcend the predicament of the absent victims, those the rescuers were unable to get out, the ones "they had to go away and leave . . . in there" (87). Although Hemingway believed that journalism sensationalized experience (Donaldson 102), "Japanese Earthquake" is not sensationalist under this definition, because Hemingway does not reduce these survivors' experience to a spectacle separate from his observer persona, so that the reader, who identifies with the journalist as well as the survivors, does not remain "safe and separate." And because the gap is closed between subject and object in this nonobjectifying or unreified practice, he avoids the universalizing ideology of the individual who asserts the truth of the world from a representative viewpoint.

This is a reflexive practice of news narrative, but it is not the practice that came to dominate the rest of the twentieth century. To see how the positivist form became hegemonic, we will look at other manifestations of objectivity in nineteenth-century journalism. Then, after tracing its development through various forms, including twentieth-century professionalized objectivity, we will explore the implications of this hegemonic version, particularly the quite rigid separation from fiction it seems to imply (and which Hersey insisted as late as 1982, in "The Legend on the License," ought to be maintained). Tracing the evolution of the dominant forms of both fiction and journalism will enable us to see why both entail a split between subject and object, observer and observed, and thus why both forms (and the distinction between them) contribute to reified modern consciousness.

Defined most simply, "objectivity" is the arbitrary imposition of a set of conventions by which we agree to accept narrative about recent events as factual. In Michael Schudson's words, it is a "belief": "a faith in 'facts,' a distrust of 'values,' and a commitment to their segregation" (*Discovering* 6). At least three working conceptions of objectivity are still invoked today, resting on three different kinds of "authority": objectivity (1) as the actions of a third party on behalf of the public, resting on the enlightened disinterestedness of the press in relation to those in power; (2) as the capability of reproducing an anterior reality in neutral form, resting on science; and (3) as the considered opinion of a trained professional elite, resting on "strategic rituals" or tradition. In order to provide a somewhat larger picture than that offered by the history of journalism in the United States, I also use examples from British newspapers.

The notion of journalism's objectivity is by now as ingrained in our consciousness as is the novel's fictionality. When we read Lennard Davis's evidence that the "news" in the sixteenth and seventeenth centuries was interchangeable with fictional ballads about repentant criminals, for example, we can hardly believe that there was no hard-and-fast distinction between these categories. According to Davis, narrative was divided into other categories besides "fact" and "fiction"; for, according to the evidence of one statute, there was no category of "uniquely fictional narrative." Apparently the general category of "historical and political works" might have included "fiction, tales, and novels as well as news and histories" (128). Even in the eighteenth century the definition of news was so arbitrary that "lawmakers defined news not in terms of its content but in terms of its mode of publication," and publishers could circumvent the tax imposed on news by changing the format and producing "nontaxable literary pages," which combined all kinds of narratives (133).

The earliest characteristics of journalism, which began appearing regularly in England in the 1620s, were its recentness and regularity, not its truthfulness. The earliest established authority for the factuality of news was the government, which licensed and censored newspapers, ostensibly to protect the people's interest in knowing the truth, but also in an attempt to control opinion, for after the hereditary succession broke down in the Glorious Revolution of 1689, politics was the paramount concern, not facts. As Anthony Smith says in his excellent, concise overview of journalism's march toward objectivity (and away from it), "there were no facts more important, nor more urgent, than the fate of factions" (158). Nevertheless, what appears to be, at least in part, self-interest on the part of the government comes to be stated as one of the first principles of objectivity in journalism, for the government's justification for using its authority to license and censor the press was to protect the people from being deceived (Siebert, Peterson, and Schramm 18ff.).[9] Thus the notion of objectivity began to be institutionalized and facts commenced to be elevated above other kinds of "truth." This principle was the source of one of the accepted beliefs about an "objective" journalism: it must be disinterested or neutral, so that the people can trust its truth value (A. Smith, "Long" 158).[10] With the advent of cheap daily papers in the 1830s in America (and decades later in England, partly owing to the continuation of newspaper duties of various kinds until after 1853),[11] this principle was extended to the public's right of protection from even the government. Journalism now served as a "third party" acting on behalf of the people, so that they would be protected from all potential abusers of truth.

The innovation of the penny papers marks the beginning of news as a business and the development of the audience for news into more than an upper-class one limited to mercantile, trade, and party interests. Because they were sold on the street instead of to a smaller number of regular subscribers, these papers were able to regard themselves as independent of both the political parties and the mercantile class that supported the earlier newspapers and as responsible only to their readers (Mott 243). According to one historian of journalism;

> In the eyes of many readers the cheap papers turned to defend the
> rights of man, through crime news especially, at a time when those
> rights seemed to be threatened by changing social relations, and when
> other institutions only turned their backs on cardinal republican val-
> ues. In particular, the belief of many republican tradesmen that knowl-
> edge, like property, should not be monopolized for exclusive use by
> private interests was expressed in the penny papers as a positive com-
> mitment to cheap, value-free information – to objective fact. (Schiller
> 10)

The absence of financial support from political parties or mercantile subscribers meant, however, that the papers had to sell a large number of copies and thereby interest many advertisers in reaching new markets. Implicit in these motivations are three reasons for the changing makeup of the paper and its growing concern with crime, human interest, and sensational news in general: such stories sold papers, at the new low prices and on the streets by hawking newsboys, who worked on commission; information about a story was easy to get, for the police blotter and court records offered easy, inexpensive access (requiring only one reporter to pick up the information); and the ideology of crime stories accommodates easily to the penny papers' avowed purpose of defending society's interests against any encroachment. It was thus an easy step toward attacking crime in any area, including official corruption, and some of these papers (most notably the *National Police Gazette*) began to expose the bribery of police, the miscarriage of justice, and the unequal application of laws.[12] This concept of objectivity persists in our notion of a so-called "watchdog" press, which we celebrate in the form of investigative reporting, which itself goes in and out of fashion depending on the people's (and the media's) approval of established institutions.

This notion of objectivity as defending "the people" against abuses of power in turn rested on a growing optimism about the efficacy of science in the nineteenth century. It also resided in the mechanism of the mass market. Papers need to attract a large readership to draw advertising, and they do so by defining a class of readers and apparently supporting its interests. Not only are science's modes of observation and the logic of its procedures and conclusions emulated, but its attitude toward language is also borrowed by the developing profession of journalism. The tendency is to subordinate language to the content or matter of science, which is regarded as separable from the "instrument" that conveys its findings (suppressing the fact that it is language that does the work). As Roland Barthes says, "On the one hand and *first* there is the content of the scientific message, which is everything; on the other hand and *next,* the verbal form responsible for expressing that content, which is nothing" ("Science" 411). Like the realism developing in American novels at about the same time, scientific or scientized objectivity is characterized by impersonal narration, emphasis on the visual, and the positivistic assertion of the world as it appears to be. The primary technological developments of the nineteenth century that made it seem possible to extend the scientific method to reporting, and thus for journalism to come under the influence of positivism and its reliance on an empirical methodology, were the telegraph, a reliable method of shorthand transcription, and the new art of photography.

The telegraph is said to have made possible the modern daily newspaper, and it seemed to promise transmission of a complete record of news about the world. The usual argument about the impact of this invention and the "wiring" of industrializing nations after 1832 is that it enhanced objectivity because of its accuracy, speed, and standardization of the news (as indeed, the wire services were founded for the purpose of serving up the same "unbiased" news to many papers). The "inverted pyramid" structure of the news story probably developed from the unreliability of telegraph lines, which led journalists to summarize their most important facts at the head of the dispatch and fill in the details in ensuing paragraphs. As Mitchell Stephens points out, this format in turn imposes its own hierarchical requirements on the material, at the expense of nuance, fullness of events, and, especially, the "temporal, historical, atmospheric or ideological connections" between the facts reported (255). According to Carey, the telegraph not only required language to be "flattened out and standardized" so that stories could be communicated uniformly to all parts of the country and to be sparse for economic transmission, but it led to the separation of the observer (the stringer or local reporter) from the writer back in the newsroom who fleshed out the bare facts (*Communication* 210–11). Another form of separation was the result of the accumulation of more and more facts. As news became distinguished from opinion, attribution was necessary, to distance the reporter from the opinions that news subjects did not always bother to separate from facts. According to Stephens, "Reporters might handle without contamination only the *independently verifiable* fact that someone held an opinion. Narrators were no longer omniscient; but the facts reporters gathered were treated as omnipotent" (258).

The impact of shorthand can best be seen in Britain, where its development was bound up with efforts to obtain press access to Parliament and its doings (A. Smith, "Long" 160–3). Shorthand notation was instrumental in changing the way the public viewed the reporters who covered speeches and public meetings and thus gave the issues involved in Britain's nineteenth-century reform movements a full airing. As Smith points out, it mystified the correspondent, setting him off from reporters (it was usually a he), providing him with an *occupation,* and giving him "the aura of neutrality as he stood between event and reader." Furthermore, this specialization gave him "the chance to feel that he represented the interests of the newspaper's clients; it connected the task of reporting to the perspective of experimental science; and it gave the writer a tool which enabled him to aspire to the status of the engineer and the philosopher" (162).

Ironically, what arose out of political passion ended up producing detachment in readers. Once shorthand transcription of debates and speeches became familiar and frequent, and news stories were rendered in impersonal, "scientific" prose, news discourse naturalized the occurrences which it reported, and readers began to forget the process which brought the news to them. This was the incipient stage of news as product, not process; what we perceive is objectified rather than remaining a perception, and this objectification makes journalism a paradigmatic instance of the separation of viewing subject from objective world. Because we take the place of the observer as we read, we assume the same detached stance not only toward the external world but toward what our own minds construct, and we take these objectified productions to be part of the external world (Porter 25). In this way we all become passive observers of society, which we experience as natural, as "already given," and thus can only contemplate (Lukacs 100).

When photography emerged in the nineteenth century, it again was devised to provide an objective lens on the world, but this illusion quickly proved a failure. Its apparent lifelikeness and uncanny accuracy are its undoing; it undermines the possibility of being objective by undermining our notion of reality itself. Such is the power of the photographic image, coupled with the widespread faith in science, that extreme claims were made for it – for example, it supposedly captured reality itself – and these claims persist in our day. Not only does the camera seem to make possible the immediate capturing of an external reality but it apparently overcomes limitations inherent in the artist's means: photographs were believed to be more accurate than drawings or paintings; they seemed free of error and thus distortion or "human fallibility" (Schiller 191); and they were both more detailed and quicker in execution. More importantly, photographic representations seemed to be the objects themselves, rather than copies of them, for they are an extreme instance of iconic signs. Because such signs are motivated – that is, they resemble their referents – we forget that we have learned to decode them, "just as we learn, at a very early age, to read their referents, figure/ground relationships in the physical world" (Nichols 45). In other words, we have naturalized this form of representation.[13]

The press photograph is a particularly "objective" image, as Barthes explains in "The Photographic Message," because it transmits "the scene itself, the literal reality"; that is, it is so powerfully denotative or analogous that we do not notice that it is connotative as well. The procedures of connotation occur at the level of production of the press photograph ("choice, technical treatment, framing, lay-out") and are increased by the text accompanying it (18–21; 25ff.).

Ironically, at the moment when journalism seemed on the verge of being able to capture and re-present reality through virtually instantaneous transmission of news in time for a daily paper (the telegraph), full transcription of the words of public events (shorthand), and an apparently perfect correspondence between reality and the representation of it (photography), its authority was undermined by characteristics inherent in each of these innovations. The camera by necessity selects, and its way of organizing perception is various and dependent on choice. It thus undermined the notion of timeless images by altering one of our "ways of seeing." As John Berger says, thanks to the camera, "it was no longer possible to imagine everything converging on the human eye as on the vanishing point of infinity" (*Ways* 18). As perception changed, so did "reality," because what we call reality is in some sense only the set of conventions by which we perceive an undifferentiated universe.

By making possible daily editions, the telegraph changed the time structures by which citizens were accustomed to apprehend "reality," because it made the "day's" news a concept (Schiller 167). It also sharply curtailed the number of points of view readers were given of a single event. Sending more than one reporter to cover an event would merely duplicate the report, for reporters are interchangeable observers under the objective model. The tendency since the end of the last century has been to "consolidate the new audience" won by aggressive marketing by turning it into a mass. This has meant giving it more instances of fewer genres, and making the news more uniform with the sharing of news through syndication, wire services, and the gathering up of local newspapers into large chains in a process Anthony Smith identifies as "rationalization through uniformity" (*Newspaper* 164–5).

The unexpected result which dampened journalism's hopes of complete fidelity to an objective reality was the overwhelming amount of "news" which first shorthand transcription and then the telegraph made available; for the first time "all the news that fits" becomes an inevitable factor in journalism. Objectivity was compromised by the need to determine what to report, how to cover it, and how much relative importance to give it, and, inevitably, by the reliance on techniques we associate with fiction (for example, condensation, representativeness) to package it for a public viewed as eager to devour it and return for more each day. Smith says that in the period following the revolutionizing of journalism by the telegraph, "The techniques of journalism became analogous to those of fiction, and lay partly in the ability to discern those elements which could be made into a transmittable artefact."[14] This function of "gatekeeping" is always ideological, because the "decision to report" can never be neutral, while the reasons for the selection are invariably suppressed ("Long" 168).[15]

Other tools which the press developed to cope with and package the information that now routinely came its way also undermined its pretense of transcribing an anterior reality: the development of specific ideological practices to manage the news, including compartmentalizing news into beats by territory (city, national desks) or by topic (women's or sports pages); imposing a rhythm of deadlines and writing to fit available space (resulting in summaries and the "inverted pyramid" news story that can be cut from the end); and relying on legitimated institutions and spokespersons and ignoring their radical, alternative, or "unreliable" counterparts.[16] The new public relations industry developed out of the opportunity some press figures (particularly Ivy Lee) saw to promote the interests of figures and businesses. It was founded on the premise that "information could itself be 'managed' " and "facts could create an impression." Under the guise of respectability, public relations became one of the media forces that "constructed the effective 'realities' of society" (A. Smith, *Newspaper* 170). In the late twentieth century, it is often indistinguishable from news.

In response to the unavoidable recognition that journalism cannot record reality but must structure it in some way, there arose the third notion of objectivity: its practice by professionals ought to preserve some domain of objective standards which would ensure credibility for the "fourth estate." This last-gasp definition, which arose in the twenties and thirties of this century (Schudson, *Discovering* 7) and is invoked quite commonly today, rests on the notion of facts as "consensually validated statements" about the world, not as "aspects" of it. In this view, journalists can no longer be expected to capture a complex reality completely, because of the limitations inherent in the positivist view; and, because newspapers are a business, they are recognized as being incapable of presenting it impartially, that is, without reflecting the interests of their advertisers.[17] Furthermore, journalists' collective disillusionment caused by the abuses of objectivity on behalf of propaganda in World War I and by the public relations machines which have dominated the press scene since then seems to have rendered them unable to believe with their former fervor in the tenets of the positivists' objectivity. However, they can at least fall back on their experience and training as professionals to ensure a modicum of dispassion, according to Schudson, and they can insulate themselves from the ordinary reader by adopting the role of the journalist and separate their professional selves, using long-standing conventions and rituals of communication, from the personal values they hold in private life (*Discovering* 8–9).

Not surprisingly, considering the dialectical movement of a democratic press between fear of loss of control and belief in consensus, this third, twentieth-century position expressing faith in objectivity contains elements of the other two: "professionalism" is merely an imitation of science's "fair and objective" methods, as in the creation of a "web of facticity" based on "supposed facts that, when taken together, present themselves as both individually and collectively self-validating" (Tuchman, "Objectivity" 86). And when editors assume that the particular "slant" or policy of their organization represents the objective position, which they tend to do in their defense of a consensually validated objectivity, they are invoking the "broader claim of journalism" as an impartial third party to justify presenting the news their way in order to protect a gullible public from a potentially less disinterested party (Boylan 61).[18]

Gaye Tuchman, a sociologist who observed the practices of what she calls "newsworkers" (reporters, editors, and other producers of news) in a variety of news organizations, found many examples of this fall-back position on objectivity, which she calls a "strategic ritual," a kind of beleaguered defense against journalism's detractors, and against inter-organizational criticism, such as that of reporters by editors. These ritualized procedures include presenting multiple explanations on two sides of an issue and supplementary evidence in support of "facts," using phrases in quotation marks to separate questionable facts from the reporter who presents them, leading with the most obvious and least arguable "facts," and segregating "fact" from "opinion" by using categories such as "news analysis" or confining feature stories to designated pages or departments ("Objectivity" 676). All these turn out to be self-justifying procedures invoked as efforts to attain objectivity, but they cannot ensure it, because they rest on such tendencies toward bias as encouraging selective attention, letting "facts speak for themselves," allowing opinion to be introduced (once the excusing quotation marks are in place), depending upon editorial policy to determine standards, and misleading the reader by suggesting that different kinds of stories and analysis can be segregated, with one as more "definitive" than another.

This sophisticated version of objectivity exists precariously. Media sociologists and critics of journalism have pointed out that the attempt to practice objective journalism reinforces the status quo: the way things are in government, economics, social practice in general. This is not only because objectivity reinforces the relations we think of as naturally existing between words and things, between news and the world (by viewing the world as outside and prior to language about it), but because by hiding the processes by which news works, objectivity asserts facts as taken for granted and becomes what Dorothy Smith calls "a *means not to know*" (quoted in Tuchman, *Making News* 179). Edward Herman and Noam Chomsky take these "strategic rituals" and show how they work in the service of dominant elites: "the observable pattern of indignant campaigns and suppressions, of shading and emphasis, and of selection of context, premises, and general agenda, is highly functional for established power and responsive to the needs of the government and major power groups" (xvi).

As Herman and Chomsky explain, despite Americans' belief in the possibility of a free, impartial press, the way the mass media work is closer to propaganda than to objectivity, for in the attempt to remove bias, the media favor elite groups – those that dominate governmental processes and private institutions and have an interest in maintaining their established power – over those who would try to "assert meaningful control over the process," such as the public (303). By treating government as inherently newsworthy (because it affects all Americans) and taking it at face value, covering it as it presents itself, journalism professionals participate in their own co-optation. As Herman and Chomsky say, when "the government's assertions are transmitted without context or evaluation, and without regard to the government's possible manipulative intent, the media have set themselves up to be 'managed.' Their objectivity is 'nominal,' not substantive" (334 n. 2).

Although Herman and Chomsky take their examples of media manipulation by government and private institutions from news events of recent decades (Latin American elections, genocide in East Timor, the attempted assassination of the pope), they take their title, *Manufacturing Consent,* from Walter Lippmann's description of propaganda in *Public Opinion* (1922). Like Herman and Chomsky after him, by the term he means not "sinister" plots, but the everyday work of government and politicians in deciding what facts they will let the people know, in order to "manufacture the consent" of the governed to the policies they have chosen, based on their access to superior information (247–8). To Lippmann, the manipulation is inseparable from the practice of democracy in a mass society, because a democratically elected government has the tools of psychological and market research, the ability to spread its message by "modern means of communication" (by which he means the "top-down" monolithic mass media), and little faith in the ability of the individual to master the broad knowledge necessary to make informed decisions.[19]

James Carey, too, has located in Lippmann's writing the source of our dominant practice of news, based on the spectator theory of knowledge; this is similar to the workings of objectivity in fiction, for Lippmann's ideal is based on visual observation (instead of conversation and listening) (*Communication* 77, 82). What's more, this way of theorizing the management of information by favoring a "specialized class" of elites who would speak for the non-expert public comes at exactly the time when Hemingway was experimenting with the rational "picture-making" techniques of Imagism in prose and developing the techniques that made his understated, objective style seem to many people to be the very embodiment of meaning. Because of the proliferation of knowledge and indeed the sheer numbers of citizens eligible to participate in democracy and needing to be informed, there is little hope that the public in general will be able to engage in any sort of considered argument (Lippmann 249). Hence "information," not argument or persuasion, becomes the goal; and scientifically verified data, rather than the passionate engagement of large numbers of ordinary citizens, are the means of eliciting consent, because the ability of the public to debate the public good has been measured against the methods of disinterested information production and found wanting. Again there is a close correlation between the professionalization of politics and that of journalism, just as there was in Crane's day, with science an influential model in both decades.[20]

As Herman and Chomsky point out, Lippmann was oblivious to the class and educational bias inherent in his proposals (322 n. 5). Other effects were probably unintended as well; he may not have been aware of the danger of framing his solution to the problem facing democracy in a mass society by emphasizing science's ability to represent or "picture" reality and professional journalism's skill in distilling it and passing it on. Nevertheless, by entrusting production of the correct information to groups of independent experts and bypassing the need to win approval or consent of the ordinary citizen, Lippmann's program results in the effective depoliticization of public discourse (Lippmann 248–9; Carey, *Communication* 76). Complex forms of argument, the process of production, and contentious politics all disappear from the main organs of public discourse – newspapers and magazines – under the influence of standards of professional objectivity based on a distinction between disinterested or universal truth, on the one hand, and mere public opinion on the other (Lasch 19).[21]

To counter Lippmann's version of the Cartesian world view, John Dewey argued (in a review of *Public Opinion* and in *The Public and Its Problems* [1927]) for a model of communication based on news discourse that would not objectify the world and separate it from a passive public receiving ever more accurate information about it. His model emphasizes hearing over seeing, for he holds "that language is not a system of representations but a form of activity, and speech captures this action better than the more static images of the printed page" (Carey 80). Dewey points to the limitations of any fixed representation (and he would not have exempted television news from this category, for its images merely illustrate the news text written to be read aloud), arguing that scientific information gathering and dissemination produces only a tool. In *The Public and Its Problems* he calls this "soliloquy," which to be effective must be taken up and processed in dialogue.

> Vision is a spectator: hearing is a participator. Publication is partial and the public which results is partially informed and formed until the meanings it purveys pass from mouth to mouth. There is no limit to the intellectual endowment which may proceed from the flow of social intelligence when that circulates by word of mouth from one to an-

other in the communications of the local community. That and that only gives reality to public opinion. (Quoted in Carey 79)

Carey emphasizes the shift from partisanship and opinion to information and the depoliticization of the national discourse as the press became more "responsible": under the information or "spectator" model of news the public is asked only to "ratify a political world already represented," one in which "all the critical choices have been made by the experts" (82). Christopher Lasch believes that this move from an open partisanship to neutrality was aided and abetted by the rise in advertising dollars and public relations peddling in the twenties. "A responsible press, as opposed to a partisan or opinionated one, attracted the kind of readers advertisers were eager to reach: well-heeled readers, most of whom probably thought of themselves as independent voters" and who did not want to read "an editor's idiosyncratic and no doubt biased view of things" (20). When a news medium takes on the appearance of objectivity, it can easily be manipulated by those with an interest, as the analyses of ideology demonstrate. Thus advertisements and press releases become indistinguishable from information, and political candidates hire media advisers not only to concoct commercials that blend into television discourse but to secure coverage that will appear as news stories. The doctrine of objectivity is powerless against such interested manipulation of its premises and standards. As Lasch says, "[A]dvertising, publicity, and other forms of commercial persuasion themselves came to be disguised as information and, eventually, to substitute for open debate" (20).[22]

Although scientific premises of journalistic objectivity contain contradictions that made it untenable just as it seemed to be about to achieve "transparency to the real" (Rorty, quoted in Carey, Communication 80), to see them the reader has to view history dialectically rather than as progressing toward accurate representations of what happened. When we do not question objectivity by showing how it trades on the assumptions of science and the primacy of visual observation, its power of illusion is similar to that of "the achievements of science and technology," which we invest "with the mantle of absolute truth, the products of experts, who become the final arbiters of the verisimilitude of scientific discoveries" (Aronowitz 47). As in science, when journalists and readers take the facts or the results for the process, they lose the history, the activity that lies behind the result, and which may have taken the form of contest or dispute. Similarly, Lippmann's leader decides "what facts, in what setting, in what guise he shall permit the public to know," although it means suppressing the history of his decisions, including alternative or oppositional positions available but not chosen.[23] Because these power relations still dominate late capitalism, it is no wonder that Lippmann's belief in a "science of society" remains influential, and no surprise that "public opinion" is simply "the statistical aggregation of the private opinions formed by the news media" (Carey 78). Journalistic objectivity, then, is just one form of the professionalization of intellectual activity; the consolidation of the study of social life into the disciplines of the "human" sciences is another.

As I suggested in characterizing the effect of the telegraph on reporting, separating the news as product from the process of uncovering and transmitting it results in reification, the objectification of conditional "truths." By being separated from the people who invented them and put them to use, the techniques of science or its instruments – photography, shorthand, telegraph – produce the illusion of honesty or truth, but not necessarily the substance of it. Therefore, as Lukacs says, journalism is an extreme example of the reification characteristic of modern life, for "it is precisely subjectivity itself, knowledge, temperament and powers of expression that are reduced to an abstract mechanism functioning autonomously and divorced both from the personality of their 'owner' and from the material and concrete nature of the subject matter in hand" (100).[24]

This analysis may make journalism seem a far different thing from fiction, which is regarded as delimited by aesthetic concerns. In the dominant view, news is regarded as one of the social sciences, and although the new "interpretive" sociology seriously undermines belief in the possibility of objectivity in journalism, this critique does not undermine readers' and journalists' belief that it contains essentially factual and truthful descriptions of "the way things are," as contrasted with literature's imaginative priorities. It is important to see this split between factual and creative genres as historically produced, therefore, as artificial rather than natural. Because objectivity is conventional, it does not define journalism; the dominant practice can consist of observing these conventions or ignoring them. Similarly, as I showed in Chapter 2, we view objectively narrated fiction as the height of literariness because of an aestheticizing process captained by Hemingway, Cather, and other modernists. Other characteristics might just have well have come to define the literary. This aesthetic had to produce an appropriate response in readers in order to persist, however. For example, it may be that Hemingway's objective style struck a responsive chord despite his early readers' inability to understand what they were reading and to fill in the gaps left by omission because of the way it reproduces the conditions of consumer society with its newly reified social relations.[25]

It is not coincidental that the procedures which construct "objective" journalism are similar to the ideological practice of advertising, and to

the ideological assumptions of the objectively narrated realist or minimalist novel, for all these forms developed simultaneously in the context
of consumer capitalism, that is, when advances in factory mechanization
and the Taylorization of the workplace in the first two decades of the
century made the creation of large numbers of consumers increasingly
desirable. News, advertising, and fictional realism "work" as ideology
because the reality they posit appears objectively real, and as viewing or
reading subjects we are effectively foreclosed from questioning their
invisible assumptions. Modern industrial society needs subjects who
function as consumers as well as producers (albeit of pieces of a total
product which means nothing to them) and who accept their diminished
place because it is not apparent to them (Althusser, *For Marx* 235).
As Catherine Belsey points out, the "conditions of existence" under
capitalism require "subjects who work by themselves, who freely exchange their labour-power for wages."

> It is in the epoch of capitalism that ideology emphasizes the value of
> individual freedom, freedom of conscience and, of course, consumer
> choice in all the multiplicity of its forms. . . . It is in the interest of this
> ideology above all to suppress the role of language in the construction
> of the subject, and its own role in the interpellation of the subject, and
> to present the individual as a free, unified, autonomous subjectivity.
> (Belsey 67)

The similarities between the novel of objective realism and the news
story are many. In the omnisciently narrated news story or novel, the
text has no visible creator, and its processes of production are hidden. In
the case of news, its processes are objectified and embedded in legitimated procedures which we take for granted. Objectively narrated novels work by powers of illusion which imply a ready-made world of
cause and effect and inevitably move toward closure. As readers of each
we are isolated from one another and from the producer of the text, the
novelist or the reporter. They may enter our homes, and in the case of a
news reporter or broadcaster this may occur daily, but we do not
interact directly with them; we "do not mutually negotiate definitions
of reality" (Tuchman, *Making* 214).

Both discourses privilege the visual and imply that the absence of bias
or interest is an advantage to the reader. Their primary values are
empiricism and professionalism (in the case of fiction, the latter takes
the form of aestheticism), and the result is lack of engagement, or
disinterest. I have shown that under this paradigm of artistic discourse
the reader is a passive one; the objectively narrated text isolates its
content from our experience by setting it off in a timeless realm, and we
are able to identify with only general human emotions, desires, and

fulfillments, which are posited as universal and absolute. By being discouraged from reading reflexively, we are isolated and left with only a personal, privatized consciousness – one which can be managed, its fears contained, its stimulated desires fulfilled in the moment (which must be repeated over and over), and its catharsis controlled through plots contrived so that we "experience only the spiritual agitation of the heroes" rather than "discovering the causal complexes of society" (Brecht 82). In the case of journalistic objectivity, its visual bias leads to the belief that reality can be captured in transparent language, or, as Lippmann would have it, "reconstructed . . . on a simpler model" before being presented to the public (16). Furthermore, news fragments history into one continuous, reiterated present ("today's stories"), thereby avoiding making connections, separating the reader from the past, and making it difficult to make sense of our experience. The reader's response to this fragmentation is indicated by the way we digest ten thousand words of information in ten minutes over coffee.

In both modes, ideology works by concealing the "mechanisms of [its] generation" (Eagleton, *Criticism* 64). As Judith Williamson says, ideology would be easier to recognize if we thought someone was " 'putting over' false ideas," but its effects are subtler.

> It is based on false *assumptions*. This can be clarified as follows: there is a big difference between saying something is true (which admits the potential of the opposite), and saying that the truth of something *need not be questioned* – which admits nothing, and claims nothing either. In ideology, assumptions are made about us which we do not question, because we see them as "already" true. (41)

We can readily see that news is ideological in this way. When it appears to reproduce a reality we think we know, without questioning it or revealing its own processes of gathering and producing it, the result is not problematic but seems to be objectively real, and therefore we think we cannot change it. As Dorothy Smith explains about ideology in general, "What ought to be explained is treated as fact or as assumption" (12). We are isolated as reading and viewing subjects by these cultural forms; we are presented "with materials for producing social structures" but with our "abilities to transform institutions and structures" forestalled (Tuchman, *Making* 196) because of our circumscribed, "subjective" (subjected) identities. We do not question the news but instead naturalize it; our "commonsense" perceptions blind us to ideological practice.

This latest practice of objectivity, rather than working to ensure the separation of value from fact, produces a set of practices for hiding how news stories are actually constructed. As a result, the attempt at objectivity, with the ostensible aim of eliminating bias and "interest," *becomes* ideological in the act of suppressing overt ideology, that is, suppressing its interest in things as they are or as they appear to be. Because facts are reified in a method of observing and reporting based on positivist science, they lose their process and their history, and so it seems possible to distinguish between fact and opinion or interpretation. This distinction, which Stuart Hall calls "one of the most profound myths in the liberal ideology" ("Determinations" 188), has become the foundational premise of objectivity, and it is almost impossible to dislodge, permeating as it does our whole ethos of a "responsible" or impartial journalism.[26]

Although it is widely conceded to be unattainable in pure form, most newsworkers deem objectivity to be worth pursuing. So long as it remains a goal, it is unlikely that a different practice will arise, for having objectivity as an ideal reaffirms the belief that the world is interpretable apart from factual discourse. Those who hold this ideal find it meaningful in itself. When John Hersey says that "there is no such thing as objective reportage," he does not contradict its inherent validity, for he means only that, because of the necessity to select, he cannot give the whole story; being human, he inevitably colors the facts he chooses with his views (*Algiers Motel* 34). In "The Legend on the License," Hersey contends that there is an important difference between leaving out "observed data" and adding "invented data," namely, that the reader expects the bias of omission, whereas when she begins to suspect additions, that is, inventions, the ground of meaning is kicked away. What he ignores is the bias inherent in omission, the ideology behind the choice of what to leave out, in journalism just as in Hemingway's strategies of omission and understatement; all decisions are political ones, and in denying them or suppressing the reasons for them they become ideological. This applies to decisions not only about what characters, events, and details to include, but about how to tell the story, indeed "the selection of this [narrated] incident to represent a whole complex chain of events and meanings" in the first place (Hall, "Determinations" 188). What Hersey ignores is that texts are nothing *but* bias, that is, perceptions from particular viewpoints. Even a historian, Lynn Hunt, has said that "there is no such thing as history in the sense of a referential ground of knowledge" (quoted in Fish 305); the world we believe to be "out there" is produced by texts and naturalized as reality or "what has happened" and "what is."

Readers experience the objectivity of realistic narratives the same way as they do that of literary journalism or documentary narratives or human interest stories or news reports; it is indistinguishable in the reading and has similar ideological effects. Why then does Hersey insist on the absolute distinction between fiction and journalism? Hersey says that the attraction of fictional form was its immediacy, the fact that the reader of fiction is conscious of the writer "*behind* the work," whereas "in journalism you are conscious of the person *in* the work." Here Hersey is referring to the journalism that is dominated by a voice who explains things to the reader, who is "always mediating between the material and the reader" ("Art" 228). In contrast, the form of fiction he has in mind is the modernist, minimalist sort that strives for pure narration and the elimination of discourse, or references to the act of storytelling.

By opposing the idiosyncratic voice of the essayist, common in the *New Yorker* of the 1920s and 1930s and in other "literary" magazines, to fiction that gives the illusion of "immediacy," Hersey sets up a contrast between journalism and fiction that is not apparent in their mainstream forms. To do this, he splits form and content, explicitly identifying his attempts at pristine factuality with the immediacy of fiction and ignoring the affinities between objective fiction and objective journalism. Hersey associates literary or fictional prose with a self-effacing narrator, and in general with narrative that hides its form; readers are not generally aware of the effect of these particular strategies on their apprehension. In sustained narratives like *Hiroshima,* "Aftermath" (the followup account published in 1985), and "Homecoming" (a 1982 report on his first visit since 1946 to his birthplace in China), Hersey adopts the techniques of fiction in order to capture its *prestige,* and the prestigious form in 1946 was (as it remains) objective narration. When this form of objective fiction is emulated by journalists, we do not hear the voice of the narrator, and our attention is not called to the fact of narrating, much as in objective journalism; the impersonal or anonymous conventions of both are highly naturalized. He is rejecting as a literary model the personal manner of the essayists who formerly commanded the line that moved toward literature via the creation of a deliberately personal style: writers like Edmund Wilson, Josephine Herbst, A. J. Liebling, E. B. White, James Thurber, and Dorothy Parker.

Thus *Hiroshima* illustrates the persisting belief in mimesis as unproblematic. Lyons and Nichols describe this concept as "based on a natural and commonsense activity, one that [does] not call into attention the act or responsibility of a person" (18). Elsewhere in his nonfiction writing, however, when Hersey thinks the truth is controversial and doubts his ability to find out the truth, as in *The Algiers Motel Incident* – the story of the murder of black youths by police in the Detroit riots of 1967 – he uses first person and exposes his involvement. This suggests that he did not regard the story of the American use of atomic weapons on a civilian target without warning (and less than a month after the first weapon was tested) as being as morally complex or ambiguous as this incident, which revealed the racism latent in U.S. society. Then too, he did not interview the six Hiroshima survivors until a year after the war ended, whereas he was much closer to participants and events as they unfolded in the Detroit case. Or perhaps between 1946 and 1967 he became less trusting of the immediacy provided by objective narration.

To the reader of "Aftermath," Hersey's essay tracing the life of all six Hiroshima victims since 1946 and published in the fortieth-anniversary edition of *Hiroshima* (once again, after its appearance in the *New Yorker*), such an "older-and-wiser" scenario seems unlikely. Like the earlier account, "Aftermath" gives the appearance of being unshaped and therefore neutral and is dominated by uninterpreted, matter-of-fact statements; Hersey forgoes interpreting these survivors' lives, even when some stocktaking by both the Japanese survivors and the U.S. airmen seems likely, because enough time had passed to put their experiences in perspective within the context of their own lives. (See the strange case of Mr. Tanimoto, discussed in Chapter 5.) The result is that Michael Yavenditti's judgment of the 1946 *Hiroshima* applies just as well to the expanded edition: "Hersey's work aroused many readers but incited few of them. It enabled American readers to reaffirm their humane sentiments and to examine their consciences, but 'Hiroshima' did not require Americans to examine the legitimacy of the bomb's use" (quoted in Sanders 20).

The reflexive reader, however, might read this objective, reified prose in terms of the "struggle to represent": that is, with an eye out to catch the writer's performance, such as his engagement with earlier writers of survivor accounts. We can also undertake an interpretation by imitating or rejecting other ways of reading (Lyons and Nichols 19, 18). In order for Hersey's account to arouse readers to imagine the scale of the destruction and then, as he says, to "extrapolate" from that to a bomb many times larger – and, what's more, to make this spectacle persist in our collective historical memory so that (as is his intention) we will work to make sure it never happens again – its political dimension must be dug out, examined, and put in context ("Art" 232). This includes such historical issues as the United States's first use of nuclear weapons, the military's predicted levels of Japanese resistance, and, after the war, changing attitudes toward the Japanese as enemy "others" because of a desire to rehabilitate their country as a market for Western industrial goods. In short, the representative survivors should not be reified as universalized fellow human sufferers but recognized as specific political and ideological subjects in a complex, dynamic relationship with the West.

The reflexive reader notes the form, questions the assertion of "what is," seeks to know what is left out and how the narrator found what he knows, and asks what other views are possible. How representative are these people of those in Hiroshima that day? of people everywhere? What interpretation is implied by the mode and form of telling, and how else might we interpret it? It is difficult to ask these questions, given the form of the narrative: the absence of references to how the stories were obtained and the omission of the narrator's own feelings and response while talking to his sources. It is, however, important for readers to see *Hiroshima* as produced, not as a faithful record of the characters and events themselves, to see the "facts" of the bomb and its effects as derived from its formulation in prose. That this prose appears transparent does not mean that it has no effect on how we view those facts, as difficult as it is to fix exactly what those effects are.

A critical reading might also see the Japanese as nonreflexive viewers of their government's propaganda. They are presented as "typical" characters who passively accept what has happened to them without blaming their government, even for the lack of aid and information in response to the disaster. For example, from the text we learn that not only did very few doctors and nurses survive uninjured but that there were no systematic efforts by the government or military to bring medical aid, food, or water, and that no organized rescue effort took place in the parts of Hiroshima our six witnesses traveled through in the days following the bombing. Rather than attributing this response to their natural or traditional stoicism, we can speculate that it is one result of the imperialistic government's having sought to produce unqualified support for its ambitious war policies. Seeing the characters as acted upon, and against, by their government, not just by the impersonal bomb (which they are depicted as having regarded as an act of fate, more like a natural disaster than a political act), makes them victims of another kind.[27] We can learn about their government's use of them in a policy of imperialism, and by implication, about our government's securing of our acquiescence in its way of making war.[28] The lesson of reading this text reflexively is that even historical characters are constructed as members of a hierarchical society that disseminates its values throughout all levels and structures, apparently in such a way that unquestioning acceptance comes to seem "simple experience and common sense" (Williams, *Marxism* 110). That is, reflexive reading encourages the recognition of the hegemonic workings of society, whereas the reading encouraged by "immediate" fiction, the kind Hersey recommends, reproduces things as they are, as "what goes without saying."

Antonio Gramsci's concept of hegemony is useful in seeing that ideology can be exposed and resisted, for it allows the description of a society as a dynamic "whole process of living" which is saturated by dominant and subordinate relations and the creation of alternative hegemonies. Because Gramsci defines ideology as "the terrain on which men move [and] acquire consciousness of their position," and thus as the site of continuous struggle among hegemonic principles, we are not simply manipulated or indoctrinated by ideological texts (377).[29] We experience meanings and values throughout our lives, in "culture" in its largest sense, which in Williams's view has to be seen as "the lived dominance and subordination of particular classes" (R. Williams, *Marxism* 110). A hegemonic class or idea dominates not simply by direct control but by winning the consent of those dominated, to the point that it is accepted as " 'normal reality' or 'commonsense' by those in practice subordinated to it" (Williams, *Keywords* 118). The term "hegemony" is useful in conceptualizing society as more than simply ruling and subordinate classes; it allows for dialectic, that is, many different forms of struggle and resistance; and it makes domination more than simple "manipulation," "indoctrination," "corruption," or "betrayal." We thus move our analysis of texts away from considerations of fictionality or nonfictionality, aesthetic or pragmatic discourse, into areas of leisure and private life, because that is where society is reproduced in each of us; here the "meanings, values and beliefs which a dominant class develops and propagates" are experienced and where we resist as well (Williams, *Marxism* 110).[30]

Furthermore, as Stanley Aronowitz points out, by reasoning that science itself is a way of knowing (a "praxis," or "set of material practices infused with the political ideologies of social classes"), Gramsci argues that there is no realm of neutral or objective knowledge apart from its practice in real material conditions. And, like other material practices, science "seek[s] political, social, and economic hegemony over other social classes" (Aronowitz 198). This is finally the reason the separation of fictional from nonfictional discourses is untenable; there is no realm of "truth" – including science – apart from the discourse and practice that produce a particular result: that is, apart from ideology, without an interest in securing hegemony. "Truth," in this view, is defined as the consequence of an ideology being "accepted by the scientific community" and becoming "hegemonic in the larger social context" (Aronowitz 148). But we can also see why the separation persists: we recognize a particular scientific proposition as "true" when it gains hegemony and reproduces its way of regarding the world (and its propositions or results) as "natural" (199). Besides, scientists themselves insist on the difference between their practice and other forms of inquiry. "Other discourses become poetry, religion, metaphysics, or whatever, but are zealously marginalized from what signifies science by those who constitute the scientific community" (148).[31]

From acknowledging that both fiction and journalism have developed in particular ways comes the realization that objectivity is not inevitable in either mode, but only conventional and privileged. There are other textual practices, which even if they are not openly oppositional, resistant, or subversive of the dominant, at least represent alternatives to it. Seeing these practices relationally, as defined by their deviance or departure from the norm, may enable us to view them positively, especially after seeing the construction of the dominant, objective modes and the way they work as ideology. Because there is no defense of objectivity that does not concede the biases involved, I would rather suggest alternatives – such as reflexive practices founded on the belief in the constructed nature of realistic or nonfictional representation – than struggle to reclaim or redeem the concept.

4

Other American New Journalisms: 1960s New Journalism as "Other"

> A clever and energetic man has lately invented a new journalism, full of ability, novelty, variety, sensation, sympathy, generous instincts; its one great fault is that it is feather-brained.
>
> — Matthew Arnold, *Nineteenth Century* (May 1887)

> Everyone has a different definition of what the New Journalism is. It's the use of fictional techniques, it's composite characterization, it's the art form that's replacing the novel, which is dying. Or it's anyone who used to write for the old *Herald Tribune* magazine, it's participation in the event by the writer, it's the transcendence of objectivity, it's anyone who makes up quotes, it's anyone who hangs out at the Lion's Head bar.
>
> — Jack Newfield, "Journalism: Old, New and Corporate" (1970)

By taking the fiction-to-journalism relationship as exemplary, we have explored one version of how the fiction–nonfiction split came to be. Now we can draw on those histories of objectivity in fiction and journalism to account for readers' and critics' sometimes vehement responses to practices that seem to blur the boundaries between these exemplary modes of literary and nonliterary discourse. Because I do not separate these categories, other than to acknowledge that literature is what we have decided to regard as such and, following Edmund Wilson, to define journalism as writing for periodicals (*Letters* 353), we are not faced with the problems of quantitative assessment and arbitrariness that plague definitions based on finding particular properties. Under the premise that generic categories are brought into being by being described, named, and defined – by gatekeepers and critics such as publishers, publicity and marketing agents, reviewers, and editors of periodicals, as well as by readers – we can approach texts and their various characteristics differently from critics who have a specific idea of the formal features of "literary journalism" or the nonfiction novel (see

120

Sims, Introduction; Zavarzadeh 56–67). Although many of the narratives discussed in Chapters 4 through 6 are widely regarded as New Journalism pieces or as "nonfiction novels," and may even be what Ohmann might call "precanonical nonfiction," others, like those by Janet Malcolm, are rarely discussed in these terms (Ohmann, *Politics* 300 n. 2).

In this and the next two chapters we will observe how various journalists use strategies that can be characterized as "dialectical" to critique the dominant practice of journalism and to demonstrate alternatives to it. Implicit in the theorizing of these counterpractices in the readings that follow (along with a brief historical outline of these "new" journalisms and of mainstream responses to them) are strategies for readers which ought to enable resistance to the positivist bias of most interpretation of journalistic narratives. We have seen that literature is in effect defined *against* other discourses, most obviously against the mass media and popular culture; here we will find New Journalism and nonfiction novels being defined against the hegemonic form of both journalism and fiction: objectivity, and objective realism. Practices that I am grouping under the term "new nonfiction" have already been identified by some as forming "crossover" or "blurred" genres, because they call attention to what has been suppressed in the separation of journalism and fiction: for example, the process of production of narratives, and the textual quality of much of our experience. I do not, then, identify examples that seem to fit this definition; I am more interested in the process by which these journalistic texts are either labeled deviant and marginal, and thus excoriated, or lifted out of their occasions to be regarded as timeless and transcendent. This is one way of asking, What happened to the New Journalism and the nonfiction novel? After all, the terms are rarely used.

To try to answer this question, I focus on the new nonfiction not as a body of works that I would privilege in turn by moving it to the position of dominant but as a potentially disruptive "ex-centric" practice (Hutcheon, *Poetics* 57). This move allows close examination of the tension between the naturalized, commonsense assumptions of objectivity (things as they appear to be) and the "unnatural" assertion of alternative, oppositional, or otherwise critical positions inherent in "interested" or political readings. Another way to conceptualize the move is as the performance of a kind of dialectical dance between interpretations, involving a refusal to substitute an essentialized new one for the naturalized one being displaced. By emphasizing the priority of narrative over events (what Hutcheon calls the "discursive nature of all reference" [119]) in reading the new nonfiction, a critic can expose the construction of the objective or factual, so that the tension between referential and reflexive levels becomes palpable.

This goes against the usual view of the sixties: that it was a decade of softening of category distinctions, of the canon's openness to crossovers from low to high, in short, of the democratization of genres. (Morris Dickstein, for example, calls it a "romantic" period in this regard [147].) In my reading, the eventual outcome, no matter how fuzzy the distinctions seemed during the sixties, was to firm up the boundaries between fiction and journalism, literature and popular discourse, for the mainstream saw these alternative practices as signifying the disorder implicit in mass culture. And because Tom Wolfe himself, as proselytizer for the New Journalism, insisted on elevating it to literary status, claiming that it outdoes the novel at the social realism it is supposed to do best, its success has usually meant its co-optation, in the Marcusean sense of the "defusing and domesticating of ostensibly oppositional forms of culture by their tolerant acceptance and commercialization" (Graff, "Co-optation" 170).

In earlier chapters we observed the separation of journalism from literature by cultural practices that designated an elite, transcendent form of objective truth. Here we trace the mechanism of a countercultural, radical, or oppositional "low" form – New Journalism – as a "mode of understanding" or "cultural analytic"; by reading this practice reflexively, we can understand not only its construction but its co-optation (Stallybrass and White 6). Peter Stallybrass and Allon White have traced a dialectic between "carnival" and the establishment of bourgeois norms from the Middle Ages to the twentieth century. I take their reading of this explosion of the excluded, "lower," or repressed as a model for regarding sixties countercultural practices, including what was labeled the New Journalism, as the "low/Other" to dominant practices – specifically, in the case of journalism, to the practice of objectivity. (This comprises both the personal "human interest" and the impersonal "news from nowhere" forms of journalistic narrative.) The finding of Stallybrass and White that is most relevant to this project is that the low/Other practice is both marginalized and co-opted, for many of its manifestations turn out to be "*symbolically* central" but "*socially* peripheral" (5). (Their example is long hair in the sixties.) Furthermore, countercultural groups, like carnival, are frequently experimental, testing boundaries and limits; even deviant or excessive practices often break through the lines containing them, in order to show where the boundaries are and, in some cases, to strengthen them in a phenomenon associated by anthropologists with the Trickster.[1]

Wolfe's practice in *The Electric Kool-Aid Acid Test* is interesting in this regard, because he shows his Prankster subjects acting out what can be called "carnivalesque" explosions of deviant behavior and alternative practices, before rounding them up via the reassertion of an objective, detached stance and moving toward narrative closure. Although at times he evokes their more outrageous behavior in appropriately excessive mannerisms, he also adopts the prose of the mainstream to assimilate their stylistic innovations in art and music and their free and loose "attitude." Does he view the "heads" as "out there," an expression of carnival needing only to be cleaned up and made presentable for boundaries to be reestablished and for them to represent no threat to the status quo? [2] Whether *The Electric Kool-Aid Acid Test* is regarded as a countercultural New Journalistic narrative or a recuperative literary treatment, an artful novel, depends to a great extent on the way it is read.

To explain this in literary-historical terms, I give the novel a trial place in the sequence of pastoral fables that Leo Marx has identified as an important tradition in U.S. writing. Marx traces the metaphor of the "machine in the garden," from Jefferson to Fitzgerald, as it dramatizes "the great issue of our culture" (353): how to respond to the increasing industrialization of a rural paradise. He says that writers since the first North American settlers have conceived of two divergent ways to view their newly discovered Edenic garden and its inevitable corruption by machinery. On the one hand is the desire to escape into a simpler, more "natural" past – for example, to go west or "light out for the territory" – and on the other is the acceptance of "the pain and responsibility of life in a complex civilization" (22). The denial of reality in a movement back to rural values Marx calls "sentimental pastoral," while "complex pastoral" is his term for texts that acknowledge the impossibility of that ideal even as they express the longing for it. Marx finds this latter form of pastoralism in many twentieth-century American writers, including Faulkner, Frost, Hemingway, and West.

> Again and again they invoke the image of a green landscape – a terrain either wild or, if cultivated, rural – as a symbolic repository of meaning and value. But at the same time they acknowledge the power of a counterforce, a machine or some other symbol of the forces which have stripped the old ideal of most, if not all, of its meaning. (363)

Even as the writers of such complex pastorals dream of a return to a more innocent past, they acknowledge historical and material changes, says Marx, and his concluding example is *The Great Gatsby,* in which "the fantasy of pleasure is checked by the facts of history," which include electric juicers, destructive automobiles, and an industrial "valley of ashes" – in short, the complexity of modern civilization (363).

If we take Wolfe's novel as a fable with an unusual solution to the problem of how to deal with encroaching civilization while returning to an earlier state of unity with the cosmos, we are likely to view it as complex pastoral. Writer Ken Kesey and his LSD-tripping Merry Pranksters, the sixties "heads" who have succeeded the Beats, plan to neutralize the threat represented by the machine by welcoming it into the garden. They believe they can harness technology's power to further the Romantic goal of living in the moment, or even use it to ride to a more exalted plane.

In the Pranksters' case, their pastoral dream is helped along by psyche-delic drugs that they believe will break down the walls separating our souls from one another and from nature. There are marked similarities between their hallucinogenic goals and the pastoral ideal; the setting is, after all, California, where the only remaining frontier lies in the consciousness. But their version of pastoral does not reject civilization wholesale; instead they pick and choose from its baggage. Their Day-Glo bus named "Furthur" is one version of the machine, but Kesey's Edenic spread at La Honda, called "the Nest," is also supremely "high-tech."

> Kesey by now had not only the bus but the very woods wired for sound. There were wires running up the hillside into the redwoods and microphones up there that could pick up random sounds. Up in the redwoods atop the cliff on the other side of the highway from the house were huge speakers, theater horns, that could flood the entire gorge with sound. Roland Kirk and his half a dozen horns funking away in the old sphenoid saxophone sinus cavities of the redwoods. (123)

In a startling inversion of the situation evoked by Hawthorne, Thoreau, and others, in which the writer has retreated to a "sleepy hollow" or idyllic bower, only to have its peace shattered by the shriek of a locomotive, Wolfe describes the accommodation of technology by Kesey and his fellow commune residents. At La Honda in 1964, new Prankster Sandy Lehmann-Haupt is exploring the redwood forest behind the house:

> Sandy suddenly came upon a fabulous bower, like a great domed enclosure, like what people mean when they talk about a "cathedral in the pines," only the redwoods were even more majestic. . . . The sun came down through miles of leaves and got broken up like a pointillist painting, deep green and dapple shadows but brilliant light in a soaring deep green super-bower, a perpetual lime-green light, green-and-gold afternoon, stillness, perpendicular peace, wood-scented, with the cars going by on Route 84, just adding pneumatic sound effects, *sheee-ooooooooo,* like a gentle wind. All peace here; very reassuring. (51)

Unlike the "ear-rending neigh" of the Iron Horse at Walden Pond, the cars that pass by La Honda merely whoosh.

In short, Kesey and his gang do not just tolerate high tech; they positively revel in it. Not only do they have the most sophisticated sound systems, with variable-lag microphones for recording as well as broadcasting, "or rapping off of," and motion-picture equipment for the Pranksters' great morass of a Movie (45 hours of their coast-to-coast bus trip alone), but they have access to the laboratory-produced chemicals, such as lysergic acid diethylamide (LSD), that make their hallucinatory trips possible and enhance their sense of being in the here and now. If the Pranksters' dream is not to be a sentimental one, there must be a different counterforce to the pastoral dream, another kind of machine threatening the garden. This opposing force is mainstream culture itself, with its mechanisms for deadening the senses, its demands for machinelike conformity, and its inhuman stifling of the forces of creativity and heightened consciousness. In other words, it is not technology or the industrial state per se but the spirit of mainstream industrialized society, with its empiricist, scientistic bias, that represents a threat to the new Eden. The Pranksters believe they can wrest technology from the soporific mainstream culture and use it to overcome the lags – sensory, social, historical, psychological – which prevent us from living in the present moment, and which make our lives in effect secondary, based on received perceptions (129–30).

Because the Pranksters' goal is to break through to a higher level of perception than that of our ordinary world of cause and effect, with its linear sense of time, their movement can be read as a form of the Romantic desire to return to our origins, away from the repressive forces of society which deny people's instinctual needs and prevent unfettered souls from merging with another in new levels of consciousness. This desire resembles numerous other "nostalgic myths of pre-modern Paradise Lost" (Berman 15) and complaints and jeremiads of "The world is too much with us" variety. It is given as a reason for modernist writers' distrust of abstract language after World War I, for example, and thus as a cause of the despair of the Lost Generation. When the writer emphasizes the egregious exploitation of nature and the natural by technology, it becomes an expression of the incredibility of reality. It is necessary to historicize this phenomenon, however; otherwise the concept enters the transcendental realm outside of history, and we lose the specificity that resists the universalist tendencies of literature in its dominant twentieth-century definition. An example of ahistorical understanding is the feeling that our reality is uniquely troubled or unreal. As Marshall Berman has noted, "People who find themselves in the midst of this maelstrom are apt to feel that they are the first ones, and maybe the only ones, to be going through it" (15).[3] Berman has traced this way of experiencing the excitement and threat inherent in what he calls "modernity" back nearly five hundred years. Indeed, insofar as the modernist acknowledges that our world is no longer Paradise, this is the defining myth of modernism.

Like other universalizing tendencies in twentieth-century criticism, this one minimizes the particular conditions producing the feeling or response and seizes on the first general explanation that transcends the particular events and causes. Because of this, the dominant explanations for the rise of New Journalism and nonfiction novels, which together I call the new nonfiction, share a similar belief in the "unreality" or absurdity of contemporary history. It may be that, as we will find in Chapter 5, the very rigidity of the categories in which we place experiences increases the effect of unreality. Rather than blurring the boundaries between fiction and reality, then, our century's (or post-World War II period's) writers and texts may be acknowledging the inappropriateness and artificiality (the "unreality") of the separation. If the new nonfiction is in any way a response to this perception of an altered reality, it is likely to be to the unreality of the way we divide up discourse.

The result of insisting on a return to the older way of demarcating life and art is a set of theories based on the same "rigid polarities and flat totalizations" that characterize twentieth-century conceptions of modernism itself (Berman 24). For example, the labels frequently applied to the new nonfiction – "literary journalism," "literary nonfiction," and "the literature of fact" (see Sims; Anderson, *Literary Nonfiction;* Weber, *Literature*) – reinforce the late-nineteenth-century notion of literature as a collection of timeless works of universal value and appeal. Such terms imply the existence of journalistic or factual discourses that are not literary; therefore, some way must be found to distinguish one category from the other, which leads to the imposition of what are invariably formalist criteria.[4]

Assimilating only formally superior examples of journalism to literature thus means accepting the dominant view of fiction's superiority to nonfictional discourse on aesthetic grounds. Furthermore, the usual definitions imply a hybrid of factual content and fictional form, leaving an example of so-called literary nonfiction liable to criticism for not being accurate or objective on the one hand or for being tied to facts or to its author's ego on the other.[5] But the biggest problem I find with the dominant definitions is that they essentialize these nonfictional examples as the result of an aesthetic practice that rises above its time and place to achieve permanence. For one thing, the aesthetic definition of literature produces a canon that does not value political and historical narrative.

The elevation of certain examples at the expense of the category of journalistic or nonfictional narrative results in the loss of the latter texts from the canon; they go out of print quickly, are not commonly read, taught, and discussed, and we lose familiarity with their historical contexts, which must be recreated by later literary and cultural historians.

In order to historicize the New Journalism, therefore, I connect it to the countercultural movements of the "much-mythologized sixties," a decade that, as Todd Gitlin notes, is itself "already fast receding either into oblivion or into convenient distortion" (*Whole World* 16). From the vantage point of the nineties, the new nonfiction, like the alternative politics of the sixties, the New Left, is easily regarded as "something that mysteriously came, made trouble, and went" (Gitlin 16). I will argue that the difference between viewing the movements of the sixties as politically relevant and legitimate and therefore perhaps of continuing value rather than assimilated or failed, depends on how the sixties as a text is habitually read. This, in turn, depends to some extent on reflexive reading of such narratives as those produced by New Journalists and nonfiction novelists.

To begin to situate the new nonfiction historically, I describe it as a category recognizable after the fact, in relation to dominant or traditional practices. Recent work by theorists of feminism, popular culture, and other noncanonical genres and discourses has shown that the dominant in any aspect of culture depends for its superior status on the identifying and scapegoating of an "other."[6] Stallybrass and White complicate the mechanism by insisting on the split between the power and prestige of excluded discourses and practices and their site or status. For example, although dominance and identity are determined on the margins, the excluded practices are not without powers of resistance and may even become constitutive (as in the return of the repressed). Another reason this is true is that the dominant may have a psychological dependence upon the Other that is opposed and excluded at the social level (5). The process is similar to Gramsci's description of the workings of hegemony (see this volume, Chapter 3, and Clarke et al. 59–62). Although there is always a question about what successful "Otherness" would be like – what specific form resistance to or subversion of dominant naturalized modes and styles would take – in 1960s New Journalism and the practices with which these writers are associated, it is safe to say they were viewed as threatening the status quo and as suggesting powerful alternative forms. Stallybrass and White conclude, "[A] challenge to the hierarchy of *sites* of discourse, which usually comes from groups and classes 'situated' by the dominant in low or marginal positions, carries the promise of politically transformative power" (201).

We can see this process of alterity within our mass society when particular phenomena become recognizable as such by being set off from hegemonic practices. The New Journalism, for example, was first defined not by the innovators in any kind of manifesto but after the fact, as a departure.[7] The closest thing it has to a manifesto is Tom Wolfe's introduction to *The New Journalism,* a collection of critical pieces written in the early seventies, several years after the innovators had been grouped together. Wolfe acknowledges that the sense of New Journalism as a group came from the attacks, which took the form of "bitterness, envy and resentment" (Introduction 24). Because he is eager to win literary status for New Journalism, he brags that what he and other New Journalists were doing was borrowing techniques from realistic fiction to write about what "actually happened"; then he sets their results up against the reigning literary genre, "The Novel," for his paramount goal is to establish this hybrid practice alongside fiction in the literary pantheon (Introduction 34, 8–9). His way of elevating the "Low Rent" form is by exaggerating his glee in the attacks, which he says came from both objective journalists (in the *Columbia Journalism Review,* which he calls "the major organ of traditional newspaper journalism") and the bastion of "older literary essayists and 'men of letters,' The *New York Review of Books*" (24). He might as well have mentioned the *New Yorker,* for two of his attackers (Renata Adler and Dwight Macdonald) were also connected with that elite literary magazine, which Wolfe had skewered in an old-fashioned, two-part, "get their goat" essay. (The series was decidedly not New Journalistic but definitely displayed his irreverence for facts.)[8] According to Wolfe, New Journalism was also called "superficial," "ephemeral," "mere entertainment," and "morally irresponsible," and its prose was denigrated as "zoot-suited" and "zippy" (37, 38).

This is not to deny that some writers who were called New Journalists were overtly critical of the hegemonic forms of journalism and deliberately subversive of those norms. Norman Mailer claims that his earliest contribution to the New Journalism was "an enormously personalized journalism where the character of the narrator was one of the elements not only in telling the story but in the way the reader would assess the experience." Although this amounted to "an all-out assault on *New Yorker* writing," Mailer insists that it was necessary, for "one of the great lies of all time" was that the "reporter pretended to be objective" (*Pontifications* 145–6). He is also well aware of the radical challenge his journalism poses to the political mainstream, and so he wears the badge of outsider proudly; it is highly visible on his combative persona. After all, this is the confessional writer who announces on the first page of the appropriately named *Advertisements for Myself,* "I am imprisoned with a perception which will settle for nothing less than making a revolution in the consciousness of our time." Mailer's inflated persona, in his political reporting from *Advertisements for Myself* (1959) to *Some Honorable Men* (1976), is thus one outstanding reason that the complaints about the New Journalists include the charge that their giant egos got in the way of their materials.[9]

New Journalism was defined by the dominant as "Other" in much the way the subcultural and countercultural phenomena that the New Journalists covered – Vietnam War protests; civil rights, Black Power, labor-organizing, and student-militancy campaigns; the "human potential" movement and Utopian communes; and the myriad subcultures revolving around race, reggae, rock, drugs, and clothing styles – were seen by the dominant culture as departing from the consensual values and practices of society as a whole. These groups and practices have some characteristics that serve to focus them as movements or identify them as groups, but one of their primary means of coherence is that they are identified in relation to a hegemonic practice or institution: as a departure from it, as an alternative, or as oppositional. Studies of how socially and politically radical groups are treated in the mass media of both the United States and Great Britain reveal the same pattern: because the press accepts the dominant view that society is unified by a "common community of interests," any group that takes exception by calling for an alteration in the system which limits its access to wealth and power is seen as deviating from the "correct" world view.

Not only were these groups in conflict with that conception but they exposed the fallacy of its assumptions – for example, by calling for the restructuring of society (Students for a Democratic Society) and by questioning the right of the president and his military and foreign-policy advisers to send Americans to fight in a war against the spread of communism. Other areas of contention revolved around sexual freedom and race and gender discrimination, with calls for fundamental reform in these areas frequently being presented by the hegemonic media as the result of youthful rebellion, or the "generation gap." Similarly, suggestions that communism might be an acceptable economic system were invariably attributed to outsiders: un-American, unpatriotic, or even subversive "others."[10]

Socially and politically radical groups would represent an uncomfortable threat if they were legitimated by being taken seriously, so they are handled by the media as gimmicky or impermanent; their representatives are characterized as immature or crazy or unnatural ("animals" was a common epithet in the sixties, whether it was being applied to members of youth subcultures or political radicals or teens cavorting sexually at rock festivals); and underlying substantive issues are handled by emphasizing the form the protest takes rather than its content. Disturbing innovations called for can be neutralized by fitting them into established categories such as "law and order," "violent protests," or "a minority spoiling the majority's good clean fun."[11]

In general, traditional journalistic discourse "empties out" the content of deviant subjects and emphasizes their form: for example, their similarities to other nonlegitimate or extremist (because nonconformist) events and their portable association with resistance or violence (see Murdock). This emphasis on easily categorized events rather than underlying substantive issues – which are complex, frequently ambiguous, and difficult to summarize under conventional news practice – is only reinforced by the doctrine of objectivity, as Graham Murdock points out, because the easiest way to satisfy this ideal is to avoid both the "partisanship implicit in the consideration of underlying issues" and the appearance of taking sides by concentrating on actions and events rather than the difficult issues and their accompanying "rhetoric of conflict" (166–7). Richard Ohmann analyzes television news in similar terms. Because it is predominantly visual, it "removes events from history, presents them as disconnected stories complete in themselves, divests politics of ideas as well as of ideology, and pictures the world from a perspective of natural hierarchy and upper-middle-class values. It is a world in which conflict and disorder make news, but only as aberrations from the underlying moral order and harmony of interests" (*Politics* 185).

What the counterculture or, especially, subcultures signify against the dominant ideology is difference; they appear to call attention to themselves, and they are seen as "deviant," abnormal, inappropriate – above all, visible and unnatural (Hebdige 101–2, 94ff.). Traditional journalism, like the classic realist novel, is lodged in the dominant order of society; both modes of realism depend on our feeling that "it goes without saying." Therefore these hegemonic discourses in literature and journalism attempt to "recuperate" deviant aspects of culture, to repair the order disturbed by a flagrant subculture or a countercultural movement, by locating even its most disturbing or critical aspects in its "natural" place. That is, Dick Hebdige explains, they reincorporate deviance as well as isolate it: "The media, as Stuart Hall ["Culture" 1977] has argued, not only record resistance, they 'situate it within the dominant framework of meanings' and those young people who choose to inhabit a spectacular youth culture are simultaneously *returned,* as they are represented on T.V. and in the newspapers, to the place where common sense would have them fit" (94). Hebdige cites a striking British example of the "domestication" of a deviant group, an article headlined "Punks Have Mothers Too" in the magazine *Woman,* meant to reassure readers that despite their outrageous appearance, these young people would eventually drop their subversive styles to settle down and become parents and bourgeois consumers themselves (98, 158–9n).

Because there is no "us" and "them" in the ideal world represented by the mainstream media, the dominant can sometimes magically elide the difference of Others by ignoring it. Where difference cannot be overlooked, it is attributed to "human nature," much as the difference of women that cannot be denied (their secondary economic and legal status, for example) is attributed to their "natural" inferiority by emphasizing their ties to nature through their role in reproduction. When groups or causes can be regarded as essentially or self-evidently factual, that is, as what they appear on the surface to be, they can readily be absorbed into the dominant belief system through tropes of biology or common sense or even patriotism. For example, what patriotic American would burn a flag? Therefore a president who calls for a constitutional amendment making such an act a "desecration" communicates an image of unquestionable patriotism, as reported by "objective" journalists, for to question the self-evident appearance of patriotism would be to move toward a partisan stance. The objectivist illusion underlying such beliefs does not encourage the questioning of cultural and political processes. Because journalism simplifies complex issues to the level of the mass reader through this naturalist reduction – whereby concepts slip from the domain of content to that of form or image – little sophisticated discussion of issues takes place. This reduction is effected by making a simple binary opposition between hegemonic values and those of the deplored group or practice, and this in turn makes it easier to neutralize, criticize, or dismiss the Other. (Todd Gitlin, in *The Whole World Is Watching,* gives a thorough analysis of one extensive example – the media's role in covering 1960s leftist politics.)

We can see processes of both incorporation and exclusion going on around New Journalism, as it was assimilated to a comfortable tradition going back to Defoe and Boswell and the form itself was equated with the human interest story, which has traditionally been distinguished from "the directness of factual news" by being acknowledged as literary journalism (Arlen, "Notes" 245–7; Hayes 262). Wolfe cooperated in his own assimilation in this sense, for he devoted pages of his "history" of the New Journalism to detailing the techniques of social realism that the novelists had abandoned in favor of fables or mythic tales and to comparing the reception of the New Journalism to the outraged response to early British novels (Introduction 28–9, 37–41).

For the most outrageous practitioners, whose antics and spectacular innovations could not be so easily naturalized, a space outside journalism was reserved. Dwight Macdonald, in an influential article in the *New*

York Review of Books ("Parajournalism, or Tom Wolfe"), defined this disreputable practice as something unnatural, outside the pale, hence "parajournalistic": "from the Greek *para,* 'beside' or 'against': something similar in form but different in function" (223).[12] Macdonald criticized Wolfe's flamboyance; his repetitiousness (exhibit A was *The Kandy-Kolored Tangerine-Flake Streamline Baby,* a collection of twenty-four pieces published in 1965); the ephemerality of his subjects; and the *"kitsch"* intimacy of his style, which "cozies up, merges into the subject so completely that the viewpoint is wholly from the inside" (226, 225).

Macdonald's attack on Wolfe, Dick Schaap, Jimmy Breslin, and Gay Talese as "parajournalists" was clearly an attempt to exclude an aberrant set of conventions from the norm. It is no wonder mainstream journalists set apart and castigated what they identified as New Journalism, for in contrast to the illusion of neutrality created by the dominant mode (represented by "Hiroshima" and similar *New Yorker* nonfiction), many of these pieces show how "the way things are" has been naturalized by conventions of realism and objectivity, and they offer an alternative in their own self-accounting form. Their practice exposes the conventions of objectivity: the structuring forms of news beats, desks, pages, and subgenres; the "operational practices" for selecting and shaping stories according to what appear as instinctive "news values" and the way these are reproduced in each generation of journalists (Hall, "Determinations" 181); and the press and broadcast journalists' role as *mediating* organizations and producers of what becomes reified as "the news" or "history."

Ed Cohen's excellent discussion of Macdonald's essay connects the latter's counterattack even more tightly to the "agonizing sting" of Wolfe's ridicule of the *New Yorker*. He emphasizes the investment proponents of " 'Literature' (with a capital 'L')" *have* in negating the challenge posed by such "bastard" forms: "it wasn't just Wolfe's writing that was at issue – it was his very authority to write." Thus, Cohen says, Macdonald's task was to "rewrite history" to exclude the radical import of Wolfe's attack, which lay in his questioning the strict opposition between fact and fiction, and what's more, the power of "legitimate" institutions to clearly mark the line – in effect, to decide what is true and what is false (3). As Cohen reads the attack, Wolfe threatened the institutions that depend on being able to clearly separate what is false from what is true. "For it is only by distinguishing 'fact' from 'fancy' that our society can determine which kinds of knowledge will be used to make social decisions. For example, if women's history or black history or chicano history or gay history is not 'true' history then it is perfectly logical to deny them a place in the great bastion of our culture, the academy – or even more importantly to ignore the *fact* of people's continuing daily oppression" (9).

To vitalize the Other that New Journalism has become, rather than exclude or minimize it, we have to "read" it dialectically by calling attention to its process. I suggest that New Journalism "works," and acquires its reputation as deviant, by seeming to adopt the style of the countercultures it reports rather than fitting them into dominant frameworks of assimilation or exclusion. In other words, because the style of these various movements and groups is "as much an assault on authority as outright confrontation" is (McRobbie 122), the "other" journalistic way to communicate their significance is to adhere closely to the inseparability of form and content. Writers identified as New Journalists and nonfiction novelists seem to produce texts that suggest the terms of their own reading. That is, we can more easily than usual see such narratives working as process, not product; they can be read as "signifying" the way subcultural style does. They signal open-ended reading strategies, for example – for resisting closure, exposing their reporting and writing processes, and deemphasizing unity in favor of contradiction, complexity, and open-endedness. Above all, they can be read to emphasize their subjectivity, rather than the objective distance between observer and observed.

To maintain this stance, writers avoided fitting experimental practices into mainstream categories which would have naturalized them. For example, countercultural journalists wrote about individuals and groups who had deviated from middle-class lifestyles – into drug, rock, politically or sexually radical subcultures – without "normalizing" them, that is, without making them conform to existing categories. This called for a form appropriate to the content. Thus some writers experimented with techniques not common in journalism. Tom Wolfe used repeated epithets ("Radical Chic," "Low Rent," the "Group Mind") as identifying ideological tags, phonetic impressions of speech, and rapid switches in point of view. (See the widely quoted opening of "Girl of the Year" in *The Kandy-Kolored Tangerine-Flake Streamline Baby*.) He and others used coinages, idiosyncratic typography, narration from inside the scene or by a collective mind, and interior monologue.

Some reporters also revived older strategies, such as composite characterization, participant observation, and overt emphasis on the story of the story. These strategies, Talese says, required long periods of "immersion" or "saturation" reporting, and were thus costly to those who published New Journalism ("When Frank Sinatra"). In some cases journalists lived as members of the subcultures or countercultural groups they were covering, earning their confidence in order to be accepted on the inside (and confirming their status as "outsiders" to conventional society as they did so). They produced such narratives as Joan Didion's "Slouching towards Bethlehem," about the Haight-Ashbury subculture in San Francisco in the late 1960s; Don McNeill's series of pieces about the analogous street scene in New York City's East Village for the *Village Voice,* collected as *Moving through Here;* Hunter Thompson's *Hell's Angels;* and Talese's *Honor Thy Father,* an account of a Mafia chieftan's life. The characteristics common to the varieties of New Journalism that led to its being identified as a phenomenon are its emphases on the writing instead of on the conventions that produce the illusion of objectivity (Dan Wakefield calls these "omniscience, self-importance, . . . the sort of pseudo-gravity that passes for 'seriousness' " [42]) and on signs of the reporter (though not necessarily in the first person or as a dramatized narrator). In these two related attributes may lie the key to what makes New Journalism seem both "new" and "other," for in relation to mainstream conventions, what is new and different will be what stands out, that is, what is not effaced or hidden. The opposite of transparent narration and invisible frames is self-conscious narration or other revelation of the process by which something is written.

The response of the mainstream to such radical departures from its conventions was probably inevitable: to minimize and question the new practice because it threatened the illusion that newsworkers could objectively capture the real. This reaction on the part of the dominant tradition is not unusual in history, even in such a specialized area as the gathering and dissemination of news. When I traced the history of American journalism in Chapter 3, I found the construction of rational belief in the factuality of the world and in the ability of newsworkers to present it to their readers. Over time, this entailed the development of means for containing the diversity of events, actors, and economic and social forces and of couching it in a dominant frame of "correctness" or normality. It is not surprising to learn that there were two earlier periods when some kind of news practice was regarded as deviant or new; what these "new journalisms" have in common with the twentieth-century form is not their discrete properties but their stance as "other" – the fact that they were greeted with the same "moral horror" by their competition, the establishment journalism of each period (Schudson, *Discovering* 88).[13]

   The "new journalism" label was first applied to the novel penny papers of the 1830s, which were innovative in many ways, most importantly in creating the modern conception of news as the transcription of events from all over, as found even in the ordinary, mundane "reality" of everyday life and expressed through the ubiquitous "human interest" story. The penny press can be regarded as counter- or antitraditional in two senses. Politically, papers like the New York *Sun* (its motto was "It Shines for All"), with their appeal to large numbers of working-class readers, undermined the dominance of an elite press. (The earlier papers were supported by political parties, featured primarily commercial and mercantile information, and sold for only six cents a copy, or no more than ten dollars for a year's subscription.) Formally, these mass-circulation dailies went against the traditional hierarchy of genres by "democratizing" the news, appealing to even the poorest, newly literate classes with crime stories and exposures of corruption among officials elected to represent "the people's" interest. (The latter innovation, of course, unites the political and the formal.) The very success of these rapidly proliferating newspapers and the growing amounts of capital needed to establish and run them eventually pushed them into the mainstream, for, then as now, advertising, not purchase price, was the source of profits.[14]

The term "new journalism" was used again in the 1880s and 1890s to describe the high-minded, crusading practice initiated by Joseph Pulitzer and William Randolph Hearst. What was "new" in this period was the emotional appeal of stories designed to call attention to the problems of the poor. Papers as widely scattered as the St. Louis *Post-Dispatch* (where Pulitzer began his editorial crusading), the *Kansas City Star,* and the *Dallas News* mixed crusades, progressive politics, sensational crime stories, and reforming zeal (M. Stephens 208–9). Edward W. Scripps is said to have conceived of his chain of papers as "classrooms for the working class" (McKerns 27). In the eyes of this journalism's detractors, however, the reporting techniques used to arouse passions of various sorts were inflammatory and were motivated more by the desire to sell newspapers than by the desire for reform. Consider, for example, how they viewed the exploits of reporters like Winifred Sweet Black ("Annie Laurie") and Elizabeth Cochrane ("Nellie Bly"), who dared such experiments as falling down in the streets of San Francisco to test emergency medical care, living in migrant-worker camps, and pretending to be insane to get admitted to New York's asylum on Blackwell's Island (Bly's *Ten Days in a Madhouse*). Instead of being admired for their activist investigative journalism, these enterprising women were invariably referred to as "sob sisters" and their crusades regarded as stunts designed to raise circulation for Hearst and Pulitzer, respectively. Undoubtedly these reporters undertook some adventures (such as Bly's trip around the world in fewer than Phineas Fogg's eighty days) largely for publicity purposes, and it may have been difficult for newspaper readers to sort out their responses to revelations about polygamy, prostitution, poor working conditions, and political corruption, which were likely to be a mixture of both titillation and indignation (Tebbell 109). But none of that ambivalent response is preserved in labeling these stories "sensationalist," and no sense of the serious investigative work these journalists undertook remains in the designation "stunt reporting."

The critical dimension of this practice was assimilated at least partly because of this new journalism's popularity, for what we view as its excesses – jingoism, sensationalism, and exaggeration of cause-effect relations – were fueled by the circulation war between Pulitzer and Hearst in the late 1890s. The infamous yellow journalism produced during their rivalry has been called "the New Journalism without its social consciousness," and its evil deeds are said to have included starting the Spanish-American War (McKerns 27). Not the least of its wrongdoings was yellow journalism's influence on imitators and successors, including the tabloids introduced in 1919, "with their black headlines and plethora of photographs" (M. Stephens 210). These tabloids, which had their heyday in the 1920s and 1930s, were accused of practicing "gutter journalism" for the sake of profit while ignoring the responsibility to inform their readers that is implicit in the First Amendment guarantee of an independent press (McKerns 31).

From our vantage point, the expansion of circulation and consolidation of capital achieved by Pulitzer and Hearst and their heirs in the twentieth century loom larger than either paper's progressive actions on behalf of "the people," for the ever-increasing capitalization needed to sustain a widely distributed, truly *popular* press moved the reporting of the large newspapers back to the center of the political spectrum and marginalized alternative and reform-movement reporting. Once again, according to Raymond Williams, history took a dialectical turn as, by the early twentieth century, "the people" and their interests become the "workers" or the "masses" and their demands. Paradoxically, the masses were marginalized, because they were identified with leftist or radical positions in a democratic society where "the people as a whole" – readers of the mainstream press and consumers in general – were conceived of as a contented homogeneous "market." The history of the term "popular press," Williams demonstrates, indicates this shift. (Although he is writing about the British popular press in the nineteenth century, the response was similar in the United States.) The radical sense of "popular" journalism as "being 'for the people,' " he says, gave way in steps, first to the meaning of "generalised political attitudes" and "reading-material of crime, scandal, romance and sport" and then to "popular" seen in "purely market terms." He shows the seamlessness of political means and financial ends: "The repression, the isolation, the containment and eventually the incorporation of an autonomous popular press . . . began as conscious political acts and continued as an effective deployment of financial resources to keep poor men's reading matter in rich men's hands" ("Press" 49–50).

The alternative to the sensationalism of yellow journalism came in the form of an emphasis on facts, and on the appearance, if not the attainment, of objectivity – as represented by the *New York Times,* after Adolph Ochs bought it in 1896 and set out to win a share of the market dominated by Pulitzer's *World* and Hearst's *Journal.* For Michael Schudson, the *Times* was the leading exponent of the "information" model of journalism, also present in other papers descended from the old penny press (in New York, the *Sun, Herald,* and *Tribune* [*Discovering* 88–9]). These papers represented the mainstream against which 1890s new journalism and the later yellow journalism of Hearst and Pulitzer were viewed. When these latter "story" forms reigned, this fact-based press, associated with "firmness, objectivity, scrupulous dispassion" (90), seemed a desirable counterpractice. The important point about the *Times*'s innovation, however, was the lip service it paid to objectivity, for once the mainstream tradition abandoned open partisanship, it also relinquished the responsibility to interpret and comment on the news; analysis and opinion giving therefore became the contested province of editorial writers, columnists, and Op-Ed-page contributors – of pundits, in other words. This group of professionals, beholden to no one, became powerful beyond their abilities, because readers depended on them to place the news in context (see Alterman 28–9).

Schudson's categories provide the framework for his view of twentieth-century journalism, for he shows this opposition continuing down to the present and dividing readers of the two modes along predominantly class lines: working-class readers supposedly want stories, while the educated middle classes seek information. According to Schudson, the "story" ideal predominates when a newspaper emphasizes pleasure and believes it can interpret the world to its readers by telling them stories that they can relate to their own lives. The format of the information model emphasizes "unframed" information, and he cites Walter Benjamin's description of information as "incompatible with the spirit of storytelling" (*Discovering* 90).

Under a reflexive model, however, these models are not different in any important way, because there is no significant difference between story and information. Storytelling is incompatible with either form of journalism, for in going from an oral tradition to one dominated by print or other technology, the overtly reflexive element, the reference to the form of the story, is suppressed. It is not just that the modern tradition of information in journalism emphasizes explanation, for it may actually explain less; but it is more likely to insist on its accuracy

(Benjamin, "Story-Teller" 88–9). Because the advantage of the story-telling tradition in its oral form was the interaction between teller and audience, the inevitable solitariness of both writer and reader of a novel and the fixed form of the printed narrative mark the demise of the "art of storytelling," with its open-endedness and lack of "explanation." As Benjamin says, "Every morning brings us the news of the globe, and yet we are poor in noteworthy stories" (89). The information contained in all journalism and books is used up as soon as it is printed, for it is completely explained, verifiable, and fixed – there are no retellings of information. Nor are novels excluded from the information model, for the rise of the novel is Benjamin's "earliest symptom" of this revolution (87).

Although we can divide news into the tendency toward either story or information (and associate particular newspapers with one emphasis or the other), the story form of journalism does not preserve the features of the oral tradition and so is not very different from information. Besides, the story form does not renege on its promise to follow objective conventions, so it does not contextualize its stories, which can be as meaningless or misleading as uncontextualized facts. The story form is evidence of the creative, constitutive nature of journalism, because the implication that there is a "story" to be dug out of or imposed on every set of materials or notes creates that story, but it works as ideology because its form is transparent and we cannot easily discover how it came to be written; by convention, the storyteller is not present. The story and information forms are readily adapted to the dominant perception of journalism as a factual genre, which is then opposed to the fictional, creative, or "literary" genres. Both journalistic models imply the existence of an objective reality; they only set about mirroring it in different ways.

These tendencies have coexisted under a paradigm of objective journalism to the end of the twentieth century. Mainstream newspapers are a mixture of "hard" and "soft" news, of information and stories. Readers respond with "the more respectable faculties of abstraction and the less respectable feelings" (Schudson, *Discovering* 119) to different parts of the same paper, rather than finding it necessary to satisfy their rational or emotional needs by buying different papers or changing television channels. This heterogeneity of the dominant mode shows the flexibility and power of the positivist world view, which can accommodate both "entertainment" and "factual" models within a form that by and large appears transparent.

The New Journalism of the 1960s and 1970s is similar to the storytelling tradition in that readers are encouraged to observe the observer, thanks to a self-conscious practice that appears in many guises. For example, a narrative persona may include the story of the assignment and give the reader up-to-date progress reports as he proceeds, as Mailer does in his Apollo 11 reporting for *Life,* which became *Of a Fire on the Moon.* Confessional strategies such as those adopted by Mailer in *Armies of the Night* (as well as the bulk of his political reporting from 1960 to 1976) and Susan Sontag in "Trip to Hanoi" enable them to show the "links between personal instinct and the structure of power" (Louvre 74). Both reject conventional historical narrative for its determinism and reductive tendencies, counterposing the subjective dimension of their instincts and their experience to the "deterministic and reductive discourse" of history; as Alf Louvre says, "what they affirm is human agency" (75). The structure of the narrative may imitate the form of the subject, as the short sections of Michael Arlen's account of the making of a Bell Telephone commercial, *Thirty Seconds,* work like commercials for his product, the narrative; besides, once we see behind the scenes to the process by which a seductive commercial is made, we are less likely to accept the illusion of reality created by his narrative without speculating in turn on *its* production. Joan Didion's jumps from story to story as well as from scene to scene in "The White Album" undermine her running commentary on her mind's attempts to impose logic, sequence, some kind of pattern on the randomly presented scenes she witnessed in one disconcerting period in California – to make events out of what stubbornly remain mere occurrences.

The reflexive reading that this New Journalistic practice facilitates can be extended to any journalism, even transparent forms. But when a narrative is viewed as literary journalism, it is easily assimilated to the dominant mode of presenting the news. Journalism does not give up its transparency or its mimetic quality by picking up the techniques of fiction, and the split between factual content and fictional form dramatized when it is viewed as a hybrid does not compromise the illusion of realism created by objectivity. To work reflexively, the journalistic narrative has to be read dialectically. When technique is overemphasized, however, the new nonfiction may appear to marginalize its subjects by highlighting their Otherness through its own eccentric formal experiments. Self-conscious or opaque narrative strategies are not necessarily countercultural or critical; they can be defensive or co-optive, ways of beating critics to the punch and thereby nullifying criticism before it is made. Of this tendency in advertisements, commercials, and movies, Pauline Kael complained in 1965, "It's as embarrassed and half-hearted a strategy as that of a fatman who makes himself a buffoon so that you can't make more fun of him than he has already" (quoted in Dunne 15). Mark Miller remarks, about the "televisual irony" whereby self-mocking formulas imply the viewer's "knowingness" as well as that of the medium, that there is almost no way to counter this "prophylactic" or self-protective irony. If attention to the process was at first a way to critique television's and other objective media's illusion of transparency, this strategy has been co-opted by the media's own self-consciousness, a form of winking at the viewer or reader to encourage backtalk, which they can easily deflect. As Miller says, "Within the televisual environment, you prove your superiority to TV's garbage not by criticizing or refusing it, but by feeding on it, taken in by its oblique assurances that you're too smart to swallow any of it" (15).

That self-consciousness is not enough to establish a legitimate alternative practice is shown by the latest new journalism, identified at the end of the 1980s. This is "tabloid television" or "entertainment TV," with its "amazing stories," unsolved crimes, true-crime docudramas, staged confrontations, and audience participation, which shares little with the New Journalism of the 1960s and 1970s except a heightened level of self-awareness. This new practice also takes advantage of freelance and bystander video footage to sell "unmediated" experience, although this illusion of direct experience is counteracted by the sensationalist promotion of the programs. The trailers for these "real-video" shows, and the programs themselves, can only remind the viewer how unusual (hence unreal and implausible) it is to view bodies at a crime scene, watch dramatic helicopter rescues, witness fatal traffic accidents, and watch the footage replayed. Most people rarely witness such incidents, and yet on television they follow one after another week after week. As the name implies, this practice has its counterpart in the ubiquitous weekly tabloid papers, with their fanciful births, UFO sightings, and reports of supernatural phenomena. Both tabloid media bring to the surface the entertainment aspects that have always been part of mainstream news practice, especially in the category of *fait-divers,* or human interest features of the "man bites dog" variety. These include formal features we associate with popular fiction, such as stereotypical characters, melodramatic plots, paradoxical causality, coincidence, and the objectification of details of people's economic and social class (see Barthes, "Structure").

This "other" journalism faces excluding and assimilating responses from mainstream practice similar to that garnered by its predecessor: television news castigates "trash TV" for its sensationalism, fictionality, and popularity, while increasing its own entertainment features, including dramatic "re-creations" on news-magazine programs and "simulations" on the nightly news. Features that could not be marginalized have been mainstreamed, probably, Rivera suggests, because of the threat to its own audience that the popular alternative represents. Because of its parodic and self-promoting methods, this latest new journalism seems to exhibit the closest thing to a postmodern consciousness that journalism can furnish. But if the possibilities for viewing it are reduced to a kind of "camp" pleasure taken in slumming around the tube and parodying *National Enquirer* headlines – that is, if it is excluded from the category of "news" and treated as a literary novelty with roots in seventeenth-century ballads and prison confessions – the mainstream incorporation of its techniques will go unchallenged. As a fictional or entertainment mode, it will be marginalized for its excesses, and its self-consciousness will pose no threat to the dominant practice of news production.

My interpretation of what are usually called "hybrid forms" or "blurred genres" illustrates the difference between objective and dialectical notions of history. An essentialist history tends to rationalize hegemonic practice by fixing categories and positing differences as absolute, whereas by reading history reflexively (which is easily done, because history is after all a narrative, rather than the events themselves) we can see why some forms of news production resist assimilation into the dominant model. In a dialectical framework, dominant and alternative practices maneuver in relation to one another over time in a process of departure and reincorporation; because the marginalized or decentered subject takes its shape in relation to hegemonic forces, there are many positions it can take up, rather than necessarily being absorbed into the dominant structure. A reflexive history also shows the limitations of the positivist model, for it reveals the way objective definitions create an either–or epistemological situation. To allow for the most possibilities, it is important not to regard Otherness as simple opposition, and not to view reflexivity as a property of texts but to conceive of it relationally, as put into play by particular reading practices. This kind of reading can overcome the separation of subject from object, and since the object is then not fixed or certain, the dynamic relationship among resistant or critical discourses and actions may become apparent.

This goes for reading individual narratives as well. To assure an interpretation that refuses either to objectify and fix its object (thus risking trivializing or essentializing the text) or to normalize the narrative by emphasizing the techniques of realistic fiction, the reader must continually read form in relation to content – analyze the effect of the self-conscious techniques on her perception of the content and try to keep from emptying out the content of the pieces – the political issues – in favor of the attention-attracting form. This is why I emphasize the tension between the two tendencies of realistic narrative: to encourage attention to its medium of language and style, and on the other hand to seduce readers into looking through it at the world we think we know (the "real" world). This reading adds to our pleasure by increasing the tension between the modes of journalism and fiction, with their different

conventions (and the knowledge that we may meet journalism's historical characters in other narratives), whereas a formalist one is likely to
resolve it in favor of one pole or the other.[15]

The Electric Kool-Aid Acid Test can serve as an example of a sixties New
Journalistic text that raises the questions of assimilation or marginalization, and of whether its author writes from a countercultural or conservative position. Does Wolfe view his subjects' style and their message as
inseparable, and thus share their "general tendency to question the values of a social consensus organized around notions of discipline, func-
tionalism, conformism, and material reward" (Whelan 74), or is he
eager to restore his subjects to their proper place, possibly even to drum
them out of the mainstream? Perhaps an even more important question
is to ask what place is offered to the reader and what reading strategies
the text suggests. According to Peter Dahlgren, "reflexivity" describes
our dialectical involvement with a text, whether as viewers or readers; it
rests on the notion that "the dialectic between society and the individual
[is] an ongoing process" and that we construct ourselves and our world
through our conscious participation in it (104). When we are not encouraged to read reflexively, this consciousness is suppressed; we are not
likely to question the text's authority, to consider social relations other
than those represented, or to dismantle the hierarchy of narrative. That
is particularly significant in considering a "doubly real," or overdetermined, narrative like a journalistic one, wherein real events are narrated
realistically, for it posits "the way things are" (105). In Dahlgren's
conception, a "non-reflexive consciousness . . . does not see itself as a
participant in the construction of the social world; it sees itself as merely
acted upon by the social world" (104).

The Electric Kool-Aid Acid Test exhibits many signs of self-conscious
or opaque narrative, yet readers sometimes find it difficult to read this
book reflexively. Many critics complain of being unable to locate
Wolfe's attitude toward his subjects. Some of his techniques seem to
naturalize the radical alternative of the Pranksters. As Thomas Edwards
notes, it is possible to read *The Electric Kool-Aid Acid Test* as giving "aid
and comfort to the oldsters it mocks," because at times Wolfe implies
that all the pranks are simply more extreme (and sexually freer) versions
of "the alcohol scene of *our* youth." If the Pranksters are not offering a
truly new reordering of society's structure, they are neither scary (to
reactionaries) nor encouraging (to radicals). As Edwards concludes, "We
won't learn much from the Pranksters, or any of Wolfe's lesser crea-
tures, if we think they're only differently costumed versions of the kids
down at the old Tappa Keg House" (544). To another critic, looking
back on the sixties, the novel seems to be about the conversion of "an

intrepid experiment with the limits of self and perception" into a form of "escape, the flower children's equivalent of the older generation's booze" (Hartshorne 154). This is to regard *The Electric Kool-Aid Acid Test* as sentimental pastoral, and indeed David Eason has labeled Wolfe an "ethnographic realist" who naturalizes the difference of his subjects "by linking the contemporary to a well-ordered, non-threatening past that promises to extend into the future (53–4).

Then, too, *The Electric Kool-Aid Acid Test* is an exemplary open or "plural" text (Barthes, *S/Z* 5) in that it clearly poses the choice between subjective and objective reading paradigms at several levels: subject (the counterculture and how to "read" it or "what to make of it"), narrator (an authoritarian third-person narrator with control of multiple points of view alternates with a dramatized first-person journalist who may be "on the bus" with the Pranksters), and the story we derive from the plot (which is affected by the reader's interpretation of the plot, or "how we learn"). A reflexive reading involves noting dialectical choices of many kinds. One is the tension between Wolfe's two tendencies – toward seeking our "absolute involvement" with the text by creating a scene and letting us in, and, on the other hand, acting as ringmaster or tour guide to the zany phenomena of the sixties he has evoked and is interpreting for us. These two narrative activities correspond to the somewhat contradictory goals of novelist and social experimenter Ken Kesey and his Merry Pranksters in this novel – to close the gap between event and experience, word and thing, and to stay out in front of the recuperating mainstream, which inevitably reduces its complexity and transforms a radical alternative into something that will fit comfortably within the dominant ideology. These tendencies are also analogous to the two possibilities for viewing subcultures like the LSD-tripping Pranksters or New Journalism itself: as truly oppositional movements or merely as old attitudes in new guise.

It must be said that there are more obvious ways of reading *The Electric Kool-Aid Acid Test* as a conservative work, even a novel of aesthetic realism, than as one demonstrating an improvisatory, productive "signifying practice" (Hebdige 117–19). For one thing, there is a level in both the Pranksters' mission and Wolfe's narrative that corresponds to the nostalgic longing for a "simpler, more harmonious style of life, an existence 'closer to nature' " (Marx 8); the novel thus smacks of sentimental pastoral. The Pranksters are bent on overcoming the gap between "the flash and the eye" with the aid of psychedelic drugs (290) and on breaking through to a new state of consciousness. Like Kesey, like Neal Cassady (who with his quick reflexes is only one-thirtieth of a second away from achieving simultaneity), and the Pranksters, Wolfe too wants to overcome the time lag, the barrier between "the subjective

and the objective, the personal and the impersonal, the *I* and the *not-I*."
The problem is, as both Kesey and Wolfe realize, "how to get it across
to the multitudes who have never had this experience themselves? *You
couldn't put it into words*. You had to create conditions in which they
would feel an approximation of *that feeling,* the sublime *kairos*" (127,
40, 205).

Simultaneity thus may be the ultimate Prankster project, and it lies
behind Kesey's attempt to overcome the linearity of writing, to escape
the trap of "syntax" by writing no more novels but experimenting with
film and other media that enable him to close the gap between himself
and the audience (*Kool-Aid* 136, 8). Wolfe may be tuned in to the
Pranksters' "trip" because of his search for the transcendent sublime,
and thus a way to define his own reception, for transcendence of the
present is one means of assuring the journalist's immortality. The more
his style is valued, the better its chances of being considered literary. In
order for him to overcome the sense of belatedness that is inevitable in
narrative and to present individual scenes as they happen, including the
nearly simultaneous experience of sight and sound that seems to be part
of the psychedelic experience, Wolfe uses devices to achieve the effect of
synchronicity, including rapid switches in point of view without signal-
ing them (which would imply sequentiality), long lists of objects and
series of adjectives, and absurdly profligate descriptions of the natural
world, with as many as ten synonyms or examples set out to illustrate
the extreme situations the Pranksters and/or Wolfe (as a narrating character) find themselves in. For example, here is a list of the disease-
causing microbes infesting the Warehouse, the Pranksters' San Francisco
headquarters: "The vermin are regaining the upper hand . . . The lice!
The pigeon fleas! The roaches! rats! scabies! impetigo! clap! piles! herpes!
all rising up out of the debris like boils" (346).

Wolfe's alliterative style also helps to give the impression of overcoming the inevitable linear nature of sentences, by making sequential actions seem simultaneous, even in simple description or scene setting: at
La Honda, "Brown dogs belly through the flea clouds outside the house,
coughing fruit flies" (138). Perhaps the most striking result of this
attempt to achieve the effect of everything happening at once is the
number of examples of "tmesis" that appear in the narrative. Tmesis
is the insertion of a word between two syllables of another word:
"unfreakingbelievable," "*in* stark stiff *medias res,*" and – describing how
the Hell's Angels traveled – "*en* mangy raunchy head-breaking fire-
pissing rough-goddamn-housing *masse*" (240, 201, 151). Although he
may have picked up this speech pattern from the "heads" he interviewed, Wolfe uses it deliberately and self-consciously, as shown by his
insertion of a whole sentence in order to delay the completion of the

Spanish sentence "Hay tiempo," meaning "There is time" (261). Wolfe may deliberately be competing with Kesey, taking up the challenge of overcoming narrative's inevitable temporal linearity and breaking all the rules Kesey feels even his first novel, *One Flew over the Cuckoo's Nest,* could not contradict (136), slyly showing Kesey how it is done and making his own bid for timelessness.

There are other signs that Wolfe is taking the Pranksters out of history and connecting them to other mythic groups on visionary quests. His style changes, too, when he resorts to old-fashioned "depth" reporting, dramatizing himself in the first person and showing off his knowledge of supposedly parallel situations in such books as Arthur Clarke's *Childhood's End* and Herman Hesse's *Journey to the East.* In such interpretative passages he sees Kesey as a charismatic leader of the mystical sort, and he quotes Joachim Wach on how religions are founded (114–15), for this is what enabled Wolfe to "understand" and find an explanatory slot for these strange goings-on with Kesey at the center. He does what Kesey refuses to do: he reads the allegorical level out into the referential world (18–19, 25). He links the Pranksters with a revival of mythical-religious feeling, much as Theodore Roszak does in *The Making of a Counter Culture.* Wolfe sometimes cannot resist treating an episode, such as the Pranksters' "Hieronymus Bosch" bus trip back east, as an "allegory of life" (65), and, as Whelan points out, he côntrols our perception of Kesey's adventures by imposing an "epic shape on the loose materials." In effect he creates a "classical tragedy" out of Kesey's rise to prominence, his becoming a larger-than-life superhero to his followers (the "Chief" is Kesey's main sobriquet), revealing the flaw of hubris in his refusal to "acknowledge limitations" imposed by straight society (Whelan 82) and failing in his attempts to break through to a new consciousness and "make this thing permanent" (290). Thus the novel ends with a small remnant of Pranksters at a club, playing, to an ever-diminishing crowd, unintelligible music with the recurring refrain "We blew it!"[16]

Wolfe is not recuperating the Pranksters on his own, of course. The most spectacular of Prankster signifying practices, their "collage aesthetic," featuring fantastic apparel and collections of colorful geegaws (145), was easily commodified by commercial culture and sold as the hippie "lifestyle." This practice not only ends the possibility of creating a separate realm of art by aestheticizing everyday life but challenges "straight" culture and its naturalized patterns of appearance by offering its explicit, attention-getting style to be "read." Hebdige borrows Breton's surrealist manifesto to describe how "the subversion of common sense, the collapse of prevalent logical categories and oppositions (dream/reality, work/play) and the celebration of the abnormal and the forbidden" signal a radical practice and bring about a new reality (105). This project is co-opted by the forces of commodification, which naturalize its defiant representations by detaching them from their meaning and encasing them in packaging so that they are inoffensive. (This is how we recognize "straight" culture: that is, we do not notice it.)

It can be argued that the purpose of the Pranksters' disruption of normal sequence and schedules, of their flag and Day-Glo costumes, of this mixing up of practices and objects from various symbol systems to form new chains of signifiers, has been simply to keep ahead of the imitators and hangers-on who would water down the intense significance of the practice and therefore render negligible the difference of the subculture from the consensual practice. The innovators also have to struggle to remain the primary group, originating practices farther out in "Edge City" (thus Kesey's movement "beyond acid") and spreading them to larger groups of people without in turn being taken over by the masses. The reason their project was so easily co-opted, however, is that their breakdown of the separate categories of work and play, the interpenetration of social life and artistic creativity, the move from separate quarters to communal living, and even the creation at moments of the "group mind," coincided with a shift in consumer culture (fed by the postwar economic boom and the perfection of commercial television programming) that led "producers to broaden the concept of commodity into the totalizing notion of life-style" (Whelan 76).

This commodification of style is possible because the signifiers – which the subculture has itself pried apart from their usual signifieds, to make new meanings and to construct an alternative discourse based on different logic and messages – are separated from their referents and sold for their style; they no longer signify "revolutionary" or "opposition" (Hebdige 102–4). For example, the Pranksters' coveralls, patched with cutouts from American flags, which Wolfe spots as ten or fifteen "flags" walking around the dilapidated San Francisco Warehouse pad, may be interpreted in various ways, but the messages all "mean" by disrupting conventional, naturalized codes (11, 13); like props in a guerrilla-theater performance, they call attention to middle-class values that run toward "regimentation and militarism" (Whelan 74).

Wolfe, too, is guilty of this commodification insofar as his effusive, excessive style fetishizes language. By calling attention to words for their own sake, as in his use of synonym or redundancy, pleonasm, and catalogs and lists, he in effect separates style from subject. To some extent, readers and critics exaggerate this effect by emphasizing his sometimes dazzling techniques for their own sake, counting the number of exclamation points or dwelling on his unusual punctuation marks (series of colons or dots)[17] and idiosyncratic typography (all capital letters, italic for emphasis). Wolfe's critics seize on these aberrations to marginalize his production, but those features may actually mask a rather traditional structure if we read *The Electric Kool-Aid Acid Test* as epic or sentimental pastoral. In this case, Wolfe gives more comfort to conservatives than to leftist readers. As Whelan points out, "Wolfe himself makes extensive note of, even while trying to minimize the importance of, these many 'mannerisms' " (84), and he is proud of being lavishly parodied (Introduction 21–2). Apparently he puts on the style as a form of disguise, so that his point of view will not be detected; even if this is not his intention, the effect is a failure to separate his point of view from those of his characters and thus to take responsibility for what he sees and says. It is here, over such matters as Wolfe's use of what he calls "downstage" narration, that critics tend to divide, and so it comes back to the reader and one's reading practice to decide whether Wolfe is a countercultural or subcultural stylist or, after all, only a sheep in wolf's clothing: a sentimental pastoralist, asserting the primacy of instinctual needs and the possibility of recovering a lost paradise.

By considering various mainstream critics' analyses of Wolfe's strategy in various narratives, we can see why it is potentially radical, that is, threatening to the status quo. According to Cohen, by "blurring" the genres that preserve the hegemony of dominant institutions (allowing them to determine "what kinds of knowledge count as social knowledge" and "what kinds of utterances legitimately serve as the basis for making social decisions or instituting social change"), Wolfe and other New Journalists are able to substitute the individual's perception for traditional societal judgments (7). They make one's "everyday experience" an interpretive frame equivalent to that of mainstream institutions such as journalism (expressed by their reviewers and critics as well as by reporters and editorial writers) in their power to determine reality, that is, what is real or true. Thus "the life of the individual becomes the primary text from which one can 'read off' the meanings that structure social relations" (8). The problem with this is that Wolfe's practice is frequently deficient in reflexivity, or in giving some idea of the individual who is "reading off" these meanings. Critics claim that he rarely separates himself from the points of view he adopts, in order to take responsibility for what he reports, either by constructing a persona or by showing the observing perspective within a particular context. He seems, Trachtenberg states, not to care whether he gives his reader enough clues to interpret; he asserts authority without showing why he is able to, which he could do by dramatizing his own participation ("What's New?" 301).[18]

When Wolfe falls in with Prankster practice, he becomes part of the "group thing" instead of remaining outside as commentator. This ability to enter into text, achieved primarily through frequent, unsignaled shifts of point of view and adoption of the tone of an unspecified character within a particular setting, is his most radical technique and makes him deviant in the eyes of mainstream journalists. In fact, because they cannot locate the Wolfean narrator in these sections, his critics assume that such a passage is "a virtual endorsement of the attitudes it mimics" (Edwards 540). Trachtenberg takes the tone of these adopted voices as equivalent to Wolfe's, whereas according to Wolfe the excited or gleeful narration comes from adopting a character's point of view or, in *Kool-Aid,* that of the group mind ("What's New" 300–1). For example, here is the collective reaction to the hallucinogens Kesey and his circle were taking early in 1960, thanks to their volunteering as guinea pigs for neuropharmacological research at the Menlo Park Veterans Administration hospital and their discovery of mail-order peyote:

> Well shee-ut. An' I don't reckon we give much of a damn any more about the art of living in France, either, boys, every frog ought to have a little paunch, like Henry Miller said, and go to bed every night in pajamas with collars and piping on them – just take a letter for me and mail it down to old Morris at Morris Orchids, Laredo, Texas, boys, tell him about enough peyote cactus to mulch all the mouldering widows' graves in poor placid Palo Alto. Yes. (41)

This passage is too demonstrably the free indirect discourse of the Pranksters to be Wolfe's attitude toward the stuff (he claims to have taken only one psychedelic – LSD – once, for research purposes, and to have found it uncomfortably disorienting), but neither is this account of the sensations attributable to a single character.

Wolfe insists (in the introduction to *The New Journalism*) that this innovative practice happened by accident, when he began to experiment with the voice of the narrator, sometimes considering it as a stand-in for the reader and letting us have a go at the subject, allowing us to "talk to the characters, hector them, insult them, prod them with irony or condescension, or whatever." "Why," he asks, "should the reader be expected to just lie flat and let these people come tromping through as if his mind were a subway turnstile?" (17). Thus his practice sometimes overcomes the subject-object split of classic realism and objective journalism, for we cannot tell where the narrator leaves off and the voice or thoughts of a character (or the characters or surroundings) begin. Cohen has shown why this ambiguity is threatening to the clear demarcation between categories such as fact and fiction, journalism and entertainment (he quotes Derrida on "The Law of Genre"): "Since genres define themselves by establishing exclusionary criteria through which they constitute themselves as 'a set of identifiable or codifiable traits,' those elements which impugn their boundaries necessarily threaten the entire classificatory system" (5). No wonder those who champion mainstream objective practices respond to such violations with cries of "impurity, anomaly or monstrosity" (Derrida, in Cohen 5).

When Kesey's outlaw status is made explicit by his flight to Mexico to avoid an almost-certain prison sentence in California on two sets of drug-possession charges, Wolfe departs his furthest from the textual equivalent of conventional society, too. He uses stream of consciousness; a "hectoring narrator" representing Kesey's paranoid voice, who counts down the seconds until an imagined rearrest; narration by a voice that sounds like the personification of the Low Rent Mexican surroundings; and all manner of typographical representation of this deviance (chaps. 21–5). It is almost as if he had said, with Kesey, "If society wants me to be an outlaw, then I'll be an outlaw, and a damned good one. That's something people need" (235). When Kesey's rampant paranoiac fantasies cause him to practice a Cornel Wilde getaway into the jungle, followed by real (or imagined) narcotics agents, Wolfe abandons conventional text boundary markers to accompany him:

> He can feel it. There is a vibration on the parasympathetic efferent fibres behind the eyeballs and it hums
> HRRRRRRRRRRAMANNNNNNNNNNNN
> Two of them one brown dumpy Mex with gold-handle butt gun one crewcut American FBI body-snatcher watching him flying like a monkey over the wall into the jungle the brown Mex holds gold gun but the brain behind that face too brown moldering Mex earth to worry about couldn't hit a peeing dog
> PLUNGE
> into the lapping P.V. fronds bursting orchid and orange the motor homunculus working perfect now powerful gallop into the picturebook jungles of Mexico (267)

The narration of these Mexican chapters represents the sentimental extreme of Wolfe's yearning for unity, or the "all" feeling of simple pastoralism. Appropriately, it is in rural Mexico that Kesey realizes his escape is a failure, and he returns to California, is arrested on the outstanding warrants, and announces the decision to go "beyond acid" (290). His flight to the wilderness has failed, as all attempts to escape to the past must fail. The decision of Kesey and his entourage to return and go beyond the "loop-the-loop of the lag" which is the LSD experience is a move toward accepting the counterforce implicit in complex pastoral; "it is either make this thing permanent inside of you or forever just climb draggled up into the conning tower every time for one short glimpse of the horizon" (290). The equivalent for Wolfe would be to acknowledge the part played by his habitual ways of seeing – for starters, his American Studies Ph.D., his personal fastidiousness and psychological uptightness (as revealed by his white suits and anachronistic style of everyday dress) – on his particular perception of Kesey and the Pranksters.

Instead, Wolfe falls back on the assertion that his are the techniques of "social realism," and that his goal is to make the screen between reader and characters disappear (Introduction 34). This goal is similar to the Pranksters' quest for simultaneity and to the "erasure of history" of postmodernist architecture and multinational corporate culture, which gives the illusion of no "before" and "after," only an integrated "now" of instantaneous communication and representation (Whelan 78, 67). Wolfe's attempt to frame his work as literary journalism is misguided. If Wolfe, like Kesey, manages to overcome the lag between experience and the representation of it, "the subjective and the objective," he will make it all present, collapse time and make history irrelevant. This is an aesthetic goal, and achieving it, as when Wolfe collapses the distance between being in the scene and depicting it from outside, or controlling the reading by emphasizing timelessness or transcendence, effectively defeats the tension necessary for reflexive pleasure.

We are back at Hemingway's theory of the journalist as constructed like a photographic plate, registering impressions that are transmitted through his typewriter until he wears out and "ceases to register when exposed." Hemingway, too, wanted to "create conditions" (to state "the real thing" "purely enough" [*Death* 2]) so that readers could experience what was impossible to put into words – *"that feeling,* the sublime *kairos"* (*Kool-Aid* 205). Wolfe develops Hemingway's behaviorist aesthetic in more detail (in a section called "The Physiology of Realism," in his introduction to *The New Journalism* [47–9]), but he follows Hemingway in his belief in objectivity. To Wolfe, "The most gifted writers are those who manipulate the memory sets of the reader in such a rich fashion that they create within the mind of the reader an entire world that resonates with the reader's own real emotions" (48). Thus, despite its characteristics of reflexivity, much of Wolfe's work ends up suppressing its readers' tendency to see themselves as "participant[s] in the construction of the social world" (Dahlgren 104) – especially when it is read, as Wolfe encourages us to do, under a paradigm of nonfiction as "what actually happened."

In contrast, Norman Mailer, comparing the journalist's and novelist's world view, says that journalism, with its empirical methods, is locked into the outmoded world view of positivism:

> Journalism assumes the truth of an event can be found by the use of principles which go back to Descartes. (A political reporter has a fixed view of the world; you may plot it on axes which run right to left on

the horizontal and down from honesty to corruption on the vertical.)
Indeed, the real premise of journalism is that the best instrument for
measuring history is a faceless, even a mindless, recorder. Whereas the
writer of fiction is closer to that moving world of Einstein. There the
velocity of the observer is as crucial to the measurement as any object
observed. (Preface, *Some Honorable Men* ix)

Unlike Wolfe, who believes that the tale of the "extraordinary decade"
of the sixties will be told "in terms of manners and morals," not history
or politics (Introduction 29), Mailer wants to change the way reporters
write about events, not simply add fictional techniques to reporting in
order to challenge novelists. By making the difference between journalism and fiction equivalent to a paradigm shift in physics, Mailer moves
the emphasis from questions of form (fiction's aesthetic superiority) or
content (its fictivity) to their interrelationship. Similarly, in the well-
known conceit at the beginning of Part 2 of *Armies of the Night,* Mailer
likens history to an instrument of observation (a telescope) and refers to
himself as "master builder of the tower" and "lens grinder of the telescopes" used to study the horizon. In sharp contrast is Wolfe's belief in
the power of social realism borrowed from novelists, which leads to his
avoidance of first person and emphasis on point of view or extensive
focalization of his characters and hence a representation of their subjectivity, not his.[19]

Once again, the political practice of countercultural journalism founders on the reflexivity-objectivity or fiction-nonfiction distinction. If
Wolfe and the reader come down on one side – the "real world" or the
representation, illusion or language – they foreclose other possibilities,
in effect making the choice that causes them, as the narrator of *Invisible
Man* says about a character who could not stand the dialectical tension
of his position as both critical outsider and essentialized Other, to fall
"outside of *history*" (Ellison 434). To be outside of time is to be outside
of history.

Wilfrid Sheed chooses the fictional side in his analysis of the effect of
Wolfe's prose. He says that Wolfe holds a mirror up to nature, but it is
a "fun-house mirror" (295). Sheed acknowledges the fictionality of
Wolfe's strategy, taking it as the sign of a novelist, whose "real subject
is his imagination" (295). According to him, no one reads Wolfe to find
out what really happened, that is, as the social realist he claims to be,
but to learn his take on cultural matters. Thus Sheed is not bothered by
what his ear picks up, which is that every Wolfean subject is treated in
similar language; he says "it obliterates uniqueness and drags everything
back to Wolfe's cave," which is "what artists do" (295). It is rather
surprising that Sheed calls this form of realism "literary," for in general,
as Hersey notes, the realistic novelist is expected to particularize charac-

ters to give the illusion they are real ("Legend" 10–12).[20] In journalism the reader is likely to be aware that a character's thoughts must be filtered through the narrator's and ought not to be surprised that it picks up signs of the mediator as it passes.

Sheed goes toward one pole: acknowledging the fictionality but attributing it to the artist's point of view, which says it does not matter whether events are true or false. If one agrees with Wolfe's ridicule of leftist and liberal movements and actions – in works like *Radical Chic and Mau-Mauing the Flak Catchers* (1970) as well as in *Kool-Aid* – this may be fine. But if the critic or reader wants to counter the politics of his position and to show that what Wolfe does in collections like *The Pump House Gang* and *Mauve Gloves, Madmen, Clutter and Vine* is also political, albeit pertaining to the politics of culture, she needs to have some strategy, some way of reading to distinguish its political position. Just because the style appears radical does not mean that the work is.

Whelan believes that the Prankster project, and by implication, Wolfe's, should be evaluated on the basis of its challenge to the autonomy of art, and thus on its continuation of the "historical avantgarde" (74).[21] The easy commodification of this conspicuous style is evidence of the co-optation of history by aesthetics, but Wolfe has not been so easily co-opted. He still poses a threat to both traditional journalism and to the cause of "moral fiction," which depends on the community's ability to distinguish fact from fiction, as demonstrated by more recent brouhahas over *The Right Stuff* and his manifesto for the new urban novel of social realism, "Stalking the Billion-footed Beast."[22] To my mind, Wolfe does not effectively challenge the separation of art from everyday practice, as the Pranksters do. Instead, he brazenly reverses the hierarchy of prose modes, making the low the high, valuing Low Rent surroundings, regarding Lumpenprole writers and genres as "seizing the power," and romanticizing the violence and sexual excesses of the Hell's Angels and other groups with working-class backgrounds (Introduction 25).[23] By celebrating the low, he in effect elevates it, and so the hierarchy is left in place and the low/Other is aestheticized, thus rendering it politically ineffective.

We can see an example of this tendency in Wolfe's treatment of the Prankster response to the only directly political encounter Kesey and the Pranksters have in *Kool-Aid,* the Vietnam Day Committee antiwar rally in Berkeley in 1965 (chap. 16). The lesson seems to be that in order to avoid co-optation by the "straight" world, even serious political action has to be mocked and "shucked." This is what Wolfe concludes as he watches Kesey undercut the rally's organizers, who have built momentum carefully throughout the day, leading to the moment when fifteen thousand crowd members will march on the Oakland Army Terminal.

Wolfe takes the Prankster leader's performance as specific instructions about reading a style. He shows Kesey watching the preceding speaker and telling first Paul Krassner and then the crowd, "Don't listen to the words, just the sound, and the gestures . . . who do you see?" The answer Krassner offers is Mussolini, and the lesson to the crowd, given in Kesey's laid-back drawl and accompanied by his twangy harmonica against his Pranksters' backup antimusic, is that the whole antiwar movement is working the way fascism does (197).

Wolfe catches Kesey's drift when he describes his performance not in terms of its referents but of its structure, just as Kesey did in keying in on Mussolini's style:

> It's not what *he* is saying, either. It's the sound and the freaking sight and that goddamn mournful harmonica and that stupid Chinese music by the freaks standing up behind him. It's the only thing the martial spirit can't stand – a put-on, a prank, a shuck, a goose in the anus. (199)

This to Wolfe is the message of the Pranksters' signifying style, their peculiar form of bricolage, or improvised response. This style cobbles together an antiestablishment stance – in the Prankster view the "establishment" includes not only the war machine but the antiwar position, which has been deauthenticated by being institutionalized and naturalized – by taking apart conventional codes (military insignia and paraphernalia) and reassembling them to signify their opposite, or perhaps merely to render them meaningless by parodying their style.

It is not the job of the viewer or reader to interpret, to locate the fixed referents of these various signifying practices, Wolfe is saying by the way he narrates this episode, but to "read" them as process, as unfinished or even disruptive to "the way it's supposed to be." If this is so, then no effective political action is possible, for Kesey's attitude is only subversive, only disruptive; it puts nothing in its place and gives the huge Berkeley crowd no impetus for action. By seeming to admire Kesey's performance that day – he does not undercut it, but rather makes fun of the organizers and of the crowd that loses its starch when confronted by troops blocking its way and, instead of marching to its goal, turns off into a park and has a picnic – Wolfe sets up his own polarities between aesthetics and politics. He takes the lesson out to society in general, in order to preserve the stability of those categories he refers to throughout his cultural journalism of the sixties and seventies: culture or politics, intellectuals versus the people, modernism or realism, myth and fable versus social realism, highbrow-lowbrow, and here, the Left as equivalent to fascism on the one hand and anarchism on the other.

In effect, he adopts the "heads" view of all large-scale demonstrations as a kind of fascism, and of oppositional organizations as implicated in the movements they are protesting. The upshot is that when we "go with the flow," when "anything goes," then nothing of significance "goes down," and political action is effectively stymied. Granted, this is a possible interpretation of Kesey's actions that day, and Wolfe did not "make up" Kesey's silence after his release from a work farm late in 1967, nor his retreat to Oregon and a more mainstream life as a writer and teacher. But Wolfe's strategy of not letting the reader in on the construction of the platform from which he observes events and fixes their interpretation in sometimes brilliant prose makes it difficult for even the perspicacious reader to see other interpretations. One alternative is to see that, as Whelan says, although "Kesey's practice has perhaps more in common with the anarchistic, libertarian tendencies of Dada than with the more coherent, Marxist intentions of surrealism or constructivism, . . . it does embody an oppositional politics, tinged with utopianism, firmly against the social status quo" (74).

Not to Wolfe, however, who must reduce oppositions to their simplest form, as when his narrator concludes that the whole countercultural movement in San Francisco had become a carnival, not politics, "because the political thing, the whole New Left, is all of a sudden like *over* on the hip circuit around San Francisco, even at Berkeley, the very citadel of the Student Revolution and all" (318). (This is 1966 he is talking about, by the way.) As the Frankfurt School theorists and Marcuse knew, it was always going to be difficult for alternative political parties and movements to develop under the dominance of what they called the "culture industry" (Horkheimer and Adorno), and certainly a large contribution of Wolfe's novel is his many riffs on the affluence of postwar society and its effects. These include not only consumerism but mass defection from repression, leading to sexual revolution, sensation seeking in drugs and rock music, and other signs of changed consciousness in response to the culture industry's deadening of the senses (see Marcuse). By narrating Kesey's early 1960s adventures in mind expansion at the Menlo Park Veterans Administration Hospital in the same inside-the-scene voice Wolfe uses to evoke Kesey's adolescent trips to the "Neon Renaissance" of drive-ins, fast cars, and the "electro-pastel world of Mom&Dad&Buddy&Sis in the suburbs" (35–7), Wolfe convincingly makes the connection between the counterculture of pleasure and the postwar boom. Indeed, one reason Marcuse became hopeful that an opposition to an "administered" society might emerge was that he believed a potentially revolutionary consciousness lay in "the substratum of the outcasts and outsiders, the exploited and persecuted of other races and other colours, the unemployed and the unemployable" (256), and these "revolutionary forces" now included "students, exploited ethnic minorities, and the peasant masses of the Third World" (Bottomore 38).

Wolfe's final attitude seems clear: the Prankster alternative is reduced to a deviant subculture, easily marginalized, with no effect save that which narratives of their experience communicate to readers. Even when it is viewed as succeeding (as Wolfe thinks Kesey did on Vietnam Day), their alternative is readily seen as complicit with the dominant group that is waging war, because it opposes only ridicule or absurdity to the former's power to coerce or win support.[24] Trachtenberg says, "By disguising itself and its procedures, by mystifying the presence of the author as a merely neutral recorder when he is in fact the only active producer of the product, Wolfe's work is a revealing instance of mass culture. The appearance of spontaneity is the product of the most archmanipulation and manufacture. By pretending to render the world always as someone's experience, from the inside, . . . [h]e converts experience into spectacle, fixes it, reifies it as a reader's vicarious experience" ("What's New?" 301).

The persistence of Wolfe's method is revealed to the reader dipping into almost any section of Richard Cramer's long account of the 1988 presidential primary and election campaigns, *What It Takes,* published during 1992. Cramer recounts the history of this campaign through the interior monologues of six candidates and their aides and families, using historical narration to tell the stories of how the candidates became the men who could say, "Not only should I be President. . . . *I am going to be President"* (viii). Cramer tells in the preface how he came by the characters' thoughts and emotions as they rode the roller coaster to the goal that all but one would lose and checked not only the words and details but the accuracy of the free indirect speech by reading every section back to the candidate involved or to an aide or spouse (ix). Once we get into the thousand-plus pages of the chronicle, we lose the identity of the chronicler; he retreats into the historian's impersonal narrator and engages in the usual expository and "placing" functions.

When Cramer shows us Gary Hart fleeing the press, as news of his extramarital escapades sent him out of the race and home to Colorado, his prose (the shouted questions from reporters, flashbulbs going off) is almost indistinguishable from Wolfe's interior monologues of astronauts facing the press in *The Right Stuff* (Cramer 470). Cramer's representation of Bush's shouted speeches in the last frenetic days of the campaign he was to win is eerily like what we heard in mainstream press accounts of the last futile speeches the incumbent gave in the closing hours of the 1992 race (1015–16). Either the gap between Bush's private incoherence and his public diatribes had closed, and reporters assigned to cover the president had picked up on the techniques of saturation reporting, or perhaps we had begun to read our impressions of these subjective accounts into "straight" ones because they have become part of the frames within which we read, watch, and listen – without our awareness of how they got there.[25] Did we hear Bush differently because satirists like Garry Trudeau and Jules Feiffer refined our ears by making a sort of poetry out of his inarticulateness?

In any case, the predominance of interior monologue and an undramatized narrator in Cramer's narrative report has a curiously ahistorical effect and contrasts highly with the campaign coverage by New Journalists Didion (in *After Henry*), Hunter L. Thompson (*Fear and Loathing on the Campaign Trail*), and above all Mailer's political reporting, beginning with "Superman Comes to the Supermarket" in 1960. We never forget the reporters who are giving their observations and analyzing them (albeit sometimes in excruciating detail) in these works.

A reflexive reading seems to be to be the only strategy to use against texts that tend to reify our experience. An approach that reads Wolfe's books about painting and architecture, *The Painted Word* and *From Bauhaus to Our House,* in terms of how he says what he does – for example, sets his dominant metaphors against the history that results – shows him to be as conservative in his approach to these arts as he is in his wardrobe. (Mary Gordon describes him as often speaking "from a position that comforts the uneasy, taking up a role that has done well by him in the past – the thinking man's redneck" [10].) We should do what Wolfe's practice indicates, not what he says – and continues to say, in his "manifesto for the new social novel" ("Stalking") and in the *Paris Review* interview conducted by George Plimpton ("Art"). We should not look through the screen between us and Wolfe's characters with an eye toward the accuracy or adequacy of the representation in comparison to the real events depicted, for the screen is not "gone," even in more transparent narrative than Wolfe's. Rather we should examine its texture, and the structures created by the narrative as a particular form of cultural configuration.

5

The "Incredibility of Reality" and the Ideology of Form

There is the story of one's hero, and then, thanks to the intimate connexion of things, the story of one's story itself . . . and the latter imbroglio is liable on occasion to strike me as really the more objective of the two.

— Henry James, *The Art of the Novel*

I was driving around the Great Plains looking at different things and I went to the Clutter house in Holcolmb, Kansas. It was kind of spooky walking around out there until I thought of Truman Capote out there on the plains, doing his reporting on their murder. This tiny figure in this landscape. And this big book he was carrying around. And I couldn't help thinking – you know, if he had written that in as well – himself, small, running round – who knows, his entire book might've been different.

— Ian Frazier, author of *Great Plains* (quoted in Als)

One of the common explanations for writers' new or revived interest in producing journalistic narratives is that in such modes they do not have to win the reader's consent to suspend her disbelief. A writer like Tom Wolfe assumes there is a built-in interest factor when the reader knows that *"all this actually happened"* (Introduction 34). Others agree that journalism is easier to produce, for the plot and characters are there for the taking, and the writer does not have to tax her powers of invention (Mailer, *Pontifications* 174–5; Malcolm, *Journalist* 153). One might well wonder, however, whether the popularity of a novel like *In Cold Blood* or a play such as Shakespeare's *Richard II* – in his time or ours – is the result of the reader's desire to hear a true story rather than a hypothetical one.

Here are two explanations to account for the pleasure and involvement we feel in viewing or reading representations of extraordinary characters and events. The first is from Johnson's *Preface to Shakespeare:*

It is false, that any representation is mistaken for reality; that any dramatick fable in its materiality was ever credible, or, for a single moment, was ever credited. . . .

. . . The delight of tragedy proceeds from our consciousness of fiction; if we thought murders and treasons real, they would please no more.

Imitations produce pain or pleasure, not because they are mistaken for realities, but because they bring realities to mind. (254, 256)

The second is from Tom Wolfe's introduction to *The New Journalism:*

[The New Journalism] enjoys an advantage so obvious, so built-in, one almost forgets what a power it has: the simple fact that the reader knows *all this actually happened*. The disclaimers have been erased. The screen is gone. The writer is one step closer to the absolute involvement of the reader that Henry James and James Joyce dreamed of and never achieved. (34)

Dr. Johnson says we are moved because we are aware that what is depicted is fictional; Dr. Wolfe,[1] arguing for the superior power of true-life narratives such as the New Journalism over traditional fiction, insists we are more involved when we know that the characters and what they do are factual. How can these two critics take such opposing (and unexpected) positions in order to explain the reader's or viewer's involvement in what are, after all, always representations? Because in reflexive reading invented and historical materials have the same status, whether in narrative or drama, I credit Johnson's explanation. Occurring in narrative, events are literary and not "real"; they seem real because "they bring realities to mind." (We should note that Johnson does not distinguish between historical subjects and invented ones in this passage, although Shakespeare used both, because he does not need to; he assumes that their status in narrative is the same.) Johnson's explanation accounts for even the frisson of pleasure we get from reading confessions in *Modern Crime* and for that felt by nineteenth-century Americans who followed trial accounts in the *National Police Gazette:* the dramatic representation moves us, when it does, because we credit it "as a just picture of a real original; as representing to the auditor what he would himself feel, if he were to suffer what is there figured to be suffered or to be done" (Johnson 255). The effect is the same whether the text is in narrative or dramatic form; Johnson assures his reader that "a play read, affects the mind like a play acted," while centuries earlier Aristotle, writing in the *Poetics* about the power of tragedy, said that "even without the aid of the eye, he who hears the tale told" will be equally moved (IX.1–3). It is not that we identify ourselves with the characters but that we are reminded of the occasions for such emotions in our lives. As

Johnson says, "We rather lament the possibility than suppose the presence of misery, as a mother weeps over her babe, when she remembers that death may take it from her" (256).

There is of course a difference in status between an actual crime or accident and a dramatization of one, but we may find ourselves responding even to the true-life incident as if it were a play or story; we react the way we do to films or novels because we have learned what to say and how to act from the many dramatizations and narrations of such events we have read and seen. This explanation for the strong emotional response we have to a classic tragedy (Aristotle's theory of catharsis, or purging of pity and fear by witnessing actions which arouse them) may also account for Boswell's reaction to the first public hanging he witnessed, for example. Aristotle writes, "Tragedy . . . is an imitation of an action that is serious, complete, and of a certain magnitude; in language embellished with each kind of artistic ornament . . . ; in the form of action . . . ; through pity and fear effecting the proper purgation of these emotions" (VI.2). And here is Boswell: "My curiosity to see the melancholy spectacle of the executions was so strong that I could not resist it, although I was sensible that I would suffer much from it. . . . There was a most prodigious crowd of spectators. I was most terrible shocked and thrown into a very deep melancholy." Two days later he was so tormented by the recollection that he could not sleep alone, but this was nevertheless the beginning of a long obsession (252–4). Although the two sets of circumstances which arouse our pity and fear are on different experiential planes, our response is the same: a vicarious experiencing of these emotions, which allows us to vent them.

The same is true of our experience of a pleasurable incident in relation to the representation of one. Who can give or receive a diamond ring without some awareness not only of how to respond appropriately but even how to *feel* at that moment, thanks to advertising as well as films, novels, and fairy tales?[2] (Indeed, why is it usually a diamond, and not an emerald or a ruby or some other token?) We have learned our response to the actual from the literary, and although we may not want to go so far as to say, with Wilde's critic Vivian, that London's fogs did not exist before the Impressionists painted them (683), who can deny that our very reactions to a wedding or disaster or a mugging we chance to witness are in a real sense "caused" by our previous experience as viewers and readers of stories?

It is more likely that narrative influences our response to experiences in our lives than that, as Wolfe insists, our knowledge that there are actual historical referents for the characters and events depicted in "true-life" narratives produces the pleasure we take in these narratives. His explanation for the appeal of these texts is misguided, for the attempt to secure admission to literature through the factual, positivist door is inevitably compromised. The dominance of positivism in literature and the social sciences is one of the causes of the subordination of the factual to the fictional or the poetic, and so an insistence on the power of that world view cannot be used to overcome this separation and elevate New Journalism to literature. Contrary to what Wolfe says, the representations of historical incidents in their textual form – in their "materiality" – are not taken for reality itself; they are brought into being by the conventions of narrative or drama. Besides, *after the fact,* events no longer "exist" but are only inferred from narrative or dramatic plots, which we read or see performed.

Texts refer to sign systems that we are accustomed to call "reality" and which appear to us to be an objective world, and therefore whether the referents of the signs (the particular named characters of a text) have actual historical signifieds or not is not an important distinction at the level of the text. These signs are embedded in what Johnson calls the "materiality of the fable," and at this level our experience of any text is the same. We read a true story and an invented one in much the same way, giving ourselves over to the illusion of reality that is created and neglecting the medium of narration, unless it becomes other than transparent. This happens when our attention is drawn by the narrative's self-referentiality (as, for example, when it takes as its subject the process of its own production) or when language is foregrounded, either by the text or the reader. We cease to look "through" language when we deliberately pay attention to the text as made of words, whether or not it attracts us with its opacity or peculiar stylistic qualities.

The differences we do perceive between a story with historical referents and one with completely invented situations and characters are largely owing to the frame, that is, the conventions of the particular genre that it belongs to and that surround its publication in a particular medium. Knowing that Crane's first-person account of his shipwreck adventure appeared on the front page of a New York newspaper, for example, affects our experience of that narrative, because there are journalistic conventions that influence both its writing and our response. Although the conventions of the various subcategories within journalism vary, normally dates and locations are specified, and persons mentioned appear under their true names. The events reported are presumed to be verifiable by other means, although it is not expected that the same story told by another person from a different viewpoint would be narrated in exactly the same way.[3] In other respects the experience of reading an invented tale is identical to that of reading a historical one. Our first reading of "Stephen Crane's Own Story" may indeed be solely to find out "what happened," but this is also true about many novels we read for the first time. The *text's* materiality is the same, whether the events outlined have externally attested counterparts or not, and whether or not the characters have historical referents.

The exploitation of newsworthy historical events in novels is not, of course, new; early English novels often imitated historical narratives, in contrast to the faraway settings of the romance. Their mixing of factual and invented materials was also a means of conveying a realistic sense of the everyday world, and thus gaining credibility for the hypothetical characters and events (see Braudy). Although according to my definition of "nonfiction novel," I would call *Journal of the Plague Year* (1721) a historical novel, because of its invented situations and imaginary narrator, this early novel is many critics' first example of the early and perennial appeal of novels about sensational or infamous historical events. Even defined as a type of narrative discourse which is a subcategory of the novel (it uses fictional conventions but confines its subject and characters to historical materials), the nonfiction novel is not a new form; Boswell's *Life of Johnson* has been read as a novel, for example (see Passler).

Critics of New Journalism and the nonfiction novel nevertheless note the resurgence of such narratives, that is, the frequency with which recent current events and biographical figures are deliberately exploited in narrative form (Hellmann 19–20; Weber, *Literature* 10–12). Mas'ud Zavarzadeh believes that this attention to empirically available "facts" by nonfiction novelists is inevitable, considering the way traditional "interpretive" fiction "reduces the charged quality of experience and consequently presents to the reader an imaginary (almost escapist) world, thin and anemic in comparison with the empirical world" (26). He lays the blame for this state of things not only on the rote methods of novelists and the form's "narrative inertia" since the high modernists but on the "changing modalities of contemporary consciousness" (26). In other words, not only reality but the way we perceive it has "deeply altered," rendering outmoded all totalizing systems and "totalistic" discourses. Zavarzadeh attributes these changes to our "technetronic" culture and the fragmentation of society as well as to the disintegration of a coherent world view largely as a result of scientific discoveries and theories (57). John Hellmann agrees that American reality underwent a "profound transformation" beginning in the 1960s (8).

The best-known version of the fictivity of the real is perhaps that expressed in 1961 by novelist Philip Roth, who lamented the absence of a credible world shared by people who watched television or read the newspapers at the beginning of the 1960s. Apparently the creation of a common, ordinary perception of life was no longer possible in fiction. In his words,

the American writer in the middle of the twentieth century has his
hands full in trying to understand, and then describe, and then make
credible much of the American reality. It stupefies, it sickens, it infuri-
ates, and finally it is even a kind of embarrassment to one's own mea-
ger imagination. The actuality is continually outdoing our talents, and
the culture tosses up figures almost daily that are the envy of any novelist. (224)

This notion has been so often repeated (and this passage quoted) that by
now it has the inevitability of fact. It has become a truism that this
"absurd" reality is a valid explanation of the abandonment of literary
realism and the turn either toward fabulism or "superfiction" or toward
documentary forms which do not attempt to re-create the world but
only to record the data it offers to the observer (Lodge, *Novelist* 33–4;
Zavarzadeh 38–43).[4] Thus we get narrative forms that resort to verifiable facts and documentary records, and assurances from authors of
"immaculate factuality" and accuracy in order to secure credibility for
their narratives.[5]

An important question is raised by these explanations: what is it that
makes our world so incredible? Surely the reality of life during war, a
famine, or a plague is horrific to the people who live through these
catastrophes, and to an enslaved or victimized people daily existence
must frequently seem preposterous. The century that has included
World War I, with its thousands of casualties in short, intense battles
and millions through the attrition of trench warfare; the Jewish Holocaust; the saturation bombing of World War II and the use of the atomic
bomb on a civilian population; and the threat of, first, nuclear winter
and, later, global warming is indeed loaded with both terrible actuality
and unspeakable possibility. But this is not what Roth is writing about,
nor are these catastrophes part of our ordinary daily experience. We
experience reality not simply as members of a large human community
but on an individual basis, and unless we are members of a persecuted
race or despised class, or suffer in prison or slavery or illness – deplor-
able situations that have always been part of human history – these
large-scale catastrophes or personal persecutions do not affect our day-
to-day experience. What is it, then, that makes life in the mid-twentieth
century so incredible?[6]

We get a hint of an answer when we learn that Roth was not the first
novelist to complain of a reality that was outdoing his textual efforts.
Nathanael West, writing in *Contact* in 1932, bewailed the press exploitation of a domain he regarded as his:

> In America violence is idiomatic. Read our newspapers. To make the
> first page a murderer has to use his imagination, he has to use a particu-
> larly hideous instrument. Take this morning's paper: FATHER CUTS

son's throat in baseball argument. It appears on an inside page. To
make the first page, he should have killed three sons with a baseball
bat instead of a knife. Only liberality and symmetry could have made
this daily occurrence interesting. (50)

Reading this complaint, written nearly thirty years before Roth's, we
realize, because both writers are using examples from the news media,
that it is not reality itself nor even one's individual experience of reality
that has become incredible or absurd but the illusion of reality as represented in textual forms – newspaper, radio, television, and film. As
Hellmann notes, "[w]e have been disoriented not merely by the surreal
events of contemporary life" but "by the insufficiently explained, unfelt,
and anonymously formulated versions of them which the conventional
media provide" (5).

When we look at Roth's influential article to see specifically what
reality he finds "unreal" (what constructed "reality" he has become
aware of himself watching), we discover that he is talking about preposterous images that have been created, not reproduced, by the enabling
forms that report them to us. His leading example is not simply a
brutal double murder case (that of the Grimes sisters) but the blitzkrieg
coverage by the Chicago newspapers that first made the girls into average "good girls" and then exploited the revelations of a suspect by
turning the case into a combination tabloid adventure chronicle and
television game show. The hoopla surrounding the case increased to the
point that mass donations poured in to the girls' mother and a contest
was held, asking, "How Do You Think the Grimes Girls Were Murdered?" In another of his examples, a radio station offers "a series of
cash prizes for the three best television plays of five minutes' duration
written by children."

Then too, in Roth's view, the preparations for the first nationally
televised presidential debates in 1960 were a circus, because the medium
of communicating them profoundly affected the objects of its attention;
Richard Nixon came to seem an invented character. To Roth, he might
as well have been a literary creation, for "as a real public image, a
political fact, my mind balked at taking him in."

> All the machinations over make-up, rebuttal time, all the business
> over whether Mr. Nixon should look at Mr. Kennedy when he re-
> plied, or should look away – all of it was so beside the point, so fantas-
> tic, so weird and astonishing, that I found myself beginning to wish I
> had invented it. That may not, of course, be a literary fact at all, but a
> simple psychological one – for finally I began to wish that *someone* had
> invented it, and that it was not real and with us. (225)

This business is not "real," but it is "with us," and has been since
popular prints and commercial photography made Abraham Lincoln the

first media president.[7] What Roth was responding to in the article he published in 1961 was the presentation, the *im*mediacy of the images entering his house via the newly ubiquitous television set, and because the perception of these manipulated images was fresh (less "real" because they were incongruous), the ones on the screen seemed to outdo the created characters in Roth's novels.

In *Pieces,* Mailer gives a witty, mock-paranoid account of his own awakening to the "betrayal" by the supposedly neutral medium of television of what he thought had been his own "splendid" appearance, with Truman Capote, on David Susskind's show "Open End" in the 1960s. Viewing a kinescope of the show allowed him to form the hypothesis "that television is not a technological process that reproduces images of real life by way of electronics, but is rather a machine (more or less cosmically operated) to anticipate the judgments and/or anathema of Limbo; the technicians pitch in with camera angles" (41). The phenomenon that certain people appear very attractive on television while others come across as evasive, untrustworthy, or detached and pompous is familiar to viewers of presidential debates since 1960; although it is couched in customary Mailerian terms of cosmic forces, it is one way to understand the effects of media on our perception of "reality" and to understand why we believe reality itself has changed significantly. "Telegenic quality" and its effect on the political process is something that statesmen and candidates appearing before mass audiences in the preelectronic age certainly did not have to worry about.

With time and familiarity, ubiquitous images become naturalized – to the point where Americans could elect an actor as president without finding his preparation for the role inappropriate and with admiration for how he read his "lines." Because of the subtle education we got, during Ronald Reagan's two terms, in the interchangeability of simulation and reality (caused by what Michael Rogin calls "the psychological shift from an embodied self to its simulacrum on film" [3]), we find it more and more difficult to distinguish what is an actual presidential statement or belief from what has been provided by a speechwriter, a photo opportunity, an aide or "handler," or a spin doctor. Thus it is almost impossible for us to understand Roth's astonishment at Nixon's conscious television strategy.[8]

What cultural critics who use the "altered nature of reality" to explain the "death of the novel" ought to emphasize is the mythicizing objectification of the world by the media through which we get much of our "news." The "reality" the mass media cover – the object of their attention – has become indistinguishable from the way they cover it. The theory Judith Williamson has developed to "decode" advertisements also explains how any public form of image transmission –

newspaper, film, television – works: shared images of the world perceived through the mass media become more "objective" than our individual experience.

> As a teenager, for example, it is really possible to live almost totally in a sort of dream world of magazine stories and images, and this *seems more real than reality* – though few people will admit it. The reason for this "reality" is that the social dream – dream though it is – is a *shared* one: what is *commonly* perceived (in the sense of a shared – though also a frequent – perception) has a more "objective" status than something particular to ourselves. People's real experience may be very similar but it remains isolated while what *is* a universal experience is the impact of media and social images. (170)

We get most of our "news" about the world from these "objectifying" sources – for example, our knowledge of politics, celebrities, crime and other social problems, even many of our ideas about our neighbors' lives – since television has frequently replaced the backyard, over-the-fence chat. For example, none of us knows "the real" Richard Nixon, but many of us know some version of him through news media; this composite presentation of his image becomes the reality for us. Consider the different "Richard Nixon" characters that we derive from texts as varied as the autobiographical *Six Crises;* Mark Harris, *Mark, the Glove Boy* (an account of covering Nixon's ill-fated run for governor of California in 1962); journalistic accounts of his press conferences, including televised versions; Joe McGinniss, *The Selling of the President;* Robert Woodward and Carl Bernstein, *All the President's Men;* Philip Roth, *Our Gang;* Robert Coover, *The Public Burning;* and the documentary *Millhouse*.[9] None of these is the "real" or original Richard Nixon, because he is not a text, but the fact that he is a historical character certainly affects our response to these plots and sends us out to the real world where he exists and to other texts with differing representations that are also interpretations.

Martin Scorsese's 1983 film *The King of Comedy* reveals the built-in constitutive powers of an apparently transparent form like television or film even more elaborately. In it comedian Jerry Lewis, an actor with a complex dramatized persona built up over scores of film, television, and telethon appearances, has the role of a famous television talk-show host, Jerry Langford, whose life is invaded by a fanatical fan named Rupert Pupkin (played by Robert DeNiro). Pupkin cannot see his hero's private identity as separate from the much more real one that comes into his home on a daily basis (just as viewers invariably read the Jerry Lewis persona into Langford). The film is so intertexual and parodic that its referentiality is continually undercut. Film and television conventions are explicitly highlighted: characters imitate other characters' actions;

actors like Tony Randall play themselves, and a director plays Langford's producer; Pupkin's mother's lines are read by Scorsese's (the director's) mother. Pupkin practices for his hoped-for television appearance by interviewing flat cardboard figures of guests. The film's self-parody makes it impossible to ignore the medium and therefore undermines the transparent illusion created by the other level of the film (as well as our our habitual suspension of disbelief while watching movies).[10]

We now generally ignore the distinction between the medium and the mediated, but at some cost. For if we give ourselves up to this shared reality, instead of distinguishing it from the form which presents it as objectively "real," we lose all chance of a "true knowledge of social realities" (Williamson 170). We begin to regard the medium as transparent, thereby missing the ideology inherent in realistic media as well as in less transparent forms. Bill Nichols says, "Ideology appears to produce not itself, but the world. It proposes obviousness, a sense of 'the way things are,' within which our sense of place and self emerges as an equally self-evident proposition" (2). With regard to advertising, television "entertainment," publicity in any form, we accept our place as subjects and viewers, that is, as receivers of information and consumers of products, and although we reserve to ourselves a choice about what we accept or reject, this choice proves to be as illusory as the "reality" presented to us in mass forms.[11]

"Reality" is not something that has changed in the twentieth century to the extent that the only way to ensure that a reader will credit a realistic account of events or characters is to reproduce it with fidelity to facts and to the sensory environment, with a goal of "zero degree of interpretation" (Zavarzadeh 41). The belief that reality is outdoing the ability of our best writers to make sense of it may actually be based on fear of the power of texts, rather than on their ineffectuality in the face of an utterly changed reality. After all, what has altered that reality (and our experience of it) so much as texts – not only scientific theories such as relativity and indeterminacy, which acknowledge the effect of perception on what we perceive, and thus shift the ground of reality itself, but the texts which apply those concepts to everything from politics and history to literature and art. (What discipline does not have an account of paradigm shifts in its history, thanks to Thomas Kuhn's landmark study *The Structure of Scientific Revolutions?*)

In other words, most thinking people are aware of the power of texts to determine what we believe, and therefore to affect actuality. But many readers do not want to acknowledge the constitutive power of texts labeled "journalism," "history," "biography." How else can we explain the resistance to theories of textuality, indeed to the narratological approach to history? If history turns out to be not simply all the things that happen (or "one thing after another") but narratives from which we recover particular ideas about the sequentiality and possible meaning of those events, then how are we to decide the authority of what "really" happened and what it ultimately means? The dominant modes of objectivity and realism in our journalistic and fictional narratives and our primary systems of visual representations (the electronic media, film, and publicity) do not enable the production of a complex "news" discourse. Consequently our experience of the world is attentuated, and we develop what Peter Dahlgren calls "non-reflexive consciousness" (104). Although his example of a news discourse that fosters nonreflexivity in its audience is television news, its aural dimension and the quality of the viewer involvement it fosters make it clearly analogous to other discourses, such as print journalism.

On the other hand, viewer (or reader) reflexivity is politically enabling. If we read self-consciously, we can visualize ourselves as "active participant[s] in the construction of the social world depicted." "Reflexivity would make it possible for the viewer to consider, in a practical and normative way, alternative possibilities to present social circumstances. The reflective consciousness is one which learns from its own shared social experiences – from its own history – to contemplate the present in a critical way" (104). Dahlgren's analysis suggests that we can become reflexive readers of texts, even those that do not encourage it, by becoming conscious of their effect on us and what kind of reader they imply, as well as of how they are structured. The notion of locating reflexivity in viewer or reader consciousness means that we who read and watch television and films can resist hegemonic values and recover almost any text for political use by relating works of literature to social conditions and working to break down the distinctions which perpetuate literature as an elitist domain. This changed reading practice is not easy, however, for what works against it is the reified consciousness that Lukacs says is endemic in modern life under capitalism. The consequence of this reified consciousness is to make what is presented appear normal, and not something we can affect. We are not encouraged to consider alternatives to the way things are, simply to accept them, or to adjust our "way of life, mode of work and hence of consciousness" to social reality as it seems to be (Lukacs 98). This reified consciousness is also behind the prevalence of the belief in the horrific quality of reality.

Whereas many people can probably accept these claims about the role of the news and entertainment media in dramatizing everyday reality, they may not agree that all narratives should be read on the model of literature, that is, reflexively, especially those describing the horrors of contemporary life – whether of a single gruesome crime and its aftermath or of war and its mass deaths "in a gas chamber or a radioactive city" (Mailer, *Advertisements* 300). Rather than treating these narratives as complex interpretations of recent history or lessons in art's power to shape realities, critics tend to regard them as documentary forms calling less on their authors' imaginative capacity than on their ability to transcribe events that have exceeded ordinary conceptual frames. George Steiner, comparing the reports and testimonial literature of World War II to the imaginative representations of World War I by Ford, Cummings, and Hemingway, says, "Fiction falls silent before the enormity of the fact, and before the vivid authority with which that fact can be rendered by unadorned report" (388).

The usual response of interpreters of this history is to reify the horror as separate from human causation. When critics assert our inability, and that of our creative writers, to come to terms with what the "Faustian urge to dominate nature" has wrought (Mailer, *Advertisements* 300), they are describing some form of reification. Fredric Jameson defines this as "a disease of that mapping function whereby the individual subject projects and models his or her insertion into the collectivity" ("Reflections" 212). The effect of this "disease" is to isolate us: according to Raymond Williams, "the active 'subject' [is] replaced by the neutral 'observer' " and separated from the "objective reality" it can only contemplate, rather than engage. One of the main causes is that language is no longer viewed as constitutive but instrumental (*Marxism* 32). The most influential theorist of reification is Georg Lukacs, who develops this concept in *History and Class Consciousness*. We noted in Chapter 3 his analysis of how objective journalism contributes to our reified consciousness by positing the separation of a neutral observer – including the reader, who is inserted into this position in reading – from the objective world. In journalism, says Lukacs, reporters lose their subjectivity, for they subordinate their "knowledge, temperament and powers of expression" to the conventions of objectivity; they act as though they can separate all these from their personal response and detach themselves from the subject they are examining and writing about. Reification is the best explanation of why reporters appear to have no "convictions": they must deny them, which means setting aside their "experiences and beliefs" (100).

Similarly, because objectivity in realistic fiction implies the separation of observer from objectified world, imagination or inner truth is regarded as separate from and on a higher level than external, objective truth. The reader experiencing a Hemingway story is like the worker or scientist contemplating not only "an objective external world" but "the objectified constructs of his own mind, which he takes to be incorpo-

rated in the external world" – Lukacs's description of reified consciousness (Porter 25). In Chapter 2 I described how the naturalization of
"things as they are" seems to result from the objective form of realism
developed by Hemingway and other modernist writers; they thus contributed mightily to the construction of the "second nature" that we
inhabit in the twentieth century. The reified world we inhabit is produced by just such naturalistic texts, multiplied and dispersed throughout in many media, including what Berger et al. call the system of
"publicity" (*Ways of Seeing* chap. 7). In Richard Peterson's view, "We
are so steeped in the conventions and assumptions of realism that we
find it difficult even when someone points it out to recognize how
thoroughly they determine our ideas of what is good art and what is
artistically 'true' " (170).

How can we expect the flat, objective, distancing strategies of either
fictional or journalistic narrative to be able to express the "integral and
pervasive political terror, social exploitation, technological dehumanization viciousness" of our century? (Widmer 142). This kind of narrative
has been aestheticized, and that is the underlying reason why critics call
the documentary style of *Hiroshima* "fictional": not that the techniques
are borrowed from fiction but that the effect they achieve has been
declared normative in modern literature or art. Modernism is committed
to the separation of art from social life, to its transcendence of history
and everyday culture. A meaningful political narrative is difficult under
such criteria, in Marcuse's definition of politics: "the practice in which
the basic societal institutions are developed, defined, sustained, and
changed. It is the practice of individuals, no matter how organized they
may be" (250).

Reification thus takes many forms, and many of them are relevant to
my discussion of the separation of fact from fiction and the various
theories of contemporary narrative that rely on a changed reality. Tom
Wolfe's division of political action into two opposed sets of beliefs or
practices, because he denies the process of sorting out the alternatives, is
a form of reification. He and Kesey hypostasize the choice open to
anti–Vietnam War demonstrators as either "Turn your back on the
whole thing" or "You are a supporter." This reduction of possibilities
to binary oppositions seems inevitable under a system that denies what
Jameson, in "Reification and Utopia in Mass Culture," calls "authentic
collective life" (140). In the absence of opportunities for collective expression of our lives in late capitalist society, the ideological alternatives
come in pairs like modernity or tradition, community versus society.
Jameson says that even the superstructure takes two forms – modernism
or mass culture – and that the two are symptoms of the reification of
modern consciousness.[12] Distinctions like highbrow and lowbrow, fic-

tion and nonfiction, fantasy and reality, arise from the same processes. This separation makes sense when we consider Karl Marx's description of the world's commodity structure under capitalism; reification describes not only the way humans are alienated from their labor but the way social relations take a "natural" form. Marx shows that "the forces of production take on the aspect of a natural alien power over humans increasingly as the latter 'forget' that the labor process has created all these forces of production" (Aronowitz 46–7). We overlook our history or, as Barthes says, turn history into nature (*Mythologies* 11).[13]

Reification is related to the literariness of texts in two ways: when we assume that narratives are produced in a fit of inspiration, as though divinely inspired; or when we treat them as part of the aesthetic world, separate from historical and social contexts. In either case we reify their real relations to a particular audience, producer, and context. For example, modernist writers and critics contribute to a reified consciousness when they respond to an increasingly commodified society, where written expression is treated like just another product, by emphasizing the division between intellectual and manual labor, or between artistic expression and pragmatic texts, reserving a place for autonomous art and artists above mass culture. In effect they contribute to the objectification of human life that they deplore, for the aesthetic definition of art arises out of the impulse to separate it from the world of commodities and mechanical reproduction, which emphasizes objects' utilitarian function (see Benjamin, "Work of Art"). In being set off from objects which retain their use value, art loses not only its function but its history, for the self-sufficiency of the autonomous artwork means that it speaks for itself. Modernist tropes for reification are familiar to us, although they are usually expressed in aesthetic terms: they include alienation; a rejection of technology, as though it, not alienated labor, were the source of the objectification of human activity; and the aesthetics of silence. But as we have found throughout this study, aestheticization in its various forms contributes to the reification of reader/spectator consciousness by its repression of the process of production. It in effect stamps out all traces of art's "relation to social life" (Wolin 188).

This expression of our inability to make sense of our experience has become commonplace, at least partly because historical explanation is one of the things reified. George Bush's use of the "vision thing" to respond to criticism that he had no visionary plan to lead us, only slogans like "1,000 points of light," reveals that a program and a political philosophy were not the objectives of his campaign for the presidency but something he knew he had to have to get elected. The imaginative framing of goals that ought to have driven his programs instead became a "thing" that he lacked and needed somehow to pick up, in order to be perceived as an effective leader. "Vision" became a public relations requirement, rather than a part of the process of leading a citizenry to act or to accept change. Similarly, the incredibility of reality has become a simple explanation for our passivity, our separation from the realm where we can affect events, determine outcomes, take control of the structures that manage our lives. Marshall Berman calls this our "broken" modernism, saying "we have mostly lost the art of putting ourselves in the picture, of recognizing ourselves as participants and protagonists in the art and thought of our time" (24).[14]

The complicated relations among art as commodity, the artist as producer, and the increasingly abstract and arbitrary "value" put on a writer's production may also contribute to this common explanation for the fact that writers seem to be turning away from attempts to depict their world comprehensively. Raymond Carver, in fact, uses the language of incomprehensibility to explain that he constructed a writing life by producing short pieces – stories and poems – because he could neither sustain his concentration nor comprehend his world well enough to write a whole novel. But what made his "world" seem incorrect, unknowable, unstable, precarious, inconsistent, and without apparent reason to exist was the condition of being a working-class parent of two children with overwhelming financial and child-care obligations. The world that did not "make sense," that "seemed to change gears and directions, along with its rules, every day," was a world where he "couldn't see or plan any further ahead than the first of next month and gathering together enough money, by hook or by crook, to meet the rent and provide the children's school clothes" (26).

The artist's expression of helplessness and frustration has taken the reified form of a perplexing reality. Can we connect that persistent strain of prose writing wherein the dominant rhetorical strategies are understatement, reticence, omission – which leads from Lincoln down through Hemingway to our postwar "aesthetics of silence" and to minimalists like Carver – to a personal grouse against one's circumstances? Is it possible that a writer belittling his own imagination and ability to concentrate in the face of contemporary events and fears is simply complaining about the demands of work and the consequences of love? The lament is usually taken as one version of art for art's sake, and we frequently detect elitism underlying such a move.

In a 1965 essay, Benjamin DeMott traces his contemporaries' celebrating a "new literary international theme" of silence in the face of degraded Western values to the devaluation of language associated with the beginnings of modernism, thereby linking the distrust of language that we noted in Hemingway to reified consciousness in another way. DeMott connects the distrust of language to the desire of writers to return to their status as privileged dispensers of the word, before the "collapse of distinctions" – between literary and nonliterary language, between mass modes and the genres that are the preserves of elites (213–16). In fact, "the very emergence of literature as a study" may "owe [its] inception in part to the desire of the clerk to repossess himself of mystery, to take language out of the public domain, to give just deserts to an age in which everyman believes he owns and understands the word" (222). He says that the strategy of the reticent writer is deliberate, though unacknowledged: "By creating silence as the only conceivable redeemer for nonliterary man, he might well restore the uniqueness stripped from him by egalitarians at the hour of the socialization of the word" (216). DeMott says we must read the claim of sixties novelists and critics that silence is the only act of integrity in a world where everyone chatters as a sign of their powerlessness, which makes them resentful, even vengeful; for to accede to their claim that this is the only appropriate response to modern civilization is to sentimentalize and, perversely, to celebrate the loss of history.

> "If one starts deploring the inadequacy of language to reality," Sartre once remarked, "one makes oneself an accomplice of the enemy, that is, of propaganda." The struggle to hold free of such complicity is, as the remark implies, a struggle for the survival of means of compelling rulers as well as rhymers to give their own word. (223)

Jacques Ellul describes silence as one of the primary techniques of modern propagandists, who prefer "to say nothing rather than to lie" and who realize that although they sometimes cannot prevent citizens from learning about current abuses, they can keep silent about past ones, thus "pervert[ing] known facts by modifying their context" (56).

Perhaps even the tendency toward sentence fragments and passive voice that any reader of student writing notes over and over again in undergraduates' expository prose is a sign of reified consciousness, for these structures may be symptomatic of our students' (perhaps, our citizens') inability to insert themselves into an "authentic collective life" (Jameson, "Reification" 140). As the object of targeted messages from those with something to sell since their earliest childhood, these young adults cannot help but be constructed as mass consumers. Since publicity itself works by ideology, by "what goes without saying," readers and viewers in their daily life become accustomed to texts with no one taking responsibility for what is said. This is only reinforced by the tendency of advertisers and public relations writers to use few complete sentences and to construct a very narrow position for their audience, isolating us from one another.

There is thus no "agency" for many of the messages we receive, and so when I write on student papers "Who is the agent in this sentence?" (in which something is being done to somebody or something), my students are usually bewildered at the form of the question. And yet many of them have been told they use too much passive voice, and they know the term "sentence fragment." To my mind, the fragments in Hemingway's Thracian dispatch that I discussed in Chapter 2 are ominous signs that the speaker does not see himself "as a participant in the construction of the social world . . . [but] as merely acted upon by the social world" (Dahlgren 104). Rather than a grammar problem, this pattern is symptomatic of a larger cultural problem. A reified consciousness is what that disembodied, detached voice expresses in "No end and no beginning. Just carts loaded with everything they owned" and "Scared sick looking at it." If it is also behind students' uncommunicative prose, we may be tackling it ineffectively by teaching them merely to recast sentences; perhaps we should encourage the use of the first person and make "real-world" writing assignments the basis of expository prose, so that, indeed, someone is perceived as acting, and so that occasionally a student feels like "an active participant in the construction of the social world depicted" (Dahlgren 104).

What expressions of the distrust of language and the retreat toward muteness have in common with other forms of reification is the absence of history. For example, Roth's shock and disappointment at what the news media do to create a story suggest he may doubt the ability of the realist novel to compete with their sensationalism, which results from exaggerating particular human interest and crime-news conventions to the point of timelessness. The various novelists he discusses in the *Commentary* essay (reprinted in *Reading Myself and Others*) do not seem to him to be adequate challengers of this sensationalism, because their characters are set against generalized backgrounds (Malamud) or are limited in subject matter and scope. They are not historically anchored, in other words, which might be the only way to counter stories that depart from their precipitating events to enter fantasy, science fiction, or the realm of the absurd. Similarly, what Joshua Meyrowitz calls "time and space saturation" by radio, telephone, and television reduces the difference between one situation and another, because these media "destroy the specialness of time and place" (124). They in effect overcome the specificity of historical memory by making events difficult to locate in a particular time and place. As Meyrowitz says, "What is happening almost anywhere can be happening wherever we are. Yet when we are everywhere, we are also no place in particular" (125). To see that this is true, one has only to think of the common form of anchoring major events in a specific time and place: "Where were you when you heard that President Kennedy was shot?" Then there is Wolfe's and other nostalgists' longing for a lost world where events can be captured in narrative, and word and thing are equivalent. This nostalgia turns out to be longing for a particular place, not time. They long, in effect, for childhood, which is ahistorical because children do not live consciously in history. They acquire historical consciousness in the process of becoming adults. That may also explain why autobiography is easily read reflexively: the thread of the narrative is the self gradually becoming aware of itself and of its particular surroundings, that is, its history. (Annie Dillard's *An American Childhood* makes this obvious in almost every section.) Here, too, the connection between history and self-consciousness or reflexivity begins to show clearly.

All these are manifestations of reification because they isolate the individual, separate subject from object, "transform human relations into an appearance of relationships between things" (Jameson, "Reflections" 212), suppress our self-consciousness, and turn the historically produced world into an objectified "second nature" (Lukacs 132). Reification is at the heart of the view that reality is incredible, for when our consciousness is reified we are unable to see our connection with the world; it does not seem a "human enterprise," merely factitious and incomprehensible (Berger and Luckmann 89). Thus reification can be seen as a way of denying responsibility for the havoc some people wreak on others, and that, individually and collectively, we wreak on our local and global environment.

One example of this denial is the reduction of evil to ordinary human behavior, as when Hannah Arendt derives the notion of the banality of evil from the ordinary appearance of Adolf Eichmann, ignoring what Norman Mailer calls the "vast power of the unconsciousness" and mistaking "the surface for the reality" (*Pontifications* 166). Mailer counters this by showing that Arendt's formulation is itself a sign of the impoverishment of the modern consciousness, that is, of its reification. As he told an interviewer, "[I]t's not the banality or the brutality of evil with which we have to contend, but its complexity, that is, the similarity of evil in others to ourselves" (*Pontifications* 166). Though Mailer believes that the "evil of true murderousness" must reside "in the most ordinary people" in order to have produced the extermination of millions of their fellow human beings in very few years, this evil cannot be explained by ordinariness; instead, repressed hatred and civilization's "divorce from the senses" are the only possible explanations for the "cold murderous liquidations of the totalitarian state" (*Pontifications* 4; *Advertisements* 318). And he challenges the fatalism of reified consciousness (what Marx identified as the way mechanical forces appear to determine social relations) by insisting on individual participation in the "collective violence we call our social order" (D. Trilling 199). "If society was so murderous," Mailer asks in "The White Negro," "then who could ignore the most hideous questions about his own nature?" (300). As Diana Trilling notes, this is a valid problem Mailer does not let us evade: "whether we can exempt the individual of responsibility for our degradation, and continue, as a culture, to feel morally superior to our collective conduct" (199–200).

From these distinctions we can understand why critics of journalistic and historical narrative use terms like "documentary narrative" and "zero-degree interpretation" to describe these texts' surface factuality; in effect, though, they reproduce the rigid categories earlier produced by reification. Thus they reinforce the separation of an "absurd" reality from our ways of knowing it. When writers like Hersey in *Hiroshima* or authors of various Holocaust narratives take a documentary approach in order to record and bear witness to multiple horrors, the results display a form of reified modern consciousness. These narratives imply that there is a separate realm of history – even of mass horrors – apart from the way we know it and communicate it to others. But James Young, author of *Writing and Rewriting the Holocaust,* finds that "[e]vents of the Holocaust are not only shaped *post factum* in their narration, but . . . were initially determined as they unfolded by the schematic ways in which they were apprehended, expressed, and then acted upon" (5). Journalism is one of the "ways" our apprehension of the Holocaust was mediated, for it mediates most current events, and is thus the starting point for the historian. We are likely to allow the historian more interpretive leeway than we do the journalist, however, because we invariably compare the latter's version to our own, whereas the events in a historian's account are likely to have receded from our memory, if they were ever there. As Young says, "This is not to deny the historical facts of the Holocaust outside of their narrative framing, but only to emphasize the difficulty of interpreting, expressing, and acting on these facts outside of the ways we frame them" (3).

Because narrative history is a process, historians continually revise the accepted or dominant interpretations of events. Even those who try to alter history by asserting that the Holocaust never happened can only be refuted and their claims repudiated. This does not discredit the theory of the textuality of events, of the notion that we derive all our knowledge of past events from narrative (including memory, which is narrativized in being recalled by our later self and certainly when it is communicated to others). It asserts the importance of analyzing and dissecting narrative and disputing or supporting its effects.[15] This concept of history as textual is useful for arguing against the assertion put forward by a few "revisionists" that the Holocaust never occurred. In order to refute this false history, we can show its construction, including its motivating anti-Semitism. Part of the refutation of the revisionists' claims must involve destroying the way their argument is made, as well as countering its assumptions with evidence. The fact that historians can say irrefutably that millions of Jews were killed in gas chambers in Germany in a few short years is the result of having established those historical facts by amassing documents, survivors' accounts, stories, and witnessing of all kinds. Because it is historically verifiable, this sequence of events to which we give the interpretive and symbolic name "the Holocaust" is meaningful in interpreting subsequent instances of anti-Semitism and, among other things, authorizes the prosecution of those who carried out the plans for genocide. The events of the Holocaust are established in U.S. law as well. For example, the decision of an editor of a college newspaper to refuse an advertisement claiming that the Holocaust never occurred is protected under the First Amendment.[16]

In sum, historical and journalistic narratives are not "the truth," although they may claim to report events accurately; they are simply partial reports of what seems to have happened, inevitably biased by being filtered through reporters, observers, researchers, and the language and forms of representation they use to communicate. My explanation for the widespread perception of modern life as incredible is based on recognizing that our experience of history and actuality is predominantly textual. What seems likely is that the news we get of horrors around the world and recovered from history, such as narratives of the experience of slavery, of life in the Gulags or under Pol Pot, or during Mao's Cultural Revolution, is actually quite credible, because one thing that has been successfuly communicated in the twentieth century is the harm human beings are capable of inflicting on one another. But the conceit is that we can hardly credit these horrors – for example, the idea that the world could end in a matter of minutes; or that genocide and forms of slavery continue in some places in the world; that state terrorism, torture, and clitoridectomies persist in incidents numbering in the millions. If we cannot credit them, after all the reports we have read and heard and seen, it can only be the result of massive denial. In this sense, "reality" outstrips, not the imagination, but the forms that have been authorized to make it manageable, that is, to order the chaos and make it acceptable as "news."

I propose a countertheory to the traditionally asserted belief that we have lost a premodern Paradise, and so no longer have the assurance offered by a meaningful and coherent world view, one which gives us a sense of order and provides the foundation for understanding our world. It is that an alternative lineage of texts, a developing series of narrative forms – from minimalist modernism to postmodern minimalism, from positivist history to cliometrics, and from objective journalism to television news – have successively reduced the range of our experience and the complexity of individual and collective responses to it. If experience is textual, then the kind of texts that dominate matters. When texts are limited in scope, depth, variety, and complexity because of the aesthetic or positivist elevation of objective narratives, our capacity to understand and communicate our experience is bound to be restricted as well. The forms of objectivity that arose and persist in this century in fiction, journalism, history, and biography have created a limited range of emotional and political expression, and it is the reifying effect of these modes of representation that produces our feeling of helplessness, which is sometimes expressed as the sense that reality has surpassed our imaginative capacity to absorb it. Roth apparently realized the limitations of high realism, too, and in response developed a series of elaborate self-conscious and autobiographical strategies that enabled him to continue to be politically as well as artistically effective, particularly in the series of novels collected in *Zuckerman Bound* (1985), *The Counterlife* (1986), *The Facts: A Novelist's Autobiography* (1988), *Deception: A Novel* (1990), *Patrimony: A True Story* (1991), and *Operation Shylock* (1993).[17]

As an example of how a limited, objective focus produces the aura of unreality that Roth and others find surrounding contemporary events, consider the essay Hersey added to *Hiroshima* in 1985, "Aftermath." One of the six survivors whose intervening story Hersey traces is the Reverend Tanimoto, a student in the United States before the war, who returned after it as a peace activist and as chaperone to the so-called Hiroshima Maidens (young women scarred by the A-bomb who were treated by plastic surgeons in New York City). On a visit to California in 1955, Tanimoto was stunned to find himself on the NBC show "This Is Your Life," with one of the surprise guests the man who had co-piloted the *Enola Gay* as it flew over Hiroshima to drop the bomb on August 6, 1945. In striving for what he believes is the immediacy of the novelist's impersonal narration, Hersey presents a scene worthy of Roth's collection of "absurd moments on TV," for Tanimoto could have stepped straight from Roth's television screen to become an example in his essay.

Not only was this program, especially the "reunion," inappropriate as entertainment, because it trivialized Mr. Tanimoto and rendered actual historical relationships irrelevant (what possible meaning is conveyed by bringing together the bomber and his victim in this framework, while providing no historical context?), but the absurdity of the effect is increased by Hersey's understated presentation. He interrupts several paragraphs describing the life-in-review format of the program with a sentence describing a sixty-second, live-commercial demonstration of a durable nail polish. These preposterous contrasts are given in the same tone in which Hersey has earlier narrated stories of extreme devastation experienced by each of the survivors. The predominant effect produced by such an objective narration is, as it is in Hemingway, irony. The narrator does not interpret or evaluate the scene in any way, and so the possibility that the reader will note other contrasts is left open.

One feature certainly worthy of notice (but given none) is the amount of money that must have been spent to gather Tanimoto's family and figures from his past and bring them to California; it would be interesting to compare it to the sum contributed to the fund for the Hiroshima Maidens by the program's viewers, who were pitched by the emcee. Another figure worthy of speculation or even research is the cost of the air time to the advertisers, such as the makers of Hazel Bishop nail polish. These factors related to the medium in cases – both the television program and the journalistic narrative – are not negligible to the overall effect. Once again, the impression that many critics call "absurd" is produced by the medium through which we perceive events and its peculiar way of looking and presenting its observations, rather than by the events themselves. This media event, while concerning a notable historical incident, explicitly denies the historicity of the occurrence. Mr. Tanimoto and the copilot of the *Enola Gay* would probably never have met except in such a contrived, artificial situation, and so there is little reason to insist on the "real" or factual basis of either the television program or Hersey's narrative reporting it. Once again we note that the incongruity of history (or biography) is exaggerated by the objective presentation – here, by its presentation as entertainment to a national audience.

If, as Berman insists, we have "lost the art of putting ourselves into the picture" (24), it is more likely that this habit of reified perception and our loss of history produces the notion that reality is absurd than that reality has significantly altered or that novelists have not kept up with it. The common response, however, is to assume that readers associate the absence of interpretation with "truth," and thus give more credence to objective factual narratives than to imaginative attempts to help us understand what happened. One can easily counter the "aesthetics of silence" position – the view that it is more important to document and disclose atrocities than to make art from factual materials – by pointing out that this is a false choice. A. Alvarez asserts that when both writer and audience are engaged, the process of making art combines form and content. This is the basis of moral decisions, too, as Alvarez makes clear in his description of what art requires: "fragile, tentative, individual discriminations." Thus the process by which a text or painting or drama or poem is produced always involves "those moral values which, if understood and accepted, would make totalitarian atrocities impossible" (25). It is rather the separation of works as autonomous artifacts from the political and social and historical conditions which spawned them that those who would be silent are responding to; and it is the consistent splitting off of documentary from imaginative artifacts and the reification of artist and viewer or reader when they are distanced as observers that leads to reticence and withdrawal. When Alvarez insists it is that very tentativeness – art's hypothetical reach, the way it calls attention to its attempts to imagine, and even its experiments in comprehension – that enables literature to function with moral imagination, he is countering the consequences of reification with a reflexive conception of art.

Reflexivity is the primary force able to counter reification; in fact, I have been substituting "reification" or "reified consciousness" in contexts where Dahlgren uses "non-reflexivity" or "non-reflexive consciousness." When we realize that reification refers to the way we view processes of production as natural, as "independent of historically situated human activity," we can begin to reclaim our products in relation to our labor or imagination by recovering the social processes from which they rose, by reminding ourselves of them or laying them bare. Just as we need to see that money and commodities are "symbols of stored-up labor, on the one hand, . . . [and] the product of the rationalized labor process, on the other" (Aronowitz 47), we can lay bare the context of the work of art, its relation to our social life.

Thus Alvarez is saying, with Mailer, that contemporary reality ought to be a challenge to the writer, whereas the silence, aestheticism, or retreat to documentary that are supposed to be the dominant responses to it are forms of submission to the dark forces in modern civilization (and, as we have seen, in failing to acknowledge the evil, they are expressions of reification). Certainly Mailer, in his historical narratives, does not fall back on neutral transcription or construct a passive audience by separating human beings from what happens to them. Although it may be more painful to confront our "collective creation" (or, as he qualifies it, at least the collective creation of the past) than to deny it, to do the latter results in "conformity and depression." And so in "The White Negro," Mailer creates an existential hero in the Hipster. He invests an outsider – the alienated psychopath, living in the moment – with energy to counter the living death of positivism's mind-numbing confinements. The solution he seeks is the means to a violent renewal of perception, a way to reinsert ourselves into the collectivity. Although in "The White Negro" the means are existentialism and rejection of the repression that produces civilization, and the substitution of individual psychopathology for the mass version that has brought us atomic destruction and concentration camps, in his journalism from 1960 to 1979

Mailer brings history and politics back to the forefront of "literary" journalism. His enabling of his readers' reflexive consciousness is his main strategy to counter the tendency of contemporary life to reify consciousness.

Various critics have noticed the tendency of a writer like Mailer toward self-examination, and toward regarding what he finds in his conscience and consciousness as "an index of the culture as a whole" (Louvre 74). "Our best fiction," says Diana Trilling, "deals merely with the massive brute social fact in its impress upon the individual consciousness" (178).[18] This is not the same thing as asserting the power of the individual personality to challenge dehumanizing forces of contemporary society but involves a dialectical relationship between self and society. In Trilling's view, Mailer "believes the social totality generates a dialectic between itself and the individual; it is therefore not merely to be endured in self-pity, it can be faced up to and changed" (178). This dialectic extends to the relationship between writer and reader, or journalist and audience, for reflexivity is not a quality of texts but the process of one consciousness engaging with another, and thereby with society. Emphasizing the relationship between narrator or journalist and reader may be an effective way to challenge the reification implied by most mass-cultural forms.

The true-crime novel might well be regarded as a challenge to this hypothesis. It seems likely, in its formulaic qualities, to reproduce the separation of observer and observed (and therefore to be a microcosm of journalism, particularly the exposé or investigative journalism, but also the human interest story) and thus to objectify the reader's consciousness. As Geoffrey Hartman and other theorists of detective, mystery, and gothic fiction have shown, these genres, especially in their popular or formulaic versions, are conservative forms "in which appalling facts are made to fit into a rational or realistic pattern" (217). By moving from mystery to disclosure, from riddle to solution, these narratives help to comfort us, control our fears and our vulnerabilities.[19] Because the narrator suppresses knowledge that, if divulged too early, would defeat the purpose of suspense and obviate our desired responses of pity and terror, they are akin to other texts emphasizing strategies of silence or reticence. Kingsley Widmer suggests that a similar need for order and rationality to counter the chaos and uncertainty of contemporary life is at the root of the documentary novel; his standards for judging this genre will be useful here. He says that this mode fails because examples tend to be unthoughtful, unreflective, and exploitative (142–3). Rather than dismissing the whole genre, however, we can take over these three categories of judgment (adding a fourth consideration, how analytical the categories are) and use them to discuss two of the best-known true-crime novels.

The two narratives are the first nonfiction novel to take that label, Truman Capote's *In Cold Blood*, published in 1965, and Mailer's *The Executioner's Song*, which won the Pulitzer Prize in 1979. The works are strikingly similar: in their subjects (violent, senseless crime; prison life; trials; punishment by execution); characters (both Perry Smith and Gary Gilmore are talented artists); and in their use of documents, interviews, and transcripts to present the past history not only of the criminals but of the settings (small towns in the West, in both cases – Holcomb, Kansas, and Provo, Utah). In addition, both use conventions of several nonfictional forms: biography, autobiography, history, and journalism. The novels are vastly different in execution and effect, however.

Perhaps the best strategy to indicate a crucial difference is to compare their stories, that is, what we infer from their extensively plotted narratives. The story of a narrative is never fully "present," and it is never known except by inference; even the story of a nonfiction novel, which comprises events from history, is never complete, because no one can ever know everything that happens. When the stories of these two novels are summarized, they are cast in the form of another narrative, and so these are not properly "story" at all. However, here is my summary of the story of *In Cold Blood:*

> A convict describes an affluent Kansas farm to a fellow inmate of Kansas State Prison, who turns the account into a fantasy and acts it out. Four members of the Clutter family are mysteriously murdered in their farmhouse in western Kansas. Detectives set about finding the killers amidst a townspeople grown suspicious of one another. They get a tip from the convict and apprehend Dick Hickock and Perry Smith, who are tried, found guilty, and executed, providing the second set of killings "in cold blood."

When we compare the story we infer from *The Executioner's Song*, it is obvious what is missing from *In Cold Blood*. The first part of this summary of the story is Mailer's (given in Aldridge [176]); the last part is mine:

> "[A] man who . . . has been in jail all his adult life, comes out, meets a beautiful girl [Nicole Baker], and has a passionate love affair that almost works, then is very unsuccessful. They break up. It's so intolerable to him that a week later he murders two men on two successive nights. Once he's back in jail, he and the girl fall in love again. It is then he comes to the conclusion that it's hopeless to stay alive in such an incarcerated existence," and when he is given a death sentence he de-

cides not to appeal. This action attracts massive amounts of publicity, and this attention from various members of the news media is inseparable from his struggle to die, to take Nicole with him in a joint suicide attempt, and to earn money to be left to his survivors by telling his story. The attempt to control the telling of Gilmore's and Nicole's story forms an equal part of the drama (and the members of the press become equal players) as events move toward Gilmore's execution by firing squad in 1977 and its aftermath.

This part of the narrative – of how the text in front of us was produced by the intervention of Larry Schiller, who signed up the rights to the principals' stories and conducted the interviews that uncovered the comprehensive details and viewpoints of the first half – takes up the whole second half of the book. We see that once the media become part of the story – of "what happens" – it is impossible to separate the product (the text) from its process (how it was produced); the text is self-accounting.

What is missing from the story of *In Cold Blood* is an awareness of its process of production, for, although many details of the story are expendable from any summary, the reader ought to learn of how the story of a nonfictional narrative became known; if we have no mention of an author or an equivalent source of the plot, we are liable to presume an omniscient author of an invented tale, or the absolute world of distant history. Here is the positivist seduction again, for a narrator who speaks in an all-knowing, positive way about events that we already assume to be "real" because of our knowledge of them from other narratives and does all this using the tropes of realism is creating a highly naturalized world, but it is triply hard for us to believe it is being created. Perhaps our summary of Capote's novel should have begun:

> In 1959, a writer, hearing of the murder of four members of a family in their farmhouse in western Kansas, sets out for the region to follow the case as a journalist. Present when the killers are apprehended, he interviews and befriends them, corresponding with them until they are executed (a scene which he witnesses), and gets to know the story from many viewpoints.

In this case, the novel would be the journalist's account of events that he has put together from these various sources.

And yet it is difficult to infer from the text of *In Cold Blood* alone this particular aspect of the story (which includes the author's six-year involvement in events, his friendship with the detective in charge of the manhunt, and his intense relationship with the killers). We get it from other versions, including interviews Capote gave and from other publicity concerning the novel (Plimpton 189–91; Long; Howard).

There is a reflexive element in *In Cold Blood:* a "journalist," whom we assume to be Capote, is present in several scenes, interviewing Holcomb residents and visiting the condemned men. A few interviews are re-created in the present tense (64–7, 76, 83). Capote reproduces certain documents and inserts them into the text with an explanation of their presence (the defendants' autobiographies, prepared for the psychiatrist who examined them, and an article from the *American Journal of Psychiatry*). He even includes psychiatric testimony that the judge did not allow to be introduced at the trial of the two killers (333–4). With the comment, "If Dr. Jones had been allowed to speak further, here is what he would have testified" (333), we are reminded of the creative role of the journalist. He has done the research which has made possible the historic narration, but instead of assimilating the evidence and turning it into an assertion of reality, in some cases he has left it as data to be interpreted. This provides some knowledge of how the text came to be produced. But most of the text's reflexivity – its accounting for itself – has been repressed by the sections that use third-person "omniscient" narration.

The primary difference between these two novels is that there is no such omniscient narrator in Mailer's masterpiece; all the news comes through an intervening consciousness or viewpoint, and the text thus enacts through its form the idea that there is no unmediated experience, no world except that created by consciousness and language. There are no "actual facts" which can be presented as they exist in the world; all we can know is what we create, primarily through language but also through other cultural structures and practices. All the creating consciousnesses of *The Executioner's Song* are enabling metaphors for this truth about experience. The journalists, writers, and public relations personnel for the prison and the state of Utah, and Larry Schiller – who wants to "own" Nicole's and Gary's story "exclusively" – demonstrate this truth on the public level of the mass media, for our "story" is our proper "self," our own property, and the only identity we have. By exposing the economic basis of the story he is telling (and by implication, his role in it, for Schiller is in part a stand-in for the author, playing the role "Mailer" plays in other texts), Mailer acknowledges not only the process of the text's production but the importance of ownership of the means of producing narrative "truth."

In contrast, Capote's attempt to keep the story of "how he got the story" out of *In Cold Blood* ends up asserting a different world view. Not only does Capote not deal with the question of the ownership of Perry's and Dick's story; he simply appropriates it and earns $4 million by telling it as if it existed objectively in the world. By asserting that what is narrated actually happened (the point of the book is "factual accuracy," says Capote [Plimpton 202]), he acts as if it exists apart from its creation by a "subjective" journalist conditioned to compose using certain patterns of words and images and in a language constructed by a complex culture. Capote is expressing the positivist belief that there is a world which can be reproduced in language, that facts have inherent meaning, and that language is a neutral instrument for recording them, and thus he denies the ideology of language and of the form of *In Cold Blood*.

Specifically, the narrative of *In Cold Blood* implies that truth is, if not simple, at least ascertainable, if we are willing to take the trouble; and that sociologists and psychiatrists have the answers to the riddle of criminal behavior. Furthermore, the reader implied by the structure of the novel learns that violent, senseless crime can be made sensible and poignant through artistic representation; and these repulsive, illiterate, antisocial criminals are rendered as literate, talented, redeemable, though flawed, personalities. (Perry is sensitive and draws, Dick has an amazing memory; both are as articulate as Dostoevsky, as Sol Yurick and others in Malin's collection have pointed out.)

The problem with *In Cold Blood* is that it assumes a world of cause and effect, of certitude, reason – in short, of common sense, and it expresses this world view via a realism characterized by verisimilitude, a historical narrator who assures the intelligibility of the text by "placing" the other narrations, and through its strong sense of closure. Then, it reinforces the dominant ideology of class: that there is an "us" and a "them," and when representatives from this underclass of poor drifters, hustlers, and convicts invade the middle-class world symbolized by the Clutters, of all people in the world "the least likely to be murdered" (102), it must be regarded as an absurdity, a phenomenon to be mastered by incorporating it in an eminently realistic narrative. The metaphor for this transformation is Detective Alvin Dewey's disappointed realization that the murderers' confessions "failed to satisfy his sense of meaningful design" (277). The novel is that "meaningful design," complete with innumerable coincidences and ironic events. For example, Mr. Clutter takes out a $40,000 double-indemnity life insurance policy the day he dies, and a surviving daughter takes advantage of the guests assembled for the funeral to have an early, quite formal, wedding ceremony. Capote also increases the number of them by his method of crosscutting, which juxtaposes images and parallel patterns, as when the early sections alternate between the Clutters' last day and the killers traveling to the farmhouse, and by skipping ahead of the story in order to view events by hindsight, thus rendering the "present" all the more poignant. The "meaningful design" also includes unbelievably "good" victims and colorful, literate killers with contrasting personalities. (In the novel, although not clearly in other narratives of the case, the sensitive one,

Smith, is the only one who kills.) The book even has a doubly ironic title.[20]

The creation of this commonsensical, meaningful, manageable world might seem inevitable in any nonfiction novel, under the prevailing view, which sees these works as tied to a reality and therefore bound to reflect it in a mimetic form, being free only to ornament its "facts" with techniques derived from realistic fiction. But there is an alternative to this kind of nonfiction novel, which Mailer's much longer, fuller account of a similar crime makes clear. In the first place, *The Executioner's Song* is overt about its fictional status: its subtitle is "A True Life Novel," and the implication of this label is that it makes no claim of absolute truth or fidelity to facts. Indeed, Mailer reminds us, in "An Afterword," that his intention that his account be "as accurate as one can make it . . . does not mean it has come a great deal closer to the truth than the recollections of the witnesses" (1020). This remark not only suggests his awareness of the difficulty of "truth telling" but should be taken as a comment on the method of narration. As in the ten monologues of Browning's *The Ring and the Book,* no "actual facts" are presented directly, that is, without our awareness of an embodying consciousness. Thus an event is never asserted to be "the way it was" by an all-knowing narrator; all the facts we get are derived from some character's viewpoint. What we have are multiple versions of events, and, as in *The Ring and the Book,* the events emerge from the differences among the various subjective accounts. Our knowledge of events in the Gary Gilmore case comes to us piecemeal; they are fragmented among the points of view of various characters; the details gradually accrete as they are filtered through an individual's recollection of them.

True, they are collected by one consciousness – what we should call the "author function," which is performed in this case by Mailer – in order to be presented to the reader. Then our consciousness reconstructs it according to our culturally structured locus or makeup. Any text works this way, and we can never be free of the illusion of an author or narrator (what Tzvetan Todorov calls the "poetic personality" or subject of the *énonciation* ["Language" 132]); in this case, however, the narrator does not assert events as real. They are allowed to emerge from the differences among subjective accounts; they do not inhere in the narrations themselves. The trick is that the narrator is himself fragmented into these points of view, for he does not make connection; only the characters or the reader does.[21] Rather than the usual seamless web of omniscient historical narration, there are only gaps between the discourses. A "visible" reminder of this is the white space between paragraphs or short groups of paragraphs on nearly every page of the novel. These blank lines also remind us that the narrative is necessarily incomplete, and therefore untrue; the narrator will not assume, and will not ask us as reading subjects to assume, that we have the "whole story" with all the blanks filled in. In this way, the novel is like the structure we impose on our experience of events; both are demonstrably fictional, that is, contrived, for in life as in this narrative, we receive impressions from various perspectives and out of sequence, and only later do we create out of them an order which is still less than a total apprehension.

Also, the reader of *The Executioner's Song* is not implied or assumed ("interpellated" is Althusser's term ["Ideology" 173ff.]) as a coherent subject of the narrative, in the way the reader of a classic realist text is, bound to receive it a certain way and to make inevitable connections. We construct the narrative of *The Executioner's Song* according to our peculiar locus within the culture and our inculcated habits of language and pattern making, which in turn depend on the particular ways we participate in society. We ostensibly do this with any narrative, but because of the assumptions certain texts make about their readers as subjects, our response is more limited in some cases than in others. It is more difficult to construct alternatives to the subordinate role that the totalized, hierarchical narrative called *In Cold Blood* implies for the reader, for example.

What is different about *The Executioner's Song* is that it is made of historical materials and yet it overcomes the positivism implied in the illusionary form of any narrative about "real" events by avoiding the assertion of a finite world, by staying open to as many interpretations as possible, by avoiding closure, and by resisting the imposition of causation on its materials. It does this by calling upon the reader to create the text along with the narrator. Take, for example, the opening paragraph of the text, which presents a miniature version of the fall from Eden, with Brenda, Gary's cousin who sponsors him so that he can be paroled, figuring as Eve.

> Brenda was six when she fell out of the apple tree. She climbed to the top and the limb with the good apples broke off. Gary caught her as the branch came scraping down. They were scared. The apple trees were their grandmother's best crop and it was forbidden to climb in the orchard. She helped him drag away the tree limb and they hoped no one would notice. That was Brenda's earliest recollection of Gary.
> (17)

Although we learn at the end of the paragraph that this anecdote is Brenda's account of her earliest memory of getting into trouble with her cousin, we cannot be sure that all the language is hers. For example, "it was forbidden to climb in the orchard" sounds more like the Old Testament God of the Mormons than a phrase Brenda might use. Does it belong to her or to an intermediary, such as an interviewer or the narrator? What this ambiguity of narration does throughout the novel is to remind us that we are constructed by language rather than masters of it. The myth of the expulsion from the perfect garden is available to all of us because it is inscribed in our culture, and a phrase such as "it was forbidden to climb in the orchard" is common "property." The important difference between a passage like this and the solemn historic narration of *In Cold Blood* is that there are many more possible interpretations for each "event" or sequence, and because the narrator has not assimilated the individual narrations but allows us to attribute them to a particular consciousness, the narrative is not hierarchically ordered or closed off or "given" to us in inevitable form.

Even the comments on characters' feelings and the occasional metaphors and similes that characterize their attitudes can be read as though they are derived from the consciousness we are in. For example, in one passage Gilmore's brother Mikal is recalling a visit Gary paid him in college during one of his rare periods of release from jail. Gary showed Mikal a pistol and asked him if he could ever use it. After a white space, the next paragraph begins, "It was like a bigger dude squeezing your machismo to see if it leaked" (493). Some critics have made it a matter of some concern that metaphoric language like this is a sign of Mailer's presence, but the ambiguity, caused by the "mutual interpenetration of reported utterance and reporting context" in free indirect discourse is a sign of dialogism, of language's social function (McHale, "Free Indirect Discourse" 263). Indeed, much of our discourse is common rather than particularized. When we tell stories we use phrases and patterns of thought that have become habitual to us because of accidents of reading and speaking – because we have been conditioned by our culture to use them, in short. This absence of a unique language for each character – in fact, much of it is paraphrase, and thus reported speech rather than dialogue – is the sign of a certain conception of character apparent in the narrative. This is how our "character" is formed, Mailer's everyday, familiar idiom says; we are all products of culture, subjects of structures – of language, family patterns, derived from the mass media, and other sources. Our customary habits of language use are not uniquely ours but produce us, cause us to appear as we do. The whole problem of the fragmented ego, the self as alienated subject, is here troped by the structure and style of the narration.[22]

Mailer says that he was first attracted to the story because of Gary Gilmore's apparent Hipster actions in acknowledging "the awareness of death as the necessary condition for every just perception" (Edmundson 443). Mark Edmundson is led to consider why the style Mailer has limited himself to is so (comparatively) flat and his voice so (for him) self-effacing, since language appropriate to Hip is energetic and intense. In "The White Negro," Mailer acknowledges the Hipster's limited vocabulary but insists that these few words are capable of expressing nuance, energy, movement, learning, flexibility, and creativity ("White" 311–14).[23] He emphasizes their appropriateness to self-definition and expression rather than repression. In other journalistic works of what Edmundson calls Mailer's "high romantic style," "the exhilaration those texts can produce in a reader derives in part from his sense that the writing possesses boundless resources and possibilities. . . . His invention will never flag, his powers of observation and analysis will persist forever" (444).

Perhaps in this novel Mailer has found the subtle style to communicate his message instead of overwhelming it. Edmundson thinks that Mailer pulled back, in *The Executioner's Song,* because as he got into the materials he realized that Gilmore might not be the embodiment of his Hipster after all; he might be merely a game player, and his act anarchism rather than an existential project. He apparently seemed to Mailer to be one who disrupts and vents, rather than showing a way out of our imprisoning, reified consciousness by pointing up the moral delusions and inconsistencies we live with. "Gilmore's minority or oppositional energies" may have no real value, hence be unable to stand against chaos, evil, and waste. Gilmore seems to be a nihilist, on the side of anarchy and entropy, rather than a philosophical anarchist, acting against them (in his attempt to control his death). Unlike Nicole Baker, who remains a heroine to Mailer, Gilmore may not be aware of the "tragic possibilities in life" (443). If, as Edmundson suggests, Mailer ends up in doubt about Gilmore rather than celebrating him as Hipster, because Gilmore simply represents chaos, "without end or allegiance," rather than the incarnation of existentialist improviser, "then Gilmore has earned the not inconsiderable distinction of being the figure who compelled America's foremost literary radical to fight culture's conserving battles for it" (446).

Chris Anderson claims that Capote too "renounces omniscience and maintains authorial silence" for much of *In Cold Blood,* "withdrawing to the point of view of an outside observer restricted to making deductions from available evidence and testimony" (53). In this view Capote does not claim to have cleared up the mystery of why Dick and Perry have killed the Clutters, or even whether they committed the murders "in cold blood." Anderson reads Capote's reticence and the "silences" and gaps in the narrative as significant, saying that it adds up to a "rhetoric of silence" (52). The difference is that we are so used to filling in these gaps that we are not likely to notice them, and we easily hear the symbolic resonance of details. (Capote's concreteness is evocative, even foreshadowing, rather than simply verisimilar.) Thus they contribute to the effect of transparency, and we feel we have had solutions to problems, answers to questions, rather than remaining puzzled.

In contrast, the process of production of *The Executioner's Song* is revealed in the narrative, since the second half (book 2) is "about" how the information in book 1 was gathered. Not only does this story of the publicizing of Gilmore's decision to be executed and his manipulation of the news media reveal to us how the witnesses came to be interviewed, the private documents of Nicole and Gary to be available – in short, how the text itself came to be – but by referring to the events of the preceding story it reinforces the fact that signs refer to other signs, not to an external reality. The reflexivity of the text inheres on several levels. First, it exists in the structure of the text, as the first half is glossed by the second. Second, it lies in the method of narration. For example, the text switches viewpoints frequently, narrating different characters' versions of the same events and incorporating some public versions of them – newspapers, and letters, for example – so that we see different perceptions constantly. These occasional reminders of how we have each bit of information or version of an experience and the absence of a totalizing narrator keep us aware of the opacity of the text and hamper our apprehension of a world "out there" beyond it. Third, the reflexivity is apparent in the subject of the narrative, which is implicitly how all our news of the world is mediated, that is, is constituted by the narrative which we usually think of as carrying or transmitting a reality to our apprehension of it.

In Cold Blood, on the other hand, represses or ignores the fact that there is no reality apart from our conception of it. In Capote's novel, interpretation and facts are asserted as "the truth about the world," and the power of the illusionary technique is not qualified by the presence of a dramatized narrator or other qualifier of the text's supposed transparency, much the way the news media or film or advertising present their images as real, not as text, because no enabling forms are visible. When the journalistic aspects threaten to surface and remind us how the story was obtained, they are overwhelmed by the "omniscient" narration. By stressing only the "technological" or recording aspects of journalism for their contribution to his detailed rendering of situation, setting, and plot, Capote is emphasizing an outmoded conception of journalism. If the history of the conventions of reporting the news has seemed to trace a growing ability to recover some semblance of reality, we have lately realized that journalism has inevitably become the art of *structuring* a reality, not representing it. We can have no understanding or appreciation of such genres as the New Journalism and the nonfiction novel unless we see that narratives in these forms must demonstrate an awareness of the constituting, creative nature of journalism, as of any discourse. Indeed, in many nonfiction novels various kinds of reflexivity are in evidence, including dramatized narrators, the exploitation of stylistic effects to call attention to the language, dominating tropes of production of meaning or text, or making the subject of the novel how the narrative came to be.

Seeing even historical and sociological narratives (for example) as fictional does not mean we have to give up the possibility of getting closer to "truth," because, although by making all discourse hypothetical we give up the idea that certain knowledge is located somewhere in reality, as Mailer says in a different context (*Advertisements* 173), "what one can always do is to compare the 'fictions' and try to see where they may lead." Although fictions do not "tell us the truth" about the world, individual fictional texts do, as Terry Eagleton says, "enunciate true propositions" ("Realism" 93) about aspects of it, which are of course subject to testing and comparison and exposure of their own contradictions. "Truth," rather than lying somewhere outside of discourse, is more helpfully imaged as lying in the gaps between competing discourses. The point is that one does not necessarily get any closer to "truth" by denying the hypothetical constructs one uses to apprehend it.

Capote denied that his narrative was hypothetical; he told George Plimpton that he decided what the truth was and always went toward that, undercutting or qualifying versions he did not agree with by how he chose to tell it. Mailer, in contrast, told William Buckley, on "Firing Line," that he "thought it might be very nice for once just to write a book which doesn't have answers, but poses delicate questions."[24] These differences are apparent within each nonfiction novel, but we cannot see these crucial differences if we insist on the separation of literary and fictional texts from nonfiction, nonliterary ones and regard the nonfiction novel as a genre that faithfully reproduces "the real."

There are many ways to consider and evaluate nonfictional narratives of sensational events apart from the deterministic categories of fact and fiction. Many of these narratives go beyond simply reflecting or reproducing a reality that has attracted the writer's attention by departing from the ordinary. The strategies themselves may be extraordinary, and thus invite the reader's attention. Such texts suggest reflexive reading strategies, rather than simply encouraging us to register what an "objective" narrative posits as real, no matter how incredible. Not only overt argument and persuasive essays arouse us to action; narrative read through the form may produce a reflexive consciousness in its readers and thus rouse them to "critical reflection and collective action" (Dahlgren 110). We do not have to take the world as given, nor do we have to retreat in dismay from the daunting task of sorting out "true-life" accounts of extraordinary events that (as some critics insist) are multiplying at a dizzying rate.

My approach to New Journalism and the nonfiction novel in some ways resembles the New Historicists' interest in the "circulation" of texts from private to public space, and of material from "social discourse to aesthetic discourse" and back without leaving either entirely behind (Greenblatt 8, 11). What the New Historicist approach offers is a way to talk about our interest in these texts without aestheticizing them. Narratives about crime, war, countercultures, and politics get significant attention, but not necessarily of the literary-critical sort, and so they do not become "literary" under the usual definition. By virtue of the fact that these narratives remain on the border between literary and nonliterary discourses, or perhaps even subvert the boundaries they help to delineate by their violation of the usual distinctions, we can account for our interest while not assuming their permanence, which tends to imply the jettisoning of their politics.

Rather than interpreting a narrative like *The Executioner's Song,* Stephen Greenblatt considers its status as a critically and financially successful novel and sketches the circulation of texts around it, including Gilmore's own story and letters to his girlfriend, which he "sold" to Schiller and Mailer; the legal maneuvers for and against his execution; Mailer's "true-life" novel with its inclusion of media coverage of the unfolding story (including Schiller's part in it) as well as of Gilmore's story itself; the televised miniseries, with Schiller directing the screenplay by Mailer; the letters from a prisoner, Jack Henry Abbott, in response to Mailer's depiction of life behind bars, which led to Mailer's supporting his parole and recommending publication of Abbott's letters as *In the Belly of the Beast;* and the murder Abbott committed soon after his release, which led to another arrest, trial, and still another text, a play called *In the Belly of the Beast* (Greenblatt 10–11). Although this congeries of texts may seem remarkable, even exceptional, the point Greenblatt is making about "the poetics of everyday behavior" (8) by pointing to a number of texts that participate in the capitalist system of production and exchange without being clearly differentiated as artistic or utilitarian discourse is easily made using other narratives on the boundaries.

One such is *Fatal Vision,* by Joe McGinniss, which seemed a rather run-of-the-mill "true-crime" novel before it was elevated to bestsellerdom by a massive publicity campaign and by the televised version. This miniseries dramatized the journalist's deceptive neutrality and apparently decided Jeffrey MacDonald, the convicted murderer of his wife and two daughters, to sue McGinniss for breach of contract, because he had hidden his conviction that the man he had befriended and whose story he had contracted to tell was indeed guilty – so that it was no longer MacDonald's "story." This civil trial in turn led another journalist, Janet Malcolm, to investigate; she generalized from McGinniss's "betrayal" of his subject's trust to the relationship of journalists and their subjects in general (*The Journalist and the Murderer*).

This circulation of texts around an actual crime gives us a chance to examine some other aspects of true-crime novels. Neither Capote's nor Mailer's novel represents the range of subjects for nonfiction novels of crime. For one thing, the criminals, in both novels, confessed to their deeds and made their stories available to the writers. (Hickock, Smith, and Gilmore gave extensive interviews before they were executed, and these version were corroborated, unlike some death-row confessions – Ted Bundy's for example.) Therefore the writers were confident they knew what had happened, and their different strategies reveal their quite disparate assumptions about their ability to explain the truth of character, motivation, and sociological explanation. For another, the victims in the *Fatal Vision* case were all female, and, as Jane Caputi reminds her reader, in a devastating analysis of recent cases involving sexual or patriarchal "terrorism," in our social and political system violent crimes against women are inevitably naturalized. They are made to seem the result of mysterious forces such as sexual urges or personality disorder, while their politics are overlooked or denied. She asserts, however, that "the murders of women and children – including torture and murder by husbands, lovers, and fathers, as well as that committed by strangers – are not some inexplicable evil or the domain of 'monsters' only. On the contrary, sexual murder is the ultimate expression of sexuality as a form of power" (439). (See also Benedict.)

Another distinction is that neither Mailer nor Capote gives the reader any embodiment, because neither dramatizes his own actions as reader or interpreter of the stories he heard. Malcolm corrects this oversight by standing in for the disbelieving reader, the one who resists McGinniss's assumptions, and she tells the story of another who disbelieved: MacDonald, as the reader of the story he "sold" to McGinniss. The furor over her generalizing to all journalists from him (and the coincidence that she was the defendant in a libel suit brought by one of her subjects over quotations he said she altered) should not obscure the valuable role she plays in bringing the journalist-subject relationship to our attention – and in attempting to theorize about it. Malcolm makes the relationship between journalist and subject overt, taking writing to the next level of reflexivity. This is the primary weakness of *The Executioner's Song*: by having a surrogate for himself (Schiller), Mailer manages to remain unimplicated. He can show the media affecting events, as

Gilmore plays to them to get what he wants, including publicity and stature, or at least significance, but he can remain aloof from this, much as Wolfe does in indicting the swarming hordes of the mass media in *The Right Stuff,* from whom he differentiates himself (see Chapter 6).

In *Fatal Vision,* not only do we have a case in which the victims are female and powerless (for, even if MacDonald did not commit the crime, he was only slightly injured), but it is radically different from the other two, because we never find out what happened at the MacDonald house in Fort Bragg, North Carolina, in January 1970. The narrative's resolution was contested by its subject, an army doctor, who objected particularly to the way McGinniss constructed the damning interpreta-tion (i.e., MacDonald said McGinniss had misused the materials and constructed a false picture of both the crime and himself). McGinniss depicted MacDonald as having killed his wife and one daughter in a fit of rage brought on by his use of self-prescribed amphetamines and as having cold-bloodedly killed his second daughter to make it look as though the family had been attacked by hippies. In Malcolm's narrative, MacDonald becomes the reader of McGinniss's text, and thus he be-comes a dramatized version (though an exaggerated one) of the reader of any nonfiction novel with a mystery at its core. In that sense, Mac-Donald's response, while understandable (he had everything to lose and nothing to gain by failing to react in shock to McGinniss's depiction of him), represents the common displaced emphasis on the error and falsity of a narrative account.[25] More desirable in a literary interpretation is Malcolm's simple acknowledgement of "the difficulty of knowing the truth about anything," the fact that there are very few incidents about which we can know what "really" happened (*Journalist* 134). "It is like looking for proof or disproof of the existence of God in a flower – it all depends on how you read the evidence" (126–7).

Malcolm is aware of the power of the text to determine MacDonald's guilt, outside of the jury's verdict (which he was still trying to appeal more than twenty years after the murders), and so she not only reads *Fatal Vision* but interviews lawyers and reads their notes and peruses letters between McGinniss and MacDonald and transcripts of both tri-als – MacDonald as defendant and plaintiff. But her final response is to throw up her hands and acknowledge our inability to know. Her atten-tion thus turns to the interactions between journalist and subject, and to the difference the guilt or innocence of the subjects makes in the narra-tive's determination of the truth. *Fatal Vision* raises the issues of truth or falsity, guilt or innocence, and makes them overlap with the narrative's determination of one side's claims. Thus the issue becomes how to determine the ground on which representation is based. Jeffrey Mac-Donald sued because he believed that McGinniss's contract to tell his story was violated. The basis of the suit was that McGinniss did not tell the truth, because he did not present as self-evident fact MacDonald's version of the story (echoing the dictum that the truth belongs to the side with the power to make its version prevail). Therefore McGinniss's novel found him guilty, along with the jury.

By treating this case wherein certainty is impossible, Malcolm also shows true-crime story's tendency toward conservation, or taming the deviance that the criminal represents, which is frequently accomplished by conventional illusionist forms. In Capote's adaptation of detective-novel conventions, sociological explanation is ultimately rendered convincing by his fictional form. In general such nonfiction novels settle for producing finite, manageable, exemplary revelations, with an omniscient narrator or figure who "knows." And yet McGinniss could not construct the scene with authority. Malcolm's account, with its messiness, points out the problem in using this kind of form for such a complex case with no certain resolution. McGinniss, indeed, got into trouble because of the inadequacy of form for what he was doing. Malcolm points this out by emphasizing the duplicity of the journalist-subject relationship, which was exaggerated by McGinniss but implicit in every such relationship. This inevitable fictivity of writing may be the repressed subject of all such interactions.

The other wrench in the machine of the smoothly functioning plot was the result of MacDonald's refusal to confess. Because many readers and viewers of *Fatal Vision* in one of its forms were convinced of his guilt by McGinniss's imagined construction of events, the inadequate form indeed affected MacDonald's life (see *Journalist* 144). Even though in the civil suit against McGinniss for breach of contract he settled out of court, after the first jury of six could not reach a verdict, he must have felt partially vindicated in receiving a settlement and knowing that five of six jurors had agreed that he was entitled to one.

To trace the journalist–novelist relationship from Crane to Mailer and Didion is to move away from the author as "immortal" creator to the writer as producer. We have seen these writers become interested in structures, conditions, and contexts, rather than simply the ideology of the individual subject (which most of news as objective narrative or as "literary" journalism embodies and communicates to the reader). Thus writers like Malcolm, Mailer, and Didion "illustrate and exemplify" their culture, rather than stepping aside from it to evaluate it (see Cain, "Realism").

These narratives keep attracting readers, presumably for the same reasons that events become part of history: we are interested in the form of the events in relation to their content – for example, in how subjects become significant as events – or we are interested in people as actors in what become events by being encoded in various explanatory conventions of historical narrative, such as similarity and repetition, cause and effect, and so on. A reflexive reader thereby becomes a kind of historiographer, exploring these journalistic narratives' textual strategies, the audience they suggest and the reading they call for, and sometimes the oppositional strategies they represent. For these reasons we can sometimes resist their assumptions and adopt alternatives (like historians who write revisionist accounts). What are the chances that sustained examination of epistemological issues in this most "aristocratic" of journalistic genres, "the long nonfiction essay" (Stimpson 899) by writers like Malcolm, Didion, and Mailer, can overcome the dominant trope of an incredible or absurd reality? An attitude of helplessness in the face of overwhelming social and political "givens" makes historical and reflexive criticism difficult, because it settles for what is instead of questioning how it got that way. The reified or nonreflexive consciousness is, after all, conceptualized as "an *object* of history" rather than the producer of it (Dahlgren 104). No narrative form can be adequate to anyone's experience of reality if it posits the existence of an objective and knowable world distinct from the observer.[26]

It is particularly difficult to read nonfiction narratives of crime or catastrophe reflexively: in the case of true-crime novels, we want the comforts of genre as an assurance that we are not capable of such acts, but we want to fathom what causes this pathology in other people.[27] In Holocaust and other catastrophe narratives, we hope that the inexplicable will be explained, perhaps even rationalized, so that we do not have to fear similar calamity befalling ourselves. In other words, reification is not something done to us; we participate in its production. Similarly, reflexivity is best conceptualized not as a quality but as an open-ended metaphor for indeterminacy, for the dialectic, for the process of making news, for making a complex reality.

6

Freud and Our "Wolfe Man": The Right Stuff and the Concept of Belatedness

> I have now reached the point at which I must abandon the support I
> have hitherto had from the course of the analysis. I am afraid it will
> also be the point at which the reader's belief will abandon me.
> – Sigmund Freud, "From the History
> of an Infantile Neurosis"

The important triad in crime nonfiction narratives, we have noted, is
made up of the criminal, the detective or prosecutor who explains the
crime by reconstructing how it "must have happened," and the journalist who reports the story, imitating or supplementing the detective by
recapitulating the solution in what becomes the privileged version.
When the true-crime story is self-consciously narrated, it is easily read
reflexively. Such a reading is likely when the journalist's relationship to
his subject forms part of the plot or when the reader begins to attend to
this relationship. An implicit concern of Janet Malcolm's analysis of
reporters' relationship to their subjects, in *The Journalist and the Murderer,*
is the effect their attitude has on the depiction of character and therefore
on the reader. She is aware that readers are influenced to accept or
reject a narrative's truth claims by the manner in which the subject is
represented. In this account of how Joe McGinniss portrayed convicted
murderer Jeffrey MacDonald in *Fatal Vision,* she is clearly appalled
that the journalist had the power to convince numerous readers of
MacDonald's guilt ("If it says so in a book, it must be true" [129]).
Malcolm's intense scrutiny of the MacDonald-McGinniss tangle in *The
Journalist and the Murderer,* and her reflections on her own lawsuit involving Jeffrey Masson, apparently led to other writers' interest in self-
accounting journalism and to speculation about the kind of reader implied by stories that do not hide the source of their authority.[1] Reporters
and critics who wrote about the controversy she ignited over journalists'
obligation to their sources, and over their right to alter quotations, also
addressed, even if indirectly, the effect on readers of laying bare the

196

author-subject relationship. Any textual or critical emphasis on readers' processes of apprehension gives us an incentive to consider our relation to the scene, rather than simply being passive consumers of a thrilling or suspenseful narrative, transparently narrated for easy consumption.

This critical approach is similar to one that poststructuralist critics have used to theorize about detective novels in general: from considering how their own desires are manipulated by particular examples, they move to readers in general and speculate about our fascination with the genre. They point to the way these narratives' structure, based on suspense and resolution by disclosure, satisfies our unconscious desire to "know": to discover our origins, to be privy to sexual secrets, even to solve the riddle of our existence. Because these are also the concerns of psychoanalysis, it is not surprising that Freudian interpretations of crime and detective fiction are common.

The psychoanalytic situation offers a parallel triad of analyst, patient, and the text that reports and theorizes the relationship. (The text is usually written by the analyst but occasionally by the patient or analysand: for example, H.D., in *Tribute to Freud*.) The narrative of psychoanalysis also implies a fourth party: the reader. Cynthia Chase comments, "The psychoanalytic project came into being with the writing that Freud carried on in supplement to his ongoing clinical practice, writings which supplemented the relationship between analyst and analysand by an invocation of readers" (64). Whereas in Chapter 5 the journalist-subject relationship took first place, here I use psychoanalytic theory to focus on the reader in relation to the other participants in the narrative transaction. The reading process is especially important when the journalist is not apparent in the text, when the narrative is highly fact-based and concerns events and characters in most readers' historical memory, and when – as is by and large the case, despite the theoretical investigations of other popular genres such as detective fiction and the romance – critics persist in discussing journalistic narratives in terms of their factuality. If we are to change the dominant conception of nonfictional texts, we must change the form of reception: change the way readers habitually read journalistic and other historical narratives.

Psychoanalytic theory supports the reflexive reading of nonfictional narratives for several reasons. First, it posits no original version of events outside of texts; the original is secondary to the text or narration. In the psychoanalytic situation, attention is focused on the present moment of the exchange, not on recapturing the past, even in memory (Malcolm, *Purloined* 42). The psychoanalyst or psychoanalytic reader takes transparent narration and makes it opaque, and so both reader/writer and analyst/analysand pay attention to the forms in which things are said. Storytellers and interpreters in both analytic situations become

self-conscious; therefore, both reader and analysand are likely to interpret personal "experiences and conflicts . . . within the context of societal arrangements" (Dahlgren 104).

Then, too, Freudian theory offers a way to talk about a different
category of reality, what Malcolm calls "neither the truth of what
happened in the past (historical truth) nor the truth of what might have
happened (narrative truth) but the truth of what the present betrays
about the past (psychoanalytic truth)" (*Purloined* 41–2). In short, "what
is believed" is more important than "what is true" in psychoanalysis,
and perhaps in relation to other texts. Most importantly, the psychoanalytic text, by enacting the process of its own discovery, makes clear the
implication of all the ways of reading reflexively we have been examining: namely, that "no position exists – including that of psychoanalysis – immune to the distortions of secondary revision involved in all
writing, no position from which writing or revision [can] be judged
with disinterested final accuracy" (Chase 63). There is no disinterested
textual position; this follows from the notion that we derive a category
of the "real" from texts.

Perhaps the best way to describe this "textual reality" is to say,
following Freud, that not only effects but memory, imagination, or
fantasy itself takes precedence over the question of the factuality of the
cause or precipitating experience. His work thus provides a model of
how to talk about reality or experience that is not solely textual, but
which we derive from texts. Evidence of this other category included,
for Freud in the 1890s, dreams, slips of the tongue and pen, and his
patients' memories or fantasies of seduction, which they narrated first
under hypnosis and then as part of what came to be known as "the
talking cure." It is thus not an exaggeration to say that, from forms of
narration and figures of speech, Freud hypothesized the existence of the
unconscious and began to describe the operations of the psyche. This
process is similar to what we do when we derive stories from narratives,
even nonfictional ones. Then, too, Freud developed his theory in self-
consciously figurative prose, turning to metaphor to describe what he
posited as the operations of the unconscious. He enables us to read
reflexively by revealing the process of production of his texts as he
writes, and he acknowledges that his theory is a kind of mythology. All
told, psychoanalysis offers another way of explaining that there is a
difference between journalistic narratives and fictional ones, but that the
difference cannot be reified as either-or categories such as real or invented, artful or innocent.

Because such key Freudian notions as repression, deferred action, and
negation are tropes of textual operations as well as of psychical ones,
they are readily adapted to criticism of narrative, and because the narra-

tives I am reading in this study are both popular and factual, I begin
with this journalist's interpretation of Freud. In her reports and critical
essays in the *New Yorker* in the 1980s Janet Malcolm offers the intel-
lectual-magazine reader clear explanations of complex psychoanalytic
concepts and a persuasive critique both of the dominant form of psychoanalytic criticism and of revisionist readings of Freud and Freudian
theory. Because in her review essays she deals with new developments
in biography and criticism and treats "newsmakers" in the narratives
and profiles, her writing is journalism in the best sense of the word, but
she is almost never grouped with other "literary journalists."[2] Her work
provides an ideal introduction to psychoanalytic criticism of journalistic
narrative, as well as being an example of "journalism that stays."

Perhaps the most important insight Malcolm offers her reader is an
understanding of Freud's foundational theory of infantile fantasy and of
how he managed to produce it, despite the habits of mind which lead
ordinary humans to favor literal or objective reality over what can
often seem the absurd productions of fantasy. Malcolm's summary and
analysis reveals how Freud negotiates the categories of the literal, the
unconscious, and the metaphorical, and resists the tendency to revise
what he discovers to conform with so-called objective reality. His practice provides a model of how to read against the ideological assumptions
of fact-based texts, or of how reflexive readers can destabilize texts that
assert their totality. The goal of developing such an alternative to the
aesthetic or idealizing form of psychoanalytic criticism is to uncover,
wherever possible, the contribution of language, fantasy, memory, and
imagination to the production of narrative. These are all ways of making
sense of experience without reducing it to only two kinds: the factual
(what really happened), or the imagined or invented (what did not
happen).

The Freudian theory discussed here is not that derived from reading the
"literary Freud" of critics such as Steven Marcus, Peter Brooks, or
Donald Spence. In my view, literariness is frequently the culprit in
normalizing readings of Freud, as well as in psychoanalytic criticism of
narratives. It leads critics to reduce Freud's complex, self-critical theories
to a set of systematic rhetorical strategies. For example, admirers of
the "literary Freud" translate his description of the operations of the
unconscious into aesthetic terms and show the equivalence of the mechanisms of the dreamwork and the tropes of classical rhetoric (White,
"The Real" 93). These literary Freudians read his case studies as modernist short stories which reveal patients struggling to master the chaos
of their lives by producing coherent explanations or "masterplots."[3]
Although Spence is a psychoanalyst, he takes a similarly literary ap-

proach by asserting that the only positive outcome of psychoanalytic therapy results from "formal interpretation": the substitution of what he calls "narrative" truth – "the truth of being coherent and sayable" – for the presumably incoherent and noncommunicable "historical" truth the patient starts out with (21–2).

The reflexive reader will easily spot the fallacy of this approach, which regards historical reality as what is past, as a repository of experiences which a person can visit to dredge up memories and fragments of stories which the analyst (or other narrator) turns into "artistic creations" (37). This does privilege narrative over events (and Spence cites the phenomenologist Merleau-Ponty's observation that thought may not exist outside of speech), but it preserves the binary categories of fact and fiction or, as Spence puts it, "what is true and what is describable" (62). This division also does violence to the concept of the unconscious, which works by condensation and displacement to "say what it want[s], but not in the way it want[s] to say it – only in softened, distorted, perhaps unrecognisable form" (Eagleton, *Criticism* 91). The coherent narrative that Spence views as a form that can "render justice to reality and make sense to the analyst" (Malcolm, *Purloined* 42) reifies the materials of the person's unconscious life as product – in this case the product of a narrative attempt to represent it by smoothing out contradictions and filling in chinks and gaps like a mason with a psychic trowel.

In contrast, the reflexive psychoanalytic reader, reading for the process, penetrates the smooth façade of the systematic narrative to focus on the conditions of its production. The source of this technique is the Freud of *The Interpretation of Dreams,* who teaches the analyst (of texts as well as dreams) "not only to lay bare the meaning of a distorted text, but to expose *the meaning of the text-distortion itself,*" that is, "the actual process of production" (Eagleton, *Criticism* 90). The lesson from this method of dream interpretation is clear, according to Terry Eagleton: "the uppermost dream layer . . . is analagous to the literary text as defined by 'normative' criticism, and as defined, as it were, by itself – the text as it would 'want' to appear, as spontaneous, complete and so as ideological" (91).[4] The implications for narrative theory are profound, for to practice normative criticism is in effect to read defense mechanisms as art, privileging the normative or noncontradictory text, rendering it authoritative and perhaps even authoritarian. Little critique is possible, and the binarisms of fiction and nonfiction, literature and nonliterary works, are preserved.

In arguing against these literary Freudians who read Freud's few case studies as examples of their thesis that psychoanalysis is "a sort of cure by narrative," Malcolm insists that Freud gave up the narrative approach in analysis early on because it depends on the patient's conscious mem-

ory and interpretation, whereas what has formed us is the way our
imagination has dealt with the vicissitudes of infancy in Oedipal and
pre-Oedipal stages (*Purloined* 28–9, 22). What psychoanalytic therapy
tries to do is "[loosen] the hold of these stories on us – by convincing
us, through the transference, that they are stories, and not the way
things 'are' " (29). In a manner of speaking, the coherent narrative is
the illness, or rather, a sign of successful defense against the chaos of
the unconscious.

> Far from presenting the patient with a well-made story, analysis seeks
> to destroy the story that the patient has for a long time believed to be
> the story of his life. Like a police investigator bent on breaking down
> the alibi of an obdurate suspect, the analyst doggedly whittles away at
> the patient's story through evidence that the patient unwittingly pro-
> vides. . . . Our lives are not like novels. . . . Psychoanalysis seeks to
> acquaint us with and free us from the tyranny of the artist within us
> who insists on an impossible order, who schemes and arranges to
> make things come out right, who commits us to a foolish, sometimes
> even dangerous adherence to *l'art pour l'art*. (45–6)

The poetic configuration of the stories we tell (including those we tell
to ourselves in inner narrative) is the result of the resistance that puts
what Malcolm calls our "mortifying memories" into our consciousness
and keeps them there; that is, they are the result of our defenses, rather
than anyone's conscious artistry (43). We are inevitably poets because
our unconscious traffics in symbols and "works" by displacement and
condensation, not because our lives are like novels (45). As Malcolm
implies, the unconscious works by mechanisms we associate with art
because they seem to have no relation to causality, sequence, plausibil-
ity, motivation, or other logic of ordinary reality; but to treat narratives
of our psychic life as we do artistic narrations, or works of art, is
to accept these productions as autonomous, rather than revelatory of
unconscious materials and grounded in the subject's particular historical
circumstances. We are not likely to subject a narrative viewed as an
artistic creation to analysis of how it came into being, which means that
we remain subject to its ideological work, just as reporting a dream
without analyzing the "dreamwork" – the process of disguise and distortion, the effects of an intervening ideological censor – leaves what
was repressed intact in the unconscious.

In contrast to the literary Freudians are the Freudian literalists, who
come in two forms: devoted followers and belligerent opponents. The
former includes the scientific positivists, who reduce Freud's ideas to
their literal explanations (penis envy, the daughter's seduction) or dream
of having psychoanalysis accepted as a science like chemistry or physiology (as indeed Freud did as well). (Freud, however, acknowledges in

Beyond the Pleasure Principle that scientific language is always figurative [see Meisel 4].) Another follower is pseudonymous Manhattan analyst "Aaron Green," the subject of Malcolm's earlier book, *Psychoanalysis: The Impossible Profession,* who thinks he is being faithful to scientific impulses of psychoanalysis when he describes the therapist "rearrang-[ing] things inside the mind . . . the way an automobile mechanic re-arranges things under the hood of the car" (108). As Harold Bloom points out, "[W]hatever his metaphors sometimes implied, Freud did not confuse the mind with the internal combustion engine" (15).

Among the anti-Freudians is Jeffrey Masson, for a brief time research director of the Sigmund Freud Archives, who takes Freud more literally (and his "original" theories more seriously) than he ever took himself. Freud was, after all, an improviser, continually revising his theories (sometimes those of the day before) to accommodate new evidence from his patients' mouths, whereas Masson believes only in Freud's earlier or "original" theses, because they appear to be based more closely on "reality." Masson shocked the psychoanalytic establishment in 1981 by denouncing Freud's turn away from the "real" world, where sexual abuse or "seduction" of infants is common, to theorize instead that his patients' Oedipal fantasies determined their neuroses (and everyone's psychosocial development). By asserting that the founder of psychoanalysis had erred in emphasizing the importance of "psychical reality" over "material reality" (Freud's own phrases in the 1925 *An Autobiographical Study,* explaining his abandonment of the so-called seduction theory), Masson was saying that psychoanalytic therapy had no empirical basis. He told the *New York Times* that if his view that Freud suppressed his belief in his patients' reports of childhood molestation carried the day, "they would have to recall every patient since 1901. It would be like the Pinto" (quoted in Malcolm, *Archives* 19).

Masson takes his stance favoring the empirical world over texts to such an extreme that it is relatively easy to see that his theory is not only untenable but ahistorical, despite his reputation as skilled researcher and revisionist historian of psychoanalysis. Sticking so tenaciously to a belief for which there is no evidence, even though it means tearing down nearly a century of developments based on the theory one is ques-tioning, is another kind of "art for art's sake." Masson's reassertion of the seduction theory makes the "real world" a kind of autonomous construction, for he ignores or suppresses evidence in support of Freud's theory of infantile sexuality and the Oedipus complex, namely, the role of fantasy in so-called normal development and the signs of the work-ings of the unconscious in the well adjusted: dreams, slips of the tongue and pen, and memory lapses (the "return of the repressed"). In William McGrath's opinion, it was the insight Freud gained from opening his mind to the possibility that his patients were expressing Oedipal desires while telling plausible tales of abuse that enabled him to blur the line between the neuroses and ordinary human unhappiness and thus to construct a comprehensive theory of human behavior (7).

By focusing too narrowly on the question of the reality or fantasy of childhood molestation, Masson leaves out the historical context which gave rise to the problem: the sometimes exhilarating, and occasionally tedious, gradual process Freud improvised for drawing out his patients, hypothesizing to fit their revelations, testing these theories against other evidence, and revising them that led to the concept of psychical reality, with its relevance to the lives of the healthy as well as the mentally ill, the "normal" as well as the abnormal.[5]

Masson is in effect criticizing psychoanalysis on the basis of its content, whereas the key to psychoanalytic thought is its attention to structure, for example, the process of producing a narrative as the "truth" of a person's reality: the form it takes, or the story the reader or analyst infers from the way it is told or from what the person is not telling.[6] This special variety of truth is "the truth of what the present betrays about the past" (Malcolm, *Purloined* 42) and is therefore anchored in each person's particular historical reality. Such attention to process does not arise from the same impetus that leads reductivist or historical revisionists to return to the Freud of the early 1890s. That Freud, torn between science and literature, despaired of curing his patients' neuroses, for they seemed grounded in the real-world ills of either traumatic sexual experience in early childhood or sexual dysfunction in adults caused by rampant venereal disease or inadequate birth control. (A draft of a paper he sent to his confidante and friend Wilhelm Fliess in 1893 reads like a prose version of Blake's "London": "society seems doomed to fall a victim to incurable neuroses . . . destroying the marriage relation and bringing hereditary ruin on the whole coming generation" [quoted in Malcolm, *Archives* 24]). As Malcolm points out, if Freud had continued down the road tracing "neurosis to disturbances of sexual life brought on by social and environmental evils, . . . he would have become the inventor of a better condom, not the founder of psychoanalysis" (*Archives* 23–4).

When therapists say that the effects of childhood sexual abuse are more important than the question of whether it actually happened or was fantasized, in a particular instance, they do not imply that it does not ever matter whether we can determine the event historically. They are acknowledging that we cannot always know what actually happened. Masson, however, makes Freud's whole theory stand or fall on the question of the reality of sexual abuse in children. With bewildering ease, he posits that Freud's shift to the inner reality – infants' imaginative experience of the care adults give them – is equivalent to saying there is no difference between fantasy and reality. He also equates it with denying the actuality of the Holocaust, insisting that psychoanalysis authorizes "the notion that there is no reality, that there are only individual experiences of it" (quoted in Malcolm, *Archives* 55–6). Thus he is appalled when an analyst asserts that he had a patient "who felt that Auschwitz had made a man of him" (82, 54–6).

This notion that "there is no reality" is not only a disturbing implication of psychoanalysis often criticized by revisionists, whether they are admirers or debunkers of Freud; it is also the issue that comes up when a writer or critic begins to question the commonsense, hegemonic assumption that reality is knowable and prior, and that texts capture it in some widely recognizable or consensually validated form. Is it important to know and remember what actually happened – to us individually, in our collective memory, in history – or is the primary question one of interpretation, how individuals and societies deal with what they think happened? The answer, of course, is that we cannot choose just one of these alternatives; both are important, indeed, intertwined, for we cannot separate what actually happened from what we think happened – from our ways of knowing, which are always textual. The fallacy in Masson's making Freud's abandonment of the theory of infantile abuse equivalent to a denial of the reality of the Holocaust is that it requires separating content (what he is asserting as reality) from the form through which we know it. In the case of infantile seduction, we can rarely know what actually happened, because in most cases we cannot verify an adult's memories from the Oedipal and pre-Oedipal period, whereas there is overwhelming textual evidence of the Holocaust: the Nazis' own records of mass slayings, survivor testimony, reports of liberating armies, and many other documents, such as photographs and drawings.[7]

According to Masson, "There are certain kinds of reality that are so overwhelming that they admit of only one interpretation" (quoted in *Archives* 55). With all our socialized belief in absolutes, our inclination at first is probably to agree with him, but unfortunately this is a wish fulfillment, a fantasy of matters being clear-cut; it may arise from a desire to avoid the "ontological crisis" toward which Freudian theory leads us. There are no realities that have only one interpretation – not the Holocaust, not four hundred years of New World slavery, not the destruction of cities by atomic bombs. Each of these catastrophes can be interpreted in many ways, for reality does not come in the categories Jeffrey Masson insists on: what is made up, and what actually happened. Although we resist this idea, psychoanalysis teaches that this very resistance is a sign of its truth. Leonard Shengold, a psychoanalyst Malcolm

interviewed, says that Masson's belief in Freud's suppression of the
reality of infantile seduction, the "trauma theory" of neurosis, is attractive because it fits most people's resistance. It allows us to blame "what
happened" for the way we are now, whereas psychoanalysis says we are
responsible for our inner life. He asserts, "The holocausts – public and
private – did and do occur. They are hard to register. But they do not
explain everything. Neurosis has turned out to be the human condition,
and not just the result of 'seduction by the father' " (Malcolm, *Archives*
83–4).

Masson also oversimplifies Freud's move from the theory of actual
seduction (social psychology) to one based on infantile sexuality, the
fantasy-of-seduction theory (depth psychology). Freud always acknowledged that cases of actual abuse in infancy caused some patients' disor-
ders, but he believed that these victims were less likely to respond to
psychoanalytic therapy.[8] As Malcolm points out, it is object-relations
theory that places more emphasis on the actual conditions of very early
childhood, particularly the "glaring facts of maternal deprivation and
abuse" of the pre-Oedipal period that cause the more severe neuroses
and psychoses that traditional Freudians are reluctant to treat (*Archives*
76–7). She says that Freud simply grew less interested in the "special
plight of the people to whom unspeakable things happen" in his interest
in explaining normal behavior as well as abnormal. In doing this he
inevitably turned from verifiable history to what I would call "posited"
truth, what we assume "must have happened" in order to explain the
way we are now. Because this is similar to the way we derive stories
from plots, the concept of psychical truth or posited reality is extremely
useful to reflexive reading of journalistic narrative.

The fact is that childhood sexual abuse matters more in its effects
than in its materiality. We can know that the Holocaust occurred, that
Auschwitz was real, but we cannot know whether everyone who reports childhood molestation actually was abused. Where the "public and
private" holocausts are similar is in their relational structure, and thus in
their effects. No one can predict why some people are seriously disabled
by experiences of what Shengold elsewhere calls "soul murder" whereas
others come out relatively unscathed. As Shengold writes (in "Child
Abuse and Deprivation: Soul Murder"), "It is in no way to condone or
minimize the often heart-breaking damage done to observe that some
victims of soul murder seem to have been strengthened by the terrible
experiences they have endured. Talents and, occasionally, creative
power can arise from a background of soul murder" (quoted in Malcolm, *Archives* 82).

Lionel Trilling believes that giving up the belief in the factual basis of
infantile seduction "established the terrain of psychoanalysis as a world

of language and fantasy free, by definition, from the domain of objective verification" (Meisel 4). This is not to say that minimizing the historical basis of seduction universalizes the theory; it only makes it general, for psychoanalytic theory enables the recognition of each individual's particular process of producing a self. All of us negotiate the perils of psychosexual development with great difficulty, but each in a different way. As Freud did, we can surmise the continuity between normal and abnormal human behavior, and see this as support for the general theory that all of us suffer childhood sexual trauma that shapes our later development (although it affects us in different ways). The central Freudian insight is "that child molesters [are not] required for the stunting of a person's psychosexual development; the potential for psychosexual catastrophe lies in wait for us all in the ordinary vicissitudes of infantile life" (*Purloined* 22).

The link between the ahistoricism of the "literary Freudians" and that of Masson rests on their similar reading practices: the literary readers deny the process of analysis, in effect offering the objectified narrative as a substitute for psychic chaos, whereas it is a defensive construction, one form the illness takes, rather than its "cure by narrative." Literal readers deny a different process; in Masson's case it is the arduous process by which Freud reluctantly abandoned his belief in actual seduction, the "years of characteristically perilous, error-fraught, uncomfortable, unpleasant creative struggle" (quoted in *Archives* 23). Instead, Masson substitutes the single moment wherein Freud is supposed to have denied evidence from reality in favor of the dynamic concept of "psychoanalytic thought," which goes beyond questions of the fantasy or actuality of belief to analyze the structural or relational *effects* of the belief. There is, finally, not much difference between the literary Freudians and the literalist ones as readers of Freud. What appeared to Spence and others to be a coherent and therefore poetic narrative is regarded by Malcolm, as it was by Freud, as a revealing text to the analyst only to the degree that its process of production can be analyzed and interpreted to learn what "the patient is not telling him." This in turn can only be inferred from "the patient's behavior toward him (transference) and from his manner of disobeying the fundamental rule of free association (resistance)" (*Purloined* 42). The story is interesting or revealing only in its incoherence, for it takes the shape it does (through secondary revision) in order to resist the insight that our behavior is the result of "the demands of inner, psychic reality" rather than "the claims of outer, material reality" (45).

Jeffrey Masson and Donald Spence thus exemplify the wrong kind of readers, but they illustrate how readers customarily approach journalistic narratives. Both approaches are ahistorical, and both lead to a model that cannot critique texts' ideology; readers find it difficult to resist the texts' assumptions because they find it difficult to refuse the position these texts offer or imply. Malcolm is a much better reader of Freud (and of her other subjects), for she historicizes him – puts his ideas in context and shows the intricate process by which he produced psychoanalysis. In turn, that theory never becomes a formula or abstract body of thought but remains dynamic. She recognizes that what makes Freud a great theorist is the "mode of psychoanalytic thought," which she calls his "essential contribution to the history of ideas" (*Purloined* 41). Furthermore, she recognizes that this way of thinking and talking about experience is in an unusual relationship to the real, which we customarily divide into historical or invented; thus it represents a dialectic, for it is neither thesis or antithesis. Unlike these others, she "materializes" psychoanalytic theory, rather than mythologizing it.

She also resists subsuming all her subjects' narratives into hers; therefore she avoids creating the illusion of a totalizing narrative which offers itself as finished product for the reader, as consumer, to take or leave. Instead of simply writing essays that explain the various principals' positions, Malcolm weaves in her explanations and defends the traditional Freudian position by presenting scenes and conversations with the principals and various commentators.

In the Freud Archives reads like a novel, with Jeffrey Masson as an iconoclastic hero, but it is one that offers the reader a choice of entering into the labyrinth where the Freudian revisionists dwell and following the process which she offers as an alternative to their positivist readings – the process by which Freud reluctantly gave up the seduction theory and founded psychoanalysis. She says to the reader, in effect, "Let's you and I get to the bottom of this matter" (although the savvy reader may also detect a hint of "Let's watch while the rogue hero does himself in"). Because the reader has a choice, she can read the book in a number of ways: for example as a "subtle comedy" with picaresque characters (Bloom 3). When it is read along with *Psychoanalysis: The Impossible Profession* and the reviews and critical essays published over a decade in the *New Yorker,* the novel seems to be about reading: how to read Freud's own analytic texts, his autobiographical histories, and case studies; how to interpret character (Anna Freud and Kurt Eissler misread Masson with disastrous results to their goals as keepers of the Sigmund Freud Archives); and how to read this account as the "cautionary tale" Malcolm says it is (*Archives* 27).

We can use this way of reading – one that resists the text as it "wants" to appear, "as spontaneous, complete and so as ideological" (Eagleton, *Criticism* 91) – to reposition ourselves in relation to a text saturated with recognizable fact, concerning events and characters within most readers' historical memory, and surrounded by the writer's own ideas about what he is doing, and thereby read reflexively or dialectically. This is important, for we cannot read journalistic narratives differently unless we can apprehend the benefits of positing the dialectical relationship of history and texts, in place of the current binary categories of fiction and fact.

To demonstrate that alternative mode of reading, I will use this reflexive form of psychoanalytic criticism to destabilize a nonfiction novel, Tom Wolfe's *The Right Stuff*. I will try to avoid simply consuming this perhaps most "normative" and popular of Wolfe's nonfiction novels by reading unself-consciously and instead model a reader who takes up a position vis-à-vis the text different from the one the text itself suggests. *The Right Stuff* is particularly difficult to read reflexively, for narratives are most seductive when they trace the contours of cultural myth that have come to stand for historical truth. Not only does Wolfe trace a strain of myth particularly resistant to criticism because of its quintessential "Americanness" – besides the space program it has a Western setting, horses, and laconic heroes exploring a new frontier – but it is also inescapably a male myth. Where does this leave readers alert to the influence of gender in any political adventure, or those interested in the more problematic aspects of the space program, such as "its cost, philosophy, technological priorities, and impact on national jingoism and machismo" (Hersey, "Legend" 12) – both of which interests the narrative, for the most part, represses? Can she or he refuse the camaraderie offered by the know-it-all narrator?[9]

The myth Wolfe recapitulates is the transformation of seven individual, competitive military aviators into a group of single-combat warrior heroes of the Cold War (summed up by the title of their collective autobiography, *We Seven*), a single unit locked into a war with the Soviet Union for supremacy of the heavens. Although he uses strategies that suggest a major rethinking, even a revisionist history, of the space race in the context of the Cold War, what comes out is simply the story of these men, in the public's eye at least, suppressing their selfish desire for personal fame and forming a cohesive group to represent the country's honor and receive its awards. Wolfe merely substitutes a more refined description of the way the news and entertainment media cooperate with government agencies and policies to perpetuate a particular illusion that becomes fact or history, without suggesting what is left out of that authoritative version that might be used to construe an alternative history. From the fact that his attention-getting style here is similar to that in many of his other reports of the clash between mainstream and countercultural activities and ideologies, we can only conclude that a writer's ostentatious style does not on its own materialize the text in order to offer the reader a critical or alternative position; the reader must read reflexively in order to produce reflexive narrative.

What we will discover, by reading this journalistic example through psychoanalytic lenses, is that trauma can exist and produce effects whether or not it is actual, that is, traceable to a historical cause. Using Malcolm's metaphor (ultimately Freud's), I want to whittle away at the text's defenses, revealing a strategy that purports to be disclosure, but turns out to be one of reticence, even repression. One repressed aspect of Wolfe's text that shows up when it is read in the light of Freudian theory is the history of the specifically masculine culture of the Right Stuff. In this text all men aspire to the Right Stuff, but it is God-given rather than earned. The narrative's defensive terms deny the historical reasons why the men who become astronauts possess this ineffable quality: the fact that they have grown up in a competitive, patriarchal society that reproduces its cultural values in individual men in different ways. The characters are reminiscent of Puritans striving to manifest in outward works the signs of an inner, spiritual grace; assuming the manner of a man with the Right Stuff might be a sign that he had it, but he could not work to achieve it. "A man either had it or he didn't!" exclaims the narrator (22).

Rather than step back to examine the effect of Wolfe's entire narrative, I begin with a pattern I noticed for the first time in Wolfe's accounts of the Project Mercury astronauts' initial flights. During the voyage of Mercury I, narrated in chapter 10 of *The Right Stuff*, Alan Shepard is trying to have the properly awed feelings he is expected to have about being the first American to view his country from space, but it is all a big disappointment. He has forgotten to change the gray filter on his periscope, for one thing (there is no window in the Mercury capsule), and so he sees the earth as "a black-and-white movie."

> There's Bimini Island and the shoals around Bimini. He could see that. *But everything looked so small!* It had all been bigger and clearer in the ALFA trainer, when they flashed the still photos on the screen . . .
> The real thing didn't measure up. It was *not realistic.* (219; ellipsis in original)

Although the narrator attributes Shepard's sensation to the effects of "precreated experience" – he is jaded from having undergone hundreds of exact simulations of space flight during training – it is strikingly akin to the psychological phenomenon Freud named *Nachträglichkeit,* or deferred action. Meaning "after the fact," *nachträglich* refers to psychic belatedness: disruptions in the temporal sequence, so that we experience events out of order, as when we alter past events according to new information, have an experience after we are supposed to have had it, or produce or derive causes from effects.

That this is what is going on becomes clear as another Project Mercury astronaut has a similar experience. John Glenn, the first American to orbit the earth, reports that what ought to have been literally a new "world view" was in fact repetitive, secondary: "He had lived it all before the event" (269). Besides the fact that Glenn was riding backward and so "saw everything after he had passed over it" (269), for the most part nothing was "novel" about his experience, because any odd sensations the first two astronauts had felt had been "*adapted out* of Glenn" by his previous exposure to a simulation of the situation that precipitated their excitement (265–6). It is only when events depart from their prefigured form that Glenn has a sense of reality, for example, when he sees something that looks like fireflies out of the capsule window or when Ground Control hints that a part of his capsule may have malfunctioned and he may burn up "like a steak" on reentry. Only the anomalous or the aberrant penetrates the feeling of déjà vu: "Real life, a crucial moment – against the eternal good beige setting of the simulation" (282).

The astronauts, in effect, had felt the sensations of space flight before they went up, with the result that the ground of experience shifted. What they measured their experience by "was not the vast reaches of the universe" but the simulators, with their photographs and drawings pasted on the windows (270). The basis for comparison became the "mock-up," against which the "actual" was found wanting. The lesson for the reader of Tom Wolfe's narrative as well as for the astronauts is that an imitative procedure can take precedence over the experience from which it was derived and which effectively "caused" it.

There is another retroactive experience in store for all the astronauts. When the narrator of *The Right Stuff* says of Glenn's flight, "No man had ever lived an event so completely ahead of time" (266), he seems to be referring to the preparatory experience Glenn gained from talking with his predecessors in space (Shepard and Gus Grissom) as well as the hours of flight simulation, but also in the background is the intense rivalry between the first seven astronauts, carried on throughout the first half of the novel, over who will be "number 1" on top of the invisible pyramid of pilots: that is, first in space. Adding to Glenn's disappointment over the inferiority of the view was his sense of coming into the field belatedly; he had been "*left behind*" when Shepard was selected to make the first (suborbital) flight (183, 207); he had lived through the first two flights with the feeling that others had taken *his* place, because each astronaut regarded himself as "number 1."

What the seven men find out after Glenn's orbital flight is that the number 3 man has actually won the race, months after Shepard's flight appeared to take priority. Because of the many postponements of the first orbital flight, the media had had an extra month to cover every aspect of the astronauts' training, and politicians like President Kennedy and Vice President Johnson were eager for the publicity any signs of the United States closing the gap in the space race would win them. From the "enormous tidal wave" of public emotion that greeted Glenn as a conquering hero, it became obvious the "holy *first flight*" (Shepard's) was not the "first" one after all; this one was. (This is made explicit in the narrative when the second group of astronauts is presented at a press conference in 1962, where the first group is canonized as the "Original Seven." They are introduced in reverse order, and NASA spokesman Shorty Powers causes riotous laughter when he introduces Shepard *last,* as "the man who's been saying for years 'But I was first!' " [330].)

After riding in ticker-tape parades and addressing a joint session of Congress, Glenn remembers his flight as the awe-inspiring, unique experience he realizes that it must have been (in order for it to have excited this enthusiastic nationwide response). His intervening knowledge has shifted events around, so that what had seemed secondary now assumes priority. To understand this we can borrow the explanation that Freud gave in the case of one of his patients, "Emma," who similarly altered a past event: "Here we have an instance of a memory exciting an affect which it had not excited as an experience, because in the meantime the change produced by [intervening developments] had made possible a new understanding of what was remembered" (Freud, *Origins* 413). (The word in Freud's text that is replaced here by the bracketed words is "puberty"; "Emma" was unable to go into shops alone because at the age of eight she had been assaulted, through her clothes, by a shopkeeper. However, she did not know the sexual connotations of this attack until a second scene at the age of twelve, when she saw two shop assistants laughing together, which she then associated with the earlier incident through the symbolism of clothes.)

Freud says that it was his patient's intervening sexual development that produced the trauma (which in her case was repressed and led to a phobia); the original event was not traumatic because she had no knowledge of sex at that time. The famous case study of the so-called Wolf Man, which details Freud's invention of this most significant mechanism, deferred action, or *Nachträglichkeit,* also places the patient's sexual enlightenment in the central place. Freud interprets the Wolf Man's dream at age four (of six white wolves in a tree outside his bedroom window) as a memory of witnessing his parents' intercourse when he was eighteen months old, a primal scene that "occurred" at full force only at the time of the dream, and which had been made possible in the meantime, Freud repeats, by "his development, his sexual excitations, and his sexual inquiries" ("From the History" 223n).

Freud concludes that the primal scene may never have happened and that the patient himself may have produced it (290). Here again is Freud asserting that the verifiability of past events is not the issue; what is of importance is their psychical reality, which may be the result of desire as well as of experience. In effect, we produce some events after the fact, as memories, in order to account for the way we are now, so that certain determining emotional effects may actually precede their causes.

Although our delayed sexual development is favorable to the operation of deferred action, a closely related phenomenon does not depend on that biological fact; this is our secondary revision of dreams, or of any past experience or memory. As a way to account for the inevitable distortion of dream-thoughts by the time they are related, even for the first time (as we wake up and "remember" our dream), Freud posited (in chapter 6 of *The Interpretation of Dreams*) a factor that he felt must operate "from the very first" – that is, within the dream itself – to recast our unconscious dream-thoughts into a form that will satisfy its conditions of representability, just as they have to satisfy the demands of condensation and of avoiding censorship and resistance. Freud explains this secondary revision as operating toward the content of dreams just as our "waking thinking behaves towards any perceptual material it meets"; that is, our thought works "to establish order in material . . . , to set up relations in it and to make it conform to our expectations of an intelligible whole" (537). In other words, secondary revision also describes our habitual consciousness, the way we structure experience by filling in the gaps, ordering it, and assuring its "representability," as though our experience were narrative.

The name Freud gives to this mechanism also reinforces its position in relation to the original; the first narration is already "secondary," and the original is always "deferred." In one of his most perspicacious essays, "Freud and the Scene of Writing," Jacques Derrida suggests that the primacy of the secondary that gives deferred action its paradoxical quality is close to the norm, rather than exceptional, in texts. He comes to this recognition by linking belatedness in its literary sense – *Nachträg* also means "postscript" – with the "supplement": "The call of the supplement is primary here, and it hollows out that which will be reconstituted by deferral as the present" (160). Derrida is glossing the last chapter of *The Interpretation of Dreams,* where Freud insists on a dynamic, rather than a topographical, representation of the psychical apparatus, because there is no actual place where the unconscious thought can exist. What this means, says Derrida, is that "the present in general is not primal but, rather, reconstituted," and "it is not the absolute, wholly living form which constitutes experience" (160). Despite our longings, we achieve a return to origins only by means of "recuperative revision"; this is "the reductive or recuperative rationalization" Freud finds not only in our ordering of absurdities of our dreams but in "systematic thought" in general (Chase 63).

What these phenomena have in common is that they throw into doubt the possibility of distinguishing the prior from the later, the "original" from the copy or repetition, and before from after. After all, it is not only scenes and seductions from infancy whose reality is undecidable. In reading journalistic narratives, we are likewise unable to recover the event itself outside of textual evidence. All the materials of journalism – documents, personal testimony, or even memories – are communicable only in a form of secondary revision. My reader will recognize this as another way of describing a category of reality that is neither historical nor fictive, for as in infants' fantasies of seduction, events may be actual without our being able to locate them in a specific time and place. For example, in the case of "Emma," we cannot locate in a particular historical moment the traumatic event that altered the girl's later memory and thus made the earlier incident causative. As Freud insists, it occurred neither in the first event (because she did not recognize the sexual element) nor in the later one, which was completely innocuous. Therefore it must have existed in the relationship between them (*Origins* 419).

Belatedness thus is an exemplary trope of journalistic narrative, because it offers multiple categories of what we usually divide into real or imaginary, fact or fiction. For example, in *The Right Stuff* we have a violation of what we usually assume is natural order: causes precede effects. The people involved are not hysterical patients who cannot separate memory from fantasy but well-trained, mentally disciplined astronauts with certifiably "normal" psychological profiles. The inference is that *all* our knowledge of past events is belated, and that the narratives from which we derive stories take priority over those events, even in the case of historical narratives, when we are able to infer these same events and characters from other narratives. The text we are reading or writing is the means of our viewing the past, and, as is the case when we recover our own past in our memory, that view is constructed or produced. Just as the Wolf Man sought his origins in a primal scene and fantasized the perfect correspondence of desire and reality, realistic texts are the result of our unconscious longing to return to a mythical place of unity, of one-to-one correspondence with reality, which Freud figured in *Beyond the Pleasure Principle* (29–32) as the restoration of "an earlier state of things," or the drive toward death.

The common plaint of modern American writers, as well as the astronauts, that reality is no longer credible or "realistic" is one expression of this longing for the original event or "primal scene" and of the realization that it is not recoverable. From this desire may come the high value we place on representation, particularly in the form of factual or documentary or realistic narratives, for realism posits the existence of the thing itself, of the prior status of the object, and of the necessary connection between word and thing that is in fact arbitrary. Always in question, furthermore, is the status of a later version vis-à-vis an earlier one (or one in another medium, which film reviewers, for example, persist in calling "the original"): will it supplant the earlier one and take precedence over it? Because of the multiple representations of reality in the mass media, we lose the ability to tell which has priority – events or their representations. The feelings the astronauts have in comparing what they experience in "reality" to the hyperreality of the simulations are only intensified versions of the way everyday experience fails to live up to the dramatized representations of events on film and television. As more than one spectator of a trial televised live on the courtroom cable channel has remarked, "It isn't 'L.A. Law.' "

It is here that questions concerning the credibility and authenticity of nonfictional narratives become valid, but they cannot be resolved by comparing the narrative to the events and characters themselves. We can only compare versions to each other, and to other texts, for "truth" cannot be found in the connection between the word and its referent (because this is always deferred); nor can it be arrived at by comparing the plot to the story we already know to have existed. This is because the facts are not there before the narrative about them; what secondary revision confirms is that there are no descriptions of events apart from narratives.

Grouping these phenomena under the concept of belatedness helps to explain how the "overdetermination" of historical materials in nonfictional narratives makes the question of truth seem to reside in the difference between "fact" on one side and fiction or imagination on the other. We tend to call nonfictional narratives "true," when all we ought to say about them is that their referents are material or historical, in contrast to imaginary or hypothetical. And the common method of criticizing a journalistic or other historical narrative – by comparing it to previous events – is less important than studying the mode of reception of all our knowledge of objects and events. This practice too gives priority to what comes after, for, as Laplanche says, "It is the *later* which is perhaps more important, and alone allows us to understand and to interpret what we persist in calling *the prior*" (25).

The Right Stuff is probably the most visibly fact-based text of those we have examined; it thus reveals the inadequacy of the usual categories of true-false, history or invention. Readers (and since 1985, viewers of the film version) must find it difficult to read nonreferentially. Reading it referentially, for "what happens," however, reifies Wolfe's narrative as authoritative; thus the form most criticism takes is to resist this authority by picking at its details, comparing Wolfe's history with what the reader or reviewer has stored in her historical memory. Then, too, experts are consulted, in the belief that insiders will have a more faithful picture in their minds. For example, in his review of the book, Apollo astronaut Michael Collins vouched for the authenticity of the description of the test pilots' lifestyle at Edwards Air Force Base. John Hersey, for his review, interviewed two astronauts, as well as a spokesman for the Johnson Space Center in Houston; all three evaluated the book as reasonably "accurate." Hersey's standards of accuracy also extend to easily verifiable facts; he lists many details that Wolfe did not check and therefore got wrong ("The kind of car John Glenn drove, . . . What operant conditioning means. The Latin name for the chimpanzee" ["Legend" 9]).

Hersey says that journalists who had covered the space program generally agreed that Wolfe had made an earnest attempt at accuracy, but "most of them thought he had been too kind to Scott Carpenter and too hard on John Glenn" (8). Hersey is clearly frustrated that there is no "ground" for determining the accuracy of character portrayal. The person depicted obviously cannot be the arbiter, for Glenn thought he "came out pretty good in the book," and this does not square with Hersey's findings. Hersey in effect makes his interpretation the basis of the narrative's reality, for he does not say simply that his view of Glenn's character is different; he says insistently, "Glenn is pictured in the book as an insufferable prig, a prude, a killjoy" (8). Like John Hersey's, our first tendency is probably to put Wolfe's representation of characters and events up against our own, without considering where either of those versions came from and how we (or Wolfe) came to hold them. We must develop this self-consciousness if we are to break out of the fiction–nonfiction bind that results in no better criticism than Hersey's relentless attempt to separate the reported from the invented.

Reading through the theoretical prism of belatedness allows us to see history as text, rather than history as the reified past. This makes it possible for the reader to regard a text as a distorted representation and to analyze, not its meaning, but the distortions, or more specifically, the significance of the form the distortions take. In other words, the text, not the characters and not Wolfe or his persona as narrator, has an unconscious which can be analyzed. Pierre Macherey describes the text's unconscious as "that of which it is not, and cannot be, aware." In Terry Eagleton's paraphrase of this notion, the relation between ideology and the text's unconsciousness is clear:

> What the text "says" is not just this or that meaning, but precisely their difference and separation: it articulates the space which both divides and binds together the text's multiple senses. . . . An ideology exists because there are certain things which must not be spoken of. In so putting ideology to work, the text begins to illuminate the absences which are the foundation of its articulate discourse. And in doing this, it helps to "liberate" us from the ideology of which that discourse is the product. (*Criticism* 90)

The first distorted representation in *The Right Stuff* that I want to discuss appears in the first chapter, "The Angels." Here the narrator overtly articulates a gap – namely, that between young naval aviators and their wives over the appropriate attitude toward death – and so would seem to affirm Wolfe's demystifying approach to the young military pilots who will become America's greatest heroes as astronauts. He also begins the book by offering the viewpoint of the aviators' wives, who are seen to provide a "reality check" by openly fearing what the men avoid acknowledging. Indeed, the chapter enacts a kind of "structural" reality: the deceptiveness of experience when it is not acknowledged by appropriate language. This story is told from the point of view of Jane Conrad, wife of Pete, one of the second group of astronauts. At Jacksonville Naval Air Station in 1955, where Pete is in Navy jet training, Jane begins to have hallucinations of being notified of Pete's death by a "Solemn Friend of Widows and Orphans," the clergyman who routinely pays such visits to inform new widows of their status. It is impossible to tell the difference between this illusion and the reality that apparently surrounds her, because life there is lived under the continual illusion that "nothing is happening," despite the fact that the men in Pete's training squadron are dying left and right in plane crashes, like Ten Little Indians, as the narrator counts them down.

Jane believes she cannot tell anyone what is happening to her, for not only is there no protocol for discussing death, but the very words necessary to speak about it have been "amputated" from the language (3). The pilots talk in a code about the frequent crashes: other pilots have "bought it" or "augered in" or "crunched," but this is in the same "breezy, slangy terminology" with which they "talked about sports." The narrator makes sure the reader knows all the horrific, gory details which describe what an incinerated pilot's corpse looks like (5–6), but this reality is denied by the pilots. Therefore Jane Conrad's hallucinations are closer to an accurate perception of reality than is the denial of death by the men, one of whom is her husband.

The women soon realize that the pilots are safer in the space program than they were in military jets. By the time we have seen each wife's parallel ordeal-by-media as her husband is launched live on television, we realize that this chapter has set up the irony that although no one wants to know Jane's story when she is truly fearful for her husband's life (while he is a member of a decimated squadron), later so many people (represented by the intrusive photographers and reporters) want to know the dreams and fears of the astronauts' wives that no such "private and personal response" is even possible (338). To the television cameras, Annie Glenn or Trudy Cooper may be what Wolfe's narrator satirizes as the "Anguished Wife at Lift-off," but her ordeal is rather different from what the press imagines: it involves nerving herself to step outside in front of the battery of cameras when she has heard her husband is safe and wondering "what kind of face should she have on?" (214–15). The emotional reality has been overtaken by its exaggerated representation. The wives must present an "appropriate" emotion to the television cameras, but it is one that has been "appropriated," for it does not match their "own" feelings. How are we able to judge which is the "true" emotion of the wives? Which is the grounding term, and what is the basis for determining factual accuracy, the truth of a witness or of one's own experience?

By seeming to substitute the wives' "correct" perception of reality for their husbands', Wolfe appears to be revising the history of the competition to be America's first astronauts and the world's leader in the race to dominate the skies. But the same problem that causes Hersey's anxiety about how we are to determine which interpretation of the men's actions and characters is the real one surfaces here: neither version is correct, for there is no primary or original place where all this history happened in a particular way. And so we cannot say that Wolfe is correcting this false impression; he is merely substituting a different one, but one that he strives to make authoritative by repressing the contradictions in his text. One of these is between theme and form: his narrative asserts the superiority of the unspoken, the laconic, and the understated, while the narrator emphasizes and even exaggerates the ineffable through such fixing and reifying strategies as hyperbole, repetition, and the ubiquitous epithet ("Low Rent," "Flying & Drinking and Drinking & Driving" and its variations). Then, too, the illusion it constructs of toppling the New Frontier myth of Project Mercury's glorious space successes and putting in its place an emphasis on Cold War maneuvering, with its subplot detailing our squabbling astronauts' jockeying for position on the great ziggurat of flying, is itself undermined by the revelations of the drive toward nothingness at the heart of the Right Stuff.

Already we are beginning to get hints of the causes of this text's indeterminacy: Wolfe does not supply a narrator who takes responsibility for the particular history he tells. He does not appear in his own voice; instead he has absorbed all the various points of view into a single composite one, while his own persona or alter ego is elusive. These variations on the actual, the substitutions of an alternative to the dominant history that accumulated through the journalistic narratives of hundreds of writers and broadcasters, all are secondary to Wolfe's self-aggrandizing narrative voice and its restoration of natural hierarchies. These are the values of patriarchal culture, extending back to the myths of early Western history, and they are based on the value of manhood, represented as racially inherited, or biological, or in some essentialist way "given."

In order to overcome the effect of his predecessors and "set the record straight," Wolfe presents the dominant myth as it was made, the process of concocting the public relations version of events. Since he is putting a different version in its place, however, the attuned reader expects his narrative to reveal its process of construction, not simply its assertion by an authoritative narrator. Wolfe's plot does show the construction of the first myth (a common strategy of revisionist historians). Because the text's primary strategies are deferral of meaning and of presence, avoidance, and the inadequacy or even absence of language ("you couldn't put it into words"), a superfluity of these figures, although striving for understatement, is a sign of repression. Indeed, Wolfe's narrative does repress its "ideological problematic"; it is "eloquent" in what it does *not* say (Eagleton, *Criticism* 89). This is obvious even in the manner in which Wolfe lays bare the behavior of the mass of reporters, who, in their primary manifestations of "Victorian Gent" on the one hand and a mass of insects swarming all over their subjects on the other, produced the myth of the heroic astronauts. By emphasizing their distortions, Wolfe effectively deflects our attention from his own exaggerated epithets and overstated metaphors describing their actions and distances himself from those journalists. He ridicules reporters who presume intimacy with the righteous warriors, violating the pilots' laconic style by pouring out details of the manly code and actually talking "about fear and bravery (they would say the words!) and how you *felt* at such-and-such a moment!" (50). The implication is that this journalist would never act in such an "obscene" or "repulsive" way, that is, say out loud the "unspoken things."

If Wolfe the New Journalist is not one of those "ravenous termites . . . taking pictures and yelling questions," nor one of the "root weevils which . . . keep their craving beaks honed in on the juicy stuff that the whole swarm has sensed" (130, 92), then where is he? The answer must be that he is the ultimate insider, that is, the narrator who critiques

previous totalizing narratives by totalizing in a different way, specifically, by elevating the writer even above the characters in his historical
narrative. We must read reflexively in order to counter this repression
and its seductive illusion of giving the total picture. Such a reading
enables us not only to "demonstrate how the text is thus 'hollowed' by
its relation to ideology" but possibly even to look around the edges of
his monolithic narrative in order to see another history. As Eagleton
says, following Macherey, "The task of criticism . . . is not to situate
itself within the same space as the text, allowing it to speak or complet-
ing what it necessarily leaves unsaid. On the contrary its function is to
install itself within the very incompleteness of the work in order to
theorise it – to explain the ideological necessity of those *'not saids'* which
constitute the very principle of its identity" (*Criticism* 89). In particular,
peering around the corners of Wolfe's text through the prism of psychoanalytic theory permits us to see the terms of this text's incompleteness.

Our analysis of Jane Conrad's hallucinations at Jacksonville has brought
results similar to those of dream analysis. What they reveal is that she
has transformed her fear into its opposite, fulfillment. As Freud (in
Beyond the Pleasure Principle) theorized about his grandson's *"fort-da"*
game ("now she's gone, now she's back," he pretended about his
mother by rolling a spool under a bed and then recovering it), she is
mastering her fear by repeatedly imagining its outcome. This is only a
more direct expression of the men's goal, for their euphemisms cover
up what for her is fulfilled in a recurring fantasy of death, Freud's
"instinct towards perfection," to which Wolfe gives the name "the
Right Stuff." This capitalized phrase, which dominates chapter 2, works
by referring not to a tangible quality but to what is marked by absence;
the Right Stuff signifies by deferral – of meaning and of death. It is
possible to define the Right Stuff only by saying what it is not: it is not
simply bravery, nor is there a single test of it. The only way to tell if a
man has it is by his difference from the others, from those who are "left
behind" or washed out, those who are "found wanting."

And yet a man with the Right Stuff paradoxically has to both defy
death and deny it. The military pilots talk about death all the time, but
only in words that have been detached from their conventional referents
and attached to new ones arbitrarily. For example, they speak in euphemisms, and they express cause-effect relations in terms of code and
example. They get themselves into corners, and "luck out of it." According to these daredevils, "there are no *accidents*" (27), which means
bad luck cannot do them in, only thoughtlessness, or lack of courage or
daring. It follows that pilots who do "buy the farm" or "auger in" must
be short the requisite amount of Right Stuff. Thus the fighter pilots

repress the fact that those late companions of theirs who are euphemistically being "left behind" or washing out are not necessarily lacking anything but in many cases are losing something: namely, their lives. They are being killed, regularly, and in ways uncomfortably familiar to the survivors. And so, Wolfe writes, these young competitors cut "the Right Stuff up in coded slices so they could talk about it . . . bowed ironically to it, stumbled blindfolded around it, groped, lurched, belched, staggered, bawled, sang, roared, and feinted at it with self-deprecating humor." But "they never mentioned it by name" (28).

Rather, defying death day after day is the primary way for a man to demonstrate that he has the Right Stuff. Repetition is also the sign of the death wish, as we know from *Beyond the Pleasure Principle.*

> Every modification which is thus imposed upon the course of the organism's life is accepted by the conservative organic instincts and stored up for further repetition. Those instincts are therefore bound to give a deceptive appearance of being forces tending toward change and progress, whilst in fact they are merely seeking to reach an ancient goal by paths alike old and new. (32)

Repetition by variation merely disguises what is inevitably the "binary choice" that defines the righteous ones. All the death-defying pyrotechnics, "pushing the outside of the envelope" and straining one's body to its physical limits (as in what Wolfe calls "Flying & Drinking and Drinking & Driving") give the illusion of bravery while merely postponing the inevitable and complicating the route to it. The pilot making his first night carrier landing on heaving seas with only three passes to make it or go back to land, or the one who has to decide in a split second whether to ignore a warning light on his panel or to eject, is choosing between the Right Stuff and death, although neither is ever mentioned. By constantly deferring mention of the subject, however, these men make it clear that the dichotomy does not consist of an opposition but of alternative routes toward the same goal.

If the Right Stuff consists primarily of denying death, of doing everything to circumvent it while coming as close as possible to it, then it can stand only for the repression of the desire for death. As Freud says in "Negation,"

> The subject-matter of a repressed image or thought can make its way into consciousness on condition that it is *denied.* Negation is a way of taking account of what is repressed; indeed, it is actually a removal of the repression, though not, of course, an acceptance of what is repressed. . . .
>   . . . To deny something in one's judgment is at bottom the same thing as to say: "That is something that I would rather repress." A neg-

ative judgment is the intellectual substitute for repression; the "No" in
which it is expressed is the hallmark of repression, a certificate of origin, as it were, like "Made in Germany." (214)

Operating as a kind of backup system, the pilots' "self-preservative
instincts" counter this "tendency to zero" (Laplanche 85). The final goal
is nevertheless still the same, for the function of these instincts "is to
assure that the organism shall follow its own path to death" (*Beyond* 33).
What the Right Stuff aces demonstrate is their divergence from the
original or "default" course of life; they are making "ever more complicated *detours* before reaching [their] aim of death" (*Beyond* 33). Thus the
Right Stuff is a displacement of the death drive, and the choice is no
choice at all, except that of which route to take.

Another trope of deferral is litotes, or understatement, which gains in
effect by contrast with Wolfe's characteristic hyperbolic narrative style.
The military euphemism for landing on the deck of an aircraft carrier is
"recovery and arrest," but in the narrative's rendering of the novice
pilots' collective free indirect speech it is a "hurtling piece of steel"
crashing onto a "heaving barbecue grill" (or "a *skillet!* – a frying pan! – a
short-order grill!"[20]). The only appropriate euphemisms for speaking
about death are understatements; thus the "hot young fighter jocks"
who fly the X-rocket planes speak of crashing and burning as "buying
the farm," "augering in," "crunching it." The master of litotes is X-1
test pilot Chuck Yeager, who is also the apotheosis of the Right Stuff.
Wolfe places him at the pinnacle of the flying brotherhood of righteous
warriors; not surprisingly, Yeager's language is exemplary. The understatement, the assurance that things are ordinary, "per usual," is the
predominant feature of his laconic speaking style. "How d'ye hold with
rockets now, son?", he asks, in what Wolfe describes as "that lazy
lollygaggin' chucklin' driftin' voice" (54), when he has just "talked
down" the pilot of a rocket plane with no visibility and no fuel. When
he becomes the first man to fly faster than the speed of sound, he signals
what has happened in code: "There's somethin' wrong with this ol'
machometer [speed indicator] . . . it's gone kinda screwy on me" (47).

The text makes much of Yeager's language and its influence on fliers,
from his compatriots at Muroc Field in California (where X-rocket
planes were tested) after World War II, on down to commercial airline
pilots today. Ironically, what had been a peculiar, idiosyncratic style of
talking, which revealed an individual approach and distinguished this
country boy (from Hamlin, West Virginia) with his colorful accent from
all other war aces, was adopted by so many macho pilots as an indicator
of the Right Stuff that they became indistinguishable from one another.
We can hear this quality today, Wolfe insists, in "the voice that tells
you, as the airliner is caught in thunderheads and goes bolting up and

down a thousand feet at a single gulp, to check your seat belts because 'it might get a little choppy.' " We may notice "a particular down-home calmness that is so exaggerated it begins to parody itself," according to Wolfe (35).

Understatement, like any rhetorical feature that is imitated or repeated, turns inside out and becomes parodic, excessive. In Yeager's case his imitators adopt the characteristics that formerly set him off from the rest of the pack, in the hope that in acquiring his manner they will also assume his skill and bravery. The features that were distinctive begin to attract so many imitators that they become dominant. What began as an absence – the avoidance of fear or excitement, the silencing of chatter – is now an ever-present phenomenon. This is a kind of deferred action in narrative, for the only way we know the unusual, the deviant, or innovative (or the avant-garde in art) is after the fact, when the deviation has become the norm, frequently taking everything along with it in a surge of dominance. This is especially apt in relation to journalism, for news narratives by definition try to tell us what is "new," but by the time some event or tendency is discussed enough to be noticed, it is no longer new; the new is therefore continually postponed. If "real" events can be so filled with indeterminacy and uncertainty, there is no way to preserve the boundaries between historical and fictional narratives, especially given the fact that so much of our experience at the end of the twentieth century is textual.

This realization, in psychoanalytic terms, is what Wolfe's coherent narrative is "defending against." The outcome of the Project Mercury astronauts' experience of belatedness is that it is repressed. These men come to believe (and Wolfe's narrative asserts it as credible truth) that their experience was unique and profound, and that to be astronauts is to be the most visible possessors of the Right Stuff. On this level the novel is the story of how what is secondary and inferior becomes central and primary, the most visible sign of righteousness. (The first astronauts, who merely sit atop rockets as they are popped up into the air, are ridiculed as "Spam in a can" by the test-pilot jocks at Edwards.) But he also admires their chutzpah in asserting their manhood despite the lack of worthy challenges to it.

Because Wolfe's viewpoint is not clearly detectable, and because the form his "New Journalism" takes in this narrative is simply to move hardly distinguishable varieties of macho men from low to high in some picturesque metaphors (climbing the ziggurat, etc.), the narrative drive seems to be just another form of seizing the power from below by emphasizing style for its own sake. The prize he would grab would be the status of literature for his Low Rent form, whether it is called popular history or New Journalism.[10] As regards the plot of that history, what he is doing most consistently is leveling the playing field to enable it to accommodate more players of the sort he approves of: namely, men, particularly those of the virile, hard-driving, good-old-boy sort; women who are "honorary men," like Pancho Barnes, proprietor of a rickety bar near Edwards, former gunrunner for Mexican revolutionaries, ace pilot (who broke Earhart's air-speed record for women in 1930), and owner of a "vulcanized tongue"; wives like Yeager's Glennis, who goes along with the hot-dogging and "nocturnal proficiency runs" back to base after hours of drinking; and any woman who accepts the Military Wife's Compact, which includes rising in rank with her husband and taking on "all the honors and perquisites pertaining thereto" while disdaining the same people the men do, especially the weevil hordes of the mass media (40–1, 332).

By elevating these particular women, either because they are "honorary men" or content to be appendages to their men, Wolfe reveals a vulnerability in his otherwise secure, totalizing narrative that the reflexive reader can use as an entry place to begin to dismantle it. Or she can take the materials and begin to construct an alternative history from his discarded or overlooked materials. As evidence that Wolfe is making a primarily ahistorical move toward myth rather than undertaking anything new or radical in the way of revisionist history, consider the formula he substitutes for the one he debunks. The mainstream media have reduced the Project Mercury wives' complex awareness that their husbands are safer in the space vehicle than they were in the jet planes to something easier to grasp, highlighting the sense of danger with the question "[W]hat are they thinking at this anguished moment?" For this, Wolfe's narrator substitutes "[W]hat kind of face should she have on?" (215). This question is no less reductive of a complex response, although it has the advantage of being deflationary, and therefore of calling attention to the inadequacy of the figure hyped by the dominant media – the Anguished Wife at Lift-off, the central figure in a wake, "not for the dead, but for the Gravely Endangered" (214) – and to its production. Although the Anguished Wife is an artificial figure, it is one easily naturalized as "real," for viewers are familiar with versions produced in the journalistic tradition of interviewing disaster survivors and victims' next-of-kin.[11] Wolfe is refreshingly satirical as he lays bare the construction of this mythology of American wifehood.

The figure which dramatizes this process of whitewashing is the *Life* cover photograph of 12 September 1959, which showed the wives' faces, from which "every suggestion of a wen, a hickie, an electrolysis line, a furze of mustache, a bag, a bump, a crack in the lipstick, a rogue cilia of hair, an uneven set of the lips . . . had disappeared in the magic of photo retouching" (130). By listing all the expurgated flaws, however, and adding a comparison to high-school photographs with a catalog of skin blemishes adolescents are prone to, which are routinely "scraped off by the photography studio," Wolfe contradicts his own metaphor of whitewashing. Instead of accepting the reconstructed image of the astronauts' wives, Wolfe restores the women, as the saying goes, "warts and all," to their distinctive, imperfect humanity. This is an instance of Wolfe having it both ways: revealing the media as complicit with NASA public relations efforts to elevate Project Mercury participants to Cold War heroes (the Victorian Gent who rewrites the wives' hesitant responses to reporters' yammerings and suppresses news of groupies seducing the astronauts one by one at Cape Canaveral), while simultaneously depicting the crowds of reporters and broadcasters as termites, fruit flies, or weevils, pesky and persistent – or as yahoos playing opposite the Genteel Beast (50, 92, 130, 187). The retouching example works similarly to Wolfe's treatment of the exaggerated understatement of Yeager's imitators: he corrects an image by addition, even to excess. As he says about Yeager's influence, "It was *Pygmalion* in reverse" (37).

This might make the reader think that Wolfe is a revisionist writer, able to show the "real" attitude of the women because he has insinuated himself into their confidence. What he purports to do is rehabilitate the wives as savvy women who have told him they knew how they were manipulated by the media. In the earlier, *Life*-constructed version, they were icons of pure womanhood; in Wolfe's alternative, they are hip to the media and to how their images are constructed. (Wolfe shows Rene Carpenter imitating the television correspondent invariably assigned to ask the doctrinaire questions about how "Primly Stable," the astronaut's wife, was holding up during the crisis [340].) It is more a facelift than a new image that Wolfe gives women, however; he merely substitutes their self-consciousness for any change in their status.

Besides, there is another striking omission in his supposedly revisionist narrative of the space race: Wolfe omits any mention of the thirteen women pilots who were "left behind" in 1961 after qualifying for the space program by performing exceptionally well in the first two phases of NASA medical and psychological testing to determine suitability for suborbital and orbital flight. (Twenty-five women pilots applied.) By omitting the story of these women pilots, several of whom performed better on the stress and sensory-deprivation tests than some of the men, and one of whom – Jerrie Croft – had flown twice as many miles as John Glenn, who led the men with 5,000 (another woman had logged 8,000), Wolfe shores up the myth of manhood that underlies the Right Stuff (McCullough 41–2).

By noting this buried story, we have evidence to support an interpretation of *The Right Stuff* as upholding the status quo. Despite the satiric signals given off by his reversals of status, which show him apparently debunking the myth of heroic astronauts, Wolfe sides with both groups of aviators against sissified NASA administrators and, indirectly, women. Revealing that women might actually have been better suited psychologically and physically to ride in the Mercury capsule would have made it difficult to perpetuate the illusion that the plane-jockeys-turned-space-pilots became heroes because they had the proper masculine stuff – and this is the ultimate goal of Wolfe's narrative, even if what they had is reduced to the machismo it took to bend NASA to their will and win a pilot's role in Project Mercury, and thus superpilot status.

By ignoring the story that women were passed over despite having proved "more durable in the face of loneliness, heat, cold, pain, and noise" (McCullough 43), Wolfe perpetuates the myths established by the astronauts and their press supporters. These asserted that only men had the Right Stuff, and, because this quality could not be defined, the men fell back on the women's inability to meet jet-testing requirements, ignoring the fact that the only reason for that was that they were simply not allowed to fly jets. (The Navy had just opened flight training for women, but even in 1974 they were not allowed to land on carriers or receive jet training.) When it was proposed to let the women check out on jets at military training bases, Jacqueline Cochran, a jet pilot and NASA consultant but not an astronaut candidate, said that although they could have completed the instruction in a short time, this was undesirable to NASA because it would have made the men, with their years of experience, "look silly" ("Letters," *Ms.* 6).

The obvious implication of ruling the women unsuitable is that there would be no way to reassert the manly code, if women could be astronauts too: it would devalue the position, the way any job takes a status dive when women do it. (At news that women were being tested, the press began to invent alternative names for them, such as "astrodolls," "spacegals," and "astrotrix"; the title "astronaut," gender neutral though it be, could not be demeaned by affixing it to women.) By neglecting to report the studies of women, including NASA's active search for women pilots to include in the candidate pool, Wolfe effectively raises the astronauts from the level of psychological subjects, "talking monkeys," to men in control of their image as well as of what were now no longer capsules but *spacecraft*. Any reader who knows this story or remembers the congressional subcommittee hearings on the matter of women's exclusion from the space program in 1962 is likely to speculate about why Wolfe left it out (especially when reading the words of a general trying to mollify an angry Pete Conrad, who is threatening to drop out of medical testing because of daily enemas: "You have a compact build, and every pound saved in Project Mercury can be critical" [77]). Many readers, however, do not know of these women's success or of the NASA spokesman who supposedly said, "Talk of an American spacewoman makes me sick to my stomach."[12]

Wolfe's omission of a subplot he surely uncovered in his research supports a particular interpretation of his novel, one that emphasizes the masculine bias not only of rocket development and space programs but of the way they are covered by journalists and historians. It does not matter whether a reader regards Wolfe as cheerleading for the astronauts or favoring the X-1 and X-15 pilots (Yeager, Scott Crosfield, Joe Walker, and Bob White) for the top of the Right Stuff pyramid. If we can see that Wolfe's representation of the astronauts suits the tendency of adventure narrative to repress the feminine and reveals the masculinist bias of the space program and its coverage, we can go beneath the surface pyrotechnics of style to see the disturbance implicit in the narrative, whether it is regarded as cheerleading or debunking criticism. In neither interpretation does Wolfe begin to consider the deeper problem of basing a billion-dollar space program on superpower competition, or comment on the preposterousness of a Cold War with its roots in nuclear rivalry, much less consider the effects on culture of denying the feminine side of experience, in individuals like the space-age warriors or in society at large. The text has universalized these tropes of negation and belatedness simply by adopting them from conventional usage. The process is similar to the acceptance of masculine models of behavior, belief, and desire as universal human ones in patriarchal society. When the text of *The Right Stuff* equates bravery and courage first with not speaking about it (or, just as likely, associates the unbrave, the washout pilot, with silence about his failure) and then with manhood itself, the narrator amplifies the reticence and the ineffable by connecting it to conditions true in all times:

> And in what test had he been found wanting? Why, it seemed to be nothing less than *manhood* itself. Naturally, this was never mentioned, either. Yet there it was. *Manliness, manhood, manly courage* . . . there was something ancient, primordial, irresistible about the challenge of this stuff, no matter what a sophisticated and rational age one might think he lived in. (22)

Rather than being learned in society, the voice of the narrator says, male qualities are inherited through some kind of racial memory.

What are the ideological ramifications of taking the desire to have the Right Stuff to be universal when it is explicitly associated with male actions and fantasies? Wolfe does not uncover the drive toward nothingness at the heart of the Right Stuff, despite all the rhetorical mileage he makes out of these figures. Even more significantly, the text's own method of reifying a particular historical reality by embodying it in a totalizing narrative – by failing to show the construction of these values and ideals, along with the process by which the men became single-combat-warrior heroes – gives it an element of mystification, despite the fact that it is obviously based on years of research. Thus *The Right Stuff* illustrates a problem many critics have with popular history and the New Journalism: it is all too easy to turn history into myth when the ultimate goal is to achieve the status of literary art.

As we have traced the process since Stephen Crane's time, deemphasizing the particular and local leads to reducing complex circumstances to simple cause-effect relations. Wolfe is guilty of this when he says the public lost interest in the astronauts because the Cold War ended and the mantle of single-combat-warrior glory fell from their shoulders (367). And how did the Cold War end? According to him, it was all over in an instant, because of the negotiation of a nuclear test-ban agreement and the installation of the hotline between the White House and the Kremlin (366). As Laurie Stone says, "Nowhere in *The Right Stuff* are Vietnam, the assassinations, or various civil rights movements ever mentioned with relationship to the space program, or American focus on it" (73). What Wolfe presents is myth, not historical analysis. There is no context except that of the Cold War, but this competition between superpowers itself has a history; it is not an event that can be summed up in a sports metaphor of sides that go ahead or fall behind. What is more, Wolfe explicitly denies that the history of the sixties can be told in anything but "manners and morals": historians will write about it not "as the decade of the war in Vietnam or of space exploration or of political assassinations . . . but as the decade when manners and morals, styles of living, attitudes toward the world changed the country more crucially than any political events" (Introduction 29).

Already, in choosing to explain the unprecedented adulation awarded the astronauts by reviving the legendary ancient champion-warriors, Wolfe has chosen to explain events in terms of myth. As Charles Ross points out, the tradition of a single warrior fighting on behalf of his people has an element of magic which is well suited to the aura of mystery surrounding space technology: "The space-race dramatized the entire technological and intellectual capability of a nation. Although it was a small skirmish, it grew in importance like magic, and the astronauts dealt in its magical stuff" (121). Then, because of the Cold War, the notion of exploration was inseparable from fear of the expansion of nuclear weapons to earth orbit. (Think how quickly the Strategic Defense Initiative became "Star Wars.") To express this dread of doomsday bombs falling from the heavens, Wolfe invokes the Norse god Thor. When news comes of two Soviet spacecraft flying in tandem orbits, the press and some members of Congress imagine "[e]ntire *formations* of Soviet space warriors, hurling thunderbolts at Schenectady . . . Grand Forks . . . Oklahoma City" (318).

Although Wolfe is writing from ten to twenty years after the fact, the effect of the downstage narrator who enters into the good-ol'-boy joshing and the spirit of the "nocturnal proficiency runs" is curiously timeless, for the narrator has gone just as smoothly into the minds of the pilots as they break speed and altitude records. All the men have the same attitude toward their activities. Several of the book's critics have pointed out that the effect may result from Wolfe's not bothering to differentiate among the voices he ventriloquizes by varying their free indirect discourse. To Laurie Stone, "because Wolfe is everywhere, he is also nowhere," and she describes the effect as "very repetitious – lots of dummy-heads but one ventriloquist" (71). As Alan Trachtenberg insists, there is no reporter's or historian's perspective. Wolfe "converts experience into spectacle, fixes it, reifies it as a reader's vicarious experience. He cheats us with illusions of deeper penetrations into segregated realities but the illusion is a calculated product that disguises what it is we are actually reading" ("What's New?" 301).

When, besides, the narrator explains the almost incomprehensible adulation the astronauts win, especially after Glenn's first flight, by citing tales of single-combat warriors feted and cosseted before the battle (in case they were not alive afterward), the effect is curiously ahistorical, even mythic. This effect is only increased by Wolfe's knowing description of the "royal treatment" accorded the astronauts and their entourage in New York City ("[y]ou had to be pretty dense not to realize what this was: a command performance! Royal treatment, point for point . . . and they were the royal families") and his exultant cry closing the section: "Oh, it was a primitive and profound thing! Only pilots truly had it, but the entire world responded, and no one knew its name" (292–3). Except Tom Wolfe, of course, for he claims credit for having figured out the reason for the unbelievable adulation showered on these seven men way back when all they had done was show up at a press conference (107). This, then, is the most pernicious effect of Wolfe's absorbing all the narratives into this totalizing one: with its opaque, repetitive manner it gives the illusion of reflexivity without offering the reader the option of easily reading for the process. The position offered to the reader is complicity in the text's all-knowingness; to read, we implicitly accept its denial of an alternative history.

This voice is distinguishable from the more subtly inflected third-person narrator of texts that blur the lines between reporter and subject and enable the reader to enter into the consciousness of a represented character, such as *The Executioner's Song* or even parts of Richard Cramer's *What It Takes* (discussed briefly in Chapter 4). *The Right Stuff* is more overtly objectifying than *The Electric Kool-Aid Acid Test,* for, as we noted in Chapter 4, that narrator occasionally says "I" and accounts for his own perceptions and interpretations. Wolfe instead assumes he knows the attitude of all the characters whose consciousness he represents in *The Right Stuff;* in fact, they all sound the same because they share *his* consciousness. Critics have noticed this same vocabulary appearing not only in various characters' free indirect discourse but in other Wolfe works, and they criticize it as emblematic of the New Journalists' overinflated egos (Arlen, "Notes"). It also puts all the characters on the same level and blurs the differences among them (Ross 119–20). The effect of this is to make everyone and everything secondary to an all-encompassing Wolfean voice. Its ideological effect is similar to that of objectivity in that it prevents the reader from entering into alternative points of view; we have to read as though Wolfe were the "one who knows" and thus accept his self-construction as authoritative narrator. But he is one who has denied us the means of evaluating what he says; he suppresses viewer reflexivity by repressing any but the "super" narrator's voice.

Despite its attempt at self-consciousness, the way in which it calls attention to its rhetoric as such, *The Right Stuff* is primarily a work of traditional realism. As Wolfe describes it in the introduction to *The New Journalism,* his goal as New Journalist is to make the screen between reader and world disappear, to make us believe in the history he has presented, in this version as what "actually happened" and in just what manner (34). We must read against the text to force it to reveal its gaps. Even a text that attempts to replicate reality can only be partial; one kind of reader resistance is to criticize what is omitted in the summarizing, symbolization, condensation, displacement, and projection invariably involved – just as in the dreamwork – in selecting from everything that has happened (history) to produce a finite (historical) text. Textual categories are also unstable, for the text as read is constantly being produced by the interaction between reader and text, and by the resistance of each.

Wolfe offers to readers only his view of what happened, only this position from which to critique. Arguing over which parts a writer "got right" in terms of accuracy is a hopeless exercise, because we have no primary or original text to compare later versions to, and these narratives are paramount in determining the history we have of events in the past; in fact, they are all we have, for we cannot retrieve the past except from texts, including our memory as a text. As Robert Rosenstone remarks in discussing *JFK*, the historical film or docudrama that is a similar combination of documentary history in dramatized form, we may of course debate the conclusions presented by such a work, that is, argue with its viewpoint. We do this by looking "from outside" the work, "from the ongoing discourse of history. . . . Any work about the past, be it a piece of written, visual, or oral history, enters a body of preexisting knowledge and debate." Therefore any historical text is not fact itself but what "engage[s] the issues, ideas, data, and arguments of that discourse" (509–10). Because in approaching *The Right Stuff* we have peered around the monolithic construction that Wolfe's totalizing voice throws up in front, comparing that either–or position it offers us as readers to Jeffrey Masson's reading of Freud, which likewise reduced complex history to "it either happened or it was made up," we can see that what is left out is an alternative reader position. Other positions or options for viewing the text are foreclosed. In Wolfe's case, his omission of the women astronaut candidates is the gap that betrays his highly defended fantasy. "What I would rather not think about" may be death for the test pilots and astronauts, but it is also the feminine principle.

There is a scene late in *The Right Stuff* which illustrates wonderfully this text's pragmatic, masculine bias toward the verifiable fact. Although the scene features Chuck Yeager, it is so paradigmatic of Wolfe's view of what is "real," and it denies so clearly the role of social or political factors in the construction of the real, that the reader is justified in regarding it as emanating from the author – especially since Yeager's free indirect discourse is no more differentiated than is that of any other character; it too has been sucked up by Wolfe's all-purpose vacuum to be spewed out through a character Wolfe deems to fit it; and of course he does not remind us of his mediation.

Wolfe's definition of the real is emblematic of his reactionary politics: what is objectively real or true is what is subject to the laws of physics in general, and aerodynamics in particular. Since Yeager is the paradigmatic possessor of the "operational" stuff, his anachronistic attempt to break an altitude record in a rocket plane after both U.S. and USSR space flights had rendered them rather meaningless ("like setting some sort of new record for railroad trains," Wolfe says) provides the perfect vehicle for Wolfe's revisionist mythology (356), which is itself a kind of technological determinism in prose. (The term "technological determinism" expresses the view that a technological invention somehow comes into being and then is used to fulfill needs, rather than being, as Ohmann says, a "social process, saturated with the power relations around it, continually reshaped according to some people's *intentions*" [*Politics* 221; see also Winner and Noble].) Wolfe's mythology (a form of recuperative revision) expresses a similar determinism: he assumes that effects appear as though demanded by their cause, but in actuality that cause-effect relation is belated, or produced because it appears necessary to account for the way things are.

In 1962 Yeager was made commandant of the Aerospace Research Pilot School (ARPS) at Edwards Air Force Base. ARPS was designed to give the military a space program focused on the X-20 and other rocket-boosted airplanes while still contributing test pilots to NASA's astronaut program. Although ARPS became in effect "Chuck Yeager's prep school" for astronauts, he took it in stride, Wolfe maintains, because "there was no steady state" on the flying pyramid; he knew, for example, that automated systems in jet fighters meant that "the age of 'the flyboys,' the stick'n'rudder fighter jocks, was about finished" (347, 352). But Wolfe insists that what finally got to Yeager was that in 1963 Washington bureaucrats, on orders from the top (President Kennedy and his brother Robert, the attorney general), insisted that a black man be in the next class of astronauts. This meant Yeager had to admit an eligible black candidate to ARPS' six-month space-flight course. He ended up admitting fourteen instead of the usual eleven, so that the black captain, who ranked fourteenth, would not be jumped above the three in front of him.

This sounds like a workable solution to anyone raised in the aftermath of civil rights legislation and court cases, from which we learned to find ways to make it possible for members of a minority group, discriminated against for centuries, to be among those benefitting from programs that may mean higher income, better education, open employment, and such intangibles as moving up in class (another invisible "ziggurat" or hierarchy which Wolfe supresses) and fame. Besides, Wolfe has just spent a chapter ("The Operational Stuff," Chap. 13) and several paragraphs detailing the perquisites and fringe benefits handed out to astronauts and their families, which make the slots decidedly worth achieving (348). Then there is the Air Force "charm school" created to help the leading candidates qualify, which even Yeager has accommodated, despite the fact that all he had ever wanted was the privilege of wearing the Air Force "Blue Suit" (348).

Nevertheless, Wolfe says that Yeager found the business of race "baffling," for "the unspoken premise was that you either had the right stuff or you didn't, and no other variables mattered." Wolfe goes into a page of rationalizing why all the Mercury astronauts and leading pilots and career military officers generally were white Protestants. The business about the need for a black astronaut, in the view of Wolfe/Yeager, is an intrusive political requirement, which simply mucks up the fair, workable competition for the race up the great ziggurat of flying which has "always" been in place. This passage is more than a diatribe against the irrelevancies of affirmative action, however, for Yeager's escape to "reality" from the unseemly pressures of the Washington apparatchiks takes the form of a new plane to test, and he turns to it with relief, Wolfe insists, in a sentence attributed to Yeager's consciousness: "All of the world's accumulated political cunning, from Machiavelli to John McCormack, wouldn't be worth a dogscratch in the NF-104 at 65,000 feet" (354–5) – as though there were nothing political about the conditions that made Yeager an Air Force colonel, commandant of ARPS, and the apotheosis of that "righteous old-time religion," with its mock dogfights, waxing one another's tail, and "locating the outside of the envelope" before stretching it a little (356, 350). The code is empirically "there" – primeval, absolute, and masculine – in the Wolfe/Yeager mind, in contrast to the "squinting and hassling" of politics despite the text's acknowledgment, just sentences earlier, that the White House was going to get a black ARPS student because the astronaut, as "single-combat warrior, had become a creature with greater political significance than any other type of pilot in history" (354). This latest "monster" rocket plane proves Yeager's undoing (forcing him to bail out for the first time since World War II), and the futility of this flight becomes the last grand gesture of the unsung "stick'n'rudder man" and Wolfe's final dramatization of the essentialist masculine myth, this time endowed with pathos generally reserved for a farmer selling his horses to buy a tractor.

Conclusion

The tropes of belatedness, as we have been using them to read *The Right Stuff*, offer a more satisfactory explanation of the appeal of journalistic narratives than the theory that nonfiction attracts us because it offers the certainty of the factual. That is, by questioning the natural relationship between narratives and the "reality" they appear to represent, a self-conscious reader, in conjunction with a text that enables it, produces a version of events that corresponds more closely to our experience of the world — especially one filled with pseudoevents and precreated experience. The complexity and ambiguity, even the uncertainty, of journalistic representations that call attention to their language, to themselves as structures of representation, or to their processes of coming into being, arouse our interest because they imitate the ongoing process of our own self-formation. By highlighting the workings of deferred action in *The Right Stuff*, I am suggesting that belatedness may be a repressed trope of journalistic narratives. If we can bring it to the conscious level of texts — or to our consciousness as we read — we may become regular reflexive readers. And what that does to our habitual practice of engaging with nonfictional or real-world texts, I look forward to seeing. Perhaps it will make a dramatic change in our consciousness, equivalent to the effect of televised reality on Philip Roth's.

This system of reading involves expanding readers' possible positions vis-à-vis a given text in order to maintain their awareness of relational categories rather than simple oppositional ones and encouraging them to take up a dialectical stance rather than fall into nonreflexive, fixed positions. Since no text is totalizing, and therefore no narrative is a perfect representation, the reader always has to keep in mind how she is positioned by the text and may reposition herself in turn. Seeing relational categories makes it possible to question the place the text has prepared for the reader and to develop an antithetical position. Because the structure of dialectic becomes obviously dynamic, there is no hard-and-fast thesis simply to accept or reject (such as "Is this real or invented?"); instead, a hypothesis is more easily kept unfixed and flexible. One can accept some aspects and reject others.

Thus I have shown various ways to resist not only the implications of particular journalistic narratives but the limited possibilities of reading under the current dispensation, which divides texts into fact or fiction, journalism or literature. This chapter, and indeed this study as a whole, reveals the tameness of the act of reading nonfiction or journalism for coherence or to "see what happened." Indeed, even to offer competing interpretations may be a similarly limited act, unless these produce a profound dissonance that locates textual gaps between ideology and explicit assertions.

Like all critical practices, mine has broader implications; one is that reflexivity is not just a way of reading. Part of my practice has been to use history as a process to avert the further reification of dominant myths, and even to demystify them and work against reductive ideological practice. Thus I favor texts in which the writer-narrator is reading some kind of text reflexively: Freud reading his patients' speech and dreams, Barthes reading cultural texts like the representation of Romans in films (*Mythologies*) or Japan's semiotic codes (*Empire of Signs*), Malcolm reading Freud and revisionist Freudians, Didion reading the coverage of the 1992 "Central Park jogger" case and linking it to the mid-nineteenth-century discourse about the park's design as a way of controlling the underclass (*After Henry* 253–319). Reflexivity *in* the text does not necessarily imply a strategy of criticism or alternative mode; sometimes it is merely a sign of self-awareness. When self-consciousness is only ironic, or when irony is the dominant trope, the narrative may be cynical, not necessarily critical, especially not self-critical (M. Miller 13–16). Although mainstream news too is apparently more self-conscious now than previously, this has not produced significantly more critical journalism. Very few oppositional strategies are offered to the reader of the *New York Times,* the *Washington Post, Newsday,* or *USA Today,* reflecting the co-opting power of the dominant form of news, which invisibly supports the establishment (see Schudson, "Sociology" 156). Nor is journalists' move toward novelistic form in their coverage of politics (Robert Woodward's *The Brethren,* David Halberstam's *The Best and the Brightest,* Cramer's *What It Takes: The Way to the White House*) necessarily either progressive or regressive; these writers may simply be running in place, for these novelistic versions of New Journalism (whether called this or not) are reminiscent of the ideal of fictional objectivity: they frequently have a totalizing narrator and construct a mythology – that is, in gathering an interpretation that will explain a complex series of events or behavior, they substitute accepted views of human nature or essential beliefs for history.

I have claimed that journalism and fiction in objective modes are quite similar – that they work similarly by ideology; perhaps the relationship holds for self-consciousness in journalism in relation to self-conscious fiction. Such journalism may become simply entertainment, merely "literary"; its critique is then easily muted. If we read *Armies of the Night* for what makes it endure as literature instead of seeing that the critique of the establishment's Vietnam policies is relevant to every other abuse of power since then (e.g., the Watergate affair; the Iran-Contra "arms-for-hostages" plan; the October Surprise; U.S. arming of Iraq before the Gulf War; BCCI money laundering; the savings and loan debacle), we in effect co-opt it, nullifying its critical lesson. And yet Mailer has given us the mechanism by which to read not only his narrative but those making up the "primary" texts of contemporary journalism as it covers events in later wars between a government with an unpopular policy and the opposition which tries to make it accountable. Mailer shows how protestors at the Pentagon in 1967 were "taken care of" by dominant groups: physically by the troops in a brutal wedge formation; politically by strategies of marginalization, isolation, dismissal; and publically by the press strategies of reduction, simplified plot, and ironic coverage, which Mailer reveals in microcosm by comparing *Time*'s coverage of his role to his own version of Mailer in D.C. Unless a text stirs readers' reflexivity, it may simply be pushing our buttons (see Schwartz).

My most general recommendation for a way to read reflexively is to re-read, with the reader (even of one's own work) remaining alert for what composition theorists are always calling ways to "re-vision" the materials. After all, one way to attend to a text's production is to be aware of how one reproduces it in reading, which is likely to happen only on a second or later reading; for finally a reflexive reading means being aware of one's own reading process, and of how all readers are complicit with the writer in producing the text. Thus reading reflexively offers the advantage that historical narrative does not have to be trans-formed into art to last; we have ways to talk about a journalistic account as a particular interpretation without aestheticizing or universalizing it. It can be both timely and timeless.

Notes

PREFACE

1. Other readings that can serve as models because they resituate texts in their context or historicize myths are those by Roland Barthes in *Mythologies*, a collection of magazine pieces (and therefore both part of and about mass media); and John Berger et al. in *Ways of Seeing*, a Marxist analysis of art history and publicity which was produced for television, then made into a paperback book. See also Stewart, who indicates how literary studies may turn into cultural studies simply by defining new problems and describing new objects of knowledge through experimental writing and pedagogical practices.

INTRODUCTION: WHAT ISN'T LITERATURE?

1. Deconstruction is the primary theory that breaks down the distinction and collapses writing into undifferentiated discourse. See especially Derrida, "Freud and the Scene of Writing" and "The Law of Genre." Doctorow says, "There's no fact or fiction any more, there's only narrative" (quoted in Clemons 76). See also Geertz.
2. See McHale on prevalent readings of *Gravity's Rainbow*, for example.
3. See the excellent, detailed survey of theories of literature in Foley, *Telling*.
4. Foley says that texts exploring "private" historical experience reveal the line between the factual and the fictive to be fine, because "the biographical and historical criteria for verifiability are not available to the average reader" ("History" 396). See also Pratt 97.
5. In a 1993 essay on the problems encountered by biographers of Sylvia Plath, Janet Malcolm points out that, paradoxically, it is not the reader of fiction who feels "epistemological insecurity" but the reader of nonfiction, for even the most accurate journalist or biographer cannot convey without mediation "the truth of what happened," whereas the novelist is constrained only by his imagination. Only fiction gives "a true report," for there are no "alternative scenarios." She concludes, "Only in nonfiction does the question of what happened and how people thought and felt remain open" ("Silent Woman" 138).

6. Compare E. D. Hirsch: "Literature includes any text worthy to be taught to students by teachers of literature, when those texts are not being taught to students in other departments of a school or university" (34).

1. WRITING AFTER THE FACT

1. Hirsch says we "know" intuitively what works are literary in most cases and then we set about searching for qualities those examples have in common (24–5).
2. See Cohn on the unrepresentative quality of Smith's passage from *Ivan Ilyich*, which overlooks the use of extensive focalization later in the novella (5–6).
3. The *Press* news accounts of 4 Jan. 1897 and that day's piece promising Crane's version are reprinted in *Stephen Crane: Stories and Tales*, along with a front-page story from the *Florida Times-Union*, Jan. 3, two other *Times-Union* stories from Jan. 4, and both "Stephen Crane's Own Story" and "The Open Boat." The last two are included in *The Portable Stephen Crane* (Katz). Page references are to the *Virginia Edition of the Works of Stephen Crane:* "Stephen Crane's Own Story" (vol. 9, *Reports of War*, 85–93), and "The Open Boat" (vol. 5, *Tales of Adventure*, 68–92). The Jan. 4 *Press* account quotes an unnamed survivor (the cook, Joseph Montgomery) who claimed there were five men in the dinghy, but Captain Murphy's version in the *Times-Union* accords with Crane's. The incorrect news story is apparently the source of the controversy, detailed in various articles, over Crane's accuracy of observation in both stories (e.g., did he exaggerate weather conditions?). For these articles see Pizer's bibliographical essay in *Fifteen American Authors* (144).
4. While White asserts the impossibility of meaningful narrative without moral authority, Teresa de Lauretis emphasizes the desire implicit in this theory of the "cultural function" of narrative: "The equation of narrative with meaning . . . is mediated by the agency of desire" (129). See also Girard and Clayton.
5. This does not make "Stephen Crane's Own Story" less "literary," of course; Christopher Benfey calls the first-person survivor story "more openly mythical and allusive" and its central action, the loss of the seven men, "more harrowing and morally ambiguous" than anything in "The Open Boat" (189): "It is a nightmare passage, its horror enhanced by the Last Judgment coloring Crane casts it in, with its demons and its doomed men consigned to the pit (the frightful maw of the ocean). The lost ones look longingly at the saved, while the guilt of the saved is assuaged only by the overstepping gesture of the demon" (192).
6. As Rader ("Defoe" 33–4 and 67 n. 3) explains the Crane–Sacks concept of represented action, characters about whom "we are made to care" are placed in states of disequilibrium which are complicated and then resolved.
7. In "The Open Boat" the focalizing character is the correspondent, and when we acknowledge the autobiographical basis of the story, we readily see why this is so. Although it is possible for a first-person dramatized narrator to use free indirect discourse to represent what other characters say (and, according to some theorists, even what they think, as in *Wuthering Heights,* for example), the possibilities for focalization and its principal technique, free indirect discourse, are for the most part limited to the first-person narrator's own mind. (See Banfield 94–5, 145, for examples.)
8. Ann Banfield has founded her theory of fiction on represented consciousness (the technique that underlies focalization) and on the belief that "no one speaks" the sentence of narration, as I show later in this chapter.

9. There is some disagreement about this, but I contend that no other single character's point of view is given by representing his consciousness. The narrator of the discourse, who gives the correspondent's speculations, occasionally takes up a superior perspective to imagine how the four men's eyes "must have glinted" and to report how the scene might have looked "viewed from a balcony" (362). This voice also speculates about what the "sharpened minds" of the four were conjuring up about those on shore who did not come to their aid (369) and other attitudes shared by the men. Nearly all our clues to what the other three men are thinking come from observations that anyone watching (most likely, the correspondent) might have made; this is true even of the captain's moodiness in the sixth paragraph. As the correspondent (or the narrator from somewhere behind him) could see, he was dejected and indifferent, and he "had on him the stern impression of a scene" of shipwreck. That is, the observer can interpret the captain's look as caused by a recent bitter memory, because he was there to witness the scene. Therefore I attribute all these representations of others' feelings to the correspondent or to the discourse of the narrator. For a different view, see Schirmer, who believes that the reader is brought close to the captain's "innermost thoughts" in this paragraph (223).

10. The first remark was supposedly uttered by Captain Murphy, assuring Crane that he had written "The Open Boat" accurately. He was overheard by a journalist, Ralph Paine, who recorded the incident in *Roads of Adventure;* Benfey (193–4), Stallman (*Biography* 257), and C. Brown (75–6) all quote Paine's version.

11. See Conder 22–30 for an interpretation that views the story as naturalistic but does not take the last statement as ironic. In this subtle reading, all the men are now interpreters, "according to their own respective professions," and the form the correspondent's interpretation takes is the story Crane titled "The Open Boat" (28).

12. Compare Colvert's description of a pattern of tension he finds in Crane: that between "the narrowing and deluding point of view of the actors and the enlarging and ruthlessly revealing point of view of the observer-narrator" ("Structure" 200). See also Holton 160–1.

13. Christopher Wilson has defined literary professionalism as more than just making a living by selling one's works. He says it came about during the Progressive Era in the United States, when writers themselves began to view their productions as the result of "technical expertise rather than inspiration" and came to regard "the market as the primary arbiter of literary value" (204n; see also 8–13).

14. Barthes's paraphrase is in "Science" (411). The linguistic explanation of this function is the projection of "the principle of equivalence" from one plane – that of selection, or the vertical – into the plane of contiguity or combination – the horizontal "speech chain" resulting from language's inevitably linear nature (Jakobson, "Closing" 358). This transfer of one mode into the other gives texts their dual quality, as when considerations of equivalence, or of sameness or difference, similarity or dissimilarity, determine the choice of a word placed next to another in a sentence.

15. The term "self-conscious" is historically broader than it has become in the context of postmodernism, where it usually suggests artificiality, such as a highly ironic, introspective style or a playfully self-dramatizing narrator. I use it as Jameson does, to characterize "the way in which a certain type of material lifts itself to awareness, not only as the object of our thought, but

also as a set of mental operations proposed by the intrinsic nature of that particular object" (*Marxism* 340). See also Hutcheon, *Narcissistic*.

16. Compare Culler: "[T]o read a text as literature is to read it as fiction" (128) and Hatlen: "Rather than thinking of English as the study of *certain kinds of texts*, I am proposing that we should instead see it as *the study of texts in a certain way*" (675).

17. Jakobson's well-known formulation of the six aspects of language is easily abridged: "The addresser sends a message to the addressee. To be operative the message requires a context referred to ('referent' in another . . . nomenclature), seizable by the addressee . . . ; a code fully, or at least partially, common to the addresser and addressee . . . ; and finally, a contact, a physical channel and psychological connection between [them], enabling both of them to enter and stay in communication" ("Closing" 353). The six functions are the *emotive* and *conative,* which correspond to sender and receiver; the *poetic,* which results from emphasizing the message; the *phatic,* or "set for contact," which serves to start, prolong, or sustain communication; the *metalingual,* which is a way of checking up on the code; and the *context,* which corresponds to the referential aspect. Although he does not ignore these other aspects (see his interesting example of the phatic function in a sample dialogue, from Dorothy Parker [355–6]), Jakobson focuses primarily on the intersection of metaphor and metonymy, the projection of "substitution" into syntax. See also his "Two Aspects of Language."

18. "The double-sensed message [resulting from imposing the poetic function over the referential] finds correspondence in a split addresser, in a split addressee, and besides in a split reference" (Jakobson, "Closing" 371).

19. In support of his thesis that Progressivism as a cultural and political movement influenced the form and dissemination of popular naturalism, C. Wilson (204n) gives David Kennedy's description (in *Progressivism: The Critical Issues*) of Progressives as "representatives of a confident new middle class eager to apply to society at large the techniques of systematization, rationalization, and bureaucratic administrative control developed in business and the professions."

20. Foley makes this claim, in objecting to Jakobson's description of the poetic function (which is her example of linguistic definitions), but her broad survey of dozens of definitions of literariness (part of an effort to posit a qualitative difference between fictional and nonfictional discourse) inevitably oversimplifies them. Besides, I use Jakobson for a different purpose: I want to extend his description of the poetic function to a general reading process that produces what some critics may want to call literature, whereas she is schematizing alternative approaches to mimesis in order to contrast them with her complexly worked out definition of the mimetic author–reader contract of documentary fiction (*Telling the Truth* 45, 42).

21. The Russian Formalists were members of two overlapping, informal literary circles that existed in Moscow for roughly the first ten years after the October Revolution of 1917. Their members included Jakobson, Viktor Shklovsky, Boris Eichenbaum, Boris Tomashevsky, Jurij Tynyanov, Jan Jkarovsky. Jakobson headed the Moscow Linguistic Circle and in 1920 emigrated to Prague, where he was leader of the Prague Linguistic Circle (Czech structuralism). See Erlich, *Russian Formalism;* Jameson, *Prison House;* and Bennett, *Formalism and Marxism.*

22. Similarly, to Louis Mink, events, or "descriptions of events," and characters "are not the raw material out of which [even nonfictional] narratives are

constructed" (147); they are functions of narrative, which we derive after the fact. Jameson puts it this way in *The Political Unconscious:* although history is "*not* a text, for it is fundamentally non-narrative and nonrepresentational," it is "inaccessible to us except in textual form" (82).

23. For fuller explanation of *sjuzet* and *fabula,* see Shklovsky, Tomashevsky, and Eichenbaum, all in Lemon and Reis, especially 57, 66–7, 116. The Formalists contrasted the two in order to show how literature is made by fashioning given materials into plot: rearranging the temporal sequence (beginning in medias res, using flashbacks), disrupting normal cause–effect relations (as in parallel plots with no connection), slowing the action, transposing parts, or adding digressions. Plot in its largest sense was to them simply one of the techniques for "making strange," for rendering the familiar world unfamiliar. See Jakobson, "On Realism"; and Bennett 20.

24. Conder, on the other hand, claims that this known background "permits a critic to merge character and author by saying that the story is the form the correspondent-author's interpretation takes" (28).

25. In commenting on the oiler's death, Cyrus Day inadvertently revealed the amusing implications of our presumed urge to fictionalize, to plot (logically and pleasingly) "what really happens" to us: "Higgins' death was made to order for Crane as correspondent and as literary artist. . . . If Higgins hadn't died, Crane would have had to kill him, or rather he would have had to kill the fictional oiler in "The Open Boat." . . . [However,] I am *not* suggesting that Crane pushed the real Higgins under in the surf, or thought of doing so, just for the sake of providing a future short story with a suitably tragic climax" (213).

26. For variations on these interpretations, see Autrey 107–8; Cady 154; D. Hoffman 172; LaFrance 298; Monteiro 330.

27. Benfey seems to have taken an insight offered by Larzer Ziff in 1966 and extended it as far as possible, as a way of seeing Crane's life as a whole. Ziff says, "Stephen Crane's expectations had a way of outstripping the event . . . [he] developed a set of responses that anticipated the reality." Benfey quotes this passage as well as citing Orvell's argument that "Crane's characters take their cues from popular culture, trying to fit their lives to its patterns" (Benfey 273n).

28. As Benfey points out, Crane kept no diaries, left few intimate letters, and seems to have revealed himself to very few, so that there is a "paucity of self-exposure" (10). The only notebook extant was published in 1969; Crane probably kept it in 1892–1893, recording his New York City wanderings.

29. Wertheim and Sorrentino (who edited the Crane *Correspondence*) have demonstrated that although suspicions arose early that Beer's Crane was a creature of the imagination, perhaps the result of overidentifying with his subject, subsequent biographers have relied on Beers's accounts indiscriminately instead of giving more credence to materials that they could have verified independently. (Beer wrote about people whom no one else could locate; no copies of most of the letters he quoted were found in his files, nor did the originals ever turn up.) See "Thomas Beer."

30. Day errs on the side of content as egregiously as the unself-conscious formalist reading does on the side of form – in, for example, emphasizing some linguistic feature for its own sake. (See Kissane for a mild example.)

31. This view of the tale has a long tradition and a distinguished origin, going back to Conrad's capsule description of it as illustrating "the essentials of life itself, like a symbolic tale" (13).

32. Called by its proponents "the journalism that acts," this kind of news was nicknamed "yellow journalism" after the main character of a popular cartoon in the *World*, whose costume was printed in bright yellow; after Hearst lured the cartoonist away, Pulitzer continued a version in the *World*, so that there were two "Yellow Kids" in the Sunday comics of both New York papers (see Milton xi–xiii; Brown 14–15).

33. As Milton points out, "yellow journalism" was a term of approbation for some, particularly those who believed the Spanish-American War was the logical outcome of "manifest destiny" (see also Brown 4).

34. As the editors of his correspondence sum up the incident, "The widespread publicity attendant upon this case, especially the charges of immorality heaped upon Crane by defense witnesses, was devastating to his reputation, already tarnished by rumors that he was a drug addict and an alcoholic" (223–4). For Crane's own account of the affair, see his "Adventures of a Novelist," in the Library of America *Stephen Crane* as well as *Tales, Sketches, and Reports* (vol. 8 of the *Virginia Edition*); and Fryckstedt.

35. See Trachtenberg, "Experiments"; Levenson, xx–xxiii.

36. Cady says that because magazine publication, not books, was the main source of income for writers of his time, Crane undoubtedly read "avidly in the great contemporary household literary magazines," viewing them as "potential markets," to see which stories worked and which did not work. He is certain that this is where "Crane got the education he all too obviously got nowhere else" (76).

37. Solomon says "'The Open Boat' is itself the story of Stephen Crane's short life, a constant battle with the stormy elements that led to both victory (his permanent art) and defeat (his early death)" (160).

38. He was "not a successful writer financially," conclude Wertheim and Sorrentino (*Correspondence* 368n), citing Stallman's biography (600), which compares average payment per word for Crane (five cents at most) and Kipling (twenty-three cents and more). No wonder he wrote to a fellow journalist in 1894, "I am living upon the glory of literature not upon its pay" (*Correspondence* 82).

39. Self-referentiality may be only an intensification of the work's aesthetic form, not really a separate characteristic, but many definitions mention it separately. For example, Todorov gives three synonyms for what he views as an extension of systematized (aesthetic) texts: "opacity," "intransitiveness," and "autotelism" ("Notion" 10–11).

40. To Dorrit Cohn, the frequent use of what she calls "focalizing techniques" inescapably marks a work as fictional, because by displacing the subjectivity of the first person to the third it "creates the reality of unreal, imaginary beings" (8). And Ann Banfield insists that representing the thought of a third person is "a signal that we have entered the realm . . . where what can be documented passes into what must always remain speculative – the inner workings of . . . another's consciousness" (259).

41. According to Rimmon-Kenan, "Perhaps most interesting are those cases where choice between an external [the narrator] and an internal focalizer [a character] is problematic or impossible" (84). The source of the focalization may be indeterminable, even when the language is that of the narrator. Deciding between them affects our interpretation, however, for if a character speaks in clichés, the language may be meant sincerely, but if the narrator is the focalizer, it becomes ironic. Rimmon-Kenan gives examples from Joyce's "Araby" (84–5).

42. Alan Trachtenberg has demonstrated how Crane overcame the problems of sensationalism and separation of detached observer in his newspaper sketches, especially "Experiment in Luxury" and "Experiment in Misery." Although he does not call this a reflexive reading, he shows how Crane "lays bare" the process of entering into the world of the Other without objectifying his subjects ("Experiments").

2. "NEWS THAT STAYS": HEMINGWAY, JOURNALISM, AND OBJECTIVITY IN FICTION

1. Hofstadter notes, "With few exceptions the makers of American realism . . . were men who had training in journalistic observation" (197). Schudson lists Dreiser, London, Crane, Norris, and Cather as novelists of this period who wrote in "a self-consciously realistic vein growing out of their experience as newspaper reporters" (*Discovering* 73). See Cowley, "Natural" 437. This view has been most recently and fully expressed by Shelley Fishkin.
2. There is no table of contents, at least as the issue is bound for libraries in a volume containing six issues. The 1897 volume includes the serialization of Richard Henry Dana's novel *Soldiers of Fortune,* as well as Dana's travel account of a spectacle in Budapest, "The Banderium of Hungary," but there are no labels characterizing them as fiction or nonfiction.
3. Crane told Cather in 1896 that he "led a double literary life; writing in the first place the matter that pleased himself, and doing it very slowly; in the second place, any sort of stuff that would sell" (quoted in Gullason 470). We are not to think that "any sort of stuff" meant only journalism, for he wrote fiction, including "The Open Boat," as easily and quickly as newspaper sketches. See Cady's introduction to *Tales, Sketches, and Reports,* volume 8 of the *Virginia Edition* of Crane's works.
4. Norman Mailer is only the latest of a series of journalist-novelists to reject the label of reporter. In *The Armies of the Night,* when Robert Lowell called him the best journalist in America, he responded, "There are days when I think of myself as being the best writer in America" (32–3).
5. See Schudson (*Discovering* 69–71), Kwiat, and the journalist-novelists' memoirs cited in Good. Although some of Good's evidence is from fictionalized versions of the writers' experience, he makes a persuasive case for their autobiographical validity and their uncensored revelations of the writers' attitudes.
6. The very fact that journalism's influence is seen as lasting so long suggests that Hemingway's minimalist kind of modernism has affinities with the practice and world view of realism. At least this is the implication of Fishkin's study, for she finds in "all of his work a concern for accurately observed and precisely recorded fact," the same values that she believes Twain learned to respect from his work as a journalist (141, 76). See Corkin (*Realism*) for evidence that Hemingway's early fiction shows the persistence of a version of the positivism that influenced Howells's criticism and fiction.
7. In *Hemingway's Art of Nonfiction,* Weber says that Fenton "overvalued" the effect of journalism on Hemingway's fiction in his influential study, *The Literary Apprenticeship of Ernest Hemingway.* From a perusal of Fenton's papers at Yale, he has discovered that Fenton omitted information that did not fit his thesis. For example, he left out a *Kansas City Star* colleague's claim

that "the *Star* taught Hemingway nothing about writing," and he failed to report that several other reporters did not remember a style book in the *Star* office (Weber 19–20). Weber believes that the more important influence of journalism was on Hemingway's "extended nonfiction" (10–11).

8. It is customary to refer to the short numbered chapters placed between the short stories of *In Our Time* as "vignettes," "sketches," or "interchapters," as well as by their chapter number. The cabled dispatches are reprinted in both *Byline: Ernest Hemingway* and *Dateline: Toronto*. Fenton reprints three of the five paragraphs sent on Oct. 20 (230–1).

9. Fenton points out that Hemingway dropped the phrase in brackets between the *Little Review* version and *in our time* (235).

10. Fenton does say that in the 1930 edition Hemingway inserted "There was" in the fourth sentence to make the first fragment into a sentence: "There was no end and no beginning" (236). Hagemann, however, regards this as an editorial change, along with the change of "kids" to children," and "kid" to "baby," in sentences 10 and 11. He insists that Hemingway – who skipped reading proofs for this edition (Scribner's first) because he was working hard on *Death in the Afternoon* – would never have countenanced these signs of the "editorial pedant," who he suspects was Max Perkins ("Collation" 44). See also Fenton 236. Hagemann calls the first American edition, published by Boni & Liveright in 1925, the preferred text (43–4). It was closely followed (that is, with these alterations reversed and the fragment allowed to stand) in recent reprintings of the 1930 edition – although Hagemann says the 1930s emendations persisted in reprintings offered for sale at the time his article was published, in 1979 [46]). (Scribner's marked its first edition by requesting an introduction from Hemingway, headed "Introduction by the Author," now entitled "On the Quai at Smyrna.")

11. Peterson (115–16) points out the contradiction in Fenton's arguing that Hemingway was working to make the sketch "more precise and specific" while regarding "the course of the revision as a move away from the 'too explicit.' " The contradiction is one I consider later on in this chapter. Peterson's analysis of Hemingway's style questions the common assumptions about the correlation between "unmodified and understated" sentences and the effects of concreteness and precision. As he insists, "[T]he relatively unmodified and understated sentence generally lacks the preciseness and specificity of the explicit" (116).

12. For example, Hemingway gives the number of refugees to be evacuated and of those already in Macedonia, mentions that the Bulgarian border was closed, and says, "There is only Macedonia and Western Thrace to receive the fruit of the Turk's return to Europe" (*By-Line* 52).

13. See the end of "War Medals for Sale" (*By-Line* 123) and the closing paragraph of "Italy – 1927." "The Chauffeurs of Madrid" was a North American News Alliance (NANA) dispatch from the Spanish Civil War that Hemingway reprinted in a collection he edited, *Men at War: The Best War Stories of All Time*. "Italy – 1927" was included in *The First Forty-Nine Stories* as "Che Ti Dice La Patria."

14. Hemingway had also transformed his observations of the Thracian refugees into the account of the retreat from Caparetto in *A Farewell to Arms* (chap. 28). "The Flight of Refugees" is reprinted in both *By-Line* and *Dateline: Toronto*, and a variorum edition appeared in *Hemingway Review* (Watson "Variorum"). Watson says he chose to do a variorum edition of this dispatch because versions existed of all the stages a dispatch could go through,

including field notes and different transcriptions or translations of the cablese.

15. Among those those who assume Hemingway was influenced by cablese is Cowley, who interprets Hemingway's goal of stating what he saw "purely enough" as meaning writing like "cabelese, with everything omitted that the reader could take for granted, and with each detail so carefully chosen that it did the work of six or seven" (*Second* 63).

16. See note 10. Although Hagemann ("Collation" 44) concludes that an editor and not Hemingway added the words to make the fragment a sentence, Fenton's inference is not irrelevant, for he does read the deliberate fragment as "surviving cablese," when it was not in the dispatch but introduced by Hemingway in 1923, 1924, or 1925.

17. The only other time Hemingway had to perform the kind of routine journalism that required the cryptic form was when he picked up additional work while covering the 1922 Lausanne Conference, held to resolve the Greco–Turkish conflict, for the *Toronto Star;* in effect he ran a round-the-clock wire service for the Universal News Service (UNS) and the INS (both Hearst agencies), sending press handouts and official reports over the wires to both and phoning general news to the chief Hearst correspondent in Paris. As Fenton says, "Almost entirely spot news, it was routine and undramatic and had a minimum of feature possibilities" (189).

18. Another process Hemingway was excessively concerned with, of course, was that of writing. Wagner says this "near-obsession" with craft came to imply the "craft of life" as well: "The right way to do a thing – whether it be bullfighting, fishing, making love, or writing – is frequently Hemingway's objective correlative, his means of characterization."

19. Fenton concludes that Hemingway's "style matured to a degree in the discipline of cabelese" (260), but at the same time he admits that the writer learned the simple declarative style outside of journalism and then practiced it in news features. For example, he says it was Gertrude Stein's influence that led Hemingway to "introduce the harsh, declarative structure of his mature prose into his feature material" (260).

20. Margaret Lewis's dissertation gives abundant evidence of Hemingway's facility with cablese and different versions of cables Watson reprints. Donaldson (96) reprints a hilarious dispatch Hemingway sent to INS in response to the agency's request for detailed records and receipts to justify payment which the correspondent felt was overdue: INTERNEWS PARIS SUGGEST YOU UPSTICK BOOKS ASSWARDS   HEMINGWAY

21. Fredson Bowers, editor of the *Virginia Edition* of Crane's works, tracing the transmission of this report after comparing ten newspaper versions of the story, sees three possibilities: that Bacheller produced a transcript from Crane's telegram, gave the carbon to the *New York Press,* then put it on the wire; that the syndicate gave the telegram to the *Press* after typing it up; or that "Crane sent the same telegrams to the *Press* and to Bacheller – a strong possibility" (Virginia Edition, vol. 9, *Reports of War* 470–1).

22. For an interesting parallel, see Zboray, who shows that despite technological innovations in book production in the United States in the mid-nineteenth century, the high price of books by American authors prevented the masses from buying them in the large numbers expected (191). High sales were possible but not inevitable. See also R. Williams, *Television* 10–14.

23. In the news story constructed as an inverted pyramid, M. Stephens remarks, facts are ranked hierarchically, "but the temporal, historical, atmospheric or

ideological connections between these facts are often weakened, occasionally severed" (255). The story he reprints as an example of this structure is from 1927 (a *New York Times* report of the execution of Sacco and Vanzetti), and he adds that this "style of newswriting had taken decades to establish its dominance" (254).

24. Christopher Wilson shows that Jack London avoided newspaper work for just these reasons – a dislike of its routine and confinement – in favor of the freedom of a self-imposed discipline. When he did reporting, it was only as a special correspondent (97).

25. See O'Brien on Cather's attempt to create an alternative "general" reader for her novels, outside the world of critics and academics but apparently superior to the "mass" reader of sentimental and romance fiction. See Fenton (169) on an editor's rejection of Hemingway's interview with Clemenceau.

26. R. Weber recognizes this strategy when he notes that Hemingway "defined writing by its opposition to journalism" (*Hemingway's Art* 28).

27. Several of Hemingway's *Toronto Star* pieces from 1922 and 1923 exhibit remarkable use of irony and other forms of understatement, stretches of dialogue, and details sketched in declarative sentences, many of which are not commented on, simply left to resonate. Some dispatches deserving of mention (besides those discussed in the text and other notes) are: "The Mecca of Fakers" (25 Mar. 1922), "Fishing the Rhone Canal" (10 June 1922), "German Inflation" (19 Sept. 1922), "King Business in Europe" (15 Sept. 1923), "Pamplona in July" (27 Oct. 1923), "War Medals for Sale" (8 Dec. 1923). All appeared in the *Toronto Daily Star* or the *Star Weekly* (its Sunday supplement) and are included in *Dateline: Toronto*.

28. See also L. Levine (216–19), who cites examples of establishing "high culture" by comparing it to the common, popular, and hence vulgar. Journalism became inherently "low," beginning in the second half of the nineteenth century, because of its numbers of readers and its ephemerality.

29. Among the many critics who see its objectivity as an important feature of Hemingway's twenties prose are Beach (110), Schorer (88–9), Halliday (175–7), and Graham (184). Beach attributes this objective tendency to "a disposition to behaviorism in fiction" and points to the requirement of such a style that "the facts shall be so rightly ordered that they will speak for themselves" (110). Kobler describes the sketches of *In Our Time* as marked by "the camera-eye technique, the flat, uninsistent quality without comment, conjecture, or emotion on the part of the author" (13).

30. C. W. E. Bigsby insists that "the attraction which Hemingway felt for the simple facticity of the countryside, . . . was simply that this was a world removed from time and the society of man" (211). See his article for an interesting argument about Hemingway's characters' and his writing generation's "flight from history."

31. It takes a little research to discover what was "left out" of certain World War I works, namely the fact that some of what was being passed off as fiction and stories and arguments for U.S. intervention in the war written by authors freely entering the publishing marketplace of ideas was actually commissioned, printed, and disseminated by the British equivalent of the Office of War Information. See Buitenhuis (xvi–xvii).

32. Compare this passage from "On the Art of Fiction" (1920): "Art, it seems to me, should simplify. That, indeed, is very nearly the whole of the higher artistic process; finding what conventions of form and what detail one can do without and yet preserve the spirit of the whole – so that all that one has

suppressed and cut away is there to the reader's consciousness as much as if it were in type on the page" (*On Writing* 102).

33. See Peterson, who sets similar passages side by side (58–9; 104–8) and says that this objective method – "understatement, irony and other forms of indirection – was virtually canonized" by the 1930s. He quotes Thomas Wolfe arguing with Scott Fitzgerald, however, against there being just this one "disciplined" way to write (108). The case for Cather as a modernist has been made by Phyllis Rose and Jo Ann Middleton; I agree that she should be grouped with these writers, but not without questioning the New Critical conception of modernism, which both critics accept.

34. This sounds a bit like Wordsworth's "emotion recollected in tranquillity," a formula Eliot considers and corrects in "Tradition and the Individual Talent" (58–9). Since his subject in this passage is "emotion which has its life in the poem and not in the history of the poet," it is worth comparing to Cather's statements on the impersonality or self-effacement of the poet in Bohlke (177–8) and *On Writing* (37). Eliot's well-known definition of the objective correlative is in "Hamlet and His Problems" (100).

35. Compare Cather: "If the novel is a form of imaginative art, it cannot be at the same time a vivid and brilliant form of journalism. Out of the teeming, gleaming stream of the present it must select the eternal material of art" (*On Writing* 40).

36. Fenton (234) and Cowley (*Second* 64) point out the importance of repetition in achieving the effects of immediacy and compression in the vignette drawn from the Thrace dispatch (*In Our Time*). Bridgman discusses the subtle use both Stein and Hemingway made of repetition while varying a single word's part of speech, form, or meaning (210).

37. Eagleton, following Adorno, says art becomes autonomous, paradoxically, "by being *integrated* into the capitalist mode of production," that is, by becoming a commodity. He explains the separation of art from the cognitive, ethical, and political spheres as the result of its move into the "anonymous freedom of the market place," where it exists "for anybody with the taste to appreciate it and the money to buy it," rather than taking its traditional place within the social functioning of "church, court and state" (*Ideology* 368).

38. Baker says that Hemingway wrote "more than a million words for newspapers and magazines" ("His Beat" 412). Kauffmann nevertheless finds "heroic" Hemingway's decision to stop working for the *Star* in order to write in a radical style he was not sure would be commercial. "With a wife and a small child to support (it would have been courageous enough without them), he turned his back on an increasingly successful newspaper career to forge himself into a serious writer" (521).

39. It is included in the *Complete Short Stories;* page references are to this edition.

40. From a letter drafted (but apparently never sent) to Edmund Wilson.

41. Nor does the predominance of dialogue establish the story as fiction, even though its use is the only aspect of form Kobler has found to distinguish Hemingway's fictional style from his journalism. Kobler also considered such factors as choice of subjects, representation of character, unity, rhetorical devices, and sentence style, concluding that "in regard to everything but the handling of dialogue, these efforts are those of craftsmanship, of rewriting, and polishing. In the fiction he simply did better what he did normally in the journalism" (124). I take that valuation to apply to the handling of dialogue as well; Kobler is not using this characteristic to define fiction, but

is describing differences in the modes he has first identified according to form of publication; that a short narrative has a preponderance of dialogue does not mean it is necessarily a short story.

42. In the "Comprehensive Checklist" in Benson, *New Critical Approaches,* fifteen citations are listed. In support of my notion that stories become fictional or literary and then enter the canon in a process of selection for publication and reprinting (as in anthologies) and then for critical and classroom attention, consider this remark by Benson in 1989 that "The Denunciation" (another Spanish story from the same period, previously neglected) has recently been treated to "particularly good" discussions and "seems to be emerging as a major story with psychological complexity" ("Criticism" 33). In other words, it is in the process of becoming "major" because critics are making it so, finding complexity in it that was presumably there even when it was not "major."

43. A collection of Hemingway's dispatches was reprinted in *Fact* as "The Spanish War."

3. NEWS THAT FITS: THE CONSTRUCTION OF JOURNALISTIC OBJECTIVITY

1. Hersey told a *Paris Review* interviewer that Harold Ross and William Shawn worked with him on editing "Hiroshima" for an intensive period lasting perhaps "ten hours a day for twenty days" ("Art" 229). Nocera mentions factual pieces by Elizabeth Drew (on the life of a U.S. senator) and Henry Cooper (on the space shuttle program) as early eighties examples of the "cold meaningless objectivity" of *New Yorker* nonfiction. In the early nineties, under the editorship of Tina Brown, nonfiction writers for the magazine seem to be less restricted by an editorial requirement that details be divorced from interpretation.

2. See Poore for a summary of the response three months after publication. He says *Hiroshima*'s extraordinary popularity can be explained by the fact that "millions of people have wanted to hear what [Hersey] has to say and to have others hear it, too" (7).

3. Indeed, Hersey reprinted *Hiroshima* in a collection called *Here to Stay* (1963).

4. I argue that journalism and fiction *should* supply this insight by laying bare the mechanisms of power in our society and encouraging their reader's reflexive consciousness. Schudson agrees that news media should "arm" us for "vigilant citizenship," but he does not think that historically they have done this; rather, they have been "a more important forum for communication among elites (and some elites more than others) than with the general population" ("Sociology" 156).

5. Its unprecedented form of publication caused an immediate sensation of a different kind: the text of *Hiroshima* took up the entire August 1946 issue of the *New Yorker* and was broadcast and reprinted in English-speaking countries all over the world within weeks (see Poore 7).

6. The similar phrasing makes me speculate that Mary Lowry Ross unconsciously adopted the novel's phrasing when in 1952 she recalled for Fenton this advice from the colleague who was a fellow sufferer under the pettiness of the Hindmarsh regime at the *Star* (Fenton 248–9). For discussions of the treatment of this avoidance of speech as central to Hemingway's aesthetic, see Lid, Portch.

7. It is reprinted along with all Hemingway's *Toronto Star* dispatches in *Date-*

line: Toronto Star; it appeared in McQuade and Atwan, a composition anthology, where I encountered it. I assume that, other than in composition, journalism, and nonfiction writing courses, teachers rarely select it for course reading.

8. Don DeLillo's novel *White Noise* makes much of our fascination with such news accounts, as when the Gladney family gathers around the television set to see disaster footage, including a videotape, replayed many times, of an airplane going down (64).

9. It is accepted by journalism historians, however, that taxes on newspapers were an effective means of continuing censorship long after the press won certain political freedoms in the seventeenth century (see Dudek 41–4).

10. M. Stephens says that impartiality or the attempt to balance viewpoints has been a goal of journalism since the first newspapers in the seventeenth century, and that facts began to crowd out opinion in the nineteenth century (256–8).

11. For an account of the effects of these "taxes on knowledge," see Lee 117–19; Dudek 53–6.

12. In his review of Schiller, Boylan says that Schiller traces this idea of "third-party" objectivity back to the penny press of the 1830s as a whole but that his definition rests on the *Police Gazette,* which was not a representative penny paper; thus he believes that Schiller's theory about the role of the penny papers in general, though interesting, is not proven by this one example.

13. Samuel F. B. Morse said that daguerreotypes were so real that "they cannot be called copies of nature, but portions of nature herself" (quoted in Rudisill 57). And compare Sontag: "Photographed images do not seem to be statements about the world so much as pieces of it, miniatures of reality that anyone can make or acquire" (*On Photography* 4).

14. Robert Darnton, a historian engaged in a cultural studies approach to forms of thought, has examined these modern news practices and the beliefs that undergird them by reflecting on his own experience as a reporter in Newark and New York City from 1959 to 1964. For my purposes his most interesting hypothesis is that the dominant model for news reporters and writers is a fictional one (in the sense of archetypally or universally "true"), because their primary narrative impulse imitates old-fashioned storytelling and the basic unit of news is the story. He says that the raw material of even financial and political news is cast into archetypal story models that go back to medieval France and England. Reporters draw on a "traditional repertory of genres" and adapt occurrences to news formulas much as one makes "cookies from an antique cookie cutter" (191, 189).

15. Although gatekeeping is an important concept in understanding how news is produced, Schudson points out that as a metaphor it reifies news as a simplified product that is merely selected; it describes neither the construction of news items "nor the feedback loops in which the agencies that generate information for the press anticipate the criteria of the gatekeepers in their efforts to get through the gate, like teenagers trying to figure out how best to talk and look in order to get admitted to X-rated movies" ("Sociology" 142–3).

16. For recent studies that describe the process of "manufacturing" or "making" news, see Fishman; Gans; Ericson, Baranck, and Chan; Manoff and Schudson; Tuchman, *Making;* and Schudson "Sociology."

17. Trade journals (e.g., computer magazines oriented toward a particular prod-

uct or market, such as the Macintosh computer) perhaps have the most obvious difficulty keeping editorial content from affecting advertising. The feminist magazine *Ms.* dropped advertising altogether in 1990 rather than depend on revenue from advertisers likely to come under attack in articles or whose images and strategies would contradict the magazine's editorial viewpoint.

18. See also Tuchman ("Objectivity 669n), who says that "superiors tend to identify 'objectivity' with the particular 'slant' or news policy of their organization."

19. See Ellul for a full discussion of this manipulation as a form of propaganda (84–6).

20. For the Progressive context of this debate, see Forcey, and Levy's biography of Herbert Croly.

21. See Alterman, who argues that the American people are the real losers, for instead of complex political debate among informed citizens we are ruled by the discourse of pundits.

22. Excellent accounts of the advertising industry are given by Tedlow and Marchand.

23. Lippmann says that wise leaders, when it is prudent, "seek a certain measure of consent. . . . But however sincere the leader may be, there is always, when the facts are very complicated, a certain amount of illusion in these consultations" (245). (Lippmann consistently uses the masculine pronoun when referring to leaders, as was the convention before the 1970s, but it is impossible to tell whether he means it to stand for "he or she" or whether he assumes all leaders to be men.)

24. Aronowitz explains how we reify "productive forces as an objective thing standing outside human control" (47): "The social relations which underlie scientific discoveries, the exigencies of capital which may determine whether a particular scientific breakthrough will be incorporated into technology and finally into modern industry, are omitted by those who impute to science and the forces of production of which it is a part the status of autonomous power. Scientific and technological power replaces social power, or, more precisely, becomes a social power" (47–8).

25. See Wagner, who says, "*The Sun Also Rises* is a difficult book to read correctly, until the reader understands the way it works" (51); Kenner, who remarks, "If this book [*In Our Time*] was so little understood for so long, one may ask why it was so respected" (150); and Peterson 66–7.

26. The fact-interpretation distinction also underlies realism itself. Hall says the "ideology of objectivity" derives from it, producing "the empiricist illusion, the utopia of naturalism" ("Determinations" 188).

27. Karl accepts Hersey's depiction of the Japanese as regarding the catastrophe "almost as part of a natural event, complaining little and, even when suffering dreadfully, not crying out" (586).

28. A brief text that opens up the question of the American government's motives at the end of World War II is Robert Lowell's letter to President Roosevelt refusing service in 1942, reprinted in his *Collected Prose*.

29. Bennett et al. add that, to Gramsci, ideology has "an 'internal' psychological dimension" and is "the way in which consciousness itself is structured" (209). These authors quote extensively from pp. 376–7 of *Selections from the Prison Notebooks,* including Gramsci's emphasis on Marx's proposition that "a popular conviction often has the same energy as a material force" (Gramsci 377).

30. Gramsci worked out the concept of hegemony while imprisoned in Italy under Mussolini from 1926 until his death ten years later. See *Selections from the Prison Notebooks* (55–8; 181–2); Bennett et al. (191–218; 219–34); and R. Williams, *Keywords* (117–18). For an interpretation of Gramsci's conception of science as praxis, which leads him to see ideology and science "as different sides of the material forces of historical change," see Aronowitz (197–200).

31. Relevant passages in Gramsci (which Aronowitz cites) are 164–5, 244–5, 350, 365–6, 376–7. This notion of literature as what is left over after other discourses have defined themselves is the basis of John Limon's intellectual history, *The Place of Fiction in the Time of Science*. He says, "To the extent that we think of literature as a discrete category, it is the result of the gradual withdrawal of all other disciplines – whose withdrawal from what comes to be literature partly constitutes them *as* disciplines – rather than of any exclusiveness that literature itself has ever mustered" (5).

4. OTHER AMERICAN NEW JOURNALISMS: 1960S NEW JOURNALISM AS "OTHER"

1. Cohn says that examples of the particular form of New Journalistic "cross-breed" she is interested in, namely the journalistic profile or biography that is told in the third person with extensive focalizing, are being "written and read for their transgressive shock value" and thus, "far from erasing the borderline between biography and fiction, bring the line that separates them more clearly into view" (11). See also Greenblatt, who says that "the effortless invocation of two apparently contradictory accounts of art [such as President Reagan's habit of quoting from his movies, with others insisting that he knew he was doing so, but delivering speeches written by others with no one feeling that he ought to acknowledge them] is characteristic of American capitalism in the late twentieth century . . . ; in the same moment a working distinction between the aesthetic and the real is established and abrogated" (7).

2. See Eason, who calls Wolfe an "ethnographic realist," able to penetrate surface confusion and fragmentation to discover reality and bind it up in narrative for the reader (53–4).

3. Foley finds "a certain myopia behind the claim that contemporary American reality is any more horrific than that of other ages or places: the European conquest of the Congo, which left millions dead, was certainly horrific from the point of view of the Congolese, while the devastation wrought by the Black Death in fourteenth-century Europe must have seemed a supremely bizarre visitation to those who endured it" ("Fact, Fiction, Reality" 394).

4. Wolfe (Introduction 31–4) and Hollowell (25–6) emphasize the number of realistic fictional techniques found in the New Journalism. Hellmann offers a formalist definition that relies on Northrop Frye's theory of the bireferentiality of writing: the final direction of meaning of a text is either centrifugal (externally referential) or centripetal (inward-looking). According to Hellmann, New Journalism is literary because its "final direction" is inward toward its own aesthetic form (23–5). And despite Zavarzadeh's intricate attempt to posit a special realm for the nonfiction novel between the poles of fact and fiction, his conception of "bi-referential" narratives that "have the aesthetic control associated with works of art" yet "remain out-referential" and "externally verifiable" is nevertheless binary (56–7). (Zavar-

zadeh treats New Journalism as a kind of journalism, and thus not in the same literary category as the nonfiction novel.)

5. The "new nonfiction" as a label has its own problems, of course, but I use "new" in the senses of "recent" and "remarkable" rather than "original" or "without precedent." Something that is new has been noticed, set off from the ordinary, and the term underlines the common etymology of "news" and "novel." There is also a connection to the political category of otherness that I develop in the next section, for novelty may be regarded as deviance, which ought to be either reincorporated into the dominant system or institution or marginalized and excluded from it. See Ericson, Baranck, and Chan, who insist that "deviance and control are the core ingredients of news" and that "most people derive their understanding of deviance and control primarily from the news and other mass media" (3).

6. The constitution of the relationship between the sexes so that man is regarded as essential and woman as inessential or incidental is the best explanation for the secondary status of women in a patriarchal society, as Simone de Beauvoir has shown ("He is the Subject, he is the Absolute – she is the Other" – xvi). Since Beauvoir, the alterity of women in the linguistic, social, and psychoanalytic orders has become a common focus in feminist criticism. Otherness is also a dominant trope in the discourse of colonialism (see Todorov, *Conquest*), and it remains a subtext in the attitude of the so-called superpowers toward the Third World.

According to Polan, some cultural anthropologists have shown that "the constitution of a society depends on that society's ability to construct some sort of Other on which to focus its disapprobation so that its own mainstream social relations may seem normal" ("Brief" 169). The concept of the Other is also important in theorizing the formation of self in philosophy (Hegel, Mead) and psychoanalysis (Freud, Lacan). For use of the term in cultural studies, see the essays in Modleski, *Studies*.

7. The two books that aroused the most sustained response and led to the wide use of the term were Capote's *In Cold Blood* (1965 – first published in the *New Yorker*) and Wolfe's *Kandy-Kolored Tangerine-Flake Streamline Baby*, a collection of his pieces to 1965. Neither author at first used this term to describe his work, although Capote claimed to have invented a new form, the nonfiction novel. Wakefield identified a buzz of interest in journalism because of these books; that is, he treated the innovations positively. For sample reviews that generalized from these two texts to define the deviant practice, see Macdonald, "Parajournalism," and Compton. (Although, strictly speaking, New Journalism is a type of journalism and the nonfiction novel a subgenre of the novel, the two are sometimes indistinguishable except for their publication form and length, and critics frequently use "New Journalism" to refer to both. I follow this usage here.) Although the term was also applied to developments viewed as positive, the practice it stuck to was the deviant one that so incensed mainstream journalists. For example, one favorable 1966 column headlined "The New Journalism," which notes "fresh directions being taken by the best of newspapers today," does not mention any names we now associate with the term; A. M. Rosenthal is cited for his *New York Times* piece, "There Is No News from Auschwitz," for example (Fixx 65).

8. This notorious attack on the *New Yorker* appeared in consecutive issues of *New York* (11 and 18 Apr. 1965); although it was more like a hoax than a seriously researched piece and not an example of New Journalism, as Wolfe

admits (Introduction 24), it brought down a barrage of counterassaults on Wolfe's head. Those responding with letters to *New York* on 25 April included Joseph Alsop, Nat Hentoff, Murray Kempton, J. D. Salinger, Muriel Spark, and William Styron (see Wakefield 43–4; Cohen 3).

9. "With his ego, he rules . . . thick lines down the edges of his own column of print" (Arlen, "Notes," 254).

10. There are clear parallels between the attack on objectivity by journalistic practices emphasizing the writer's subjectivity, this antiestablishment critique by students and the New Left, and the Frankfurt School thinkers who theorized mass culture long before both journalists and political analysts got around to it in the sixties. According to Bottomore, "The social-philosophical outlook which suffused all Frankfurt School theory was a 'defence of subjectivity' against the idea of an objective, law-governed process of history; and it was this which evoked an enthusiastic response in the student movement of the 1960s, directed above all against 'the system' " (49).

11. For analysis of these reincorporating techniques, see Murdock; Hall, "Determinations"; and Phillips. See also the editors' introductions to the three parts of Cohen and Young; and Hebdige 92–9.

12. Wolfe has always aroused the ire of leftist critics for his cultural conservatism, and his notorious 1965 attack on the *New Yorker,* which, as Wolfe says, was not an example of New Journalism (Introduction 24), probably inspired Macdonald to launch a counteroffensive. (See also Adler and Jonas.) Nevertheless, the terms of Macdonald's abuse of Wolfe effectively illustrate the techniques by which the mainstream marginalizes deviant practices.

13. Because in my framework New Journalism is "what is regarded as deviant," my identification of precedents is of course different from others who have asked "How new is the New Journalism?" (And I must add that my identification of earlier "new" journalisms is not exhaustive. I could have made the history much longer by citing muckraking journalists of the Progressive era and radical journalists of the 1930s and explaining what happened to these "other" journalisms.) While Wolfe is anxious to prove that there was really no exact predecessor to the sixties form (Introduction), Connery regards New Journalism as only the latest manifestation in a long but ignored tradition of literary journalism going back to Mark Twain. His useful introduction not only mentions scores of literary journalists working in nearly every decade for one hundred fifty years but reviews dozens of definitional, critical, and historical articles and books in an attempt to define the protean field and make both words in the term "literary journalism" appropriate. When he seems to settle on a definition, it is Barbara Lounsberry's identification of four features essential to "literary or artistic nonfiction": "(1) documentable subject matter; (2) exhaustive research (immersion, saturation); (3) the scene; and (4) fine writing" (Connery 5). (He nevertheless prefers "journalism" to "nonfiction" as the correct term for the category, for reasons he gives on p. 15.)

14. Large circulation became important to attract advertisers, but it also mattered who was buying the paper, that is, how much spending power those readers had. "As the decades passed, there came times when it seemed too many publishers had again become captivated by the charms of a 'respectable,' monied readership, when newspaper prices crept higher and their pages grew more 'serious.' But then the journalistic world again would be refreshed by a new wave of 'popular' journalism, bringing new readers and even larger circulations" (M. Stephens 208).

15. An exception to this generalization is Hellmann, who reads many examples of new nonfiction reflexively (and excellently), despite his formalist definition. See Schuster for a reflexive reading of nonfiction by John McPhee.

16. This "authoritarian" narrative is especially ironic in view of Kesey's technique, which Whelan describes as "by nature decentered, outward moving, oriented toward the 'further.' Wolfe, on the other hand, makes a neat structure of . . . events, with the acid tests as the summit of the 'rising action' " (82). Whelan's essay offers a complex analysis of the works of both Kesey and Wolfe as a "synecdoche or sample" of late-1960s counterculture, a phenomenon which he believes should be read as seriously as we read literary works in the ordinary sense (64).

17. Wolfe calls what appear to be ellipsis points "syncopations" or "dots"; he says he uses them lavishly (along with other marks, such as dashes and exclamation points) "to give the illusion not only of a person talking but of a person thinking" (Introduction 22).

18. Wolfe may not respect his audience, but this is not to say that he regards his audience as deficient in culture or education, which is how Macdonald characterizes "parajournalism's" readers. Macdonald implies that this may be a consequence of New Journalists' reordering their priorities so that entertainment becomes more important than information, in which case fiction triumphs over fact out of its interest in holding readers' attention ("Parajournalism" 229; see Cohen 7).

19. It is ironic that Wolfe is rather like Hemingway in his belief in objectivity, while Mailer, supposedly the disciple, recovers the personal voice of the more voluble Hemingway. Apparently Mailer models his reporting on what Papa does, not on what he says, in passages like the one just quoted; it is Hemingway's expansive journalistic voice, not his objective fictional style, that reappears in Mailer's prose. The younger writer has detected what Brom Weber notes, particularly in nonfiction like *Death in the Afternoon,* that "Hemingway's famous stylistic economy frequently seems to conceal another kind of writer, with much richer rhetorical resources to hand" (151).

20. Because of the predominance of zero-degree narration and the prominence of objective realism in popular and canonical narratives, many writers and critics assume that the advantage of point of view is the transparency made possible by the "invisible" narrator. See Banfield, and Barthes, *Writing.* (Consider also the other primary term for point of view: "focalizing.")

21. The term "historical avantgarde" comes from Bürger (53–4), who distinguishes it from high modernism. Whereas the modernists insisted on the separation of art, avant-garde movements challenge its autonomy with examples of the aestheticization of everyday life. See also Huyssen (21–2) and the excellent discussion of these matters in Whelan.

22. See Hersey ("Legend") and the "Letters" columns in *Harper's,* which printed "Stalking."

23. For egregious examples, see his evocation of Arthur Koestler's "Ahor," the ancient horror from boyhood, in the "genteel suburban kid" at the gas station who spies on the mechanics telling dirty jokes in the "primordial Shellube pits" (56); he also uses it to explain the Pranksters' fascination with the Hell's Angels (Chap. 13).

24. This brings home once again why the form of historical narrative is so important, for it is in their textual form that events are meaningful as history, as "what happened." One has only to recall the continuing argument over the effect of Lili Riefenstahl's Nazi propaganda films to see how

difficult this analysis is and how hard it is to "prove" the correctness of one interpretation over the other.

25. According to Stevenson, "Cramer takes toward George Bush a stance of novelistic curiosity rather than moralistic condemnation, and his portrayal is all the more damning for not having been drawn as an indictment" (476).

5. THE "INCREDIBILITY OF REALITY" AND THE IDEOLOGY OF FORM

1. Wolfe holds a Ph.D. in American Studies from Yale University, 1957.
2. Cf. Richard Howard's "Note on S/Z," in Barthes S/Z: "Literature is like love in La Rochefoucauld: no one would ever have experienced it if he had not first read about it in books." We ought to amend this maxim to substitute "advertising" for "books." For an analysis of how advertising provides a structure capable of making such transformations in objects and in our responses, see Williamson.
3. A sampling of newspaper reports of the wreck of the *Commodore* makes this point indelibly.
4. Hellmann believes that New Journalists combine the self-reflexive techniques of fabulist novelists with attention to a "journalistic world" to create a genre that is finally fictional. In his section on the absurdity of contemporary reality, Zavarzadeh quotes, along with Roth's essay, the accounts of Seymour Krim and Larry King, who contrive "fictions" from contemporary journalism and then reject them as "unpublishable" for their aura of improbability (21–3).
5. Capote told George Plimpton that he had invented a form that used "all the techniques of fictional art but was nevertheless immaculately factual" (189). See also Hellmann (19–20); Hollowell (5–10); Weber (*Literature* 189).
6. Foley suggests that events since World War II may be leading writers to nonfiction out of a desire to document a world so incredible that it might not be believable to later generations. If so, African-American literature in general is a "legitimate forebear" of these documentary novels: "While many white writers in post-World War II America have indeed experienced marked difficulties in representing a historical world that encompasses, within recent memory, Auschwitz, Hiroshima, the political assassinations of the 1960s, the Democratic National Convention of 1968, My Lai, Woodstock, and Attica, it could be argued that, for most black writers . . . 'reality' in this country has always had a certain horrific quality" ("History" 390).
7. See Holzer, Boritt, and Neely, and A. Smith's mention of Theodore Roosevelt pursuing "the politics of the image" during his administration (*Newspaper* 168). Close scrutiny of Presidents by the media began with the administration of Theodore Roosevelt (Meyrowitz 274n). See Cornwell for a history of presidential manipulation of public opinion.
8. For the use of a specific example from Rogin's book to illustrate how we are implicated in this blended universe, and thus the difficulty we have in separating the boundaries of fiction and fantasy usually drawn in political life, see Greenblatt 6–7. He says that Reagan's entire "political career has depended upon an ability to project himself *and his mass audience* into a realm in which there is no distinction between simulation and reality" (6). (Italics added.)
9. This list puts Nixon's protest of the television docudrama "The Final Days" (1989) in perspective, for one source of the extra frisson of pleasure we get

at running into some version of the Nixon character in a narrative or dramatic presentation is wondering whether the historical character has read or seen it and how he feels about it; in the case of the docudrama, as Wines reports, he fumed publicly.

10. Pauline Kael says that "what DeNiro is doing might be based on the War-holian idea that the best parody of a thing is the thing itself" (123).

11. Again, here is Mailer: "a particular man or as easily all Americans can believe consciously that they are superior to advertising while in fact they suffer an unconscious slavery which influences them considerably" (*Advertisements* 171).

12. "Capitalism systematically dissolves the fabric of all cohesive social groups without exception, including its own ruling class, and thereby problematizes aesthetic production and linguistic invention which have their source in group life. The result . . . is the dialectical fission of older aesthetic expression into two modes, modernism and mass culture, equally dissociated from group praxis" (Jameson, "Reification" 140).

13. As Carolyn Porter asserts, paraphrasing Lukacs, "[B]oth aspects of reification – an alien world of commodities with a life of their own, and an alienated consciousness which can only contemplate this independent and autonomous process, moving in accord with its own 'natural laws' – are repeated in bourgeois consciousness as a whole." And she quotes Lukacs (100): "Not only does man 'become the passive observer of society; he also lapses into a contemplative attitude vis-à-vis the workings of his own objectified and reified faculties' " (Porter 25).

14. Where we have not lost it, according to Noam Chomsky, is in relation to sports; he told an interviewer that people who call "talk radio" shows about football games, for example, engage in high-level analysis of coaching strategies and show a mastery of details and accumulated knowledge of the subject that they do not exhibit when discussing foreign and domestic politics, although these subjects are not much more complicated. The problem, to Chomsky, is getting people to exhibit "normal skepticism" and use their analytical skills "to take apart the illusions and deception that prevent understanding of contemporary reality," rather than reserving them to suggest "what, say, the New England Patriots ought to do next Sunday" (19).

15. Theories premised upon the textuality of history should not be feared as much as the false history they can be used to combat, because theory cannot be used to prove what did not happen. Viewing history as a text undeniably weakens the authority of positivist history, but that is all to the good, because authority is always based, implicitly or explicitly, on the power to have one's views disseminated and taken to be legitimate, rather than on some abstract idea of justice or transcendent idea of truth.

16. The decision to refuse these ads is not a form of censorship, for writing (whether journalism or advertisements) is not protected as free speech when it is demonstrably false. See the *New York Times* Op-Ed piece by Oshinsky and Curtis. They also report the case of *Mermelstein* v. *Institute for Historical Review,* in which the plaintiff was awarded the money promised to "anyone who could 'prove' that Jews were exterminated at Auschwitz." The presiding judge declared that the fact of the mass killings was not "subject to dispute" but quite "simply a fact." For a comprehensive account of the growing influence of Holocaust deniers and a vigorous rebuttal of their "antihistory," see Lipstadt.

17. Consider as evidence Roth's response to Wolfe's characterization of "Writ-

ing American Fiction" as a directive to writers in the 1960s and 1970s to "avert their eyes" and turn from realism (in Wolfe's "Stalking"). Roth insists he was "identifying a postwar literary trend, not proselytizing for it" (Letter to *Harper's*, Feb. 1990: 4). Judging from the letters from novelists in response to Wolfe's manifesto of November 1989, Wolfe's mistake in calling for novels to come back to the comprehensive novel of social realism was to define realism too narrowly. He missed the point that what Roth was lamenting was the dearth of fictional forms sufficient to deal with contemporary history; the classic realist novel is demonstrably not that.

18. In Chapter 4 I mentioned briefly one strand of New Journalism whose practitioners tend to concentrate the self as a prism (Mailer's telescope metaphor) and make the individual ego the primary index of the culture. See also Edmundson, who regards Mailer as a quintessential American Romantic, in the Emersonian tradition of "self-destroying self-invention" (435).

19. Hartman ends up indicting the popular detective novel or mystery story for reasons similar to those Widmer employs in disparaging documentary novels: issues are trivialized, the genres' realism lacks context, and solvers of mysteries get off easy. The guilty are too obviously that, and truth is less complex than it ought to be. He says, "Thus the trouble with the detective novel is not that it is moral but that it is moralistic; not that it is popular but that it is stylized; not that it lacks realism but that it picks up the latest realism and exploits it" (225).

20. When Smith and Hickock are found by the state to have killed the Clutters "in cold blood," a judgment questioned by the narrative, they are put to death with the same dispassion. It is also possible to read the title as referring to the book itself: Capote, too, made "a killing," to the tune of a "cool" $4 million, when he marketed his account six years later (Long).

21. Schleifer says "the momentary indirect discourse [Mailer] hears never quite achieves melody beyond its individual voices, its indirect moments" (137).

22. For the notion of the self as other, see Lacan, and Wilden, "Lacan and the Discourse of the Other," in *The Language of the Self*.

23. Mailer describes the dozen or so Hip words as follows: "Like most primitive vocabularies each word is a prime symbol and serves a dozen or a hundred functions of communication in the instinctive dialectic through which the hipster perceives his experience, that dialectic of the instantaneous differentials of existence in which one is forever moving forward into more or reatreating into less" (314).

24. "Crime and Punishment: Gary Gilmore," on "Firing Line," host William F. Buckley, Jr., broadcast on PBS, 4 Nov. 1979; quoted in Hellman 60. Schleifer also quotes this passage and adds, "What Mailer discovered was that a vision of America, unlike a vision of Russia or France, cannot produce answers and explanations." He also found that there are "aspects of human and social life that [are] not susceptible to intelligent responses" (132).

25. Daniel Kornstein (McGinniss's lawyer in the civil trial) attempted to make the validity of Malcolm's narrative stand or fall on the basis of factual errors and misinterpretations of the legal issues. This tradition of tedious recital of error has a long and dreary history. Earlier we noted Day's attempt to prove what literally happened to Crane off the coast of Florida in 1897 and Hersey's diatribe against the latest productions of Capote, Mailer, and Wolfe in 1980 ("Legend"). There are numerous articles detailing what both Capote and Mailer invented surrounding their subjects; indeed at least one reviewer of true-crime nonfiction novels invariably feels obligated to set the record

straight by pointing out false facts rather than reading carefully to note how the writer has made the material speak. As Malcolm says, "The material does not 'speak for itself' " (*Journalist* 127).

26. Stimpson says that although Malcolm bravely tackles epistemological issues, her theory is not adequate to the issues. In insisting on significant distinctions between fiction and a more "virtuous" nonfiction, Malcolm "retains the illusion of the existence of 'the actual,' an uncontaminated referent, a pure realm that exists *out there* and that our discourse has not already interpreted for us" (901). This narrowing of the options for reader reflexivity contrasts sharply to a work like Didion's "Sentimental Journeys," on the historical, political, and linguistic "transgressions" surrounding the Central Park Jogger case of 1989, in *After Henry*.

27. To Hartman, the formulaic quality of both characters and "the plot itself, which moves deviously yet inexorably toward a solution of the mystery," is a sign of the detective novel's inevitable conservatism (217).

6. FREUD AND OUR "WOLFE MAN": *THE RIGHT STUFF* AND THE CONCEPT OF BELATEDNESS

1. Jeffrey Masson is the primary subject of *In the Freud Archives,* her 1984 account of Freudian revisionists running amok just where the title says: Masson was a psychoanalyst with highly unorthodox views who nevertheless became research director of the closely guarded Freud Archives. Malcolm discusses this lawsuit in the afterword to the paperback edition of *The Journalist and the Murderer*.

2. Groping for terms to describe Malcolm's two books on the psychoanalytic establishment, Harold Bloom calls them "essays in personality," " 'fictions' of the Age of Freud and Proust" that transcend their genre of "superb reportage" (3).

3. Brooks quotes Marcus on Freud's "Dora" case study: "Human life is, ideally, a connected and coherent story, with all the details in explanatory place, and with everything . . . accounted for, in its proper causal or other sequence. And inversely illness amounts at least in part to suffering from an incoherent story or an inadequate narrative account of oneself" (282).

4. Eagleton is giving Pierre Macherey's ideas on text-ideology; he shows the parallels between the way Macherey reads texts and the Freudian process of dream interpretation. His ultimate goal is to suggest an encounter between Marxist criticism and Freudian theory (*Criticism* 89–92).

5. Deriving the operations of normal consciousness and behavior from the abnormal is not a sign that any particular mechanism is universal, that is, that the same cause will produce the same effect in everyone (although Freudian theory is often universalized this way, particularly in Anglo-American ego psychology). What Freud is suggesting is that all humans have an unconscious; that the existence of sex and death drives or instincts, as well as their repression, is universal; that we all dream; and that early experiences thus influence our later development. These effects are historically variable, but in order to theorize he must look for patterns (which means finding similarities and repetitions) and expressing them in a coherent argument that imposes generalizations, and hence universal implications. As Chase points out, although Freud is able to see "systematic thought" in general as reductive and recuperative, he repeatedly neglects to acknowledge

that this is true about his own system. She says (63) that this tendency to resist applying the "critique of theory" to his own theory – that is, his lapse in self-consciousness – is a weakness of Freud's works from *Project for a Scientific Psychology* (1895) to *Negation* (1925).

6. Laplanche uses the term "structural" to denote this category of "psychical reality" or experience: he describes it as "something which would have all the consistency of the real without, however, being verifiable in external experience" (33).

7. See Felman and Laub for the use of Freudian theory to theorize the way memories and witnessing become factual through testimony.

8. In his twenty-third Introductory Lecture (1917), Freud noted that "the question about whether fantasy or reality has had the greater share in these events of childhood could only be resolved by understanding their 'complementary relations' " (quoted in McGrath 7).

9. See Fetterley (xx) on the position offered to female readers by such a totalizing text, which offers only a male point of view.

10. Trachtenberg says that Wolfe's "writing asks to be noticed, to have conferred upon it the status of 'style,' and now of 'art' " ("What's New" 300); he adds, "His *lumpenprole* revolution is no more than a botched theft of what he thinks is the prize jewel of the intellectuals, the label of 'art' " (301).

11. Part of the pleasure of *The Right Stuff,* as in most of Wolfe's journalistic narratives, is that the reader watches the construction of these epithets and other shorthand notations of situations. For Louise Shepard, the first "Mrs. Commander Astronaut at Home," considerable detail is given (214). When we get to Betty Grissom, "It was the Danger Wake business again," and she is tagged as "the Honorable Mrs. Captain Second American in Space" (245). Annie Glenn, who has to endure the media circus twice, because John's first flight is postponed after he has been atop the Mercury rocket for five hours, has a particular reason to be fearful: she is a stutterer, and so her sense of "impending catastrophe" concerns how she will get any words out to the microphones. Wolfe gives a whole paragraph to the set speech television reporters declaim which he has reduced to "Anguished Wife at Lift-off"; it includes the description of her "sharing the anxiety and pride of the entire world at this tense moment but in a very private and very crucial way that only she can understand" (259).

12. The possibility of having women eligible to be astronauts at the inception of the space program slipped down a memory hole and was probably generally unknown, unless one remembered the hearings and the brouhaha in the press, until an article by Joan McCullough in *Ms.* in 1973. *Ms.* editor Gloria Steinem's women's-history feature in the *New York Times* in March 1992 refers to it; Steinem says she remembered the story while watching a television screening of Philip Kaufman's film version of *The Right Stuff,* which also leaves the women out.

Works Cited

Abbott, Jack Henry. *In the Belly of the Beast: Letters from Prison.* New York: Random House, 1981.

Adler, Renata. *Reckless Disregard.* New York: Knopf, 1986.

Adler, Renata, and Gerald Jonas. Letter. *Columbia Journalism Review* 5 (Winter 1966): 32–4.

Aldridge, John W. "An Interview with Norman Mailer." *Partisan Review* 47 (1980): 176.

Als, Hilton. "My Lunch with Ian: Practicing Personable Journalism." Rev. of *Great Plains,* by Ian Frazier. *Village Voice* 20 June 1989: 59.

Alterman, Eric. *Sound and Fury: The Washington Punditocracy and the Collapse of American Politics.* New York: Harper, 1992.

Althusser, Louis. "Ideology and Ideological State Apparatuses." *Lenin and Philosophy and Other Essays.* Trans. Ben Brewster. London: Monthly Review P, 1971. 127–86.

———. *For Marx.* Trans. Ben Brewster. Harmondsworth: Penguin, 1969.

Alvarez, Alfred. "The Literature of the Holocaust." *Beyond All This Fiddle: Essays 1955–1967.* New York: Random House, 1969. 24–33.

Anderson, Chris. *Style as Argument.* Carbondale: Southern Illinois UP, 1986.

Anderson, Chris, ed. *Literary Nonfiction: Theory, Criticism, Pedagogy.* Carbondale: Southern Illinois UP, 1989.

Andrews, Edmund L. "FCC Proposes a TV System That Interacts with Viewers." *New York Times* 11 Jan. 1991, natl. ed.: C5.

Aristotle. *Poetics: Aristotle's Theory of Poetry and Fine Art.* 4th ed. Trans. S. H. Butcher. New York: Dover, 1955. Chap. 9.

Arlen, Michael. "Notes on the New Journalism." *Atlantic* May 1972. Rpt. in *The Reporter as Artist.* Ed. Ronald Weber. New York: Hastings, 1974. 244–54.

———. *Thirty Seconds.* New York: Penguin, 1981.

Arnold, Matthew. "Up to Easter." *Nineteenth Century* May 1887: 638–9.

Aronowitz, Stanley. *Science as Power: Discourse and Ideology in Modern Society.* Minneapolis: U. of Minnesota P, 1988.

Autrey, Max L. "The Word out of the Sea: A View of Crane's 'The Open Boat.' " *Arizona Quarterly* 30 (Summer 1974): 101–10.

Baker, Carlos. *Ernest Hemingway: A Life Story*. New York: Scribner's, 1969.

———. *Hemingway: The Writer as Artist*. Princeton: Princeton UP, 1972.

———. "His Beat Was the World." Rev. of *By-Line: Ernest Hemingway. New York Times Book Review*, 28 May 1967: 1, 16. Rpt. in *Ernest Hemingway: The Critical Reception*. Ed. Robert O. Stephens. N.p., Burt Franklin, 1977. 412–13.

Banfield, Ann. *Unspeakable Sentences: Narration and Representation in the Language of Fiction*. Boston: Routledge, 1982.

Barnett, Lincoln. "Einstein's Relativity." *The Universe of Doctor Einstein*. New York: Morrow, 1972. Rpt. in *A World of Ideas*. Ed. Lee A. Jacobus. New York: St. Martin's, 1983.

Barthes, Roland. "Historical Discourse." *Social Science Information* 6.4 (1967). Trans. Peter Wexler. Rpt. in *Introduction to Structuralism*. Ed. Michael Lane. New York: Basic, 1970. 145–55.

———. *Mythologies*. Trans. Annette Levers. New York: Hill & Wang, 1972.

———. "The Photographic Message." *Image Music Text*. Trans. Stephen Heath. New York: Hill & Wang, 1977. 15–31.

———. "Science versus Literature." *TLS* 28 Sept. 1967. Rpt. in *Introduction to Structuralism*. Ed. Michael Lane. New York: Basic, 1970. 410–16.

———. "Structure of the *Fait-Divers*." *Critical Essays*. Trans. Richard Howard. Evanston: Northwestern UP, 1972. 185–95.

———. "Syntagm and System." *Elements of Semiology*. Trans. Annette Lavers and Colin Smith. New York: Hill & Wang, 1967. 58–88.

———. *S/Z*. Trans. Richard Howard. New York: Hill & Wang, 1974.

———. *Writing Degree Zero*. Trans. Annette Lavers and Colin Smith. New York: Hill & Wang, 1967.

Beach, Joseph Warren. *American Fiction, 1920–1940*. New York: Macmillan, 1941.

Beauvoir, Simone de. *The Second Sex*. Ed. and trans. H. M. Parshley. New York: Knopf, 1952.

Beegel, Susan. *Hemingway's Craft of Omission: Four Manuscript Examples*. Ann Arbor: UMI, 1988.

Beer, Thomas. *Stephen Crane: A Study in American Letters*. New York: Knopf, 1923.

Bell, Daniel. *The End of Ideology: On the Exhaustion of Political Ideas in the Fifties*. Glencoe, IL: Free, 1960.

Bell, Millicent. "*A Farewell to Arms*: Pseudoautobiography and Personal Metaphor." *Ernest Hemingway: The Writer in Context*. Ed. James Nagel. U of Wisconsin P, 1984. 107–28.

Belsey, Catherine. *Critical Practice*. London: Methuen, 1980.

Benedict, Helen. *Virgin or Vamp: How the Press Covers Sex Crimes*. New York: Oxford UP, 1992.

Benfey, Christopher. *The Double Life of Stephen Crane*. New York: Knopf, 1992.

Benjamin, Walter. "The Author as Producer." *Understanding Brecht*. Trans. Anna Bostock. London: New Left, 1977. 85–103.

———. "The Story-teller." *Illuminations*. Trans. Harry Zohn. New York: Harcourt, 1968. 83–110.

——. "The Work of Art in the Age of Mechanical Reproduction." *Illumina-tions*. Trans. Harry Zohn. New York: Harcourt, 1968. 219–54.

Bennett, Tony. *Formalism and Marxism*. New York: Methuen, 1979.

Bennett, Tony, et al., eds. *Culture, Ideology and Social Process: A Reader*. London: Batsford/Open University P, 1981.

Benson, Jackson J. "Criticism of the Short Stories: The Neglected and the Oversaturated – An Editorial." *Hemingway Review* 8.2 (1989): 30–5.

——. "Ernest Hemingway as Short Story Writer." *The Short Stories of Ernest Hemingway: Critical Essays*. Ed. Benson. Durham, NC: Duke UP, 1975. 272–310.

——. *Hemingway: The Writer's Art of Self-Defense*. Minneapolis: U of Minnesota P, 1969.

Benson, Jackson J., ed. *New Critical Approaches to the Short Stories of Ernest Hemingway*. Durham, NC: Duke UP, 1990.

Benveniste, Emile. *Problems of General Linguistics*. Trans. Mary Elizabeth Meek. Coral Gables, FL: U of Miami P, 1971. 205–15.

Berger, John. "Another Way of Telling." *Journal of Social Reconstruction* 1.1 (1980): 57–75.

Berger, John, et al. *Ways of Seeing*. London: Penguin, 1972.

Berger, Peter L., and Thomas Luckmann. *The Social Construction of Reality*. Garden City, NY: Doubleday, 1966.

Bergon, Frank. *Stephen Crane's Artistry*. New York: Columbia UP, 1975.

Berman, Marshall. *All That Is Solid Melts into Air: The Experience of Modernity*. New York: Simon, 1982.

Bigsby, C. W. E. "Hemingway: The Recoil from History." *The Twenties: American Writing in the Postwar Decade*. Ed. Frederick J. Hoffman. New York: Viking, 1955. 203–13.

Birkerts, Sven. *American Energies*. New York: Morrow, 1992.

Bloom, Harold. Rev. of *In the Freud Archives*, by Janet Malcolm. *New York Times Book Review* 27 May 1984: 3, 15.

Bohlke, L. Brent, ed. *Willa Cather in Person: Interviews, Speeches, and Letters*. Lincoln: U of Nebraska P, 1986.

Boswell, James. *London Journal, 1762–1763*. Ed. Frederick A. Pottle. New York: McGraw, 1950.

Bottomore, Tom. *The Frankfurt School*. New York: Tavistock/Methuen, 1984.

Bové, Paul. *Destructive Poetics*. New York: Columbia UP, 1980.

——. *Intellectuals in Power: A Genealogy of Critical Humanism*. New York: Columbia UP, 1986.

Boyce, George, James Curran, and Pauline Wingate. *Newspaper History: From the Seventeenth Century to the Present Day*. London: Constable, 1978.

Boylan, James. Rev. of *Objectivity and the News*, by Dan Schiller. *Columbia Journalism Review* 20 (Sept.–Oct. 1981): 61–63.

Bradbury, Malcolm. Rev. of *By-Line: Ernest Hemingway*. *New Statesman* 22 Mar. 1968: 386–7. Rpt. in *Hemingway: The Critical Heritage*. Ed. Jeffrey Meyers. London: Routledge, 1982. 523–5.

Braudy, Leo. *Narrative Form in History and Fiction*. Princeton: Princeton UP, 1970.

Brecht, Bertolt. *Aesthetics and Politics.* Essays by Bloch, Lukacs, Brecht, Benjamin, and Adorno. London: New Left, 1977.

Bridgman, Richard. *The Colloquial Style in American Literature.* New York: Oxford UP, 1966.

Brooks, Peter. *Reading for the Plot: Design and Intention in Narrative.* New York: Knopf, 1984.

Brown, Charles H. *The Correspondents' War: Journalists in the Spanish-American War.* New York: Scribner's, 1967.

Buitenhuis, Peter. *The Great War of Words: British, American, and Canadian Propaganda and Fiction, 1914–1933.* Vancouver: U of British Columbia P, 1987.

Bürger, Peter. *Theory of the Avant-Garde.* Trans. Michael Shaw. Minneapolis: U of Minnesota P, 1984.

Cady, Edwin H. Introduction. *Tales, Sketches, and Reports.* Vol. 8 of *The Virginia Edition of the Works of Stephen Crane.* Ed. Fredson Bowers. Charlottesville: U of Virginia P, 1971.

———. *Stephen Crane.* Rev. ed. Boston: Twayne, 1980.

Cain, William E. *The Crisis in Criticism: Theory, Literature, and Reform in English Studies.* Baltimore: Johns Hopkins UP, 1984.

———. "Realism, Naturalism, and the New American Literary History." Rev. of *The Gold Standard and the Logic of Naturalism,* by Walter Benn Michaels. *Review* 10. Ed. James O. Hoge and James L. W. West III. Charlottesville: UP of Virginia, 1988. 73–83.

Canary, Robert, and Henry Kozicki, eds. *The Writing of History.* Madison: U of Wisconsin P, 1978.

Capote, Truman. *In Cold Blood.* New York: NAL, 1965.

Caputi, Jane. "The Sexual Politics of Murder." *Gender and Society* 3 (1989): 437–56.

Carey, James W. *Communication as Culture: Essays on Media and Society.* Boston: Unwin, 1988.

———. "The Communications Revolution and the Professional Communicator." *Sociological Review Monograph* 13 (1969): 23–38.

Carter, Everett. *Howells and the Age of Realism.* Philadelphia: Lippincott, 1954.

Carver, Raymond. *Fires: Essays, Poems, Stories.* Santa Barbara: Capra, 1983.

Cather, Willa. *Not under Forty.* New York: Knopf, 1936.

———. "When I Knew Stephen Crane." *Library* 1 (1900): 1718. Rpt. in *Stephen Crane: A Collection of Critical Essays.* Ed. Maurice Bassan. Englewood Cliffs, NJ: Prentice, 1967. 12–17.

———. *On Writing.* New York: Knopf, 1949.

Cawelti, John. *Six-gun Mystique.* Bowling Green, OH: Bowling Green State UP, 1971.

Chase, Cynthia. "Oedipal Textuality: Reading Freud's Reading of *Oedipus.*" *Diacritics* 9 (1979): 54–68.

"The Chicanery of *Silkwood.*" *New York Times* 25 Dec. 1983: 12E.

Chomsky, Noam. *Chronicler of Dissent.* Interview, by David Barsamian. Monroe, ME: Common Courage, 1992. Excerpted as "Monday-morning Policy Wonks." *Harper's* March 1993: 19.

Clarke, John, et al. "Sub Cultures, Cultures and Class." *Culture, Ideology and Social Process: A Reader.* Ed. Tony Bennett et al. London: Batsford/Open University P, 1981. 53–79.

Clayton, Jay. "Narrative and Theories of Desire." *Critical Inquiry* 16 (1989): 33–53.

Clemons, Walter. "Houdini, Meet Ferdinand." *Newsweek* 14 July 1975: 73–6.

Cohen, Ed. "Tom Wolfe and the Truth Monitors: A Historical Fable." *Clio* 16 (1986): 1–11.

Cohen, Stanley, and Jock Young. *The Manufacture of News.* Beverly Hills, CA: Sage, 1973.

Cohn, Dorritt. "Fictional versus Historical Lives: Borderlines and Borderline Cases." *Journal of Narrative Technique* 19 (1989): 3–24.

Collins, Michael. "So You Want to Be an Astronaut." Rev. of *The Right Stuff,* by Tom Wolfe. *Washington Post Book World* 9 Sept. 1979: 1, 8.

Colvert, James B. Introduction. *Reports of War.* Vol. 9 of *The Virginia Edition of the Works of Stephen Crane.* Ed. Fredson Bowers. Charlottesville: U of Virginia P, 1971. xix–xxix.

———. "The Origins of Stephen Crane's Literary Creed." *University of Texas Studies in English* 34 (1955): 179–88. Rpt. in *Stephen Crane's Career: Perspectives and Evaluations.* Ed. Thomas A. Gullason. New York: NYU P, 1972. 170–80.

———. "Structure and Theme in Stephen Crane's Fiction." *Modern Fiction Studies* 5 (1959): 199–208.

Compton, Neil. "Hijinks Journalism." *Commentary* Feb. 1969: 76–8.

Conder, John J. *Naturalism in American Fiction.* Lexington: UP of Kentucky, 1984.

Connery, Thomas B. Introduction. *A Sourcebook of American Literary Journalism.* Ed. Connery. New York: Greenwood, 1992. 3–37.

Conrad, Joseph. Introduction. *Stephen Crane,* by Thomas Beer. New York: Knopf, 1923.

Corkin, Stanley. "Hemingway, Film, and U.S. Culture: *In Our Time* and *The Birth of a Nation. A Moving Picture Feast.* Ed. Charles M. Oliver. New York: Praeger, 1989.

———. *Realism and the Birth of Modern America.* In press.

Cornwell, Elmer E., Jr. *Presidential Leadership of Public Opinion.* Bloomington: Indiana UP, 1965.

Cowley, Malcolm. "A Natural History of American Naturalism." *Kenyon Review,* Summer 1947. Rpt. in *Documents of Modern Literary Realism.* Ed. George Becker. Princeton: Princeton UP, 1963. 429–51.

———. *A Second Flowering.* New York: Viking, 1973.

Cowley, Malcolm, ed. *After the Genteel Tradition: American Writers, 1910–1930.* Carbondale: Southern Illinois UP, 1964.

Cramer, Richard Ben. *What It Takes: The Way to the White House.* New York: Random House, 1992.

Crane, Stephen. *The Correspondence of Stephen Crane.* Ed. Stanley Wertheim and Paul Sorrentino. 2 vols. New York: Columbia UP, 1988.

——. "Howells Fears Realists Must Wait." *Tales, Sketches, and Reports.* Vol. 8 of *The Virginia Edition of the Works of Stephen Crane.* Ed. Fredson Bowers. Charlottesville: U of Virginia P, 1970. 635–8.

——. "The Open Boat." *Tales of Adventure.* Vol. 5 of *The Virginia Edition of the Works of Stephen Crane.* Ed. Fredson Bowers. Charlottesville: U of Virginia P, 1970. 68–92.

——. *Poems and Literary Remains.* Vol. 10 of *The Virginia Edition of the Works of Stephen Crane.* Ed. Fredson Bowers. Charlottesville: U of Virginia P, 1975.

——. *The Portable Stephen Crane.* Ed. Joseph Katz. New York: Penguin, 1969.

——. *Reports of War.* Vol. 9 of *The Virginia Edition of the Works of Stephen Crane.* Ed. Fredson Bowers. Charlottesville: U of Virginia P, 1971. 85–93.

——. *Stephen Crane: Prose and Poetry.* Ed. J. C. Levenson. New York: Library of America, 1984.

——. "Stephen Crane's Own Story." *Reports of War.* Vol. 9 of *The Virginia Edition of the Works of Stephen Crane.* Ed. Fredson Bowers. Charlottesville: U of Virginia P, 1971. 85–93.

——. *Stories and Tales.* Ed. Robert Stallman. New York: Vintage, 1955.

——. *Tales of Adventure.* Vol. 5 of *The Virginia Edition of the Works of Stephen Crane.* Ed. Fredson Bowers. Charlottesville: U of Virginia, 1970.

——. *Tales, Sketches, and Reports.* Vol. 8 of *The Virginia Edition of the Works of Stephen Crane.* Ed. Fredson Bowers. Charlottesville: U of Virginia, 1973.

Culler, Jonathan. *Structuralist Poetics.* Ithaca: Cornell UP, 1975.

Dahlgren, Peter. "TV News and the Suppression of Reflexivity." *Mass Media and Social Change.* Ed. Elihu Katz and Tomas Szecski. Beverly Hills, CA: Sage, 1981. 101–13.

Darnton, Robert. "Writing News and Telling Stories." *Daedalus* 104 (1975): 175–94.

Davis, Lennard J. "A Social History of Fact and Fiction." *Literature and Society.* Ed. Edward W. Said. Baltimore: Johns Hopkins UP, 1980. 120–48.

Davis, Richard Harding. *Notes of a War Correspondent.* New York: Scribner's, 1910.

——. "Our War Correspondents in Cuba and Puerto Rico." *Harper's Monthly* May 1899: 938–41.

Day, Cyrus. "Stephen Crane and the Ten-foot Dinghy." *Boston University Studies in English* 3.4 (1957): 193–213.

DeFalco, Joseph. *The Hero in Hemingway's Short Stories.* Pittsburgh: U of Pittsburgh P, 1963.

De Lauretis, Teresa. *Alice Doesn't: Feminism, Semiotics, Cinema.* Bloomington: Indiana UP, 1982.

DeLillo, Don. *White Noise.* New York: Viking, 1985.

DeMott, Benjamin. "Dirty Words?" *The American Novel since World War II.* Ed. Marcus Klein. New York: Fawcett, 1969. 210–23.

Derrida, Jacques. "Freud and the Scene of Writing." *Writing and Difference.* Trans. Alan Bass. Chicago: U of Chicago P, 1978. Rpt. in *Freud: A Collection of Critical Essays.* Ed. Perry Meisel. Englewood Cliffs, N.J.: Prentice, 1981. 145–82.

———. "The Law of Genre." Trans. Avital Ronell. *Glyph* 7 (1980): 202–32.

Dickstein, Morris. *Gates of Eden: American Culture in the Sixties.* New York: Basic, 1977.

Didion, Joan. *After Henry.* New York: Simon, 1992.

———. *Slouching towards Bethlehem.* New York: Farrar, 1968.

———. *The White Album.* New York: Simon, 1979.

———. "Why I Write." *New York Times Book Review* 1976. Rpt. in *Eight Modern Essayists.* Ed. William Smart. New York: St. Martin's, 1980.

Dillard, Annie. *An American Childhood.* New York: Harper, 1987.

Doctorow, E. L. *The Book of Daniel.* New York: Signet, 1971.

Donaldson, Scott. "Hemingway of *The Star.*" *Ernest Hemingway: The Papers of a Writer.* Ed. Bernard Oldsey. New York: Garland, 1981. 89–108.

Dreiser, Theodore. *A Book about Myself.* 5th ed. New York: Boni, 1927.

Dudek, Louis. *Literature and the Press.* Toronto: Ryerson, 1960.

Dunne, Michael. *Metapop: Self-referentiality in Contemporary American Popular Culture.* Jackson: UP of Mississippi, 1992.

Eagleton, Terry. *Criticism and Ideology: A Study in Marxist Literary Theory.* London: Verso, 1978.

———. *Ideology of the Aesthetic.* Oxford: Blackwell, 1990.

———. *Literary Theory: An Introduction.* Minneapolis: U of Minnesota P, 1983.

———. "Realism and Cinema." Rev. of *Realism and the Cinema,* ed. Christopher Williams. *Screen* 21.2 (1980): 93–4.

Eason, David. "The New Journalism and the Image World." *Critical Studies in Mass Communication* 1 (1984): 51–65.

Edel, Leon. *Henry James: The Master, 1901–1916.* 1972. Rpt. New York: Discus-Avon, 1978.

Edmundson, Mark. "Romantic Self-Creations: Mailer and Gilmore in *The Executioner's Song. Contemporary Literature* 31 (1990): 434–47.

Edwards, Thomas R. "The Electric Indian." Rev. of *The Electric Kool-Aid Acid Test,* by Tom Wolfe. *Partisan Review* 3 (1969): 533–44.

Egan, Kieran. "Thucydides, Tragedian." *The Writing of History.* Ed. Robert H. Canary and Henry Kozicki. Madison: U of Wisconsin P, 1978.

Eichenbaum, Boris. "The Theory of the 'Formal Method.' " *Russian Formalist Criticism.* Ed. and trans. Lee T. Lemon and Marion J. Reis. Lincoln: U of Nebraska P, 1965. 99–139.

Eliot, T. S. *The Sacred Wood.* London: Methuen, 1920. Rpt. New York: Barnes, 1960.

Ellison, Ralph. *Invisible Man.* 1952. Rpt. New York: Vintage, 1989.

Ellul, Jacques. *Propaganda: The Formation of Men's Attitudes.* Trans. Konrad Kellen and Jean Lerner. New York: Knopf, 1965.

Epstein, Edward Jay. *News from Nowhere: Television and the News.* New York: Vintage, 1974.

Ericson, Richard V., Patricia M. Baranck, and Janet B. L. Chan. *Visualizing Deviance: A Study of News Organization.* Toronto: U of Toronto P, 1987.

Erlich, V. *Russian Formalism.* The Hague: Mouton, 1955.

Ewen, Stuart. *Captains of Consciousness: Advertising and the Social Roots of the Consumer Culture.* New York: McGraw, 1976.

Faludi, Susan. *Backlash: The Undeclared War against Women*. New York: Crown, 1991.

Fekete, John. *The Critical Twilight: Explorations in the Ideology of Anglo-American Literary Theory from Eliot to McLuhan*. London: Routledge, 1977.

Felman, Shoshana, and Dori Laub. *Testimony: Crises of Witnessing in Literature, Psychoanalysis, and History*. New York: Routledge, 1992.

Fenton, Charles A. *The Apprenticeship of Ernest Hemingway*. New York: Farrar, 1954.

Fetterley, Judith. *The Resisting Reader: A Feminist Approach to American Fiction*. Bloomington: Indiana UP, 1978.

Fish, Stanley. "Commentary." *The New Historicism*. Ed. H. Aram Veeser. New York: Routledge, 1989. 303–16.

Fishkin, Shelley Fisher. *From Fact to Fiction: Journalism and Imaginative Writing in America*. Baltimore: Johns Hopkins UP, 1985.

Fishman, Mark. *Manufacturing the News*. Austin: U of Texas P, 1980.

Fixx, James F. "The New Journalism." *Saturday Review*, 12 Feb. 1966: 65.

Flora, Joseph M. *Ernest Hemingway: A Study of the Short Fiction*. Boston: Twayne, 1989.

Foley, Barbara. "Fact, Fiction, Fascism: Testimony and Mimesis in Holocaust Narratives." *Comparative Literature* 34 (1982): 330–60.

———. "Fact, Fiction, and 'Reality.'" *Contemporary Literature* 20.3 (1979): 389–99.

———. "History, Fiction, and the Ground Between: The Uses of the Documentary Mode in Black Literature." *PMLA* (1980): 389–403.

———. *Telling the Truth: The Theory and Practice of Documentary Fiction*. Ithaca: Cornell UP, 1986.

Forcey, Charles. *The Crossroads of Liberalism: Croly, Weyl, Lippmann, and the Progressive Era, 1900–1925*. New York: Oxford UP, 1961.

Freud, Sigmund. *Beyond the Pleasure Principle*. Trans. James Strachey. New York: Norton, 1961.

———. *Dora: Fragment of an Analysis of a Case of Hysteria*. Trans. James Strachey. Ed. Philip Rieff. New York: Collier, 1963.

———. "From the History of an Infantile Neurosis." *Three Case Histories*. Trans. James Strachey. New York: Collier, 1963. 187–316.

———. *The Interpretation of Dreams*. Trans. James Strachey. New York: Avon, 1965.

———. "Negation." *General Psychological Theory*. Trans. Joan Riviere. New York: Collier, 1963.

———. *The Origins of Psychoanalysis*. Trans. Eric Mosbacher and James Strachey. New York: Basic, 1954.

Fryckstedt, Olov W. "Stephen Crane in the Tenderloin." *Studia Neophilologica* 34 (1962): 135–63.

Frye, Northrop. *The Anatomy of Criticism*. Princeton: Princeton UP, 1957.

Gans, Herbert. *Deciding What's News*. New York: Pantheon, 1979.

Garrick, John. "Hemingway and *The Spanish Earth*." *A Moving Picture Feast*. Ed. Charles M. Oliver. New York: Praeger, 1989. 76–90.

Geertz, Clifford. "Blurred Genres." *Local Knowledge*. New York: Basic, 1983.

Gilkes, Lillian. *Cora Crane: A Biography of Mrs. Stephen Crane*. Bloomington: Indiana UP, 1960.

Girard, René. *Deceit, Desire, and the Novel: Self and Other in Literary Structure*. Trans. Yvonne Freccero. Baltimore: Johns Hopkins UP, 1965.

Gitlin, Todd. "The Politics of Communication and the Communication of Politics." *Mass Media and Society*. Ed. James Curran and Michael Gurevitch. London: Arnold, 1991. 329–41.

——. *The Whole World Is Watching: The Mass Media and the Making and Unmaking of the New Left*. Berkeley: U of California P, 1980.

Godden, Richard. *Fictions of Capital: The American Novel from James to Mailer*. Cambridge: Cambridge UP, 1990.

Going, William T. "William Higgins and Crane's 'The Open Boat': A Note about Fact and Fiction." *Papers on Language and Literature* 1 (1965): 79–82.

Good, Howard. *Acquainted with the Night: The Image of Journalists in American Fiction, 1890–1930*. Metuchen, NJ: Scarecrow, 1986.

Gordon, Caroline, and Allen Tate. *The House of Fiction: An Anthology of the Short Story with Commentary*. New York: Scribner's, 1950.

Gordon, Mary. "Letters." *Harper's*, Feb. 1990: 10.

Gossman, Lionel. "History and Literature." *The Writing of History*. Ed. Robert H. Canary and Henry Kozicki. Madison: U of Wisconsin P, 1978.

Graff, Gerald. "Co-optation." *The New Historicism*. Ed. H. Aram Veeser. New York: Routledge, 1989. 168–81.

——. *Professing Literature: An Institutional History*. Chicago: U of Chicago P, 1987.

Graham, John. "Ernest Hemingway: The Meaning of Style." *Modern Fiction Studies* 6 (1960): 298–313. Rpt. in *Ernest Hemingway: Critiques of Four Major Novels*. Ed. Carlos Baker. New York: Scribner's, 1962. 183–92.

Gramsci, Antonio. *Selections from the Prison Notebooks*. Ed. and trans. Quintin Hoare and Geoffrey Nowell Smith. New York: International, 1971.

Grebstein, Sheldon. *Hemingway's Craft*. Carbondale: Southern Illinois UP, 1973.

Greenblatt, Stephen. "Towards a Poetics of Culture." *The New Historicism*. Ed. H. Aram Veeser. New York: Routledge, 1989. 1–14.

Griffin, Peter. *Less Than Treason: Hemingway in Paris*. New York: Oxford UP, 1990.

Gullason, Thomas A. "Stephen Crane's Short Stories: The True Road." *Stephen Crane's Career: Perspectives and Evaluations*. Ed. Gullason. New York: NYU Press, 1972. 470–85.

Hagemann, E. R. "A Collation, with Commentary, of the Five Texts of the Chapters in Hemingway's *In Our Time*, 1923–38." *Critical Essays on Ernest Hemingway's In Our Time*. Ed. Michael S. Reynolds. Boston: Hall, 1983. 38–51.

——. "Sadder than the End: Another Look at 'The Open Boat.' " *Stephen Crane: Centenary Essays*. Ed. Joseph Katz. DeKalb: Northern Illinois UP, 1972. 66–85.

Hall, Stuart. "Culture, the Media and the 'Ideological Effect.' " *Mass Communication and Society*. Ed. J. Curran et al. London: Arnold, 1977. 315–48.

————. "The Determinations of News Photographs." *The Manufacture of News*. Ed. Stanley Cohen and Jock Young. Beverly Hills, CA: Sage, 1973.

Halliday, E. M. "Hemingway's Narrative Perspective." *Sewanee Review* 60 (1952): 202–18. Rpt. in *Ernest Hemingway: Critiques of Four Major Novels*. Ed. Carlos Baker. New York: Scribner's, 1962. 174–82.

Hämburger, Kate. *The Logic of Literature*. Trans. Marilynn Rose. 2nd ed. Bloomington: Indiana UP, 1973.

Hankiss, Elemér. "Semantic Oscillation: A Universal of Artistic Expression." *The Sign in Music and Literature*. Ed. Wendy Steiner. Austin: U of Texas P, 1981: 67–85.

Hartman, Geoffrey H. "Literature High and Low: The Case of the Mystery Story." *The Poetics of Murder: Detective Fiction and Literary Theory*. San Diego: Harcourt, 1983. 210–29.

Hartshorne, Thomas L. "Tom Wolfe on the 1960's." *Midwest Quarterly* 23 (1982): 144–63.

Hatlen, Burton. "Why Is *The Education of Henry Adams* 'Literature' While *The Theory of the Leisure Class* Is Not?" *College English* 40 (1979): 665–76.

Hayes, Harold. "Editor's Notes on the New Journalism." *Esquire* Jan. 1972. Rpt. in *The Reporter as Artist*. Ed. Ronald Weber. New York: Hastings, 1974: 154–60.

Hebdige, Dick. *Subculture: The Meaning of Style*. New York: Methuen, 1979.

Hellmann, John. *Fables of Fact: The New Journalism as New Fiction*. Urbana: U of Illinois P, 1981.

Hemingway, Ernest. "The Art of Fiction XXI." *Paris Review* 18 (1958): 61–89.

————. *By-Line: Ernest Hemingway*. Ed. William White. New York: Scribner's, 1967.

————. *The Complete Short Stories of Ernest Hemingway*. Finca Vigia Edition. New York: Scribner's, 1987.

————. *Dateline: Toronto*. Ed. William White. New York: Scribner's, 1985.

————. *Death in the Afternoon*. New York: Scribner's, 1932.

————. *A Farewell to Arms*. New York: Scribner's, 1934.

————. *In Our Time*. New York: Scribner's, 1930.

————. *A Moveable Feast*. New York: Scribner's, 1964. Rpt. New York: Bantam, 1965.

————. *The Nick Adams Stories*. Ed. Philip Young. New York: Scribner's, 1972.

————. "The Old Man at the Bridge." *Ken* 1.4 (19 May 1938): 36.

————. *Selected Letters, 1917–1961*. Ed. Carlos Baker. New York, Scribner's, 1981.

Hemingway, Mary. *How It Was*. New York: Knopf, 1976.

Herman, Edward S., and Noam Chomsky. *Manufacturing Consent: The Political Economy of the Mass Media*. New York: Pantheon, 1988.

Hernadi, Paul, ed. *What Is Literature?* Bloomington: Indiana UP, 1978.

Hersey, John. *The Algiers Motel Incident*. New York: Knopf, 1968.

————. "The Art of Fiction XCII." *Paris Review* 28 (1986): 211–49.

————. *Hiroshima*. New York: Knopf, 1946. Rpt. Knopf, 1985.

————. "The Legend on the License." *Yale Review* 70 (1980): 1–25.

Hirsch, E. D. "What Isn't Literature?" *What Is Literature?* Ed. Paul Hernadi. Bloomington: Indiana UP, 1978. 24–34.

Hoffman, Abbie. "The Sixties Revisited." Symposium. Vanderbilt University, 5 Apr. 1990.

Hoffman, Daniel. *The Poetry of Stephen Crane.* New York: Columbia UP, 1957.

Hofstadter, Richard. *Age of Reform: From Bryan to FDR.* New York: Knopf, 1955.

Hollowell, John. *Fact and Fiction: The New Journalism and the Nonfiction Novel.* Chapel Hill: U of North Carolina P, 1977.

Holton, Milne. *Cylinder of Vision: The Fiction and Journalistic Writing of Stephen Crane.* Baton Rouge: Louisiana State UP, 1972.

Holzer, Harold, Gabor S. Boritt, and Mark F. Neely, Jr. *The Lincoln Image.* New York: Scribner's, 1984.

Horkheimer, Max, and Theodor W. Adorno. *Dialectic of Enlightenment.* Trans. John Cumming. New York: Herder, 1972.

Hough, Graham. *The Last Romantics.* London: Duckworth, 1949.

Howard, Jane. "How the 'Smart Rascal' Brought It Off." *Life* 18 Feb. 1966: 70–6.

Howe, Irving. "Mass Society and Post-modern Fiction." *The American Novel since World War II.* Ed. Marcus Klein. New York: Fawcett, 1969. 124–41.

Howells, William Dean. *Criticism and Fiction, and Other Essays.* Ed. Clara Marburg Kirk and Rudolf Kirk. New York: NYU P, 1959.

———. *Editor's Study.* Ed. James W. Simpson. Troy, NY: Whitston, 1983.

———. *W. D. Howells as Critic.* Ed. Edwin H. Cady. London: Routledge, 1973.

Hughes, Helen MacGill. *News and the Human Interest Story.* Chicago: U of Chicago P, 1940.

Hutcheon, Linda. *Narcissistic Narrative: The Metafictional Paradox.* New York: Metheun, 1984.

———. *The Poetics of Postmodernism.* New York: Routledge, 1988.

Huyssen, Andreas. *After the Great Divide: Modernism, Mass Culture, Postmodernism.* Bloomington: Indiana UP, 1986.

"Invention." *Princeton Encyclopedia of Poetry and Poetics.* Ed. Alex Preminger. Princeton: Princeton UP, 1965.

Ireland, Doug. "Press Clips." *Village Voice* 5 March 1991: 8.

Jakobson, Roman. "Closing Statement: Linguistics and Poetics." *Style in Language.* Ed. Thomas Sebeok. Cambridge, MA: MIT P, 1960.

———. "On Realism in Art." *Readings in Russian Poetics.* Ed. & trans. L. Matejka and K. Pomorska. Cambridge, MA: MIT P, 1971: 38–46.

Jakobson, Roman, and Morris Halle. "Two Aspects of Language and Two Types of Aphasic Disturbances." *Fundamentals of Language.* The Hague: Mouton, 1956. 69–96.

James, Henry. "Gustave Flaubert." *The Art of Fiction.* By James, New York: Oxford UP, 1948. 124–53.

Jameson, Fredric. *Marxism and Form: Twentieth-Century Dialectical Theories of Literature.* Princeton: Princeton UP, 1972.

———. *The Political Unconscious.* Ithaca: Cornell UP, 1981.

————. *The Prison House of Language*. Princton: Princeton UP, 1972.

————. "Reflections in Conclusion." *Aesthetics and Politics*. Essays by Bloch, Lukacs, Brecht, Benjamin, and Adorno. London: New Left, 1977. 196–213.

————. "Reification and Utopia in Mass Culture." *Social Text* 1 (1979): 130–48.

Johnson, Samuel. "Preface to Shakespeare." *Rasselas, Poems, and Selected Prose*. By Johnson, Ed. Bertrand H. Bronson. New York: Rinehart, 1958.

Josephs, Allen. "Hemingway's Spanish Civil War Stories." *Hemingway's Neglected Short Fiction: New Perspectives*. Ed. Susan Beegel. Ann Arbor: UMI, 1989: 313–28.

Kael, Pauline. Rev. of *King of Comedy*. *New Yorker*, 7 March 1983: 123–8.

Karl, Frederick. *American Fiction: 1940–1980*. New York: Harper, 1983.

Katz, Joseph, ed. Introduction. *The Portable Stephen Crane*. New York: Penguin, 1969.

Kauffmann, Stanley. Rev. of *By-Line: Ernest Hemingway*. *New Republic,* 10 June 1967. Rpt. in *Hemingway: The Critical Heritage*. Ed. Jeffrey Meyers. London: Routledge, 1982. 519–22.

Kazin, Alfred. *Bright Book of Life*. Notre Dame, IN: U of Notre Dame P, 1980.

————. *On Native Grounds: A Study of American Prose Literature from 1890 to the Present*. New York: Reynal, 1942.

Kennedy, David. *Progressivism: The Critical Issues*. Boston: Little, 1971.

Kenner, Hugh. *A Homemade World: The American Modernist Writers*. New York: Knopf, 1975.

Kissane, Leedice. "Interpretation through Language: A Study of the Metaphors in Stephen Crane's 'The Open Boat.' " *Rendezvous* 1 (1966): 18–22. Rpt. in *Stephen Crane's Career: Perspectives and Evaluations*. Ed. Thomas A. Gullason. New York: NYU P, 1972. 410–16.

Knightley, Philip. *The First Casualty*. New York: Harcourt, 1975.

Kobler, J. F. *Hemingway: Journalist and Artist*. Ann Arbor: UMI, 1985.

Kornstein, Daniel J. "Twisted Vision: Janet Malcolm's Upside Down View of the *Fatal Vision* Case." *Cardozo Studies in Law and Literature* 1.2 (1989): 1–22.

Krieger, Murray. "Introduction: The Literary, the Textual, the Social." *The Aims of Representation*. Ed. Krieger. New York: Columbia UP, 1987. 1–22.

Kwiat, Joseph J. "The Newspaper Experience of Stephen Crane." *Stephen Crane's Career: Perspectives and Events*. Ed. Thomas A. Gullason. New York: New York UP, 1972. 161–9.

Lacan, Jacques. *Four Fundamental Concepts of Psychoanalysis*. Trans. Alan Sheridan. Rpt. New York: Norton, 1981.

LaFrance, Marston. *A Reading of Stephen Crane*. Oxford: Clarendon, 1971.

Laplanche, Jacques. *Life and Death in Psychoanalysis*. Trans. Jeffrey Mehlman. Baltimore: Johns Hopkins UP, 1976.

Lasch, Christopher. "The Lost Art of Political Argument." Excerpt from "Journalism, Publicity, and the Lost Art of Argument." *Gannett Center Journal,* Spring 1990. Rpt. in *Harper's* Sept. 1990: 17–20, 22.

Lauter, Paul. *Canons and Contexts*. New York: Oxford UP, 1991.

————. Introduction. *Reconstructing American Literature*. Ed. Lauter. Old Westbury, NY: Feminist, 1983.

————. "Race and Gender in the Shaping of the American Literary Canon: A Case Study from the Twenties." *Canons and Contexts.* By Lauter. New York: Oxford UP, 1991.

Lazere, Donald. "Literacy and Mass Media: The Political Implications." In *Reading in America.* Ed. Cathy Davidson. Baltimore: Johns Hopkins UP, 1989. 285–303.

————. "Literary Revisionism, Partisan Politics, and the Press." *Profession 89.* New York: MLA, 1989. 49–54.

Lee, Alan. "The Structure, Ownership and Control of the Press, 1855–1914." *Newspaper History: From the Seventeenth Century to the Present Day.* Ed. George Boyce et al. London: Constable, 1978.

Lemon, Lee T., and Marion J. Reis, eds. and trans. *Russian Formalist Criticism.* Lincoln: U of Nebraska P, 1965.

"Letters." *Harper's.* Jan. 1990; Feb. 1990.

"Letters." *Ms.* Nov. 1973: 6; Jan. 1974: 406; June 1974: 73–4.

Levenson, J. C. Introduction. *Tales of Adventure.* By Stephen Crane. Vol. 5 of *The Virginia Edition of the Works of Stephen Crane.* Ed. Fredson Bowers. Charlottesville: U of Virginia, 1971. xv–cxxxii.

Levine, George. *The Realistic Imagination.* Chicago: U of Chicago Press, 1982.

Levine, Lawrence W. *Highbrow/Lowbrow: The Emergence of Cultural Hierarchy in America.* Cambridge, MA: Harvard UP, 1988.

Levy, David W. *Herbert Croly of the New Republic: The Life and Thought of an American Progressive.* Princeton: Princeton UP, 1985.

Lewis, Margaret Calien. "Ernest Hemingway's The Spanish War." Diss. U of Louisville, 1969.

Lewis, R. W. B. *Edith Wharton: A Biography.* New York: Harper, 1975.

Lewis, Robert O. " 'Long Time Ago Good, Now No Good': Hemingway's Indian Stories." *New Critical Approaches to the Short Stories of Ernest Hemingway.* Ed. Jackson J. Benson. Durham, NC: Duke UP, 1990. 200–12.

Lid, Richard W. "Hemingway and the Need for Speech." *Modern Fiction Studies* 8 (1962–3): 401–7.

Liebling, A. J. "The Dollars Damned Him." *New Yorker* 5 Aug. 1961: 48–72. Rpt. in *Stephen Crane: A Collection of Critical Essays.* Ed. Maurice Bassan. Englewood Cliffs, NJ: Prentice, 1967. 18–26.

Limon, John. *The Place of Fiction in the Time of Science: A Disciplinary History of American Writing.* Cambridge: Cambridge UP, 1990.

Lippmann, Walter. *Public Opinion.* New York: Harcourt, 1922.

Lipstadt, Deborah E. *Denying the Holocaust: The Growing Assault on Truth and Memory.* New York: Free Press, 1993.

Lodge, David. *The Modes of Modern Writing.* Ithaca: Cornell UP, 1977.

————. *The Novelist at the Crossroads and Other Essays on Fiction and Criticism.* Ithaca: Cornell UP, 1971.

Loewenberg, Bert James. *American History in American Thought.* New York: Simon, 1972.

Long, Barbara. "In Cold Comfort." *Esquire* June 1966: 124–6.

Lounsberry, Barbara. *The Art of Fact: Contemporary Artists of Nonfiction.* Westport, CT: Greenwood, 1990.

Louvre, Alf. "The Reluctant Historians: Mailer and Sontag as Culture Critics." *Tell Me Lies about Vietnam: Cultural Battles for the Meaning of the War.* Ed. Louvre and Jeffrey Walsh. London: Open University P, 1988. 73–87.

Lowell, Robert. *Collected Prose.* Ed. Roubert Giroux. New York: Farrar, 1987.

Lukacs, Georg. *History and Class Consciousness: Studies in Marxist Dialectics.* Trans. Rodney Livingstone. Cambridge, MA: MIT P, 1971.

Lyons, John D., and Stephen G. Nichols, eds. *Mimesis: From Mirror to Method, Augustine to Descartes.* Hanover, NJ: University P of New England, 1982.

McCullough, Joan. "Thirteen Who Were Left Behind." *Ms.,* June 1973: 41–5.

Macdonald, Dwight. *Discriminations: Essays and Afterthoughts, 1938–1974.* New York: Grossman, 1974.

———. "Hersey's 'Hiroshima.' " *Politics* 3 (Oct. 1946): 308.

———. "Parajournalism, or Tom Wolfe and His Magic Writing Machine." *New York Review of Books* 26 Aug. 1965: 3–5. Rpt. in *The Reporter as Artist.* Ed. Ronald Weber. New York: Hastings, 1974. 223–33.

———. "Parajournalism II: *The New Yorker* and Tom Wolfe." *New York Review of Books* 3 Feb. 1966: 18–24.

McGinniss, Joe. *Fatal Vision.* New York: Putnam's, 1983.

McGrath, William J. "Rescued from His Protectors." Rev. of *The Complete Letters of Sigmund Freud to Wilhelm Fliess, 1887–1904.* Ed. and trans. Jeffrey Moussaieff Masson. *New York Times Book Review* 28 Apr. 1985: 7, 9.

McHale, Brian. "Free Indirect Discourse: A Survey of Recent Accounts." *PTL: A Journal for Descriptive Poetics and Theory of Literature* 3 (1978): 249–87.

———. "Modernist Reading, Post-modern Text: The Case of *Gravity's Rainbow.*" *Poetics Today* 1.1–2 (1979): 85–110.

———. "Unspeakable Sentences, Unnatural Acts: Linguistics and Poetics Revisited." *Poetics Today* 4.1 (Autumn 1983): 17–45.

———. " 'You Used to Know What These Words Mean': Misreading *Gravity's Rainbow.*" *Language and Style* 18 (1985): 93–118.

McKerns, Joseph P. "The History of American Journalism: A Bibliographical Essay." *American Studies* 15 (1976): 17–34.

McNeill, Don. *Moving through Here.* New York: Knopf, 1970.

McQuade, Donald, and Robert Atwan. *Popular Writing in America.* 5th ed. New York: Oxford UP, 1993.

McRobbie, Angela. "Settling Accounts with Subcultures." *Screen Education* 34 (1980). Rpt. in *Culture, Ideology and Social Process.* Ed. Tony Bennett et al. London: Batsford/Open University, 1981: 111–23.

Mailer, Norman. *Advertisements for Myself.* New York: Perigee-Putnam, 1959.

———. *The Armies of the Night: History as a Novel/The Novel as History.* New York: NAL, 1968.

———. *The Executioner's Song.* New York: Warner, 1979.

———. *Of a Fire on the Moon.* Boston: Little, 1970.

———. *Pieces.* Boston: Little, 1982.

———. *Pontifications: Interviews.* Ed. Michael Lennon. Boston: Little, 1982.

———. *Some Honorable Men: Political Conventions, 1960–1972.* Boston: Little, 1976.

———. "The White Negro." *Advertisements for Myself.* New York: Perigee-Putnam's, 1959. 299–330.

Malcolm, Janet. *In the Freud Archives*. New York: Knopf, 1984.

——. *The Journalist and the Murderer*. New York: Vintage, 1990.

——. *Psychoanalysis: The Impossible Profession*. New York: Knopf, 1981.

——. *The Purloined Clinic: Selected Writings*. New York: Knopf, 1992.

——. "The Silent Woman." *New Yorker*. 23 and 30 Aug. 1993: 84–159.

Malin, Irving, ed. *Truman Capote's* In Cold Blood: *A Critical Handbook*. Belmont, CA: Wadsworth, 1968.

Manoff, Karl, and Michael Schudson, eds. *Reading the News*. New York: Pantheon, 1986.

Marchand, Roland. *Advertising the American Dream: Making Way for Modernity, 1920–1940*. Berkeley: U of California P, 1985.

Marcus, Steven. *Representations: Essays on Literature and Society*. New York: Random House, 1975.

Marcuse, Herbert. *One-dimensional Man: Studies in the Ideology of Advanced Industrial Society*. Boston: Beacon, 1964.

Marx, Leo. *Machine in the Garden: Technology and the Pastoral Ideal in America*. New York: Oxford UP, 1964.

Masson, Jeffrey Moussaieff. *The Assault on Truth: Freud's Suppression of the Seduction Theory*. New York: Penguin, 1985.

Matejka, L., and K. Pomorska, eds. *Readings in Russian Poetics*. Cambridge, MA: MIT P, 1971.

Meisel, Perry. *The Myth of the Modern*. New Haven: Yale UP, 1987.

Meisel, Perry, ed. *Freud: A Collection of Critical Essays*. Englewood Cliffs, NJ: Prentice, 1981.

Meyers, Jeffrey. "Hemingway's Primitivism and 'Indian Camp.' " *New Critical Approaches to the Short Stories of Ernest Hemingway*. Ed. Jackson J. Benson. Durham, NC: Duke UP, 1990. 300–8.

Meyrowitz, Joshua. *No Sense of Place: The Impact of Electronic Media on Social Behavior*. New York: Oxford UP, 1985.

Michaels, Walter Benn. *The Gold Standard and the Logic of Naturalism: American Literature at the Turn of the Century*. Berkeley: U of California P, 1987.

Middleton, Jo Ann. *Willa Cather's Modernism: A Study of Style and Technique*. London: Associated University Presses, 1990.

Miles, Josephine. *Major Adjectives in English Poetry: From Wyatt to Auden*. U of California Publications in English 12.3. Berkeley: U of California P, 1946.

Miller, J. Hillis. *Fiction and Repetition*. Cambridge, MA: Harvard UP, 1982.

Miller, Mark Crispin. *Boxed In: The Culture of TV*. Evanston: Northwestern UP, 1988.

Milton, Joyce. *The Yellow Kids: Foreign Correspondents in the Heyday of Yellow Journalism*. New York: Harper, 1989.

Mink, Louis O. "Narrative Form as a Cognitive Instrument." *The Writing of History*. Ed. Robert H. Canary and Henry Kosicki. Madison: U of Wisconsin P, 1978. 129–49.

Mitchell, Lee Clark. *Determined Fictions: American Literary Naturalism*. New York: Columbia UP, 1989.

——. "Naturalism and the Language of Determinism." *Columbia Literary History of the United States*. Ed. Emory Elliott. New York: Columbia UP, 1988. 525–45.

Modleski, Tania. *Loving with a Vengeance: Mass-produced Fantasies for Women.* Hamden, CT: Archon, 1982.

Modleski, Tania, ed. *Studies in Entertainment: Critical Approaches to Mass Culture.* Bloomington: Indiana UP, 1986.

Monteiro, George. "The Logic beneath 'The Open Boat.' " *Georgia Review* 26 (1972): 326–35.

Mott, Frank Luther. *American Journalism–A History: 1690–1960.* New York: Macmillan, 1962.

Murdock, Graham. "Political Deviance: The Press Presentation of a Militant Mass Demonstration." *The Manufacture of News.* Ed. Stanley Cohen and Jock Young. Beverly Hills, CA: Sage, 1973.

Nelson, William K. *Fact or Fiction: The Dilemma of the Renaissance Storyteller.* Cambridge, MA: Harvard UP, 1973.

Nichols, Bill. *Ideology and the Image.* Bloomington: Indiana UP, 1981.

Noble, David. *America by Design: Science, Technology, and the Rise of Corporate Capitalism.* New York: Knopf, 1977.

Nocera, Joseph. "How Hunter Thompson Killed New Journalism." *Washington Monthly* 13 (Apr. 1981): 44–50.

O'Brien, Sharon. "Becoming Noncanonical: The Case against Willa Cather." *Reading in America.* Ed. Cathy Davidson. Baltimore: Johns Hopkins UP, 1989. 240–58.

Ohmann, Richard. "A Kinder, Gentler Nation: Education and Rhetoric in the Bush Era." *Journal of Advanced Composition* 10 (1990): 215–30.

———. *Politics of Letters.* Middletown, CT: Wesleyan UP, 1987.

———. "Speech Acts and the Definition of Literature." *Philosophy and Rhetoric* 4 (1971): 1–19.

Oldsey, Bernard. "Always Personal." Rev. of *By-Line: Ernest Hemingway. Journal of General Education* 19 (1967): 239–43. Rpt. in *Ernest Hemingway: The Critical Reception.* Ed. Robert O. Stephens. N.p., Burt Franklin, 1977. 423–4.

———. "Hemingway's Beginnings and Endings." *Ernest Hemingway: The Papers of a Writer.* Ed. Oldsey. New York: Garland, 1981. 37–62.

———. *Hemingway's Hidden Craft: The Writing of* A Farewell to Arms. University Park: Pennsylvania State UP, 1979.

Ortega y Gasset, José. *The Dehumanization of Art.* Garden City, NY: Doubleday, 1956.

Orvell, Miles. *The Real Thing: Imitation and Authenticity in American Culture.* Chapel Hill: U North Carolina Press, 1989.

Oshinsky, David M., and Michael Curtis. "The truth appears to be . . . ." "Op-Ed." *New York Times* 11 Dec. 1991. Natl. ed. A15.

Parker, Hershel. "Textual Criticism and Hemingway." *Hemingway: Essays of Reassessment.* Ed. Frank Scafella. New York: Oxford UP, 1991. 17–32.

Passler, David L. *Time, Form, and Style in Boswell's Life of Johnson.* New Haven: Yale UP, 1971.

Pater, Walter. Preface. *The Renaissance.* By Pater, 1877. Rpt., ed. Harold Bloom. New York: NAL, 1974.

Perelman, Chaim. *The Realm of Rhetoric.* Trans. William Kluback. Notre Dame, IA: U of Notre Dame P, 1982.

Peterson, Richard K. *Hemingway: Direct and Oblique*. The Hague: Mouton, 1969.

Phillips, Damien. "The Press and Pop Festivals: Stereotypes of Youthful Leisure." *The Manufacture of News*. Ed. Stanley Cohen and Jock Young. Beverly Hills, CA: Sage, 1973. 323–33.

Pizer, Donald. "Stephen Crane." *Fifteen American Authors before 1900*. Rev. ed. Ed. Earl N. Harbert and Robert A. Rees. Madison: U of Wisconsin P, 1984. 128–84. *New York Times Book Review* 16 Jan. 1966: 2. Rpt.

Plimpton, George. "Truman Capote: An Interview." in *The Reporter as Artist*. Ed. Ronald Weber. New York: Hastings, 1974. 188–206.

Poirier, Richard. *The Performing Self: Compositions and Decompositions in the Languages of Contemporary Life*. New York: Oxford UP, 1971.

Polan, Dana. "Brief Encounters: Mass Culture and the Evacuation of Common Sense." *Studies in Entertainment*. Ed. Tania Modleski and Andreas Huyssen. Bloomington: Indiana UP, 1986. 167–87.

———. "Bertolt Brecht and Daffy Duck: Toward a Politics of Self-reflexive Cinema?" *American Media and Mass Culture: Left Perspectives*. Ed. Donald Lazere. Berkeley: U of California P, 1988. 345–56.

Poore, Charles. "The Most Spectacular Explosion in the Time of Man." *New York Times Book Review* 10 Nov. 1946: 7, 56.

Portch, Stephen R. "The Hemingway Touch." *Hemingway Review* 2 (1982): 43–7.

Porter, Carolyn. *Seeing and Being: The Plight of the Participant Observer in Emerson, James, Adams, and Faulkner*. Middletown, CT: Wesleyan UP, 1981.

Pratt, Mary Louise. *Toward a Speech Act Theory of Literary Discourse*. Bloomington: Indiana UP, 1977.

Rader, Ralph. "Defoe, Richardson, Joyce and the Concept of Form in the Novel." *Autobiography, Biography and the Novel*. By William Matthews and Ralph Rader. Berkeley: U of California P, 1973.

———. "Literary Form in Factual Narrative." In *Essays in Eighteenth-Century Biography*. Ed. Philip P. Daghlian. Bloomington: Indiana UP, 1968.

Radway, Janice. *Reading the Romance*. Chapel Hill: U of North Carolina P, 1984.

Reviews of *Hiroshima:* By R. S. Hutchison, *Christian Century* 63 (1946): 1151. In *Kirkus* 14 (1946): 471. By Louis Ridenour, *Saturday Review* of Literature 2 Nov. 1946: 16. In *TLS* 7 Dec. 1946: 605.

Reynolds, Michael S. *Hemingway's First War: The Making of* A Farewell to Arms. Princeton: Princeton UP, 1976.

———. "Two Hemingway Sources for *in our time*." *Critical Essays on Hemingway's* In Our Time. Ed. Reynolds. Boston: Hall, 1983. 31–7.

Rimmon-Kenan, Shlomith. *Narrative Fiction: Contemporary Poetics*. New York: Methuen, 1983.

Rivera, Geraldo. "Nonfiction TV." "Op-Ed." *New York Times* 16 Dec. 1988: A39.

Rogin, Michael Paul. *"Ronald Reagan," the Movie: And Other Episodes in Political Demonology*. Berkeley: U of California P, 1987.

Romano, Carlin. "The Grisly Truth about Bare Facts." *Reading the News*. Ed. Robert Karl Manoff and Michael Schudson. New York: Pantheon, 1986.

Rondel, William. "From Slate to Emerald Green: More Light on Crane's Jacksonville Visit." *Nineteenth-Century Fiction* 19 (1965): 357–68.

Rose, Barbara. "Wolfeburg." Rev. of *The Painted Word,* by Tom Wolfe. *New York Review of Books* 26 June 1975: 26–8.

Rose, Phyllis. *Writing of Women: Essays in a Renaissance.* Middletown, CT: Wesleyan UP, 1985.

Rosenfelt, Deborah. "The Politics of Bibliography." *Women in Print* 1 (1982): 21.

Rosenstone, Robert A. "*JFK:* Historical Fact/Historical Film." *AHR* Forum. *American Historical Review* 97 (1992): 506–11.

Rosenthal, Andrew. "Bush's In-flight Show: Pique, and Bumpy Ride for the Press." *New York Times* 16 Feb. 1990, natl. ed.: A9.

Ross, Charles S. "The Rhetoric of *The Right Stuff.*" *Journal of General Education* 33.2 (1981): 113–22.

Roszak, Theodore. *The Making of a Counter-Culture.* Garden City, NY: Doubleday, 1969.

Roth, Philip. "Writing American Fiction." *Commentary* Mar. 1961: 223–33.

Rovit, Earl. *Ernest Hemingway.* Rev. ed. Boston: Twayne, 1986.

Rudisill, Richard. *Mirror Image.* Albuquerque: U of New Mexico P, 1971.

Said, Edward. "Opponents, Audiences, Constituencies and Community." *The Anti-Aesthetic: Essays on Postmodern Culture.* Ed. Hal Foster. Seattle: Bay, 1983: 135–59.

Sanders, David. *John Hersey Revisited.* Boston: Twayne, 1991.

Saussure, Ferdinand de. *Course in General Linguistics.* Trans. Wade Baskin. New York: Philosophical Library, 1959. Excerpted in *The Structuralists from Marx to Lévi-Strauss.* Ed. Richard DeGeorge and Fernande DeGeorge. Garden City, NY: Doubleday, 1972: 59–79.

Schiller, Dan. *Objectivity and the News.* Philadelphia: U of Pennsylvania P, 1981.

Schirmer, Gregory A. "Becoming Interpreters: The Importance of Tone in Crane's 'The Open Boat.' " *American Literary Realism* 15 (1982): 221–31.

Schleifer, Ronald. "American Violence: Dreiser, Mailer, and the Nature of Intertextuality." *Intertextuality and Contemporary American Fiction.* Ed. Patrick O'Donnell and Robert Con Davis. Baltimore: Johns Hopkins UP, 1989.

Scholes, Robert. "Decoding Papa: 'A Very Short Story' as Work and Text." *Semiotics and Interpretation.* New Haven: Yale UP, 1982. 110–26.

———. *Textual Power.* New Haven: Yale UP, 1985.

Schorer, Mark. "The Background of a Style." *Kenyon Review* 3 (1941): 101–5. Rpt. in *Ernest Hemingway: Critiques of Four Major Novels.* Ed. Carlos Baker. New York: Scribner's, 1962. 87–9.

Schudson, Michael. *Discovering the News.* New York: Basic, 1978.

———. "The Politics of Narrative Form: The Emergence of News Conventions in Print and Television." *Daedalus* 111 (1982): 97–112.

———. "The Sociology of News Production Revisited." *Mass Media and Society.* Ed. James Curran and Michael Gurevitch. London: Arnold, 1991: 141–59.

Schuster, Charles. "Mikhail Bakhtin as Rhetorical Theorist." *College English* 47 (1985): 594–607.

Schwartz, Tony. *The Responsive Chord.* Garden City, NY: Doubleday, 1973.

Searle, John. "The Logical Status of Fictional Discourse." *New Literary History* 6 (1975): 319–32.

Sheed, Wilfrid. "A Fun-house Mirror." *New York Times Book Review* 3 Dec. 1972: 2. Rpt. in *The Reporter as Artist*. Ed. Ronald Weber. New York: Hastings, 1974. 294–8.

Shklovsky, Viktor. "Sterne's *Tristram Shandy*: Stylistic Commentary." *Russian Formalist Criticism*. Ed. and trans. Lee T. Lemon and Marion J. Reis. Lincoln: U of Nebraska P, 1965. 25–7.

Shulman, Robert. "Community, Perception, and the Development of Stephen Crane: From *The Red Badge* to 'The Open Boat' " *American Literature* 50 (1978): 441–60.

Siebert, Fred, Theodore Peterson, and Wilbur Schramm. *Four Theories of the Press*. Urbana: U of Illinois P, 1963.

Sims, Norman, ed. Introduction. *Literary Journalism in the Twentieth Century*. New York: Oxford UP, 1990.

———. *The Literary Journalists*. New York: Ballantine, 1984.

Slotkin, Richard. *The Fatal Environment*. New York: Atheneum, 1985.

Smith, Anthony. *Goodbye Gutenberg: The Newspaper Revolution of the 1980s*. New York: Oxford UP, 1980.

———. "The Long Road to Objectivity and Back Again." In *Newspaper History: From the Seventeenth Century to the Present Day*. Ed. George Boyce, James Curran, and Pauline Wingate. London: Constable, 1978: 153–71.

———. *The Newspaper: An International History*. London: Thames, 1979.

Smith, Barbara Herrnstein. *On the Margins of Discourse: The Relation of Literature to Language*. Chicago: U of Chicago P, 1978.

Smith, Dorothy. "The Ideological Practice of Sociology." 1972 manuscript, excerpted as "Theorizing as Ideology." *Ethnomethodology*. Ed. Roy Turner. Baltimore: Penguin, 1974.

Smith, Paul. *A Reader's Guide to the Short Stories of Ernest Hemingway*. Boston: Hall, 1989.

Solomon, Eric. *Stephen Crane: From Parody to Realism*. Cambridge, MA: Harvard UP, 1966.

Sontag, Susan. *On Photography*. New York: Farrar, 1977.

———. "Trip to Hanoi." *Styles of Radical Will*. New York: Farrar, 1969, 205–74.

Spence, Donald P. *Narrative Truth and Historical Truth*. New York: Norton, 1982.

Stallman, R. W. *Stephen Crane: A Biography*. New York: Braziller, 1968.

Stallman, R. W., ed. *Stephen Crane: Stories and Tales*. New York: Vintage, 1955.

Stallman, R. W., and E. R. Hagemann, eds. *The War Dispatches of Stephen Crane*. New York: NYU P, 1964.

Stallybrass, Peter, and Allon White. *The Politics and Poetics of Transgression*. London: Methuen, 1986.

Steiner, George. *Language and Silence: Essays on Language, Literature, and the Inhuman*. New York: Atheneum, 1967.

Stephens, Mitchell. *A History of News: From the Drum to the Satellite*. New York: Viking, 1988.

Stephens, Robert O. *Hemingway's Nonfiction: The Public Voice.* Chapel Hill: U of North Carolina P, 1968.

Stevenson, Diane. "Different from the Rest." Rev. of *What It Takes: The Way to the White House,* by Richard Ben Cramer. *Nation* 26 Oct. 1992: 474–7.

Stewart, Susan. "The Interdiction." *Profession 89.* New York: MLA, 1989: 10–14.

Stierle, Karlheinz. "The Reading of Fictional Texts." Trans. Inge Crosman and Thekla Zachran. In *The Reader in the Text.* Ed. Susan Suleiman and Inge Crosman. Princeton: Princeton UP, 1980. 83–105.

Stimpson, Catharine R. "The Haunted House." Rev. of *The Journalist and the Murderer,* by Janet Malcolm. *Nation,* 25 June 1990: 899–902.

Stone, Laurie. "Spaced Out." Review of *The Right Stuff,* by Tom Wolfe. *Village Voice* 10 Sept. 1979: 71, 73, 76.

Suleiman, Susan. *Authoritarian Fictions: The Ideological Novel as a Literary Genre.* New York: Columbia UP, 1983.

Talese, Gay. *Honor Thy Father.* New York: Fawcett, 1972.

———. "When Frank Sinatra Had a Cold: A Reflection on the Cause of Today's Common Journalism." *Esquire* 6 Nov. 1987: 161–6.

Tanner, Tony. *Reign of Wonder: Naivety and Reality in American Literature.* Cambridge: Cambridge UP, 1965.

———. Rev. of *By-Line: Ernest Hemingway. London Magazine* May 1968: 90–5. Rpt. in *Hemingway: The Critical Heritage.* Ed. Jeffrey Meyers. London: Routledge, 1982. 526–30.

Tebbell, John. *The Life and Good Times of William Randolph Hearst.* New York: Dutton, 1952.

Tedlow, Richard S. *New and Improved: The Story of Mass Marketing in America.* New York: Basic, 1990.

Thompson, Hunter S. *Fear and Loathing: On the Campaign Trail '72.* San Francisco: Straight Arrow, 1973.

———. *Hell's Angels: A Strange and Terrible Saga.* New York: Ballantine, 1967.

Thompson, Thomas H. "Freud Redux: Psychoanalysis Turned Inside Out." *North American Review* Dec. 1984: 15–28.

Todorov, Tzvetan. *The Conquest of America: The Question of the Other.* Trans. Richard Howard. New York: Harper, 1984.

———. "Language and Literature." *The Structuralist Controversy.* Ed. Richard Macksey and Eugenio Donato. Baltimore: Johns Hopkins UP, 1972: 125–33.

———. "The Notion of Literature." *New Literary History* 5 (1973): 5–16.

———. *The Poetics of Prose.* Trans. Richard Howard. London: Blackwell, 1977.

Tomashevsky, Boris. "Thematics." *Russian Formalist Criticism.* Ed. and trans. Lee T. Lemon and Marion J. Reis. Lincoln: U of Nebraska P, 1965. 61–95.

Tompkins, Jane. "Criticism and Feeling." *College English* 39 1977: 169–78.

———. "The Reader in History: The Changing Shape of Literary Response." *Reader-response Criticism: From Formalism to Post-Structuralism.* Ed. Jane P. Tompkins. Baltimore: Johns Hopkins UP, 1980. 201–32.

Trachtenberg, Alan. "Experiments in Another Country: Stephen Crane's City

Sketches." *Southern Review* 10 (1974): 265–85. Rpt. in *American Realism: New Essays.* Ed. Eric J. Sundquist. Baltimore: Johns Hopkins UP, 1982. 138–54.

———. "What's New?" Rev. of *The New Journalism,* by Tom Wolfe. *Partisan Review* 41 (1974): 300–2.

Trilling, Diana. "The Moral Radicalism of Norman Mailer." *Claremont Essays.* London: Secker, 1965. 175–202.

Tuchman, Gaye. *Making News.* New York: Free, 1978.

———. "Myth and the Consciousness Industry: A New Look at the Effects of the Mass Media. *Mass Media and Social Change.* Ed. Elihu Katz and Tomas Szecski. Beverly Hills, CA: Sage, 1981. 83–101.

———. "Objectivity as Strategic Ritual." *American Journal of Sociology* 77 (1973): 660–79.

Volosinov, V. N. *Marxism and the Philosophy of Language.* The Hague: Mouton, 1972.

Wagner, Linda W. *Hemingway and Faulkner: Inventors/Masters.* Metuchen, NJ: Scarecrow, 1975.

Wakefield, Dan. "The Personal Voice and the Impersonal I." *Atlantic,* June 1966. Rpt. in *The Reporter as Artist.* Ed. Ronald Weber. New York: Hastings, 1974. 39–48.

Walcutt, Charles Child. *American Literary Naturalism: A Divided Stream.* Minneapolis: U of Minnesota P, 1956.

Waldhorn, Arthur. *A Reader's Guide to Ernest Hemingway.* New York: Farrar, 1972.

Watson, William B. " 'Old Man at the Bridge': The Making of a Short Story." *Hemingway Review* 7.2 (1988): 152–65.

———. "A Variorum Edition of Dispatch 19." *Hemingway Review* 7.2 (1988): 93–109.

Weber, Brom. "Ernest Hemingway's Genteel Bullfight." *The American Novel and the Nineteen-Twenties.* Stratford on Avon Studies 13. London: Arnold, 1971. 151–64.

Weber, Ronald. *Hemingway's Art of Nonfiction.* London: Macmillan, 1990.

———. *The Literature of Fact: Literary Nonfiction in American Writing.* Athens: Ohio State UP, 1980.

Weber, Ronald, ed. *The Reporter as Artist.* New York: Hastings, 1974.

Weimann, Robert. "History, Appropriation, and the Uses of Representation in Modern Narrative." *The Aims of Representation: Subject/Text/History.* New York: Columbia UP, 1987. 175–215.

Wellek, René, and Austin Warren. *Theory of Literature.* 3rd ed. New York: Harcourt, 1962.

———. "What Is Literature?" *What Is Literature?* Ed. Paul Hernadi. Bloomington: Indiana UP, 1978.

Wertheim, Stanley, and Paul Sorrentino. "Thomas Beer: The Clay Feet of Stephen Crane Biography." *American Literary Realism* 22.3 (1990): 2–16.

Wertheim, Stanley, and Paul Sorrentino, eds. *The Correspondence of Stephen Crane.* 2 vols. New York: Columbia UP, 1988.

West, Nathanael. "Some Notes on Violence." *Contact* (1932). Rpt. in *Nathanael*

West: A Collection of Critical Essays. Ed. Jay Martin. Englewood Cliffs, NJ: Prentice, 1971. 50–1.

Whelan, Brent. ' 'Furthur': Reflections on Counter-Culture and the Postmodern." *Cultural Critique* 9 (1988–9): 63–86.

White, Hayden. "The Real, the True, and the Figurative in the Human Sciences." *Profession 92*. New York: MLA, 1992: 15–17.

———. "The Value of Narrativity in the Representation of Reality." *On Narrative*. Ed. W. J. T. Mitchell. Chicago: U of Chicago P, 1981.

White, William. Introduction. *By-Line: Ernest Hemingway*. New York: Scribner's, 1967.

Widmer, Kingsley. "American Apocalypse: Notes on the Bomb and the Failure of Imagination." *The Forties: Fiction, Poetry, Drama*. Ed. Warren French. DeLand, FL: Everett/Edwards, 1969. 141–51.

Wiebe, Robert. *The Search for Order: 1877–1920*. New York: Hill & Wang, 1967.

Wilde, Oscar. *The Decay of Lying*. 1889. Rpt. in *Critical Theory since Plato*. Ed. Hazard Adams. New York: Harcourt, 1971.

Wilden, Anthony. *The Language of the Self*. Baltimore: Johns Hopkins UP, 1981.

Williams, Raymond. "Base and Superstructure in Marxist Cultural Theory." *Problems in Materialism and Culture*. London: New Left, 1980.

———. *Culture and Society*. Harmondsworth, UK: Penguin, 1963.

———. *Drama in a Dramatized Society*. Cambridge: Cambridge UP, 1975.

———. "Isn't the News Terrible?" *What I Came to Say*. London: Hutchinson, 1989.

———. *Keywords: A Vocabulary of Culture and Society*. 2nd ed. New York: Oxford UP, 1984.

———. *Marxism and Literature*. Oxford: Oxford UP, 1977.

———. "The Press and Popular Culture: An Historical Perspective." *Newspaper History: From the Seventeenth Century to the Present Day*. Ed. George Boyce et al. London: Constable, 1978. 41–50.

———. *Television: Technology and Cultural Form*. New York: Schocken, 1975.

Williamson, Judith. *Decoding Advertisements*. London: Marion Boyars, 1978.

Wilson, Christopher. *The Labor of Words: Literary Professionalism in the Progressive Era*. Athens: U of Georgia P, 1985.

Wilson, Edmund. *Letters on Literature and Politics, 1912–1972*. New York: 1972.

———. *The Wound and the Bow*. New York: Oxford UP, 1965.

Wines, Michael. "ABC Rejects Nixon Effort to Stop Show." *New York Times* 22 Sept. 1989: C11.

Winner, Langdon. *Autonomous Technology: Technics-out-of-Control as a Theme in Political Thought*. Cambridge, MA: MIT Press, 1977.

Wolcott, James. Rev. of *The Purple Decades,* by Tom Wolfe. *New York Review of Books* 4 Nov. 1982: 21–3.

Wolfe, Tom. "The Art of Fiction CXXIII." *Paris Review* 33 (1991): 93–121.

———. *The Bonfire of the Vanities*. New York: Farrar, 1987.

———. *The Electric Kool-Aid Acid Test*. New York: Bantam, 1969.

———. Introduction. *The New Journalism*. Anthology. Ed. Wolfe and E. W. Johnson. New York: Harper, 1973. 3–52.

————. *The Kandy-Kolored Tangerine-Flake Streamline Baby*. New York: Farrar, 1965.

————. *Radical Chic and Mau-Mauing the Flak Catchers*. New York: Farrar, 1970.

————. *The Right Stuff*. New York: Bantam, 1980.

————. "Stalking the Billion-footed Beast: A Literary Manifesto for the New Social Novel." *Harper's* Nov. 1989: 45–56.

Wolfe, Tom, and E. W. Johnson, eds. *The New Journalism*. New York: Harper, 1973.

Wolin, Richard. *Walter Benjamin: An Aesthetic of Redemption*. New York: Columbia UP, 1982.

Wood, Michael. Rev. of *The New Journalism*, by Tom Wolfe. *New York Times Book Review* 22 July 1973: 21.

Young, James E. *Writing and Rewriting the Holocaust*. Bloomington: Indiana UP, 1988.

Young, Philip. *Ernest Hemingway: A Reconsideration*. New York: Harcourt, 1966.

Yurick, Sol. "Sob-sister Gothic," *Nation* 7 Feb. 1966: 158–60. Rpt. in *Truman Capote's* In Cold Blood: *A Critical Handbook*. Ed. Irving Malin. Belmont, CA: Wadsworth, 1968.

Zavarzadeh, Mas'ud. *The Mythopoeic Reality: The Postwar American Nonfiction Novel*. Urbana: U of Illinois P, 1977.

Zboray, Ronald J. "Antebellum Reading and the Ironies of Technological Innovation." *Reading in America: Literature and Social History*. Ed. Cathy N. Davidson. Baltimore: Johns Hopkins UP, 1989. 180–200.

Ziff, Larzar. "The Social Basis of Hemingway's Style." *Ernest Hemingway: Six Decades of Criticism*. Ed. Linda Wagner. East Lansing: Michigan State UP, 1987. 147–54.

Index

285